YOUR CAREER ADVENTURE

Exploring and Planning for Tomorrow

Second Edition

Roger LeRoy Miller
Institute for University Studies
Arlington, Texas

West Educational Publishing
an International Thomson Publishing company I(T)P®

Cincinnati • Albany, NY • Belmont, CA • Bonn • Boston • Detroit • Johannesburg • London • Los Angeles
Madrid • Melbourne • Mexico City • New York • Paris • Singapore • Tokyo • Toronto • Washington

About the Author . . .

Roger LeRoy Miller, Institute for University Studies, Arlington Texas, graduated Phi Beta Kappa from the University of California at Berkeley where he also won the departmental prize in economics. He was a Woodrow Wilson Honor Fellow, National Science Foundation Fellow, and Lilly Honor Fellow at the University of Chicago, where he received his Ph.D. in Economics in 1968.

Dr. Miller has taught at the University of Washington, the University of Miami, and Clemson University. He also has taught methodology to teachers of high school economics through the Joint Council on Economic Education.

Among the more than 100 books he has written or co-authored are works on economics, statistics, law, consumer education, and government. Dr. Miller also has operated several businesses and served as a consultant to government agencies, private corporations, and law firms.

Production Credits

Team Leader	Robert Cassel
Project Manager	Lynda Kessler
Production Editor/Designer	Carole Balach
Photo Research	Jan Seidel
Permissions	Elaine Arthur
Illustrations	Matt Thiessen
Copyediting	Mary Berry
Index	Terry Casey
Proofreading	Bette Holzer
Cover Images	©PhotoDisc, Inc.
Composition	Parkwood Composition Services, Inc.
Prepress Services	Clarinda Company

Printed in the United States of America

06 05 04 03 02 01 00 8 7 6 5 4 3

Student Edition: ISBN 0-314-22322-3
Teacher's Wraparound Edition: ISBN 0-538-42380-3

Photo Credits Follow Index

CONTENTS

CHAPTER 3
MAKING DECISIONS 42

CHAPTER 4
LEARNING PERSONAL SKILLS 56

PART TWO
EXPLORING CAREERS 71

CHAPTER 5
How To Research Careers 72

CHAPTER 6
Agribusiness and Natural Resources Careers 90

CHAPTER 7
Business and Office Technology Careers 107

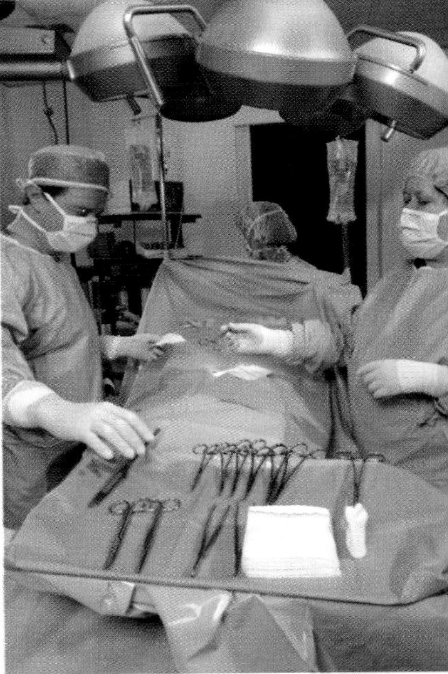

CHAPTER 17
MARKETING AND DISTRIBUTION CAREERS 262

CHAPTER 18
PERSONAL SERVICES CAREERS 277

CHAPTER 19
PUBLIC SERVICES CAREERS 291

Tickets
NEW YORK

FEATURES

Attitude Makes a Difference

Careers for Tomorrow

From School to Careers

From School to Careers, continued

Thinking About Yourself

Working Online

♦ INTRODUCTION ♦

Your Career Adventure, Exploring and Planning for Tomorrow, Second Edition, has been written for you. You are on the verge of making educational decisions that will affect the rest of your lives. As you read the textbook and do the hundreds of activities, you will learn a great deal about yourselves, the world of work, and the importance of education. You will learn how to make decisions, improve your basic skills, and develop positive attitudes.

The text includes 25 chapters organized into three major parts: *Part One*: Looking Forward to the World of Work; *Part Two*: Exploring Careers, and *Part Three*: On Your Way to Success.

Your Career Adventure contains over 200 pages of information about occupations. In *Part Two*: Exploring Careers, you will be introduced to the fifteen career clusters (groups) developed by the U.S. Office of Education. For each cluster you will read "What Would It Be Like," imaginary conversations between different workers in a particular career cluster. "Job Families," "At the Heart of . . .," and "Skills, Training, and Experience" complete the discussions about each cluster. You will also read about job duties, transferable skills, and the employment outlook for occupations in that cluster. At the end of each of these career cluster chapters is a list of occupations within that cluster with their *DOT* numbers so that you can continue career research outside the classroom. You will be introduced to several publications along the way that will help you with your career research. Two of these are *The Occupational Outlook Handbook* and the *Dictionary of Occupational Titles* (*DOT*).

You will learn from and enjoy doing the many activities found within the chapters as well as at the end of the chapters. You will enjoy reading *Your Career Adventure*, and find lots of stories about young people just like yourselves, who have had real-life experiences to which you can relate and from which you will learn. The content is written in a lively, modern style that will capture your attention and hold it.

As you read through the text, you should be aware of three major themes carried throughout *Your Career Adventure*. One theme is the *importance of developing a positive attitude*. The textbook works hard at promoting a positive attitude about yourself, your work, and other people. You will find interesting stories to get you thinking about the importance of attitude in the feature called "Attitude Makes a Difference."

The second theme is the *importance of education and training*. Not only have we devoted a full chapter to education and training, but you will also find practical examples of the many different ways that you can get the most from your educational experience in the feature "From School to Careers."

The third major theme is *self-understanding*. In addition to Chapter 2, "Who are You? Values, Interests, and Abilities," and Chapter 4, "Learning Personal Skills," you will find the feature "Thinking About Yourself" in most chapters. This feature attempts to get you to question your own values, skills, and interests in terms of the different careers being explored.

The author and West Publishing Company believe that you will like reading *Your Career Adventure* and will start to think seriously about your future and develop the career decision-making skills and knowledge you will need for a lifetime.

Acknowledgements

The author and publisher would like to thank the following teachers for their helpful suggestions and recommendations during the revision of this textbook.

Skyne Betha
Warsaw Middle School
Warsaw, NC

Sheryl Gasaway
Stamps High School
Stamps, AR

Brenda Graham
A. C. Reynolds Middle School
Asheville, NC

Carol Ann Harrold
Madison Middle School
Madison, OH

Connie Martin
Tecumseh Junior High School
Lynnville, IN

Janet Scott
Lindbergh High School
St. Louis, MO

Stacie Sparks
Lee Academy
Marianna, AR

Kay Spurlock
East Junior High School
West Memphis, AR

A special thanks to Janice Hanlon, Program Manager at the Arkansas Department of Workforce Education for her continued support and assistance. Finally, our sincere thanks to Linda Cegiel, who spent most of her free time over the last couple of months contributing all of the creative material for the *Teacher's Wraparound Edition*.

DARE TO DREAM

Do you have dreams and hopes for the life you would like to live someday? Do they sometimes seem impossible? Do you wonder how you can plan your future when you don't know what will happen?

It might seem too early to start thinking so far ahead, but it's never too early to think about your future. In the next few years you will be making more and more of your own decisions. These decisions will have a big impact on your life. You will make decisions about what future courses to take during the next few years, decisions about what after-school activities to participate in, and decisions about what you'll do with your free time and who you'll do it with.

As you make these decisions, you'll be determining much of what will happen the rest of your life. You will be writing your own script for the movie that will be your life. It's up to you how you will make your decisions and write your script. It's not too early to think about your future.

You need a *plan* if you are to reach your dreams and hopes. You need to include in your plan some high expectations of yourself, even though they may seem out of reach right now. If you don't set your *goals* high, you may miss out on some great life experiences. Your goals are what you want to accomplish. So start out big and *dare to dream*.

Almost everyone has dreams. We dream of where we'd like to go for a vacation. We dream of how we'd like to celebrate our birthdays. We dream of hitting the game-winning homer in the ninth inning with two outs. But it's when we start thinking about jobs and careers that we believe we should stop dreaming. Others often tell us to "be realistic."

Never mind "being realistic" for a while. Dream on. Eighty percent of the workers in this country (which means eight out of every ten people who work) are *underemployed*. This means they are working in jobs that are less than they are capable of doing, and therefore, they are not as happy as they could be. Perhaps they were being "too realistic" when they chose their jobs. Even experts agree that the more you listen to your dreams, the more you increase your chances of being able to do what you've always wanted with your life.

Are there any adults you've met who do not like their jobs? How do you know this? You probably know it because they complain about having to work too hard or having a nasty boss. In any event, you know there are lots of people who do not like their jobs. That should just tell you how important it is for you to end up working in a job that you really like.

You live in a giant world with lots of possibilities. Dreaming is like taking a trip around the world. When you want to land, you have to decide where, and pick a specific place. Before you pick a good place, you have to know many things about the area and what it will be like to land there.

Before you pick a place to land with your career, you have to know many things about yourself. You have to know many things about all the different careers from which you can choose. You have to discover what you like to do best. You have to discover what you do well.

In this book you are going to take a long trip. You can go wherever you want and stay as long as you want, because this book is about *you*. You are going to dream about your future, especially your future in the world of work. You are also going to learn about yourself and about careers so that you can pick a good place to land. You may decide you like the place where you land first, or like most people, you may decide to go to other lands. But whether you stay or go, the important thing is that you will have begun your career adventure, and that you will be the person at the controls, making your own informed career decisions.

Career Decision-Making Activities

Take a few minutes to dream up an ideal job for yourself. You may want to do a warm-up exercise to get those dreams going. Write the following information about your ideal job on a sheet of paper. Be ready to talk about your answers in a class discussion.

- What is the title of your ideal job?
- Describe a twenty-four hour day from the time you get up, go to work, get off work, and so on.
- How much income are you making?
- How did you get to work?
- What did you wear to work?
- How much education and training did you need to get the job?
- What high school subjects helped you to prepare for the job?
- How did these subjects help you prepare for the job?

PART ONE

LOOKING FORWARD TO THE WORLD OF WORK

CHAPTER 1 A WORKING ATTITUDE

◆ Chapter Objectives ◆

After completing this chapter you will be able to do the following:

- ◆ Define the terms listed under "New Career Terms."
- ◆ State reasons why people work.
- ◆ Explain the difference between a job and a career.
- ◆ Give reasons why a positive attitude is important.
- ◆ Describe how school courses and schoolwork can affect a person's career and life.

◆ New Career Terms ◆

In this chapter you will learn the meanings of the following career terms:

- ✔ Work
- ✔ Job
- ✔ Occupation
- ✔ Career
- ✔ Goal
- ✔ Attitude
- ✔ Self-concept
- ✔ Work ethic

Do you realize that one morning, in the not-too-distant future, you'll wake up and you will no longer be going to school? You will have graduated from high school, or college, or whatever the last school you attend should happen to be. Believe it or not, school does not last forever. It will be over. You'll be free to do whatever you want.

That particular morning is not far off. It could be only three or four years away, or eight years. But it won't be long. It certainly won't be long in relation to the rest of your life. If you are between the ages of eighteen and twenty-five when you finish your formal schooling, you should live for another fifty to seventy years.

Do you know what you will do after you've graduated from your last school? You probably know that you'll do what almost everyone else does—you will *work.*

But what kind of work will you do? Where will you do this work? And how much income will you earn for doing the work? Do you know the answers to these questions?

You should answer these questions very carefully. Why are they so important? Because you will spend so much time and so many years of your life working. Whether or not you enjoy your work will be a major factor in how happy you are throughout your life. Can you see how important choosing your work is?

In this chapter you will begin thinking about work. You will learn why people work and the difference between jobs and careers. Most important—you will examine your attitude about yourself and work. You will also learn how to improve your attitude if it needs improving.

◀ There are hundreds of job possibilities to choose from.

> ***work***
> productive activity resulting in something useful.

WHAT IS WORK?

Work is a hard word to define. One standard dictionary takes over thirty lines to define it. Most of the definitions refer to *useful, productive activity* and the *labor by which a person earns a living.*

How would you define *work?* What sorts of activities would you classify as work? Obviously, a part-time job at a local fast-food restaurant would qualify as work. But what about drying the dishes for your mother? Or fixing your broken computer? Or cleaning the garage? And how about baby-sitting the neighbor's kids? If you spend all day trying to get your car running, but fail, have you done any work?

Go ahead and write your own definition of *work* on a sheet of paper. Compare your definition to those written by friends and classmates. What differences do you see in the ways you perceive work?

As you read through this book, your attitude toward work will probably change. You will develop a deeper understanding of the many different types and kinds of work that exist. You will begin to appreciate, if you don't already, the many benefits of work. Because you will probably spend thirty or forty years working full-time, you might as well learn to enjoy this hard-to-define activity. You may never be a workaholic, but you can be someone who has a happy, fulfilling life, largely due to a *positive working attitude.*

Career Decision-Making Activities

1. For two days keep a diary of all the things you do before and after school. After completing the list, put NW (for nonwork) next to the activities you don't consider to be work. Put W (for work) next to all the activities you consider work. Compare your list with your classmates' lists. Were any of the same activities considered work by some people but nonwork by others? How do you explain the differences?
2. Ask three working adults you know to define *work* in their terms. Then ask them if they consider everything they do on their jobs to be work, or if they consider some of their tasks to be fun rather than work. Report your findings to the class.

WHY DO PEOPLE WORK?

You might think that the only reason people work is to earn money. You might feel that no one in his or her right mind would keep working at a job if there were no need for the money income.

It's true that people work for money. They need money to buy necessities such as food, clothing, and shelter. They want money so that they can buy luxuries such as jewelry, digital video games, and vacation trips to faraway places. They also work for money so that they can be independent and make their own choices about how and where they will live.

Chances are, however, that you can think of some people you know about who work for reasons other than money. Have you ever heard about people who have inherited large sums of money—enough to support them for the rest of their lives—but have still continued to work? Do you know any senior citizens who work part-time for little pay even though their retirement benefits are more than adequate? Have you read stories about famous entertainers or business leaders who continue working even though they've already made millions, even billions, of dollars? How many people can you name who seem to be working for something other than money income?

▲ Work gives you an opportunity to meet and get to know people. If you enjoy social contact, you will have an advantage in the world of working.

Why do these people work? If you took a poll, you would probably get answers like these:

1. *People like to be with people.* "I was lonely at home all day with nobody to talk to. I needed some companionship." Many people work so that they can be with, and communicate with, other people. Most people like social contact. They want to have friends to share their interests with and tell their problems to. People like people. After they graduate from school, work is their best opportunity to meet and socialize with others.
2. *People want to be fulfilled.* "I felt worthless. I wasn't doing anything worthwhile. I needed to feel that I was accomplishing something." Many people work because they find their jobs fulfilling. Their work helps them feel good about themselves. Work satisfies the basic human need for self-esteem. After all, when two adults meet for the first time, one of the first questions in their conversation is, "What do you do?" Many people are identified by their work. For some, accomplishing something worthwhile is satisfaction enough. For others, there is a need to do more than they've done before—to expand their skills or be creative. Still others feel good about themselves because work gives them an identity.
3. *People need direction and purpose.* "When I was not working, I just didn't seem to get much done in my life." Most people like to have direction in their lives. Working gives them that direction, for they have certain things they must accomplish every workday. There is an old saying that if you want something done, ask a busy person to do it. The reason is because busy people do not usually waste much time. They get things done in life.

So you see, people work for lots of important reasons other than money income. These reasons can be described in many ways, but they basically have to do with people's needing to feel good about themselves.

How does work make them feel good? It gives them an opportunity to socialize with others. It gives them an identity. It makes them feel useful. It gives them an outlet for their creativity. Work can make people happy in many different ways—in addition to providing money to pay the bills.

Career Decision-Making Activities

1. Survey three working adults to find out their main reasons for working. If they had to pick one of the following as the main reason for working, which would they pick? What would be their second pick?
   - To have money to buy necessities.
   - To have money to buy luxuries.
   - To be with other people and make friends.
   - To feel good about myself because I am accomplishing something worthwhile.
   - To feel good about myself because I expand my skills and knowledge through my work.
   - To feel good about myself because work gives me a sense of identity.

   After completing your survey, summarize your results and report them to the class.
2. Make a list of five jobs—both paying and non-paying jobs—that people you know have. For each job, give the main reason they have that job, using reasons listed in Activity 1. What would be their most frequent reason for working? Their second most frequent reason?

A JOB OR A CAREER?

When you work for a living, you might say that you work at either a *job* or a *career.* A job and a career are not, however, the same thing. One good way to understand the difference is by examining your feelings about friendships.

▶ Starting out in entry-level positions will give you an opportunity to be trained for advancements.

Do you have friends you want to know for the rest of your life? If so, you feel they are your best friends and a big part of your life. In contrast, are there other people you like, but don't really picture yourself knowing for the rest of your life? You don't feel as close to these acquaintances as you do to your best friends.

This comparison between best friends and acquaintances is similar to the difference between jobs and careers. A job is like the person you meet and spend some time with, but probably won't know very well. A career is like a best friend whom you want to keep knowing and learning about all your life. Of course, just as anyone you meet could turn into a best friend, any job could turn into a career.

JOBS

A **job** is a group of work tasks that you agree to perform for an employer. You make an agreement with the employer when you accept a job. You agree to be responsible for work that is important in the employer's business. In return, the employer agrees to pay you for the work you do.

Another word you need to learn is **occupation.** This word is often used in place of the word *job.* An occupation is actually a *group of jobs* involving similar tasks. For example, suppose you have jobs in three different grocery stores while you're in high school. At each store your main task is to stock shelves. Your other tasks vary from store to store. The jobs would be different, but the occupation—stock clerk—would be the same.

Your first jobs will probably require only a few skills and will not necessarily be your only occupation or lifelong career. As you develop more skills, you may find you work at jobs that you want to turn into a career.

This does not mean that some jobs or occupations are important and worthwhile, and that others are not. All jobs are important and

job
being employed by a person or company to perform certain tasks and being paid for the work.

occupation
the type of job a person is employed in.

FROM SCHOOL TO CAREERS

Lifelong Learning

When you were in the first grade in school, you learned to read and write. In middle school you prepare a course of study for high school. In high school you prepare a course of study for college and begin to think about the future. Your school experiences are the beginning of your career ladder. Each future step up your career ladder will be the result of learning—whether it be in school or on the job. (See the representation of a career ladder on page 11.) Education and training provide the boosts that take you closer to your dream career. They are truly some of the greatest opportunities you will have in life.

needed, or they wouldn't exist. All work has *dignity*—honor and prestige. But for you to be happy and get the greatest possible reward for the work you do, you may need to think in terms of a career.

CAREERS

career
work done over a period of years in one area of interest

A **career** is the work you will do over a period of years. You will probably have lots of different jobs. You will probably also work in many different occupations. You can think of your career as the total of all the jobs and occupations you will ever have.

You may start out in a company with a position requiring only a few skills. You might then work your way up the career ladder to a highly skilled job within the same company. Many presidents of major companies in the United States started out with less skilled positions. They then worked their way up to more highly skilled jobs, with each new job along the way requiring more skills and education.

PLANNING A CAREER

goal
an objective or target to be reached by directing your thoughts and energy

A **goal** is something that you want to obtain and that you work to achieve. A goal can be the big picture of things you would like to accomplish in your lifetime. Achieving an important goal usually takes many steps and hard work.

CAREER GOALS

Consider the following possible career goals:

- You might dream of owning a fishing cabin in the mountains, a boat, or a farm.
- You might dream of a workshop with tools to work on computers, video game players, or cars.
- You might dream about solving mysteries, understanding scientific things, or acquiring the knowledge to solve some of the world's problems.
- You might dream of creating new things using science and technology; finding new ways to do things; or adding beauty to the world with art, writing, or music.
- You might dream of serving others, teaching people better ways to do things, and helping them solve their problems.
- You might dream of owning your own business, going into politics, or being a good leader for people.

All of these dreams are career goals. They will take time to achieve. To reach them you will need to make decisions and plan ahead. You will learn a great deal about decision making and planning in this book.

A career, like a best friend, is a goal. Remember at the beginning of this book, when you were asked what kind of work you thought

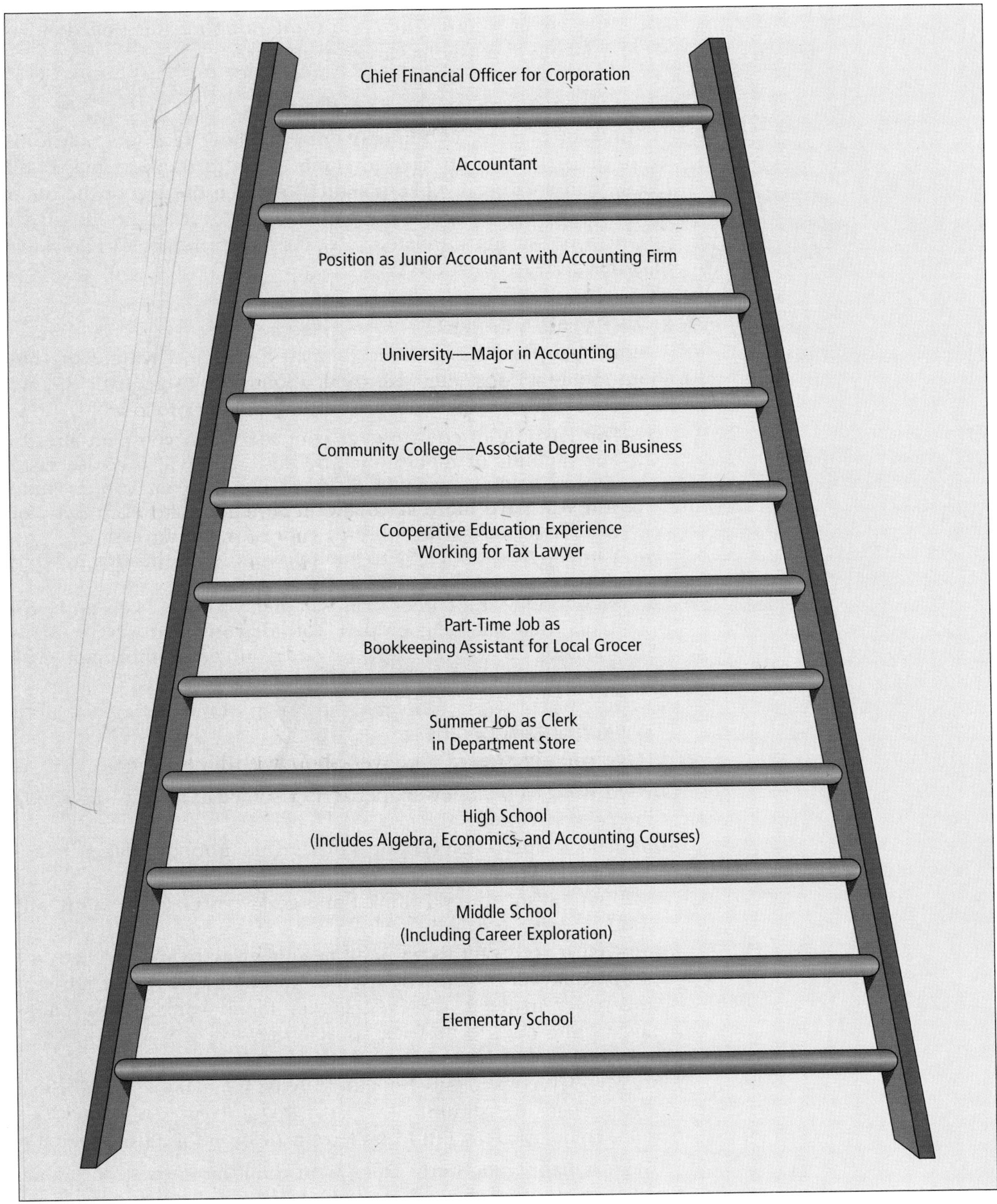
Chief Financial Officer for Corporation
Accountant
Position as Junior Accounant with Accounting Firm
University—Major in Accounting
Community College—Associate Degree in Business
Cooperative Education Experience
Working for Tax Lawyer
Part-Time Job as
Bookkeeping Assistant for Local Grocer
Summer Job as Clerk
in Department Store
High School
(Includes Algebra, Economics, and Accounting Courses)
Middle School
(Including Career Exploration)
Elementary School

▲ Your school counselor is a good source in your career journey. Find out which classes will help you reach your career goal.

you were going to do? When you thought about this question, you were thinking about your career goals.

A MOUNTAINTOP OR HILLS TO NOWHERE

Think of a career as a mountain trail. Think of a job as one hill along the pathway you have to climb to get to the next higher hill. If you plan a career, it's like planning to reach the top of the mountain someday by climbing up a pathway and over all the hills. If you just plan on having unrelated jobs, it's like planning to climb over hills that lead to nowhere.

WHY PLAN A CAREER?

Some people never bother to plan a career. They never think about mountaintops. They just think about how to get over the next hill. Some of the advantages of planning a career follow:

1. You have more control over your life when you plan ahead.
2. The amount of money income you earn will increase faster, because each new job will be higher on your career ladder. You will have more skills and experience with each new job, which will be worth more to your new employers.
3. You will be more likely to end up working in the area in which you are most interested.
4. Each job in your career plan will give you new skills and experience that will help prepare you for your next job.
5. You will be able to work toward your most important goals. You can plan to reach mountaintops.

ONLY YOU CAN DECIDE

Have you ever heard a conversation like this?

Carol: I want to be a newspaper writer someday. I want to write for the sports section.

John: That's dumb. Everybody knows that nobody makes it as a newspaper writer.

Carol: But I want to try. I think I'm a good writer, and I know a lot about sports.

John: Well, if you want to be poor and unhappy all your life, go right ahead. I have a cousin who tried to be a sportswriter for ten years and never made it. It's even harder for a woman. Newspapers always hire men to be their sportswriters.

Carol: Really?

John: Yes. My cousin says he should have gone into computer sciences. That's the future.

Carol: Maybe you're right. I don't want to be poor all my life.

What is happening here? Does John think he knows more about Carol than she knows about herself? Does Carol know herself well

Attitude makes a difference

A Dream That Didn't Happen

All during junior high school June thought about being a nurse. She was always good at taking care of her brothers and sisters when they were sick. She was interested in medicine and health.

When she was in tenth grade, her cousin said she could help June get a job as an aide in a local hospital in which she worked. June turned down the job because it didn't pay enough. She went to work in a department store where she could earn more money. June was clearly looking at today, and not ahead.

A year later, June still wanted to be a nurse. She talked about it constantly. Her counselor suggested that she take some science courses that would help her later. June said they were too hard and took other courses instead. Her cousin again offered to help her find a job as an aide with the local hospital during the afternoons. June turned it down again. Instead, she got a job mowing lawns, because she wanted to be outside to get a suntan.

When June graduated from high school she went to a local beauty school, because there wasn't a school with a nursing program nearby. She didn't want to travel to the next city, because it took too much time.

She dropped out of the beauty school and went to work in her friend's boutique selling clothes. She quit after two weeks and went to work as a cashier in a bowling alley.

June doesn't like her job and is unhappy. She doesn't know what to do. She still wants to be a nurse but has no experience and has not taken classes that could help her get a job at the hospital.

What Do YOU Think?

Has June really planned a career? What could June have done differently? What could she do now?

---

enough not to be influenced by John? Should Carol give up her dream before she even tries? Should she try computer sciences instead?

Keep in mind that you have to know what it is *you* really want. If you don't, someone else along the way is going to try to tell you. Just remember that *you* are the main source of information about yourself. No one else on earth cares as much about what happens to you as you do. Your parents, teachers, and counselors can be very helpful. Their opinions are important to listen to carefully. Once you have listened to them, though, then listen to yourself last. Only you can decide.

Career Decision-Making Activities

1. Write a short career plan to help June (page 13) develop her skills and meet her career goals. Begin your plan assuming that June is still in junior high. Include as many specific details as possible in your imaginary plan. Select another student from the class to role-play June. Read your career plan to June, and have her respond to it.

2. Visit your school library, and ask the librarian for the *Occupational Outlook Handbook.* Look up the reporter, correspondent, writer, and editor careers. What information can you find for each of these careers? Report your findings to the class. You will also learn more about these careers in Chapter 8.

YOUR ATTITUDE

Have people ever told you they don't like your attitude? That you have a bad attitude? That you have a negative attitude? Maybe you've said this to friends when you saw them acting like grouches or criticizing others.

Your friends' negative behavior may mean they don't like themselves very much. When people don't like themselves, they don't treat other people well. Additionally, they don't give themselves a chance to succeed. Because they think they will fail, they are almost certain to do so.

Has anyone ever told you he or she likes having you in a class or on a team because you have a good attitude? That you are fun to be around because you have a positive attitude? That he or she wants you on the team because you have a great attitude? This probably means you like yourself.

People who like themselves think they can do what they set out to do. They think they are capable of achieving their goals. This attitude improves their chances for being successful. Your **attitude** is your basic outlook on life. It is your own personal way of looking at the world around you and all the people in it.

attitude
a person's outlook on life, usually positive or negative.

self-concept
the way in which a person views his or her own self-worth and personal abilities.

SELF-CONCEPT

Your **self-concept** is the way you see yourself. It is your feelings about your own worth and value. Of course, your self-concept and attitude change a little from day to day. When you are satisfied that you have done something well, your self-concept improves. For example, if you get an A on a test, your teacher and parents congratulate you. You usually feel pretty good about yourself.

When you make a mistake and someone criticizes you, your self-concept goes down. For example, if you strike out or drop an easy fly ball in a baseball game, your team members may criticize you. You may feel like a clumsy failure for a while.

Attitude makes a difference

Learning to Run a Restaurant

James had a long-term goal of owning his own restaurant someday. When he was in seventh grade he frequently volunteered to help out as a dishwasher after school in his uncle's restaurant. During really busy times he also helped the busboys. He watched carefully how the waiters treated the customers. He learned what kinds of things made customers happy and caused them to come back to the restaurant (and give good tips).

During his junior year in high school James got a job in another restaurant as assistant to the cook. He took on more and more responsibility, and eventually learned how to prepare many dishes by himself.

The next year James was hired as an assistant to the cook in a much larger and nicer restaurant. He also used the skills he had learned as busboy to work one night a week as busboy in the new restaurant. After a few months he was promoted there to waiter. He made twice as much money as he had made being a busboy.

For the next three years James worked for the restaurant as a waiter and part-time host. He knew so much about working in different areas of the restaurant that he was soon promoted to assistant manager. One year later he was manager of the restaurant.

James has saved his money and has many years of experience in the restaurant business. He is going to buy his own restaurant next year and has lots of ideas about how to make it the most successful restaurant in town.

What Do YOU Think?

What can you tell about James's attitude toward working in a restaurant? Do you have the same attitude when your parents ask you to do a chore around the house? How did James "work his way up"?

These kinds of ups and downs are normal. Try not to let your self-concept go down too much or for too long. Your general, ongoing self-concept is what is important. This self-concept is the picture you have in your mind about what kind of person you are. You should like the person you are, even though you make mistakes and don't always act the way others think you should.

Do you give yourself the credit you deserve, without exaggerating your good points? Do you like the person you are? If you don't, you should discuss your feelings with your parents or your counselor.

YOUR ATTITUDE AND WORK

Perhaps the most important factor in your job success will be your attitude toward work. What is your attitude about work? You probably have a general one, whether you know it or not. This attitude has probably been influenced by your parents and by other adults in your life.

work ethic a set of values based on hard work.

Many people believe in the **work ethic**—a set of values based on hard work. These people believe that work is good. They believe that all people should work, and work hard. Their attitude toward work is that work is something we are all supposed to do and that work is good for us.

Other people are not such strong believers in the joys and benefits of work. They see work as a "necessary evil" and do only the minimum to survive. For some reason these people do not see the positive side of work that others do.

POSITIVE AND NEGATIVE ATTITUDES

Attitudes are often classified into two general types—positive and negative. People with positive attitudes usually look forward to what they do. They are usually cheerful and energetic, see the bright side of things, and treat other people well. You probably know people with positive attitudes and know how nice they are to be around. When you feel down, they point out the positive aspects of you and your life, and you feel better.

People with negative attitudes usually complain a lot. They seem angry much of the time and see the bad sides of most things. They don't get along very well with most people. You may know people with negative attitudes who are not very nice to be around.

Career Decision-Making Activities

1. Are you a good worker in school? Keep a journal for a week evaluating your own work habits in school. At the end of each day rate yourself on the following qualities that employers value. Rate yourself from 1 to 5, with 1 being poor performance and 5 being outstanding performance.

- Cooperation (trying to get along with everyone).
- Honesty.
- Initiative (finding things to do without being told).
- Willingness to learn.
- Willingness to follow directions.
- Dependability (being there every day, on time).
- Enthusiasm (having an energetic, positive attitude).
- Ability to accept criticism.
- Loyalty (supporting the teacher).

At the end of the one-week period, write a short essay describing your work habits.

2. Are your basic skills average, below average, or above average? Talk to your math and English teachers, and ask them to tell you which of the following skills need the most improvement.

- Writing.
- Reading.
- Speaking.
- Listening.
- Basic math.
- Solving word problems.
- Making decisions.

Make a plan for improving one or two of your basic skills.

YOUR ATTITUDE AND YOUR SUCCESS

How well you do in your job will depend to a large degree on your attitude. Your attitude will affect the way you get along with your boss and with other people with whom you work. If you have a negative attitude, others will act negatively toward you. If you have a positive attitude, they will act positively toward you.

One of the main reasons workers lose their jobs is that they have a negative attitude and cannot get along well with others. Remember that even though your attitude is positive, you may have to work with people who have negative attitudes. Keep your attitude positive, and chances are these people will start being more positive, at least while they are around you. Positive attitudes are contagious.

If you have a positive attitude, you are already on your way to a successful career. If your attitude is negative, you can change it. The younger you are and the harder you work at it, the easier it will be to acquire a more positive attitude.

Besides, there are many things about work to enjoy if you have the right attitude:

- You will make new friends with interests similar to yours.
- You will accomplish things of which you can be proud.
- You will be making money to spend on things you like.
- You will grow as an individual and learn new skills.
- You can even have a lot of fun while you work.

Start off with the right attitude. Think positively about work. Attitude always makes a difference.

Three Ways to Start

You're reading this book for a good reason. The decision makers at your school believe that you can increase your chances for a happy, satisfying life by getting to know yourself better now. They believe that the decisions you make about the courses you take in high school and college and the attitude you have about your schoolwork will affect your entire life. And these people are right. You can make school count, and you can begin now, if you haven't already.

1. *Make better choices.* How do you make school count? First, you use a book like this one to help you get to know yourself better, explore career choices, and learn to make decisions. After reading this book you will be able to make wise, informed choices about your education. You will be able to choose the courses that will help you the most after you graduate. Your course selections won't be based on a friend's suggestion or a wild guess. They'll be choices that make sense to you because you know who you are and where you are going.
2. *Develop a positive attitude.* A second way

you can make school count is by developing a positive attitude toward work now and putting it to use in school. School is good practice for work. Your study habits often become your work habits. If you are a person who gets the most out of school, you are probably a person who will get the most out of work and life. In other words, you can use school as a training ground for your career, which increases your chances for success.

3. *Improve your basic skills.* A third way you can make school count is by improving your basic math, communication, thinking, and decision-making skills. All employers emphasize the importance of basic skills. No matter what career you choose, you must be able to read, write, speak, and listen. You must be able to do basic math calculations using fractions and percentages. And you must be able to think critically to solve problems and make decisions. These are basic skills needed in all jobs and professions. And guess what?—these are exactly the skills that your teachers will be focusing on throughout the rest of your school years.

So make school count. Work hard in this course so that you can begin to give your life a direction. Work hard in all your courses so that you develop good work habits that will carry over into your career. And work especially hard on improving your basic skills. Your choices for success and happiness are tied directly to these skills—no matter which career path you choose.

Career Decision-Making Activities

1. What kind of attitude do you have? Take out a piece of paper. Write in one column the word *positive* and in the other column the word *negative.* Now read down the following list of positive and negative attitudes. Each time you have a positive attitude, put a check mark in the positive column on your sheet of paper. Do the same each time you have a negative attitude. Try to be honest about yourself.

Positive Attitude	**Negative Attitude**
I smile easily.	I seldom smile.
I don't complain very often.	I complain a lot.
I listen to other people's opinions.	I am always right.
I am willing to change for the better.	I don't want to change anything.
I will admit if I'm wrong.	I blame others for mistakes.
I seldom make excuses.	I make excuses
I seldom criticize other people.	I criticize other people.
I am considerate of other people.	I think only of myself.
I am responsible for my own mistakes.	I can't be held responsible for my own mistakes.
I think a job can be interesting and fun.	I don't like work.
I am willing to try new things.	I don't want to try new things.
I like most people.	I don't like most people.

Now add up the check marks in each column. Do you have more positive or negative checks? If your score is 12 positive checks and 0 negative, you obviously have a very positive attitude. If your score is the other way around, you obviously have a very negative attitude. One of your goals, then, should be improving your attitude. You *can* improve your attitude!

Review and Enrichment

Summarizing the Chapter

Summarizing information is a critical thinking skill that will help you succeed in the world of work. Write a summary of what you learned in Chapter 1. Focus on the main points of the chapter. Then in a class discussion, compare your summary with the summaries done by your classmates. Can you improve your summary?

Improving Your Career Vocabulary

Learning to use new vocabulary terms will improve your communication skills, which are important in almost all areas of work. Write definitions for the terms listed below. Then for each term, write an original sentence about yourself in which you use the term correctly.

- work
- job
- occupation
- career
- goal
- attitude
- self-concept
- work ethic

Finding the Facts

Finding exact information is a frequently used skill in many careers. Find the answers to the exercise below, and write the answers on a separate sheet of paper.

1. Give three reasons why people work.
2. List at least three advantages to planning a career.
3. Who or what is the main source of information about you?
4. Does a person's self-concept change from day to day or remain constant over a period of years?
5. Attitudes can be classified into what two general types?

Thinking for Yourself

To complete the exercise below you will need to use critical thinking and communication skills, which are skills valued by all employers. Write out your answers or be prepared to discuss them in class, depending on your teacher's instructions.

1. Explain in your own words the difference between a *job* and a *career.*
2. Only you can decide which career to pursue, but many people can offer good advice. From whom will you seek career advice? What reasons can you think of for your parents being good sources of career guidance?
3. Do you think most of the people you know have a positive, negative, or in-between attitude? Why do you think this is so?
4. What relationship do you see, if any, between your friends' attitudes and their success and popularity? Explain.
5. Do you think school has prepared you for the world of work? How will you be better prepared after finishing high school? Explain.

Practicing Your Basic Skills

Your career success depends greatly on your basic math and communication skills. Work hard at improving in the areas where you have trouble with the following exercises.

Math

1. There are five sets of numbers below. The numbers represent, in order, the number of years a person attended school full-time, the person's age on completing school and starting a full-time job, and the person's age at retirement. How many more years did each person work full-time than go to school full-time?
   a. 13 - 19 - 60
   b. 15 - 21 - 66
   c. 17 - 23 - 65
   d. 22 - 28 - 64
   e. 21 - 27 - 68
2. Ryan has been offered five jobs. Below are the number of hours per week he'd work and the hourly rate for each job. How much would Ryan make per week in each job? If Ryan's only reason for working were to make as much money as possible, which job should he take?
   a. 20; $5.45
   b. 15; $6.25
   c. 25; $4.35
   d. 22; $4.87
   e. 30; $3.90
3. To baby-sit one child, Jacob charges $2.50 per hour. For *each* additional child he charges one-

half that amount per hour. How much should Jacob be paid in each situation below?

a. 2 children; 7 hours
b. 4 children; 6 hours
c. 3 children; 8 hours

Reading and Writing

1. Read newspapers and magazines for one week looking for articles about people who have achieved success in their careers. Take your favorite article to class. Write a paragraph summarizing the reasons why that person has been successful.
2. Scan the business section of your local newspaper each day for one week. Make a list of all the jobs that come to mind as you scan the articles. Which job seems the most interesting to you? Write a paragraph explaining why this job more than any other sounds the most interesting to you.

Speaking and Listening

1. Give a one-minute speech to your class. Base your speech on one of your readings from the reading suggestions above. Pretend that an employer will either hire you or not, depending on how well you deliver your speech.
2. Listen closely to each of your classmates' speeches. Take notes. After each speech, compare notes. Did you "hear" everything your classmates heard?

Activities Working with Others

In almost all careers you must be able to get along well with other people to be successful. Work with your classmates to do the following activities. As you work together, pay attention to how well you get along. If necessary, work hard at improving your ability to do your part and to cooperate.

1. Work with your classmates to design and create a bulletin board collage of pictures and drawings representing the ideal careers of the class members. Each person must find or draw a picture for someone else's ideal career.
2. All jobs are important, but some have more prestige (high value in people's minds). As a class, compile a list of the twenty most prestigious careers. Work out a system for resolving differences of opinion so that the final list represents the majority viewpoint.

Decision Making and Problem Solving

You will be a big help to your employer if you can make decisions and solve problems. List all the possible ways of resolving the situations described below. Then pick the best alternative (possible choice), and tell why you chose it. If you need help, you might want to refer to Chapter 3.

1. A new person in school asked you to sit with her at lunch. You've just met this person and like her, but several of your friends don't like her. You know they'll give you a hard time if you eat lunch with her. The new girl doesn't seem to have any friends, though, and you know your sitting with her would mean a lot to her. What will you do?
2. You're really interested in clothes, and you'd like to get a part-time job working in a clothing store. You'd even be willing to work a few hours a week for no pay just so you could get the experience. The problem is that you don't know anyone who could help you get such a job. The only thing you can think to do is go to all the clothing and department stores and ask if they need any help. This would be hard to do since you are shy, especially with strangers. What will you do?

CHAPTER 2

WHO ARE YOU? VALUES, INTERESTS, AND ABILITIES

◆ Chapter Objectives ◆

After completing this chapter you will be able to do the following:

- ◆ Define the terms listed under "New Career Terms."
- ◆ Explain the difference between life values and work values.
- ◆ Identify your most important and least important values.
- ◆ Identify your major interests.
- ◆ Give examples of how interests match up with careers.
- ◆ Explain the difference between aptitudes and skills.

◆ New Career Terms ◆

In this chapter you will learn the meanings of the following career terms:

- ✔ Values
- ✔ Life values
- ✔ Work values
- ✔ Conflict of values
- ✔ Interest
- ✔ Interest inventory
- ✔ Aptitude
- ✔ Skills

Rebecca promised her best friend, Maggie, that she would celebrate her birthday with her. They made plans two weeks ago. Rebecca is going to take Maggie to a concert featuring one of Maggie's favorite bands and then to a restaurant, where she has ordered a cake. Maggie's birthday falls on Friday, but they have decided to celebrate on Saturday night so Maggie can be with her boyfriend on Friday night.

Two days before Maggie's birthday, Rebecca receives a phone call. She is surprised and happy to hear the sound of Jim's voice. She has met him on several occasions over the past year. He is the school's number one track star and very smart.

Every time Rebecca meets Jim she thinks about how much she would like to go out with him. She never dreamed he would ask her. He tells her he is having a special party on Saturday night. He would like Rebecca to be his date.

Rebecca accepts Jim's offer and makes a date for his party on Saturday. After she hangs up, she calls Maggie and explains. She promises to take her out the following Saturday night to celebrate her birthday. She apologizes and says she will make it up by buying her a belt that she knows Maggie has wanted for a long time.

Did Rebecca make the right decision? What would you have done? What are the reasons for your decision?

More than likely, how you judge what Rebecca did depends on your values.

VALUES

Your **values** are personal standards that you believe are important and worthwhile. These are the rules you make for yourself and by which you want to live. They are what feels best for you.

Life values represent what is important to you in life. These values include family values, social values, and so forth. **Work values** represent what is important to you in work. These values could include how much money you earn, job security, your work environment, and so on. If your life and work values are the same, or you learn to balance them, you will be able to meet your life values through your work.

Consider the life values facing Jeffrey in the next example:

Jeffrey faces a problem. Jeffrey has been painting since he was five years old. He has always dreamed about being a painter. His family and friends have always encouraged him. His work has been praised by the local paper, and he has won several state awards.

When Jeffrey is in his junior year in high school, he begins to make plans for attending an art college in a big city that is two thousand miles from where his family lives. It is the best college for what he wants to do and the college from which he is most likely to get a scholarship.

Jeffrey's uncle owns a very successful jewelry store in Jeffrey's hometown. One morning his uncle asks him to visit the store.

values
personal views or ideas that a person feels are important.

life values
things that are important in your life such as family values and social values.

work values
represent what is important in work such as the money you earn, job security, and your work environment.

Jeffrey's uncle asks him to come to work for him when he graduates. He tells Jeffrey that he has such an artistic eye that he could be very successful in the jewelry business. Jeffrey could count on rapidly advancing and possibly managing the store one day. Also, the job would provide a secure income, and he would be near his family.

What should Jeffrey do? What values should he identify in himself?

LISTEN TO YOUR OWN VALUES

Listen to your own values. You probably learned many of them from your parents, and they have been developing inside you all your life. They have become a big part of what is right for you.

When you are true to your values, you are in *harmony* with yourself. You will have found an internal calm. Your values can give you direction and make you feel comfortable with your choices. If you don't listen to your values, you will feel it inside yourself. It's like eating food you know will make you sick.

Values affect career choices and should be taken with you during your career adventure. Your values will give you *signals* about how happy or successful you can be in particular careers.

Here is a list of some values you need to think about:

- **Money.** Is it important to you to earn a lot of money? Do you want to be able to buy a big house or a nice car? Would you give up making a lot of money for other things that were more important to you?
- **Independence.** Do you want to work for yourself or have a job where you make most of your own decisions? Do you want to be free to take vacations whenever you want to?
- **Security.** Do you like knowing you can count on having your job from day to day? Does earning a regular salary make you feel secure?
- **Education.** Is it important to you to continue learning about the world? Are you curious? Is it important to be able to talk to many people about many things? Would you like to have an education that could get you a job in a professional area, such as law or medicine, where you could earn more money, or have more security, or have more independence?
- **Being creative.** Do you feel the need to create things? Would you give up security for a chance to create something? Would you give up making a steady income to be an artist?
- **Making changes in your community.** Are you concerned with what is happening in your town? Would you like to see your town cleaner, or would you like to see less crime or drug use? Would you like to take part in

▶ If you choose a career requiring a college education, life there will be different from high school. It is the first environment in which you personally will make choices based on your values.

efforts to help make these things happen? Would you be willing to do volunteer work or work with little pay to help other people?

- **A regular schedule.** Do you want a schedule that is the same every day? Do you want to go home at the same time every day to spend time with your family? Is having time off more important than money you would make working overtime?
- **Having a high profile, or being recognized.** Do you want a career that could make you famous, or a career that puts you in a high position where lots of people recognize you? Is prestige (high standing) or being well known important to you?
- **Putting personal life ahead of job.** Do you want to stay close to your family members? Would you pursue a career that didn't give you enough time to spend with your family? Or a career that left you too tired to have energy to do things with your family?
- **Being a leader.** Do you like being the boss instead of taking orders? Or do you prefer that someone else make the decisions and take the responsibility?

There are many more values you might consider. Knowing what your values are and which ones are most important will help you make wiser decisions. Knowing your values can also help you reduce the chances of your different values conflicting (see the next section) or your values conflicting with those of other people.

Remember that your values may change. You may begin to question the values you grew up with. As you have new experiences, some values may become more or less important.

CONFLICT OF VALUES

Have you ever wanted two things at the same time? Have you ever been in a situation where if you have one thing, then you can't have the other? Both things were important to you, and you had trouble deciding which one was most important. If so, you may have been having a conflict of values.

A **conflict of values** is when you hold one or more values that you can't stay true to at the same time. For example, your friends might plead with you to go somewhere you'd like to go, but your parents have told you that place is off limits. In this case your family values would be in conflict with your social values.

conflict of values
when you have one or more values that you can't satisfy at the same time.

At the beginning of the chapter, Rebecca was facing a conflict of values. What values were in conflict for her?

Career Decision-Making Activities

1. Each of the following statements shows how you could have a conflict of values. Rewrite the statements on a separate sheet of paper, filling in the blanks with something that is important to you. Then share your answers with a classmate. Also discuss in class some possible solutions to the conflicts.
   a. You want to spend time with your friends, but you also want to get a weekend job to earn money to buy a __________.
   b. You want to get good grades, but you don't want to take time away from __________ to study.
   c. You want to be in great shape for ________, but you don't want to do the ________ you must do.
   d. You think it's important to be honest, but your best friend asks you to __________.
   e. You want to impress your friends, but you don't want to endanger or hurt yourself by __________.
   f. You want to please your parents, but your friend wants you to __________.
2. Where do you stand on different values questions? Below are a number of statements that people often read or hear. As a class, vote either that you *agree* or *disagree* with each statement. Keep track of your own votes. How do your personal opinions compare with the class majority opinions?
   a. There are times when cheating is all right.
   b. School should be optional.
   c. If you don't have money, you won't be happy.
   d. Health is more important than anything else.
   e. Women should not work outside the home if they have small children.
   f. Men should not work outside the home if they have small children.
   g. Children should have to work for an allowance.
   h. The government should spend more money on clean air.
   i. Family always comes first.
   j. You don't get ahead by being nice.
   k. Having a steady job is the most important thing about working.
   l. You should tell your parents anything they ask you.

In making decisions, it is important to be aware of your values and which ones are most important. It is also important to be aware of how other people's values influence the decisions you make.

Your values belong to you. Only you can know for certain what you value the most.

YOUR INTERESTS

Imagine getting paid for what you like to do. Imagine taking what you are interested in and turning it into a job. Imagine doing the things that you have fun doing and turning them into a career. Imagine doing what you like best for the rest of your life.

Did you know that many famous photographers first took pictures only as a hobby? That many successful airplane mechanics started out fixing bicycles for fun? That famous comedians started out as young children making people laugh? That many builders of famous buildings started out designing houses from Popsicle sticks for class projects? Did you know that some of the founders of the most successful computer companies in the United States started out as kids playing around with computers?

These are examples of people who took what they were interested in and turned it into a lifelong career. They are probably good at their jobs. They are probably happy and satisfied.

You may have heard people say, "This job is so boring I can't stand it," "Thank goodness it's Friday," or "I can't stand to get up in the mornings and go to work." These people have jobs in which they aren't interested. They probably aren't very good at their jobs, either.

▶ Most people find it easiest to develop skills in things they enjoy doing.

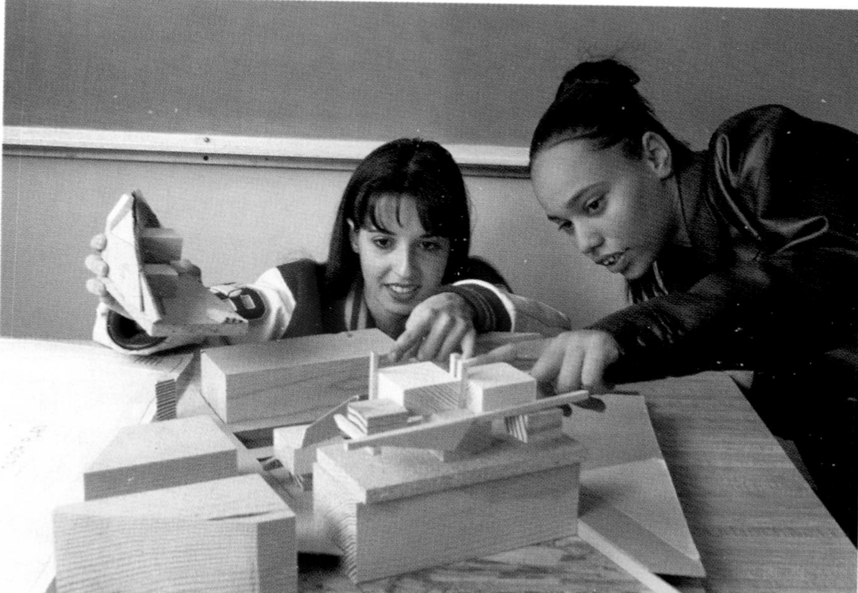

When you do what you're interested in, you have a better time. When people are having a good time, they naturally do better. When you think about careers, think about having a good time.

DISCOVERING YOUR INTERESTS

An **interest** is a positive feeling you have about something. Your interests are what you like to do.

interest
something a person enjoys doing or thinking about.

Finding out what you like to do is a search inside yourself. This search can help you identify your life goals. No one else can tell you what your life goals should be.

Don't think of searching inside yourself as hard work or homework. Think of it as fun. Exploring the inner world of yourself and unwrapping your skills is like unwrapping presents on your birthday.

Close your eyes, and think about what you like doing more than anything else—your major interest. You're probably smiling about it. You probably also know that you're good at what is on your mind. You're probably also curious about it and would like to do it better and more often.

There are many other interests about which you might have been thinking. If you couldn't recall any, think about what you like to do with your friends. Also think about what friends you like to be with, because you often choose friends who have the same interests as you do.

WHAT DO YOU WATCH AND READ?

Think about what television programs you watch or what books or magazines you read. Do you like watching programs about police, or programs about animals? Are your favorite programs about science, or about teachers? Is the only station you like MTV?

When you go to the movies, do you like seeing movies about foreign countries? Do you like old Westerns about cattle ranchers? Do you like reading books about hospitals or private detectives or boating? Do you like to read magazines about race cars or woodworking

Career Decision-Making Activities

1. Read the two quotes below:
   "Work is the crabgrass in the lawn of life." (Snoopy)
   "Work is love made visible." (Kahlil Gibran)
   Which quote do you think comes from someone whose job involves doing something he or she enjoys? Which quote comes from someone who isn't interested in his or her job? Make up your own quote about work. Be prepared to explain what your quote means to you in a class discussion.

Attitude makes a difference

Debra Starts Selling Cars

When Debra graduated from high school she was a mechanic in her father's service station in her hometown. It was a small town, and she lived in a house in the nearby countryside with a horse and a dog. She earned a fair salary and had a group of friends who liked to ride horses together.

Debra was offered a job by a car dealer in a big city as a car salesperson. She realized it was an opportunity to make more money.

She gave up living with her family and her animals and rented an apartment in the city. Within two months Debra was the best car salesperson in the entire car dealership.

What Do YOU Think?

How did Debra's decision affect the way she lived? Do you think Debra had a good attitude about work?

▼ If band is your favorite class, you should investigate careers related to music.

or computers? What section of a newspaper do you turn to first? All these choices that you make every day can give you clues about your interests.

WHAT CLASSES DO YOU LIKE?

Think about the classes you like. Are you good in math? Do you like the classes that discuss the business world? Do you think you would do well in a vocational class? This is a class that teaches you skills in a trade, such as carpentry or auto mechanics. You will learn more about these kinds of courses later in this book.

Perhaps you have developed a strong interest in one of your classes. Ask yourself, "If I could take any class I wanted without having to worry about a grade, what would it be?" If you are really good in one of your classes, there is a chance you could be successful pursuing a career in that area.

WHAT ARE YOUR HOBBIES AND DREAMS?

Think about your *hobbies.* Hobbies are usually strong interests that have developed into activities you do regularly for pleasure.

Think about what daydreams you have and about what is on your mind before you go to sleep at night. Maybe you dream about being a famous scientist, or senator of your state, or a movie star.

Career Decision-Making Activities

1. You need to pinpoint your interests. On a separate sheet of paper, list the five interests from the following list that most appeal to you. Keep your interest list in your notes as you continue reading this chapter. Consider some of the following, and ask yourself if they are your interests:

- Listening to music.
- Reading books.
- Taking care of children.
- Taking care of animals.
- Looking at the stars.
- Playing sports.
- Talking to people.
- Exploring the Internet.
- Keeping a diary.
- Cooking.
- Building science projects.
- Drawing.
- Volunteering to help others.
- Playing a musical instrument.
- Collecting baseball cards.
- Fishing.
- Playing video games.
- Telling stories.
- Attending religious services.
- Gardening.

2. You may have many interests but can't decide which are the most important to you. Make a list of all your interests. Consider all the areas mentioned in the text, such as television, books, hobbies, and friends. Then look over your list, and decide which are your top ten interests. Make a list (like Shawn's, which follows), and put your most important interests first.

Shawn's Top Ten Favorite Interests

1. Following the local football team.
2. Listening to music.
3. Playing tennis.
4. Playing with friends.
5. Working on the school newspaper.
6. Watching favorite television shows.
7. Doing projects in art class.
8. Playing interactive CD-ROM games.
9. Going to movies.
10. Surfing the Internet.

INTEREST INVENTORIES

Perhaps you've given a party or helped someone else plan a party. You might have made a list of every item you would need to make it a fun and successful party. The list helped you identify and keep track of everything you would need. It helped you remember and keep in mind what you had to work with. This list was a form of *inventory.*

If you take an inventory of your interests, it will also help you to identify and keep track of yourself so you can have a fun and successful career. An **interest inventory** is a list that helps you pinpoint and rank your interests. It will help you find out which interests are the most important to you.

interest inventory a questionnaire that helps people determine what their interests are.

Interest inventories allow you to choose your favorite activities. The activities you select are then placed in groups. Each group of interests can be matched to specific careers. In this way an interest inventory can give you clues about what careers might be interesting to you. A sample interest inventory appears on page 30.

Sample Interest Inventory

This is just a sample inventory. **Do not write in your book**. If you were taking the inventory, you would mark "L" for the activities you *Like* and "D" for those you *Dislike*.

Realistic	**L**	**D**
Fix electrical things	☐	☐
Repair cars	☐	☐
Raise dairy cows or beef cattle	☐	☐
Use metalworking or machine tools	☐	☐
Be a hunting or fishing guide	☐	☐
Take woodworking course	☐	☐

Total No. of L's ☐

Investigative	**L**	**D**
Read scientific books or magazines	☐	☐
Work in laboratory	☐	☐
Study a scientific theory	☐	☐
Read about special subjects on my own	☐	☐
Take physics course	☐	☐
Take chemistry course	☐	☐

Total No. of L's ☐

Artistic	**L**	**D**
Sketch, draw, or paint	☐	☐
Act in a comedy or play	☐	☐
Design furniture, clothing, or posters	☐	☐
Play in a band, group, or orchestra	☐	☐
Write for a magazine or newspaper	☐	☐
Read or write poetry	☐	☐

Total No. of L's ☐

Your school guidance counselor may give you an interest inventory. This is a test that doesn't require studying, because there are no right or wrong answers. Such tests are designed to help you get to know yourself better. They might help you choose a career about which you can be excited.

MATCHING INTERESTS TO CAREERS

You can find a career that involves many of your interests. On page 29 in the "Career Decision-Making Activity," there was a list of possible interests. You selected five and wrote them on a piece of paper. Do any of your top five interests appear in the following list? Can you think of other careers that might match your top five interests?

You can probably think of some actual careers that might be possible given the responses in your interest inventory.

INTERESTS	CAREER POSSIBILITIES
Talking to people	Salesperson, personal assistant, manager, teacher
Taking care of animals	Pet store employee, veterinarian, veterinarian's helper, farmer, rancher
Drawing	Commercial (advertising) artist, illustrator, architect, draftsperson
Cooking	Chef, chef's assistant, restaurant manager, fast-food cook
Playing a musical instrument	Musical group manager, musician, music composer, music teacher
Building science projects	Computer engineer, multimedia designer, chemist, physicist
Keeping a diary	Office clerk, bookkeeper, librarian, writer
Volunteering to help others	Nurse, teacher, social worker, counselor
Exploring the Internet	Web page designer

HOW TO AVOID A BORING JOB

Wouldn't it be better to be interested in your job and be enthusiastic about it rather than being bored or complaining the way some people do? Most of these people could have chosen a career that would have made them happier. They started out just like you. They had the freedom to discover their interests and choose between many careers. If they had thought more about their interests and had chosen a career in which they were interested, they probably wouldn't be complaining so much.

Also remember that it's important not only to find out what interests you but also to find out what *doesn't* interest you. This way you will know ahead of time which careers would not match your interests.

Use your freedom of choice to discover and develop your interests. Explore and find new interests.

You can say, "Thank goodness it's Monday morning." You'll say that because you like your job.

Career Decision-Making Activities

1. Make a list of twenty activities in which you are *not* interested.
2. Narrow your list to ten.
3. Put the interests in order from 1 to 10, with number 1 being your least favorite activity.
4. For each of your ten least favorite activities, write the names of three jobs that would involve those activities.
5. Look over your completed list, and ask yourself if these look like jobs you should avoid.

APTITUDES AND SKILLS

aptitude
ability or potential for learning new skills.

skill
ability to perform a certain activity well.

An **aptitude** is the potential or readiness to develop a skill or ability. If you have an aptitude for something, it means that you have the natural ability to learn a certain skill more easily than some other skills. Your **skills** are your abilities to do things.

If the first time you hit a baseball, it was easier for you than for most people, then you might have an aptitude for learning baseball skills. If the first time you did a science project you came up with a good idea before most people, then you might have an aptitude for science. If you think you understand more than your classmates about a book you read, then you might have an aptitude for English and reading.

You may know people who learn how to solve math problems very quickly. You may know others who have a more difficult time learning. The people who learn more easily have an aptitude for math. The others may learn math just as well, but they have to work a little harder. Chances are those people have an aptitude for learning other things more easily, such as playing the guitar or drawing.

Remember that just because you can't do something the first time doesn't mean you will never be able to do it. If you have enough

◀ It takes many aptitudes and skills to successfully stage any production—many of them "behind the scenes."

interest, then keep trying. Chances are you will be able to do it better than most people.

Don't be discouraged if someone tells you that you don't have an aptitude for something. People have different aptitudes and skills, just as they have different interests. And different jobs require different aptitudes and skills. That is why you want to identify your own aptitudes and skills and the jobs that use them.

DISCOVERING YOUR APTITUDES

You probably know some of your aptitudes, but not all of them. You probably don't even realize you have an aptitude for some activities, because you haven't tried them yet. If you think you might be good at something, you should try it to find out.

How can you find out what your aptitudes are? You can do several things. A good place to start is with yourself. What do you think your strongest abilities are? Are you good at painting pictures? Are you good at figuring out the answers to math problems? Are you good at convincing people?

Your grades are one indication of your aptitudes. Which subjects do you get the best grades in? Of course, if you don't try very hard in school, you may have more aptitude for certain kinds of work than your grades indicate. Also, you may not have taken courses yet in subjects for which you have the greatest aptitude.

You might discover your aptitudes outside of school. You might find you have an aptitude for singing by singing in a choir, or an aptitude for dancing by taking dancing lessons, or an aptitude for electronics by fixing a cassette deck.

Sometimes it's hard to recognize our own aptitudes, so it might help to ask your family and friends what they have noticed are your apptitudes. Usually your teachers and guidance counselors can let you know if they think you have an aptitude for certain kinds of work.

There are also tests to help you understand what your aptitudes are and exercises that tell you what skills are required for different careers. Your counselor may give you an aptitude test.

One of the most widely used aptitude tests lists eleven basic aptitudes. These eleven aptitudes and brief descriptions of each are listed here:

- **General.** The ability to learn—intelligence. Being able to understand instructions, facts, and reasons. The ability to reason and make judgments. Closely related to doing well in school.
- **Verbal.** The ability to understand meanings of words and ideas. Being able to present information and ideas clearly.
- **Numerical.** The ability to perform arithmetic operations quickly and accurately. The ability to solve mathematical story problems.
- **Spatial.** The ability to "see" how objects in flat drawings or pictures would actually look in three dimensions. Being good at visualizing shapes, heights, widths, and depths mentally.
- **Form perception.** The ability to notice detail in objects. The ability to see differences in shapes and shadings of figures, and in widths and lengths of lines.
- **Clerical perception.** The ability to observe detail and recognize errors in numbers, spelling, and punctuation in written material. The ability to observe differences in copy, to proofread words and numbers.
- **Finger dexterity.** The ability to move the fingers to work with small objects rapidly or accurately.
- **Manual dexterity.** The ability to move the hands easily and skillfully. The ability to work with the hands in placing and turning motions.
- **Motor coordination.** The ability to coordinate eyes and hands or fingers rapidly and accurately in making precise movements with speed. Includes tasks such as guiding objects into position and assembling parts.
- **Eye-hand-foot coordination.** The ability to move the hands and feet together when a signal indicates response needed. Includes tasks such as piloting a plane or driving a car.
- **Color discrimination.** The ability to see likenesses or differences in colors or shades. The ability to match and select colors that go together.

Sample Aptitude Test Questions

Listed below are sample questions from an aptitude test. Experts can use the results from such a test to point you toward a career area that will make use of your strengths.

1. An eclipse of the sun throws the shadow of the
   A. moon on the sun
   B. moon on the earth
   C. earth on the sun
   D. earth on the moon

3. How many 36-passenger buses will it take to carry 144 people?
   A. 3
   B. 4
   C. 5
   D. 6

10. 60 ÷ 15 =
   A. .3
   B. 4
   C. 5
   D. 6

25. A car uses too much oil when which parts are worn?
   A. pistons
   B. piston rings
   C. main bearings
   D. connecting rods

26. The saw shown is used mainly to cut
   A. plywood
   B. odd-shaped holes in wood
   C. along the grain of the wood
   D. across the grain of the wood

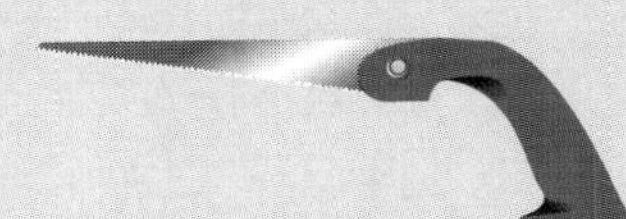

28. What is the area of this square
   A. 1 square foot
   B. 5 square feet
   C. 10 square feet
   D. 25 square feet

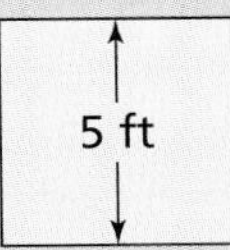

29. Which post holds up the greater part of the load?
   A. post A
   B. post B
   C. both equal
   D. not clear

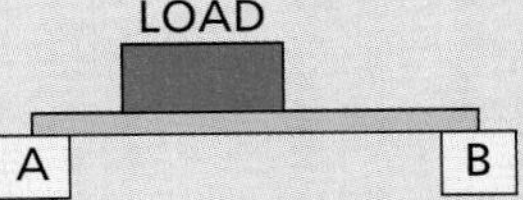

30. In this arrangement of pulleys, which pulley turns fastest?
   A. A
   B. B
   C. C
   D. D

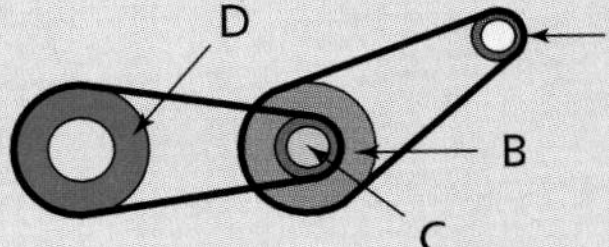

31. Which of the following has the least resistance?
   A. wood
   B. iron
   C. rubber
   D. silver

32. In this schematic vacuum tube illustrated, the cathode is element
   A. A
   B. B
   C. C
   D. D

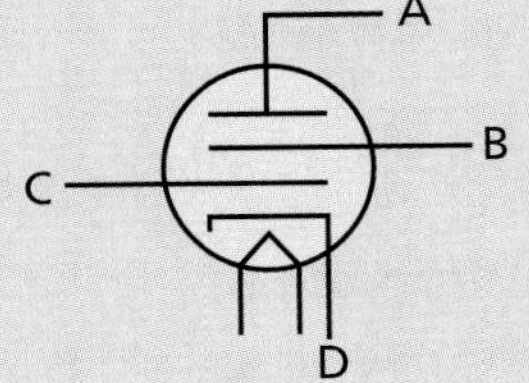

Samples from the Armed Services Vocational Aptitude Battery (ASVAB)

Career Decision-Making Activities

1. On a separate sheet of paper list the eleven aptitudes just described.
2. Next to each aptitude, write a number from 1 to 5 to indicate how strong you are in that aptitude, with 5 being the strongest aptitude and 1 the weakest.
3. For each aptitude, write one or two sentences telling why you rated yourself as you did.
4. Discuss your ratings with your guidance counselor or teacher.

DISCOVERING YOUR SKILLS

People aren't born with any skills, but they can learn hundreds. You, for example, may not realize it, but you have hundreds of skills. How many can you name?

You may know how to flip a skateboard, or use a computer, or play the saxophone. These are skills. You may know how to sew, or shoot baskets, or bake pies. You may know how to dance, or ride a horse, or do crossword puzzles. These are all skills. Having a natural aptitude for certain kinds of skills will make those skills easier for you to develop and perfect than other skills.

It is important that you know your skills. You don't want to choose a career only to find out that you'll be expected to do tasks that you don't know how to do. Because you constantly learn new skills, you must frequently re-ask yourself, "What skills do I have now?" Your list of skills will grow and grow as you have new experiences.

A VARIETY OF SKILLS

PEOPLE	FACTS	THINGS
Teaching young children	Adding numbers	Typing letters
Persuading others	Finding information	Hitting baseballs
Organizing meetings	Keeping records	Running obstacle courses
Interpreting messages	Sorting numbers	Assembling parts
Leading discussions	Analyzing reports	Building furniture
Initiating group activities	Remembering dates	Weeding gardens
Giving instructions	Setting up filing systems	Cooking
Listening to others	Classifying information	Washing cars

Listed on page 36 are just a few of the hundreds of skills you might have. Read through the list to get a better idea of what you can count as a skill. Remember—these are just a few examples. The skills are divided into three groups to help you think of additional skills.

TIPS TO KEEP IN MIND ABOUT APTITUDES AND SKILLS

Read and put to use the following suggestions about aptitudes and skills:

- **Just because you may not now have a certain skill doesn't mean you can't learn to be good at it.** If you want to do something badly enough, chances are you will be able to learn. Don't be discouraged if people tell you that you don't have an aptitude for something you really want to learn. Just be prepared to work harder.
- **Everyone is different.** Just as everyone has different interests, not everyone has the same skills. Even people with the same skills will want to use them in different ways.
- **Just because you are strong in a skill doesn't mean you don't have to work at it anymore.** You can't just sit back and relax. Keep working on your skills and get better at them, just the way an athlete keeps trying to break personal records. As you get older there will be more people with the same skills competing with you.
- **Keep trying to learn skills you don't have.** Even if you don't have an aptitude or interest in some areas, you will need to develop some skills in them. You need many skills just to survive without too many problems and without having to depend on other people. For example, even though you might not like your English class, you will still have to be able to read so you can understand written instructions. You will have to learn how to write so that people will know exactly what you mean to say. Even if you don't like math, you will still want to be able to balance your checkbook, figure out a budget, or measure a room to put in a rug.
- **Most people find it easier to develop skills in things they enjoy doing.** If you have a great interest in certain areas, chances are you can develop skills in those areas. If you don't seem to be particularly skilled in any area, let your sense of enjoyment guide you to learning skills.

This chart will help you understand how interests, aptitudes, and skills are related to one another and to particular occupations.

OCCUPATION	INTEREST	APTITUDE	SKILL
Automobile mechanic	Likes fixing things	Moving the eyes and hands together to perform work correctly	Repairing automobile engines
Chemist	Likes knowing more	Being able to reason and make judgments	Setting up laboratory experiments
Interior decorator	Likes creating new, attractive things	Selecting colors that go well together	Helping customers pick out paint, furniture, drapes, and carpets
Day-care worker	Likes children	Understanding the meaning of words and ideas	Giving instructions for children's games
Store manager	Likes to be a leader	Using words to present ideas clearly	Showing new workers how to do their jobs
Bookkeeper	Likes to keep things organized	Doing math problems quickly and correctly	Keeping financial records for a company
Crane operator	Likes working outdoors	Moving the hands and feet together in response to visual signals	Placing steel beams on a new building

SPECIAL TALENT

In many careers, especially those involving music, art, and sports, a great deal of natural talent is needed. A talent is a "superior," natural ability or skill. When people refer to the natural talent of another, they often use the word *gift.* People such as Ludwig van Beethoven, Albert Einstein, George Washington Carver, Georgia O'Keeffe, and William Shakespeare are examples of people who had special talents. Whom do you think of when you think of special talents?

As any talented person would probably tell you, talent alone is not enough to be successful. Successful people also worked very hard and devoted themselves to their work. They spent many years studying, training, and practicing. Thomas Edison, for example, said that genius was 1 percent inspiration and 99 percent perspiration. Even those people with special talents made mistakes and had disappointments along the way.

Do you think you have any hidden talents that you haven't developed?

Career Decision-Making Activities

After studying the example on page 35, write answers to the following questions on a separate sheet of paper.

1. What aptitude from the chart is strongest for you?
2. What is the title of an occupation (other than the one listed) that would use the aptitude you selected in Question 1?
3. Briefly describe how you would use this aptitude in the occupation you have selected.
4. Have a class discussion, and compare your answers with those of other students.

Review and Enrichment

Summarizing the Chapter

Summarizing information is a critical thinking skill that will help you succeed in the world of work. Write a summary of what you learned in Chapter 2. Focus on the main points of the chapter. Then in a class discussion, compare your summary with the summaries done by your classmates. Can you improve your summary?

Improving Your Career Vocabulary

Learning to use new vocabulary terms will improve your communication skills, which are important in almost all areas of work. Write definitions for the terms listed below. Then for each term, write an original sentence about yourself in which you use the term correctly.

- values
- life values
- work values
- conflict of values
- interest
- interest inventory
- aptitude
- skills

Finding the Facts

Finding exact information is a frequently used skill in many careers. Find the answers to the exercise below, and write the answers on a separate sheet of paper.

1. Name five values that can be applied to one's work.
2. What purpose does an interest inventory serve?
3. What is the difference between an aptitude and a skill?
4. List three of the eleven basic aptitudes.
5. What two things did Thomas Edison say genius consisted of?

Thinking for Yourself

To complete the exercise below you will need to use critical thinking and communication skills, which are skills valued by all employers. Write out your answers or be prepared to discuss them in class, depending on your teacher's instructions.

1. Tell in your own words what you think happens when a person does things that go against his or her values.
2. Think of one or two people you know who seem fairly satisfied with their jobs. How do their interests and jobs match up?
3. Do you have an aptitude you've never developed? Do you think it could be useful in a career? If so, what do you plan to do about it?
4. Think of two skills you possess that you have improved during the past year. What caused this improvement? Do you plan to develop these skills further in the future?

Practicing Your Basic Skills

Your career success depends greatly on your basic math and communication skills. Work hard at improving in the areas where you have trouble with the following exercises.

Math

1. Look at the list of top ten interests you made in response to the Activity on page 29. What percentage of your interests involves interacting with other people? With things? With facts?
2. Juan is working part-time at a gas station. He has an interest in auto mechanics and wants to take a course in it at his community college. His boss says he can work extra hours to help pay for the course. The course costs $150, and Juan makes $5.75 an hour. How many extra hours will Juan need to put in to pay for the course?
3. Teresa enjoys cooking. She wants to triple the following chili recipe for a party. How much of each ingredient will she need altogether?
   - 1½ lb. hamburger
   - 2½ c. chili beans
   - ¾ c. chopped celery
   - 1¼ c. onions
   - 1 t. cumin
   - 1¼ t. oregano
   - 1½ t. chili powder
   - ¼ t. salt
   - 2¾ c. tomatoes

Reading and Writing

1. Find a book at your library that has to do with an interest you think might play a part in your future career. Write a brief report on the book telling whether or not others with the same career interests should read it, and why.
2. Many newspapers feature articles about jobs in at least one issue each week. Check through several

Review and Enrichment, continued

back issues. Find at least one article about a job, event, or trend that might pertain to your job interests or aptitudes. Read the articles and report on what you learned to the class.

3. Ali is a skilled artist and would like to be a fine painter someday. His teachers say he has talent, but his parents are against his plan. They say only a few painters are successful enough to make a living at it. Besides, Ali has been irresponsible lately and has neglected his other studies. Write Ali a letter suggesting ways he might convince his parents to let him develop his talent.

Speaking and Listening

Part of your effectiveness in getting a job will be due to the impression you give an employer. Over the next twenty-four hours, pay attention to the ways in which you speak. Do you slur your words, use a lot of slang, or use bad grammar? Choose two ways in which your speech can be improved and work on them during the next week.

Activities Working with Others

In almost all careers you must be able to get along well with other people to be successful. Work with your classmates to do the following activities. As you work together, pay attention to how well you get along. If necessary, work hard at improving your ability to do your part and to cooperate.

Choose a skill that you are good at, such as math, swimming, or storytelling. Write an advertisement telling about your skill and post it on the class bulletin board. When all class members have posted their ads, read them and find someone with a skill you'd like to learn or improve. Arrange to spend one hour with that person for a tutoring session sometime during the next two weeks. Be prepared to tutor someone yourself for the same amount of time.

Decision Making and Problem Solving

You will be a big help to your employer if you can make decisions and solve problems. List all the possible ways of resolving the situations described below. Then pick the best alternative (possible choice), and tell why you chose it. If you need help, you might want to refer to Chapter 3.

1. Your best friend has just told you she is interested in being a singer. The only problem is that she can't carry a tune. You don't want to hurt her feelings or discourage her if there is any way for her dream to come true. But you can't lie to her either. What will you do?
2. Your dad is a salesman for a big department store. He says he can get you a job there for the summer. You both think it would be good business experience for you and would bring in some extra money. However, your friend Julie is starting a rock band and needs you to be the drummer. If the band gets any jobs later on, they will conflict with the hours when you have to be at the store. Your career goal is to be a talent agent, and you'd like to make the choice that would benefit you the most. What will you do?

CHAPTER 3 MAKING DECISIONS

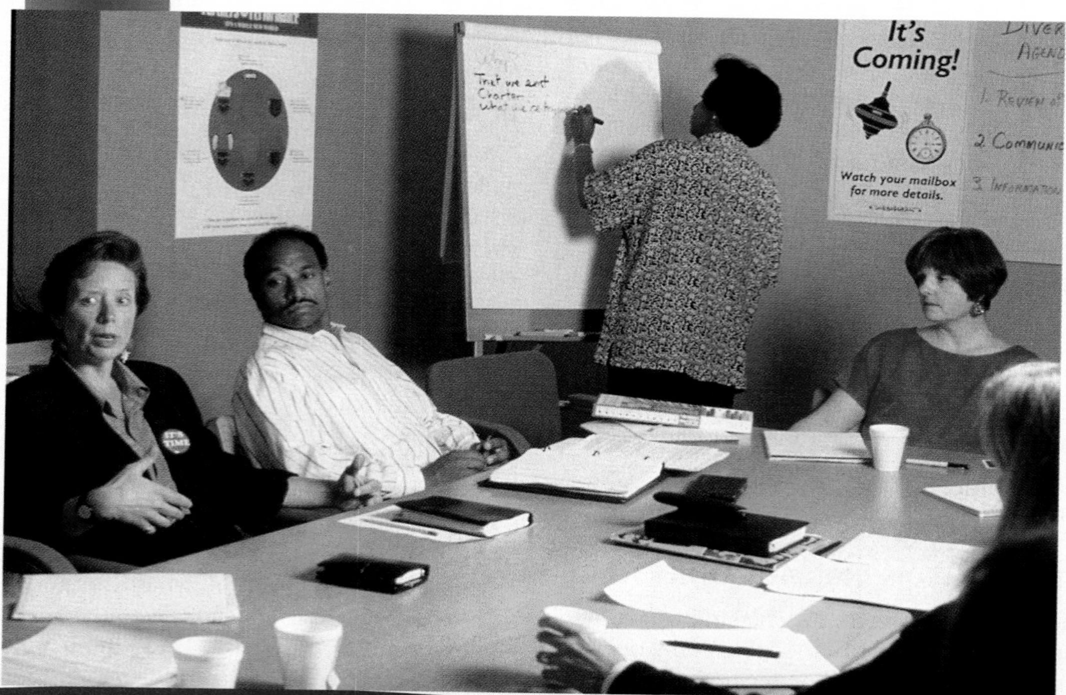

◆ Chapter Objectives ◆

After completing this chapter you will be able to do the following:

- ◆ Define the terms listed under "New Career Terms."
- ◆ Explain why decision making can be difficult.
- ◆ Explain the importance of career decision making.
- ◆ List and describe the seven steps in the decision-making process.
- ◆ Give an example of how someone can use the decision-making process to make career decisions.
- ◆ List and describe seven hints for making wise decisions.

◆ New Career Terms ◆

In this chapter you will learn the meanings of the following career terms:

- ✔ Decision
- ✔ Decision-making process
- ✔ Needs
- ✔ Wants
- ✔ Resources
- ✔ Evaluate
- ✔ Plan
- ✔ Tentative

Paula was sitting around in the cafeteria one day with a group of her friends. They were talking about what to do that night. One friend suggested they go to an outdoor fireworks display. Another wanted to go see a new movie. Paula thought she might want to stay home and read.

Then Patrick came up and asked Paula if she would like to go out to dinner with him and his sister.

Paula didn't know what to do. She had several choices.

Paula faced several choices and had to choose only one. She had to decide. She had to make a **decision** (choice).

decision
choosing between two or more possibilities.

How do you react to situations similar to Paula's? Do you have a hard time making decisions, or do they usually come easy?

Any time you have more than one choice, you are in a situation where you must make a decision. You must decide what your choice will be. As soon as you open your eyes in the morning you start making decisions. You decide whether or not you want to get out of bed, what color clothes to wear, how to comb your hair, and what to eat for breakfast.

Then you begin to make decisions that will affect your whole day. Should you come home early and finish a science project after school, or stay late and study for an English test? Sometimes your decisions will affect your whole week, such as whether or not to play in a big softball tournament.

Imagine sitting at the breakfast table and making a decision that would affect your *whole life!* Imagine making a decision that might change the way you lived for years to come and might make the difference in how happy you would be.

Does such a decision sound important? Your career decision is one of the most important decisions you will ever make in your life. That may sound scary. It doesn't have to be. Decision making is a skill. Just like any skill, it can be learned, and you can get better at it as you practice.

DECISIONS, DECISIONS

Life is full of decisions. Whenever there is more than one thing that you can do, you must make a decision. Some decisions are simple. They take only a second to make, such as when someone offers you either a glass of orange juice or water. There are only three good choices here. You take the orange juice, the water, or nothing at all.

Most of your important decisions, however, will have more than two or three choices. Selecting from among the choices may be more difficult. Choosing will take more time and thought on your part.

Every time you make a decision, you know that you are giving up other choices. When you make a choice, you are saying *no* to the choices you have ruled out. Nobody likes to give anything up. The more you feel you are giving up, the more difficult it is to make a decision.

HOW DO YOU MAKE ONLY ONE CHOICE?

You often must decide on only one choice in a decision. For example, have you ever gone into a restaurant and looked at a menu filled with all your favorite foods? You have trouble deciding what to order, because you would like ten different things. It's difficult to decide, because there are too many things from which to choose. You know you can't order them all, because you can't eat them all. And you can't pay for them all. So you are forced to make a decision. Otherwise, you will have to leave the restaurant and stay hungry.

Have you ever gone to pick out a new shirt for a party and found five or six that you would love to have? They all fit perfectly and match the color of your eyes. You can choose only one, because you only have enough money to buy one.

Do you close your eyes and point to one? Do you ask a friend which one looks best on you? Do you choose the least expensive or the most expensive? Do you get too frustrated and leave without buying any of them? Do you try them on again and make a choice?

Do you hate that feeling you get inside yourself when you don't know how to decide?

FROM SCHOOL TO CAREERS

What Classes to Take

Manuel wants to have his own printing business someday. He has an aunt who has a very successful printing company and who has encouraged him. She has even told him that all business or math skills he can learn in school will help him in the printing business later.

When Manuel signed up for next year's classes, he told his guidance counselor about the printing business he would like to have someday. The counselor suggested that Manuel take an extra math course and a course in business next year. She told him they were not required courses, but that they would help him in opening up and running a business.

Manuel had just made the track team and knew it would take up a lot of his time. He chose not to take the extra courses his counselor suggested. He signed up for an extra shop course instead, because he knew he wouldn't have any homework in that class. He would have more time for track practice.

What Do YOU Think?

Did Manuel make a good decision? Is Manuel making school count?

The reason these decisions seem difficult is because by choosing one food item from the menu or one shirt, you give up the others. It's natural to want everything, but you can't have everything. When you try, you usually end up with nothing.

Making decisions is part of knowing yourself and what you want. The more you discover about your interests and your personality, the easier your decisions will become. The more you know about making decisions, the easier they will be.

WHY BOTHER LEARNING TO MAKE DECISIONS BETTER?

You might be thinking that decisions just come naturally. You've been making them all your life. It's easy to make decisions. Why bother learning how to do it better?

How would you like it if your teacher told you to drive from Florida to Alaska, but told you not to use any maps or look at any road signs? What if he or she told you to just take off down the road and see what happens?

It would probably take you a very long time to get to Alaska, if you got there at all. You would be lost most of the time. You would be confused and unhappy.

Most people wouldn't go on a journey like that. Yet many people do the same thing with a much more important journey—their career journey. They don't use a road map, but just fall into one job or another by accident. They just let things happen, or play it by ear.

That is one reason why so many people are unhappy with the way their lives have turned out. It is also one reason to learn how to make good decisions.

◀ Everything works best if you plan ahead—whether it's a family vacation or a career decision.

Have you ever played around setting up dominoes? You line up the rectangular wooden blocks in a row or in a pattern. Then you push over the first domino. This domino hits the next one, and on and on, until all the dominoes have been knocked down. The whole thing started with that first domino.

A decision is like pushing over the first domino. Each one crashes into the next. All the decisions you make now affect the decisions you will make all your life. The decisions you are now facing will have an impact on you for many years. It's important to get a good start.

Career Decision-Making Activities

People use all types of methods to make their decisions. Remember that early in this book, you learned about the different types of values, interests, and abilities that people have. These differences in people cause them to use different decision-making methods. Let's look at a few methods people use to make decisions. As you read the list, try to think of people you know who use these methods.

1. The first idea you get is usually the best! Don't worry, just do it.
2. It's best to follow someone else's plan. After all, it worked for her. I'll do what she did.
3. It just seems like the best thing to do. It feels right. I'll follow my instincts.
4. Looking at all the possibilities is overwhelming. I don't know what I'll do. I'll just cross that bridge later. I'll forget it for right now.
5. Things will work out. Leave it up to fate. Things will be what things will be.
6. I'll develop a plan so I'll be sure to end up being satisfied. I'll have a good balance between how I feel about the decision and all of the possible choices.

THE DECISION-MAKING PROCESS

decision-making process steps that can be taken to help you make the best decision.

The **decision-making process** is the method you follow when you make a decision, or choice, among options. It is a series of *steps* to take that will lead you to a decision that is right for you.

Have you ever had a lot of trouble making a decision? Have you ever said, "I just can't decide"? Have you ever made a decision and known it was wrong for you even as you were making it?

There is a way to make decisions easier for you. If you follow the steps you're about to read, you will learn to be happier with the decisions you make. These steps can give you a road map that will save you time and keep you from getting lost along the way on your career adventure. They will help you reach your dreams.

No matter what kind of decision you are making, this decision-making process can help you. The steps can help you make decisions about which shirt to buy, which classes to take next year, what movies to see, which sports to play, or what to do next weekend. But they are especially helpful when you make big decisions that will affect your life.

The following are the seven steps in the decision-making process. They are summarized in Figure 3.1.

1. **Define what you need or want.** Try to pinpoint what it is that you need and want first. **Needs** are things you must have to survive. **Wants** are things that you'd like to have—luxuries—but don't have to have.

   Be as specific as you can. When you go into a restaurant, you have already identified what you want. You want something to eat or drink. When you go to the store to buy a shirt, you have taken the first step. You want a new shirt.
2. **Look carefully at your resources.** Your **resources** are everything you have available to you to get what you want. Resources can be your strengths, your skills, or your talents. They are also things such as money that you need to exchange for what you want.

   You should be sure of what your resources are before you make a decision. Before you choose an item on the menu, you'd better know how much money you have to pay for it. Not knowing what your resources are can be embarrassing.
3. **Identify your choices.** The third step is very important. If there is a decision to be made, there are at least two choices,

needs
things you must have to survive.

resource
any skill or advantage you have.

wants
things you would like to have, but don't have to have—luxuries.

Figure 3.1 Decision-Making Steps

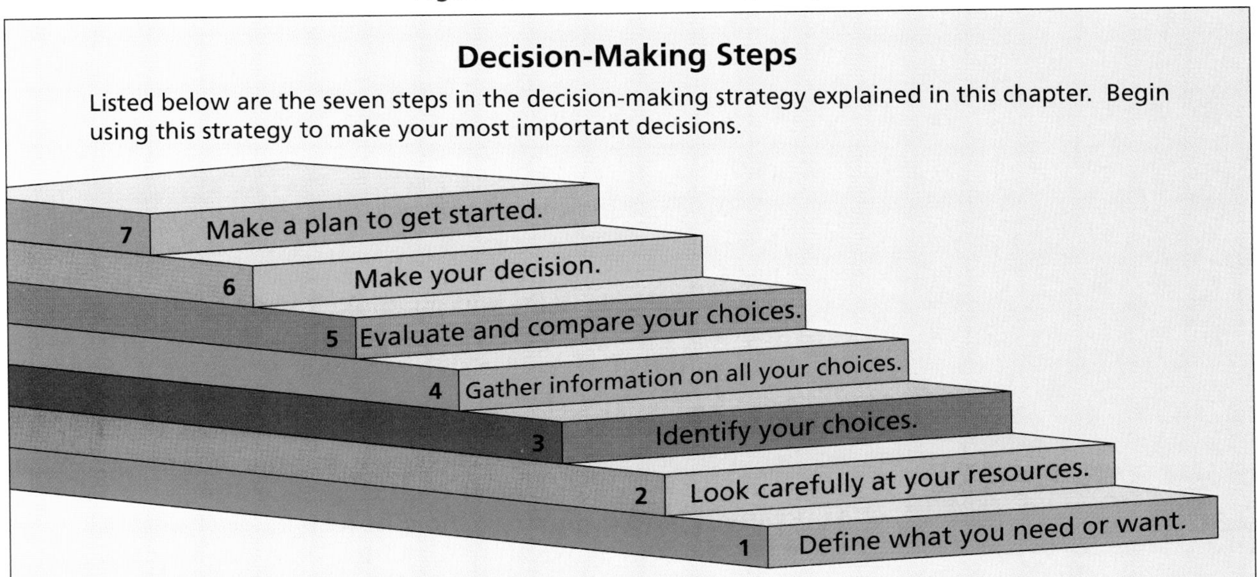
Decision-Making Steps
Listed below are the seven steps in the decision-making strategy explained in this chapter. Begin using this strategy to make your most important decisions.
7 Make a plan to get started.
6 Make your decision.
5 Evaluate and compare your choices.
4 Gather information on all your choices.
3 Identify your choices.
2 Look carefully at your resources.
1 Define what you need or want.

and usually many more. Sometimes it is not easy to see them all immediately. When you go to find a shirt for a party, you might want to look in more than one store. You might want to check a catalog.

Identifying *all* the choices takes some effort. You may not be aware right away of all the choices. Some could be unknown to you. And you might be able to create several choices.

One way to be certain you know about all your choices before you make your decision is to write down the following:

- The decision you are making.
- How much time you have to make your decision.
- All of the choices you already know about.
- Some places where you might learn about additional choices.

Then, depending on the time available, identify as many additional choices as possible. Don't eliminate any choices yet. Think of as many as possible. You'll separate the good choices from the bad ones later.

For example, suppose that Chien's alarm clock didn't go off, and he was late getting up. By the time he was ready for school, he knew he would miss first period and barely make second. Chien's parents had already left for work, and he was alone in the house. There was a second period pep assembly that Chien didn't want to miss. He knew he should check in with the principal's office about being late or he would get a detention. If he took the time to do that, though, he would miss part of the pep assembly. Chien realized that he must decide what to do. How many choices does Chien have? See how many you can list. Remember, don't eliminate any choices yet. Write down every choice that comes to mind.

evaluate
to look at closely and judge.

4. **Gather information on all your choices.** After you've listed all the possible choices in your decision, take a good look at each one. Consider the advantages and disadvantages of each choice. Think about the effect each choice will have on you. Some choices will have a desirable effect. Others will have an undesirable effect.

   If you are choosing a meal in a restaurant, for example, find out how it is made or what kind of sauces it comes with. If you are choosing from a group of shirts, find out how each one fits, how the color suits you, and how it would coordinate with clothes you already have. Also, think about how the price compares with that of similar shirts in other stores.

   Now try this information-gathering step with Chien's choices. You may want to discuss the advantages and disadvantages of each of his choices with your classmates. What would be the end result of each choice for Chien?

▼ Any time you have more than one choice, you must make a decision.

5. **Evaluate and compare your choices.** To **evaluate** means to judge the value or worth of something. Use the information you

have found about your choices to evaluate them. Then compare your choices with one another, and see which one comes out on top. Think about which one has the best chance of getting you what you need or want.

Remember the wants you identified in the first step. Perhaps you want a shirt that is going to be the most colorful and flashy one at the party. So line them up and take a good look at each. Choose the flashiest, if you can afford it.

6. **Make your decision.** Which choice came out on top? Which one is the best choice for you? Which one will get you what you want?

   Keep in mind that one choice may not come out way ahead of the others. There may be two or three that tie. Don't get discouraged. At least you have narrowed your choices down. A decision won't be nearly as difficult now.

7. **Make a plan to get started.** Your decision-making process isn't complete until you make a **plan** (a method for achieving something). Your plan may be as simple as planning to go to the store where the best shirt is, buying it, bringing it home, and wearing it to the party.

   We will talk later about how to develop a plan that will work for you.

plan
the method or course you decide to take after going through the decision-making process.

Career Decision-Making Activities

1. On a separate sheet of paper, make a list of your next ten purchases. Identify each purchase as either a need or a want. Read your list in class. Did anyone make the same purchase but classify it differently? Discuss the reasons for this difference.
2. In different decision-making situations you will identify different resources (skills and advantages). For each of the following decision-making situations, write all your skills and advantages that will affect that decision. Compile a complete list in class. Did your classmates think of resources you forgot to list?
   a. Accept a baby-sitting job, or hang out with friends at the mall on Saturday night.
   b. Go out for the soccer team, which means after-school practice four nights a week; or take piano, guitar, drum, or horn lessons, which require two nights a week after school.
   c. Buy a new pair of tennis shoes, or buy a new sweater for the same price.
   d. Try to do a difficult homework problem on your own, or ask for help from a classmate who you're sure can do the problem but with whom you feel uncomfortable.
   e. Ride your bike to school, or take the bus.
3. Pick one of the decision-making situations from Activity 2 above. Choose the situation that is closest to a decision you have actually made recently. For each of the two choices, list as many advantages and disadvantages as you can.

APPLYING THE DECISION-MAKING PROCESS TO CAREERS

The steps in the decision-making process will take more time when you use them to choose a career. Using the decision-making process, with its seven steps, will help you make all of your important career decisions. It will also increase your chances of making the right choices.

IT'S NEVER TOO EARLY

It may seem too early to make a career decision. You may not know what you want to do yet. You may not be sure you can make the right choice. It's natural to feel this way.

tentative
the best decision you can decide on at a certain time, which can be changed later as you learn more.

But it's better to go ahead and make a **tentative** decision now. A tentative decision is not definite. You know you may change it later. It's not always your *final* decision, but it may be the *best* decision you can make at the time you make it.

Your tentative career decision will be the best decision you can make now, given all you know about careers and about yourself so far.

Making a career decision, even this tentative one, will have a positive effect on your life. This decision will give you a sense of what you would like to work toward—a feeling for the direction you would like your life to take.

You can always change this decision later. When you get new information and learn more about yourself, you may want to go through the decision-making process again. The thing to remember is that changing a decision is much better than never making a decision at all.

▼ Do you think this young woman, used the seven steps in her career choice?

You are going to be doing a lot of career decision making in this book. This is especially true for Chapters 6 to 20. In these chapters you will learn a great deal about many different kinds of careers. At the end of each chapter you will decide whether or not you would enjoy a certain kind of career.

Use the decision-making skills you are learning in this chapter to make your decisions. And don't put off or avoid these decisions. *Decide* what you would like and what you wouldn't like. Narrow your career choices to the one or two kinds of careers that seem best for you right now. Make the best decision for you at this time.

JESSICA USES THE SEVEN STEPS TO DECIDE ABOUT HER CAREER

Jessica loves the outdoors. She has always liked hiking, camping, and outdoor sports. She usually takes along a book on wildflowers to identify each one when she goes hiking. She is also interested in different kinds of plants and trees in the forest and what makes them grow in certain places.

Step 1. Recently Jessica has started thinking about a career. All she knows is that she wants to work outdoors. Jessica has taken *Step 1*. She has defined what she wants. She wants to find a career that will allow her to work outdoors.

Step 2. Jessica thinks about what she already knows. She has some skills in identifying wildflowers and plants. She has taken a biology course that taught her about plants and animals. She has been to a summer camp for two summers and has learned about safe camping and hiking. She knows how to use a map and a compass. Jessica took *Step 2* by taking a look at what her resources are.

Steps 3 and 4. Jessica decided to talk to some people in the community who work in a nearby national forest. She explained to them that she might be interested in a career working in a national forest and would like to know more about it. They loved talking about their work and invited her to visit. They took her on a tour and told her about what forestry workers do, what wildlife workers do, what game and fish wardens do, and what pollution-control technicians do.

Afterwards, Jessica decided to do some research with her guidance counselor on other types of outdoor jobs. She read about being a resort area manager, a ski instructor, a logger, and a veterinarian. She started thinking that the careers of forestry worker, game and fish warden, and veterinarian were probably the most interesting to her.

She has taken *Step 3* by identifying her choices. She has also taken *Step 4* by gathering information about her choices.

Step 5. Jessica sat down and reviewed her choices with her guidance counselor. Her counselor helped her find out more about each career, such as how much it pays, how many jobs are available, and what the working conditions are like. Jessica also found out how much training and education she would need for each job. She thought about how she would like her life to be and compared her three choices. Jessica has taken *Step 5* by evaluating and comparing her choices.

Step 6. As Jessica reviewed her choices, she decided that she really wanted to work more with trees, plants, and flowers than she did with animals. Fish and game wardens and veterinarians work mainly with animals. Forestry work looked like the kind of job that would fit her personality and her interests. She decided to work toward being a forestry worker. She has taken *Step 6* by making a decision.

Step 7. Jessica discussed her decision with her guidance counselor. He suggested that she take another biology course. He also gave her a brochure for a horticulture program offered at another school. In addition, he told her about a summer program in the nearby national forest where she could be a camp counselor teaching younger children about the forest. She decided on her own that she would take a first-aid course so she would be prepared if anyone were hurt while hiking. She has taken *Step 7* by making a plan to get started.

▶ Your peers can help you identify things you do well, but *you* must make your final career choice.

PLANNING AND DECISION MAKING CONTINUE

Jessica will need to begin her educational plan now. She will need to consider questions such as the following:

- Will I need a college degree to reach my tentative career goal?
- Could I reach my tentative career goal with a two-year program in a junior college or technical school?
- Could I obtain enough skills to begin my tentative career in a high school program?
- Could I take the high school program and still have enough time in my high school schedule to take the necessary courses to get into a good college?
- What high school courses should I take to prepare me for the next step in my educational plan?

As Jessica finds out more about herself and the career she wants, she may decide to go through the decision-making process again. She may make a new decision.

For now, she has made a tentative decision, and she feels much better about herself. She has an idea of what she would like in her future. She has a sense of the *direction* she would like to go. She has a *goal* to work toward. She understands what she needs to do to get there. Jessica now has a better chance of reaching her dreams.

SEVEN TIPS ABOUT MAKING BETTER CAREER DECISIONS

With practice, you can become skillful in using the decision-making process. The more skillful you become, the better able you will be to make a good career decision.

Remember that some decisions will give you trouble. If you have trouble, some of these tips might help you:

1. **Remember that other people, such as your friends and parents, will put pressure on you to do what *they* want you to do.** Although you should consider their opinions, remember that a career decision is one that only you—not they—will have to live with for the rest of your life.
2. **Don't be afraid of failure.** You may be able to do much more than you think. You will be able to develop many skills and learn many things that seem impossible right now. There will be obstacles, but you can get around them.
3. **Pay attention to the decisions you make every day.** Start practicing the decision-making process with simple decisions you make. This will make it easier when you get to the bigger ones.
4. **Remember that decisions have both good and bad outcomes.** A good decision has more good results than bad. Good decisions will get you closest to what you want, but their outcomes will never be perfect in every way.
5. **Accept the outcome.** If you made the best decision you could, and things still don't work out, don't worry. Your next decision will be better. You will know more about yourself and about the decision next time.
6. **Remember, you can change decisions.** Decisions are not usually set in cement. Sometimes things change, and you may want to change your decision. Don't be afraid to change.
7. **Don't depend on luck.** The more control you have over your decision, and the more planning you do, the more likely you will be able to reach your dreams.

Career Decision-Making Activities

1. Make a tentative career decision *now*. Suppose that you had to decide right now what career you'd have for the rest of your life. What would it be? Do not do any research. Base your decision on what you know now about yourself and about career possibilities. You may want to review what you've learned about yourself in the first few chapters of this book. Write your decision on a piece of paper. Also write three or four reasons why you chose that career. Save the sheet of paper to see if you want to revise your decision after you have explored career clusters in Chapters 6 to 20.
2. Practice making school and career decisions. Suppose that several of your best friends are going to sign up for a certain course next year. The course meets only during fourth period. Another course, which you think will help you more after you graduate, also meets only during fourth period. No one you know, however, is taking the course you think you should take. What will you do? Be honest with yourself, and make a decision. Use the first six steps of the decision-making process. Discuss the decision and your reasons for making it with your classmates.

Review and Enrichment

Summarizing the Chapter

Summarizing information is a critical thinking skill that will help you succeed in the world of work. Write a summary of what you learned in Chapter 3. Focus on the main points of the chapter. Then in a class discussion, compare your summary with the summaries done by your classmates. Can you improve your summary?

Improving Your Career Vocabulary

Learning to use new vocabulary terms will improve your communication skills, which are important in almost all areas of work. Write definitions for the terms listed below. Then for each term, write an original sentence about yourself in which you use the term correctly.

- decision
- decision-making process
- needs
- wants
- resources
- evaluate
- plan
- tentative

Finding the Facts

Finding exact information is a frequently used skill in many careers. Find the answers to the exercise below, and write the answers on a separate sheet of paper.

1. What must you define before you make a decision?
2. Give three examples of resources.
3. What things should you note to be sure you know about all your choices?
4. Give the seven steps in decision making.
5. Give three tips that can help you make better decisions.

Thinking for Yourself

To complete the exercise below you will need to use critical thinking and communication skills, which are skills valued by all employers. Write out your answers or be prepared to discuss them in class, depending on your teacher's instructions.

1. Tell in your own words why a person should learn to make better decisions.
2. Describe a decision you made in the last six months. How did you go about it? Could you have made a better decision? If so, how?
3. Do you think most people make careful decisions using the seven steps? Why do you think this is so?
4. Which steps in the decision-making process seem like ones people would neglect? Why?
5. How do you think a positive attitude could contribute to decision making?

Practicing Your Basic Skills

Your career success depends greatly on your basic math and communication skills. Work hard at improving in the areas where you have trouble with the following exercises.

Math

1. José had to make three decisions within twenty-five hours. The first decision involved a job and was more important than the other two. He felt he should spend three times as much time on the job decision. He would divide the remaining time between the other decisions. How much time did he spend on each?
2. Marcia had a choice between two jobs in two different cities. One job paid $18,900 a year. In that town, rent for apartments averaged $425 a month. The second job paid $21,000, and apartments in that town averaged $700. After Marcia pays the rent for an apartment, which job would leave her the most money?
3. Sa'ad has a chance to go to college if he can get a loan. Which of the following loan choices will cost him the most in interest the first year?
   a. $15,000 at 8% interest for 4 years
   b. $10,000 at 10.5% interest for 4 years
   c. $12,000 at 9.5% interest for 3 years

Reading and Writing

1. Read an article or book on a successful person. Discover an important decision the person made. Write a paragraph telling why the decision was made and what happened.

Review and Enrichment, continued

2. Write a one-minute TV commercial selling people on using the seven steps in the decision-making process.
3. Write a paragraph evaluating your own ability as a decision maker.

Speaking and Listening

1. For the next twenty-four hours, listen to your family and friends as they make decisions. How many of the seven steps do they use?
2. Talk to at least two people about a decision they made regarding a career. Ask them how they came to the decision and how it turned out.

Activities Working with Others

In almost all careers you must be able to get along well with other people to be successful. Work with your classmates to do the following activities. As you work together, pay attention to how well you get along. If necessary, work hard at improving your ability to do your part and to cooperate.

1. With a classmate, design and make a poster telling about the decision-making process.
2. Your teacher will divide the class into small groups. In your group, make two lists: *Easy Decisions* and *Difficult Decisions.* Think of as many decisions as you can for each category. Discuss each decision with your classmates as to what makes it easy or difficult before adding it to the list.

Decision Making and Problem Solving

You will be a big help to your employer if you can make decisions and solve problems. List all the possible ways of resolving the situations described below. Then pick the best alternative (possible choice), and tell why you chose it.

1. You are out shopping with your friends, and you see a sweater you really like. All you have in your wallet is $20, and the sweater costs $39. You think your mother will give you the extra money, but you try calling her and she's not home. The sweater is such a good buy you are sure it will sell quickly. What will you do?
2. You and your eight-year-old sister are home alone. While you are in the kitchen making lunch, she disappears. You look all over the house and then go out in the yard and call to her, but you can't find her. You think she may have gone to the store or to the neighbor's. If something is wrong, though, you don't want to waste precious time looking in the wrong places. What will you do?

CHAPTER 4

LEARNING PERSONAL SKILLS

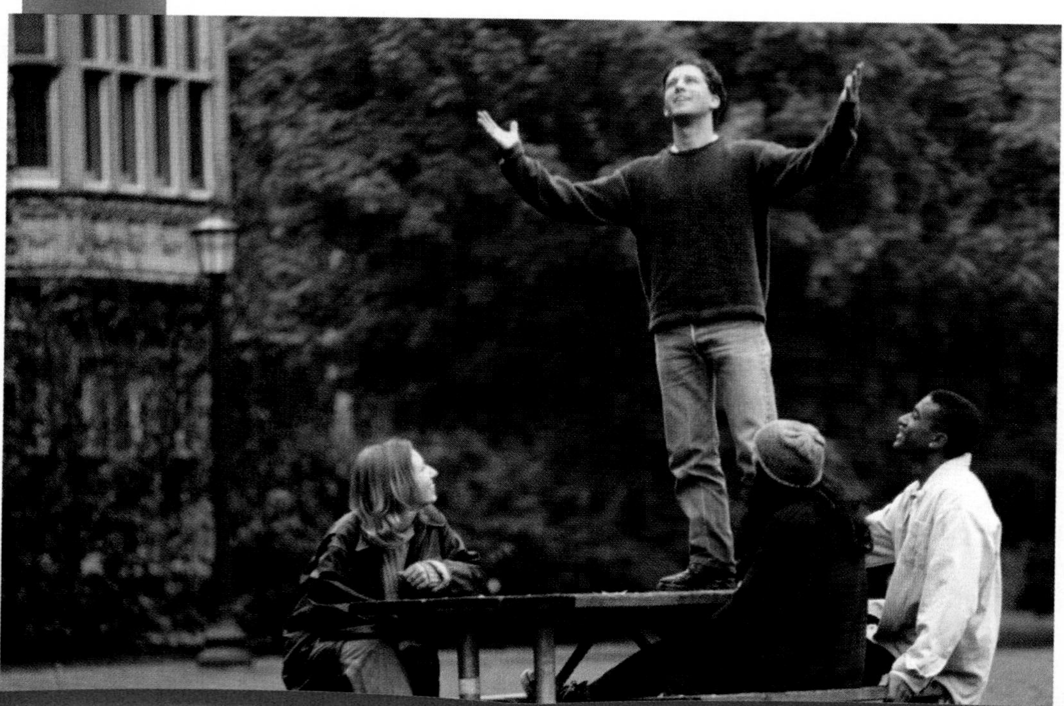

◆ Chapter Objectives ◆

After completing this chapter you will be able to do the following:

- Define the terms listed under "New Career Terms."
- Explain the benefits of having high self-esteem.
- List ways you can improve your self-esteem.
- Discuss why you must accept individual responsibility.
- List the ways to improve your self-management.
- Name six ways to become a good listener.
- State the benefits of having integrity.

◆ New Career Terms ◆

In this chapter you will learn the meanings of the following career terms:

- ✔ Self-esteem
- ✔ Body image
- ✔ Sibling
- ✔ Perfectionist
- ✔ Mass media
- ✔ Individual responsibility
- ✔ Chain of command
- ✔ Self-management
- ✔ Sincerity
- ✔ Distractions
- ✔ Integrity
- ✔ Ethics

Brinn was never on time for anything. She had lost several baby-sitting jobs because of this problem. She knew that other people were annoyed by her lateness, but she did not realize the full extent of the problem until she began losing friends. When Brinn was supposed to go somewhere with her friends and she was not ready, they began to go without her. The second time this happened, Brinn talked to her mother about the problem.

Her mother explained that being late was inconsiderate because it wasted others' time. She reminded Brinn of the lost baby-sitting jobs. She made Brinn realize that being late for those baby-sitting jobs was almost like stealing time from the parents for whom she was baby-sitting. When she made her friends wait for her, she was taking time away from whatever activity was planned. Brinn decided to find out how to get organized so that she could get to places on time.

You probably know someone like Brinn. You may even have some of her characteristics yourself. Being late for work (or for anything, for that matter) means wasting your time and someone else's, too. It also means that you have not mastered two key personal skills—*self-management* and *individual responsibility*—that you'll learn more about in this chapter.

To succeed in the world of work, and in life in general, you need many personal qualities in addition to self-management and individual responsibility. You must have the right attitude, be able to manage others when necessary, be sociable, and have integrity. Before you can even consider those personal qualities, though, you have to feel good about yourself. This is called having **self-esteem.**

self-esteem
to have a high regard for, or feel good about, yourself.

body image
the way you look, and a mental picture of how you *think* you look.

SELF-ESTEEM

Your self-esteem is composed of your feelings about all areas of your life. Part of your self-esteem relates to your **body image**—how you look and how you *think* you look, kind of like a mental picture of your body. Some people's body images are unrealistic. For example, some young people think that they are overweight even though their weight is actually normal. People's body images change over time as they mature. What you see in the full-length mirror today may be quite different from what you will see two years from now.

Besides your body image, your self-esteem also involves your mind, your behavior, and your relationships with others. Self-esteem touches all areas of your life.

If we say a person has *high self-esteem,* we mean that she basically likes herself, even though she realizes that she is not perfect. If a person has *low self-esteem,* he is generally unhappy with his self-concept, or his image of himself. (You learned about self-concept in Chapter 1.) Sometimes low self-esteem can have tragic results.

Young people, particularly females, who are unhappy with their body images may sometimes adopt a completely unrealistic view of

▼ Do you think this girl has high self-esteem? Why or why not?

themselves. They look in the mirror and think they are overweight, even if they are not. They refuse to eat or eat only a little bit at each meal. Their weight continues to drop. When they look in the mirror, though, they still see themselves as too fat.

HOW SELF-ESTEEM IS FORMED

sibling
a brother or sister.

perfectionist
a person who is uncomfortable with mistakes or flaws.

The core, or basis, of your self-esteem was probably formed by the time you were about three years old. This core of self-esteem is the result of your interactions with parents, grandparents, **siblings** (brothers and sisters), and other significant people in your life. If you were treated with love and respect as a young child, your core of self-esteem is probably high.

If, however, your early interactions with others were mostly negative, you may have some self-esteem problems. If your parents were perfectionists, for example, you may have felt that nothing you did was good enough in their eyes. (A **perfectionist** is someone who is uncomfortable with mistakes or flaws.) If your parents had many problems of their own or were too preoccupied or too busy to give you the attention a young child needs, your self-esteem may have suffered.

In any event, if you have low self-esteem, you are not destined to be unhappy forever. Fortunately, you can improve your self-esteem. You will read about ways to improve your self-esteem later in this section.

VARIATIONS IN SELF-ESTEEM

Your self-concept and self-esteem can change a little from day to day. When you do something well and someone compliments you, your self-concept improves. When you make a mistake and someone criticizes you, however, your self-esteem goes down for a time. Small changes such as these are normal.

Variations in self-esteem tend to increase during the teen years, because so much in life is changing. Your body is changing from a child's body to an adult's. Your thoughts and feelings are also maturing. Your relationships with your parents and friends change during adolescence because you are growing up.

mass media
means of communication by which information is distributed to the general public (newspapers, magazines, radio, television, the Internet).

You may also be paying more attention to media images than ever before. The way singing stars and movie actors look can influence your image of yourself. Not every celebrity is thin and beautiful. However, the **mass media,** especially in their advertisements, have emphasized the importance of a perfect body. (The mass media are newspapers and magazines, radio programs, television broadcasts, and other forms of communication aimed at huge numbers of people.)

Finally, worries about the future also put stress on you. These concerns may affect your self-esteem.

BENEFITS OF HIGH SELF-ESTEEM

Ups and downs in your level of self-esteem are normal. What is important is not your level of self-esteem on any given day but rather your general, ongoing feelings about yourself. Everyone has strengths and weaknesses. Everyone makes mistakes at some time or other. If you have a high level of self-esteem, you can accept the fact that you are not perfect. You won't let your mistakes get you down for long. You will basically like the person you are, even though you don't always act the way you and others think you should.

HOW TO IMPROVE YOUR SELF-ESTEEM

If your self-esteem is very low, if you often feel depressed or angry, or if you don't feel worthwhile, you may need a professional's help to improve your picture of yourself. Your teacher, school counselor, or religious leader (for example, minister, priest, or rabbi) can assist you in finding a counselor who can help you feel better about yourself. If your self-esteem problems aren't severe, however, you can do several things to improve your self-esteem.

ACCEPT YOURSELF AS YOU ARE

One of the most important things you can do to improve your self-esteem is to learn to accept yourself as you are. Accepting yourself as you are means feeling okay about the fact that, for example, your hair is straight rather than curly, you prefer reading books to playing baseball, or your family doesn't have as much money to spend as you would like.

◀ Many types of counselors can help you develop and maintain high self-esteem.

Accepting yourself as you are doesn't mean that you *can't* change. For example, if you have a problem controlling your temper, you need to find ways of bringing it under control. Your behavior is something you can regulate. People with high self-esteem have learned to accept what they cannot change, but they aren't afraid to try to change what they can.

PAY ATTENTION TO YOUR STRONG POINTS

Although you should accept the fact that you have both good and bad points and certain strengths and weaknesses, you can improve your self-esteem by paying more attention to your strong points than to your weak ones. Then use your strong points to help others. If you are good with children, for example, you can volunteer at a daycare center. If you have an aptitude for basketball, you can help others improve their games. Helping others is a great way to feel good about yourself.

LEARN TO ACCEPT PRAISE

Learning to accept praise will go a long way toward improving your self-esteem. When someone tells you, for example, that you have pretty eyes, do you smile and say, "Thank you," or do you say, "Oh, they're really nothing special"? If someone pays you a compliment, accept it. File the words away in your mental storehouse. Then someday, when you are feeling down, remember the compliment. Those kind words will remind you that there is something about you that someone else likes, and this will help. You will feel better.

LEARN TO BE KIND TO YOURSELF

Sometimes we are harder on ourselves than we are on others. We think that it is okay for other people to make mistakes. If we make a mistake, though, we are not willing to excuse ourselves. Do you find, for example, that it is easier to excuse a friend when she breaks a promise than it is to forgive yourself for similar behavior? People with high self-esteem have learned to be kind to themselves. They treat themselves as valuable people worth loving.

GET INVOLVED

Another way to improve your self-esteem is to participate. People with high self-esteem get involved. For example, Sandrine is the goalie on the hockey team and a volunteer who brings flowers to hospitalized patients. Bob sings in the choir and makes the costumes for the school play. Inga mows an elderly neighbor's lawn and teaches Sunday school. Getting involved gives you less time to dwell on your shortcomings and makes you feel good. Some other suggestions for improving your self-esteem are given in Figure 4.1.

Figure 4.1 Improving Your Self-Esteem

- **RELAX**
  Give yourself permission to fail. Learn how to relax your mind and body.
- **SEND YOURSELF "FEEL-GOOD" MESSAGES**
  Tell yourself you are pretty, or smart, or funny. Write encouraging notes to yourself, and hang them in your locker or on your mirror.
- **TRY TO LOOK YOUR BEST**
  When someone looks good, he or she usually feels good.
- **LEARN TO ENJOY LIFE**
  Find at least one good thing about each day.
- **LEARN TO HANDLE TROUBLE**
  Don't avoid or ignore problems. Take responsibility for your life.
- **LIVE IN THE PRESENT**
  Plan for the future, but don't worry excessively about it. Today is what you have. Try to make the most of it.

Career Decision-Making Activities

As you read in the text, ups and downs in the level of self-esteem are normal. The important thing is the ongoing feelings you have about yourself. On a separate piece of paper answer the following statements to develop a plan to improve your self-esteem.

a. List ways that you can relax.
b. Plan the best time during each day to relax.
c. List five "feel-good" messages about yourself.
d. Describe some ways that you could improve your appearance and make plans to do so (i.e., free makeover, purchase new clothing, etc.)
e. What are some ways you can improve your enjoyment of life?
f. Start a list by writing down one good thing that happens each day. What is a good thing that happened today?
g. List some things that cause trouble in your life and how you can deal responsibly with each of the troubles.
h. Write out a weekly schedule for the coming week. Remember to include time for relaxation (#2) and enjoyment.

INDIVIDUAL RESPONSIBILITY

Lei Chang has no siblings. Her mother is a physician, and her father works in a bank. Both parents work long hours. Lei is involved in several after-school activities. She is a cheerleader. Once a week she has a dance lesson. Her parents feel that Lei should do the family laundry, keep her room clean, and make dinner every night during the week. Mr. Chang cooks on

▲ Do you have assigned tasks at home?

individual responsibility being accountable, or responsible, for ourselves and our actions.

weekends and cleans the rest of the house. Mrs. Chang does the shopping and pays the bills. They hire someone to cut the grass. If repairs need to be done, the Changs pay someone to do them.

Lei doesn't feel that the chores her parents want her to do should be her responsibility. She resents having to come home from cheerleading practice to make dinner. She dislikes handling the soiled clothes on Saturdays when she does the laundry. She thinks her family should hire someone to do these jobs, just as they pay someone to cut the grass. Lei's parents, however, think that it is good for Lei to do work around the house. While growing up, both of them worked to help their families.

Many parents are like Lei's. They believe that their children should do a specified number of chores around the house. They are right to believe this, for all of us have to learn **individual responsibility** (being accountable, or responsible, for ourselves and for the actions that we take). The only way to learn individual responsibility is to have chores, or tasks that we should do on a regular basis.

In school, you have homework assignments. At home, you have chores. In the world of work, you'll have many actions that you must do. These are your job tasks. If you haven't learned individual responsibility, you won't be able to complete these tasks. You'll do poorly on the job.

You must learn to accept responsibility now, not later. When your parents tell you to clean up your room, asking "Why?" doesn't get you anywhere. When you say something silly like that, you are avoiding individual responsibility. When your teacher gives you an assignment that you do not do on time (or at all), you are not accepting individual responsibility.

If you don't accept what you must do in life, it is usually because you have a bad attitude. You learned about this subject in Chapter 1. You've also been reading about attitudes in the feature entitled "Attitude Makes a Difference," such as the one below. This feature will continue to appear throughout the book.

SELF-MANAGEMENT

Jabari has a problem. Three weeks ago, his family had the latest two-hundred-channel interactive cable TV installed, and Jabari can't stay away from it. He can now play every video game he ever wanted to play. He can also listen to (and record) digital-quality music through a special box. There are hundreds of educational programs and movies for him to watch. He has never had so much information and so many entertainment possibilities at his fingertips. Every spare moment, Jabari spends glued to the TV—or to the TV listings guide, which is as thick as his English textbook. Whenever he can, he even eats dinner in front of the TV screen.

His parents complain that they never see him anymore. His friends are beginning to ignore him, because he never wants to go anywhere with them or even talk to them for more than a minute or two on the phone.

Jabari never gets around to doing his homework now. He knows his grades will suffer as a result. He keeps trying to convince himself (and his parents) that he can learn much more from this new cable system than he can from books anyway.

Right now, Jabari doesn't know how to manage himself. He has not mastered the important personal skill of **self-management** (directing, controlling, or organizing oneself).

Jabari, like you, will need the skill of self-management as he goes on in school and enters the world of work. Let's see how the skill of self-management can be developed. We'll start at the beginning.

self-management
a key personal skill—organizing your time so as not to waste yours or that of others.

Attitude makes a difference

Accepting the Chain of Command

Tashana does volunteer work at a nursing home. Mrs. Zobiek supervises the volunteers. She reports to Ms. Washington. Tashana felt that Mrs. Zobiek didn't like her. She often asked her to empty bedpans and mop floors, jobs that the volunteers were only supposed to do in an emergency. Tashana made an appointment to talk about the situation with Ms. Washington.

When Tashana's father learned of the situation, he said that Tashana probably should not talk to Ms. Washington. He told Tashana that she should follow the **chain of command**—the way that authority is distributed in an organization. In other words, Tashana should talk first to Mrs. Zobiek. Tashana tried, but when she approached her, Mrs. Zobiek said she didn't have time to talk. Tashana then kept her appointment with Ms. Washington.

Tashana's father was right when he said that an employee should follow the chain of command when there is a problem. In this case, however, Tashana didn't think she had much choice.

What Do YOU Think?

Do you think that Tashana had the right attitude? What would you have done if you were Tashana?

SETTING LONG-TERM AND SHORT-TERM GOALS

The first step in self-management is to set out goals, both short term and long term. You learned about goals in Chapter 1. Is Jabari's long-term goal to become a video game designer? Or a teacher? Or a small-business owner? Whatever Jabari's career goal (and yours, too), he knows he'll have to complete high school and perhaps college.

Each long-term goal carries with it a series of short-term goals. These short-term goals will tell Jabari what he has to focus on right now, right at this very moment. Glued to the front of a two-hundred-channel interactive TV will not really help Jabari attain his long-term goal, whatever it may be.

FOCUS

After you have decided on a long-term career goal, the list of short-term goals usually becomes quite obvious. But it's not enough simply to list and know these goals. You have to work all of the time toward achieving them. One of Jabari's short-term goals is to focus on his schoolwork and graduate. This would be one of the first steps to take on the way to achieving his overall long-term goal. When you are constantly thinking about how to achieve your short-term goals, you are focused. Focus is a key part of self-management.

Not everyone is born a genius. Indeed, some people have limited abilities. But even with limited abilities, it is still possible to succeed. How? By learning to focus on goals. Even the brightest student can fail if he or she does not focus on getting done that which is most important.

DISCIPLINE AND THE AVOIDANCE OF DISTRACTIONS

distractions anything that draws attention away from what you really want to be doing.

Focusing on a necessary short-term goal still is not enough. You have to be able to avoid **distractions.** You can do so only if you impose discipline on yourself. In Jabari's case, the distraction was the new interactive TV system. Other distractions might be friends who want you to hang out with them at the mall, movies you want to see, sports you want to play (or watch on TV), video games, music—there is no end to the list.

Part of self-management, then, involves the discipline of avoiding distractions. You can avoid distractions in several ways. You can set very, very short-term goals with rewards after each one is accomplished. Say you want to finish your math homework after dinner. You can tell yourself that you will watch one television show after you have done your homework. The TV show is your reward. Or you might have a research project to complete over the weekend. Your reward for finishing it might be a few hours hanging out at the mall with your friends.

The important thing is that rewards come after, not before, you have finished a short-term goal.

What is the reward for completing a long-term career goal? It is doing work that you like. It may also be a better life.

Career Decision-Making Activities

You can do a simple exercise to improve your self-esteem. Write down ten things that you like about yourself. They can be talents, things at which you have succeeded, personality traits you like, or things you want people to see in you. Then write down two or three good things that you did in the past week. Doing this exercise *regularly* will help you focus on the positive things about yourself.

MANAGEMENT OF OTHERS

If you have mastered self-management, you can then learn how to manage others. Anytime you are in charge of any activity that involves others, you have to manage them. If you are put in charge of organizing a school cleanup program, you have to know how to manage others.

To manage others, you have to be a good leader. Read the ways to become a good leader in Figure 4.2.

You'll find that managing others is easier if they like you. That means you have to be sociable.

Figure 4.2 How to Be an Effective Leader

- Show enthusiasm about the work and the members of the group.
- Work with the group to get things done. Try to solve any problems that might arise.
- Give the members of the group responsibility.
- Praise group members.
- Treat all members fairly and considerately.
- Make decisions after receiving information from group members and discussing the options.
- Show respect for each person's ideas and opinions.

▲ Being sociable is important in the world of work just as it is in school.

BEING SOCIABLE

Marnie, a new girl in school, has a locker near Françoise's. Marnie has made several attempts to be friendly. She has talked to Françoise when the girls were at their lockers and has walked to class with her. When Marnie asks Françoise if she wants to go to a movie with her on Saturday, Françoise says, "Sure," and also tells Marnie that she is glad to finally have a friend to do things with.

After the movie, the girls stop at a local diner. Françoise avoids looking directly at Marnie and responds in one-syllable words when Marnie talks. Françoise keeps her arms crossed in front of her body. Marnie is confused about how Françoise feels.

It's never easy to meet new people. In the world of work, though, you'll be meeting new people all of the time. How you interact with them will be important. It may even determine how well you succeed at your job.

Being sociable, or being friendly to others, is an important skill in the world of work. One of the first things you need to learn in order to be sociable is how to be a good listener.

THE IMPORTANCE OF LISTENING

Have you ever met someone who couldn't seem to stop talking? After a while, you probably wanted to be elsewhere. The cold fact is that no one wants to just hear other people talk. Most of us want to talk, too. So if you're going to be sociable, you have to learn to listen. Figure 4.3 lists some ways to become a good listener.

CARING ABOUT OTHERS

sincerity
honest or genuine feeling.

Another important way to be sociable is to really care about others. If you only think about yourself all the time, you can't show much interest in others' problems. If you only think about yourself, you can probably never become a good listener. After all, if you really don't care about others, you won't show much **sincerity** (honest or genuine feeling). A sincere friend is one who cares from the heart. An insincere friend is one who makes believe he or she cares about your problems.

No one can force you to care about others. You'll find, though, that if you do, your life will be richer and more rewarding. You'll also find that if you show genuine concern about others, they will do the same with you.

Figure 4.3 How to Be a Good Listener

- **MAINTAIN EYE CONTACT WITH THE SPEAKER**
  Don't let your eyes wander around the room or look to see who just came in.
- **LISTEN ATTENTIVELY**
  Give your attention to what the speaker is saying. Hear the words in your mind. Think about the words as you hear them.
- **REMEMBER WHAT YOU ARE HEARING**
  Try to remember and translate into your own words what the speaker is saying.
- **GIVE VERBAL AND NONVERBAL CUES (SIGNALS) TO SHOW YOU ARE LISTENING**
  Nod or smile at appropriate times. Ask a question or make a comment that indicates you are interested and want to learn more about the person's thoughts and feelings.
- **TRY TO FIGURE OUT THE OTHER PERSON'S POINT OF VIEW**
  Try to discover the feelings beneath the words. What assumptions is the speaker making? (What is he or she taking for granted?)
- **GIVE APPROPRIATE COMMENTS OR ASK QUESTIONS WHEN THE SPEAKER HAS FINISHED TALKING**
  Respond to what the speaker has said.

INTEGRITY

Lance had a part-time job interviewing people over the telephone for a company that was conducting a survey. He was supposed to call people and ask them what kind of soap they used. One evening, while he was working, Sabina, one of his friends, stopped by his office while he was making his phone calls. Lance began chatting with Sabina and didn't notice how much time was passing.

At the end of the evening, he realized that he should have made about twenty-five more calls than he actually had. Lance decided to write on his chart that he had made the calls anyway. He couldn't remember very many kinds of soap, though, so his reports seemed a bit odd.

Lance's supervisor asked him about the calls. Lance told the truth. He was told that the next time he did anything wrong at work, he would be fired.

When Lance put down the false information about calls he didn't make, he was lying. Every time you lie, you are showing a lack of **integrity.** Integrity is the quality of being honest, both to yourself and others. Integrity relates to your personal values. If you value being honest, you would not do what Lance did. As Lance discovered, integrity is important at work.

Sometimes we say that acting honestly means acting ethically. Indeed, your integrity also relates to your personal set of **ethics.**

integrity
the quality of being honest, both to yourself and others.

ethics
the rules or principles by which a person lives.

▶ A person's ethics play an important role in many of today's service-oriented occupations. These customer service operators must perform their jobs with little direct supervision.

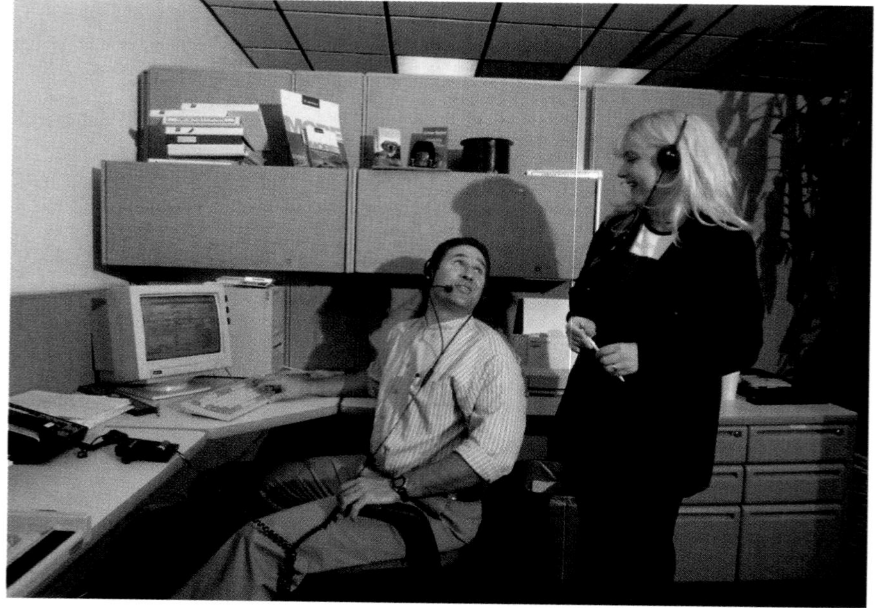

Ethics are the rules or principles by which you live. One rule might be not to lie. Another rule might be not to steal. Yet another rule might be to try to make others feel good.

There is an old saying, "What goes around, comes around." It means that if you treat people badly, at some time you will be treated badly, too. But if you treat people nicely, you'll be treated nicely, as well. If you maintain your integrity, you'll be rewarded. People will respect you more. When you work, people will know that they can count on you. You'll have an easier time succeeding.

Career Decision-Making Activities

Pick a famous person, living or dead, whom you think of as someone with a special talent. Research this person's career to find out what that person had to do to make use of his or her talent. Did success come easily? What especially difficult obstacles did the person have to overcome? Write a one-page essay describing the person's talent and the greatest challenges the person faced in developing and using that talent.

Review and Enrichment

Summarizing the Chapter

Summarizing information is a critical thinking skill that will help you succeed in the world of work. Write a summary of what you learned in Chapter 4. Focus on the main points of the chapter. Then in a class discussion, compare your summary with the summaries done by your classmates. Can you improve your summary?

Improving Your Career Vocabulary

Learning to use new vocabulary terms will improve your communication skills, which are important in almost all areas of work. Write definitions for the terms listed below. Then for each term, write an original sentence about yourself in which you use the term correctly.

- self-esteem
- body image
- sibling
- perfectionist
- mass media
- individual responsibility
- chain of command
- self-management
- sincerity
- distractions
- integrity
- ethics

Finding the Facts

Finding exact information is a frequently used skill in many careers. Find the answers to the exercise below, and write the answers on a separate sheet of paper.

1. What personal qualities do you need to succeed in the world of work?
2. List the five ways to improve your self-esteem.
3. What is the first step to improve your self-management?
4. What are the ways to be an effective leader?
5. What the six ways to become a good listener?

Thinking for Yourself

To complete the exercise below you will need to use critical thinking and communication skills, which are skills valued by all employers. Write out your answers or be prepared to discuss them in class, depending on your teacher's instructions.

1. Explain in your own words how you think a person's self-esteem can affect his or her work life.
2. Write a paragraph about how you think the mass media affects your own body image.
3. Explain briefly why self-management is important in reaching personal goals.

Practicing Your Basic Skills

Your career success depends greatly on your basic math and communication skills. Work hard at improving in the areas where you have trouble by using the following exercises.

Math

1. John wants to change his lifestyle, and the first step is to buy a flashy car. The car he wants costs $27,675. He can come up with a down payment of $2,500. The car dealer will loan him the rest at 13¼ percent interest over three years. How much in interest will John pay altogether?
2. Write each of these percentages as decimals:

17%	25%	6%	3.5%
150%	½%	310%	0.5%

3. Susan is experiencing a conflict of values. Usually she saves 10 percent of her salary each month. However, she wants to buy a radio this month that costs $215. If she doesn't put the 10 percent in her savings, she'll have just enough to buy the radio. How much does Susan earn each month?

Reading and Writing

1. Many people don't write well because they have poor vocabularies. The following five words have to do with people's values or personalities. Copy them down. Look their meanings up in the dictionary. Learn to spell them correctly, and then write each one in a sentence.
   a. integrity
   b. aesthetics
   c. conscience
   d. exuberant
   e. extravagant
2. Write a paragraph describing your ideal lifestyle. Tell where you will work and live, who your friends will be, and how you will dress.
3. Read a magazine article about someone with a lifestyle similar to one you think you'd enjoy. Afterward, write a short paragraph telling about

Review and Enrichment, continued

the things you *don't* think you'd like about that person's lifestyle.

Speaking and Listening

1. For one day, listen carefully to how other people speak. Make notes as to how their speaking habits reveal their personalities. Share your discoveries with the class without mentioning any names.
2. How you pronounce words is important to being understood. Practice saying the following words, which are often mispronounced. If you're not sure of a pronunciation, look it up in the dictionary. Use each of the words in sentences at least three times during the day.

   often   applicable   asked

Activities Working with Others

In almost all careers you must be able to get along well with other people to be successful. Work with your classmates to do the following activities. As you work together, pay attention to how well you get along. If necessary, work hard at improving your ability to do your part and to cooperate.

1. Go to the library and find a magazine from the 1920s and one from the 1950s. How has our concept of an attractive body image changed? What is considered an attractive body image today? How important is this ideal image to a person's self-esteem? Present your findings to the class.
2. Prepare a five minute oral presentation on one of the following topics.
   a. Parents must be the leaders.
   b. Everyone is a leader.
   c. Getting along with people is (is not) important if you are to be a successful leader.
   d. The most often overlooked quality of leadership is. . . .

Decision Making and Problem Solving

You will be a big help to your employer if you can make decisions and solve problems. List all the possible ways of resolving the situation described below. Then pick the best alternative (possible choice), and tell why you chose it. If you need help, refer to Chapter 3.

1. You are working as a clerk in a grocery store. A customer has just paid for her groceries and left the store, but the bagger missed a candy bar, which is lying on the counter. The candy bar has already been paid for. What will you do?

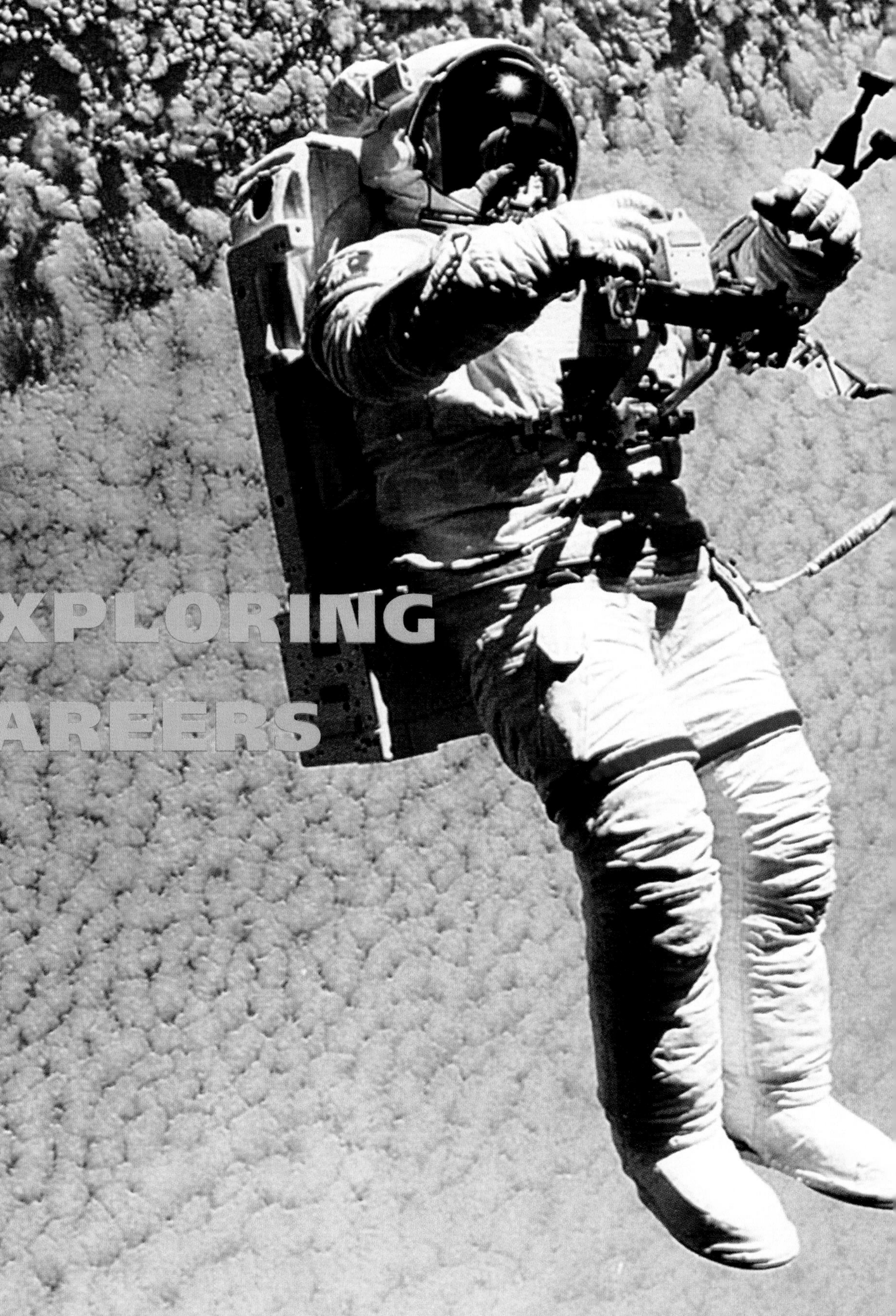

PART TWO

EXPLORING CAREERS

CHAPTER 5

HOW TO RESEARCH CAREERS

◆ Chapter Objectives ◆

After completing this chapter you will be able to do the following:

- ◆ Define the terms listed under "New Career Terms."
- ◆ List the three main career resource books published by the U.S. government.
- ◆ Name the eight types of information found in each *OOH* article.
- ◆ List at least five sources of career information, in addition to the three main government sources.
- ◆ Give examples of the types of questions a person should ask in interviewing a worker.
- ◆ List and describe at least five ways to research careers.
- ◆ Use a nine-point checklist to research careers.

◆ New Career Terms ◆

In this chapter you will learn the meanings of the following career terms:

- ✔ Research
- ✔ *OOH*
- ✔ *DOT*
- ✔ Job duties
- ✔ *GOE*
- ✔ Online
- ✔ Experience
- ✔ Volunteering
- ✔ Temporary job
- ✔ Part-time job
- ✔ Work-study programs
- ✔ Entry-level job

Sarah's mother has worked as a travel agent for as long as Sarah can remember. Sarah has already thought about a career in the travel ***agency business.***

She knows that her mom works regular hours. She's always been home to fix breakfast and dinner. Sarah also knows that her mother gets to take a lot of trips. She doesn't have to pay much for them. Sarah thinks being a travel agent would be a good career choice.

After school Sarah usually doesn't do things with her friends. She likes to stay home and read. In fact, a few times Sarah has not gone to parties because she is uncomfortable talking with strangers.

Sarah thinks she wants to be a travel agent like her mother, but does she really know what that career is like? She hasn't discussed it with her mom. She hasn't talked it over with her guidance counselor. She hasn't done much **research** on her own. This means that she hasn't investigated or collected information about the topic.

research
finding out more by reading and talking to people.

Sarah isn't absolutely certain about what career is best for her. Perhaps there are other careers for which she might be better suited. For example, much of the job of a travel agent is talking—talking with both strangers and acquaintances. If Sarah did some career research, she would find out about this. She might question whether being a travel agent is the occupation (career) for her.

To begin her research about travel agents, Sarah might do the following:

◆ Spend a day at work with her mother, and talk with different workers at the travel agency about their jobs.

Careers for Tomorrow

ROBOTICS TECHNICIAN

Robots used to be considered science fiction. They aren't today. Over 80,000 robots are currently working in U.S. manufacturing plants. Some experts predict that in ten years there could be as many as 300,000 robots at work.

Robots carry out human functions, but they're still just machines. They have computers inside them, with motors and all sorts of other mechanisms, to make them move the way humans move. Many robots even look like humans. The people who make them sometimes give them human names.

The science of robot technology is called *robotics*. There is a growing need for technicians—people who fix things—in the robotics industry. If you are mechanically minded and like the idea of working with robots, you might consider a career as a robotics technician.

For more information, check out robotics on the Internet.

Robotics technicians are in demand in today's manufacturing occupations.

- Obtain some travel brochures at the travel agency to study the type of information customers will expect to receive.
- Ask how the travel agency determines the cost of a tour.

Can you think of other things Sarah might do to find out about this career possibility?

Visiting job sites, talking with workers, and seeing what a real workday is like are good ways to begin your career research for any occupation. You will usually find that people are glad to have you visit. Just be sure to phone for an appointment first and show a sincere interest in their career area.

Researching careers can be fun. When you research careers, you will find out what people do on their jobs. You're going to find out that people are doing lots of interesting things—many of which you've never heard of. The other enjoyable part of career research is that much of it involves talking to people, visiting work sites, and trying out some jobs. There's a lot more to career research than reading books in the library or working on the Internet. In this chapter you will learn several different ways to research careers.

RESEARCHING CAREERS AT THE LIBRARY

Your school and local libraries contain many outstanding books, magazines, pamphlets, and other resources dealing with careers. Your library can also order books from other libraries and from publishers about careers in which you are especially interested.

As you'll learn later in this chapter, actual work experiences and talking to workers about their jobs are the two best ways to explore careers. But there are tens of thousands of different jobs in the United States. You probably don't have time to work at thousands of different jobs or talk to thousands of different people. This is why reading about careers is a good way to begin your research. Reading helps you quickly find out which kinds of careers you would and would not enjoy. Reading helps you narrow the field so you can do your best research on the careers you are most likely to enjoy.

Of course, you are beginning your career reading with this book. Chapters 6 through 20 especially provide lots of information on careers. The sections that follow describe some of the most useful career books available in print. The first three books mentioned are all published by the U.S. government.

OCCUPATIONAL OUTLOOK HANDBOOK (OOH)

One source of general information about occupations is the *Occupational Outlook Handbook* **(OOH).** This book describes about 250 occupations in detail. These occupations account for about 85 percent of all jobs.

Look at the partial page duplicated from the handbook in Figure 5.1. Every article about an occupation has the same headings. These headings and the kinds of information found under each one are listed below:

1. **Nature of the Work.** Tells what workers do on their jobs; gives you the common **job duties,** the tasks that make up the jobs.
2. **Working Conditions.** Describes the work settings and the hours worked.
3. **Employment.** Tells the number of jobs available and where they are.
4. **Training, Other Qualifications, and Advancement.** Tells the required skills and knowledge, the ways to get needed education and training, and the chances for advancement.
5. **Job Outlook.** Tells whether the number of jobs is expected to go up or down.
6. **Earnings.** Gives average earnings and range of earnings.
7. **Related Occupations.** Lists occupations with similar skills, interests, and education requirements.
8. **Sources of Additional Information.** Tells where to go for more information.

Just make sure that before you use the handbook, you read the introductory section entitled "How to Get the Most from the Handbook." Also make sure you have the most recent edition of the *OOH.* There's a new edition every two years.

OOH
Occupational Outlook Handbook—a guide for researching careers.

job duty
a task you are expected to perform on the job.

Figure 5.1 Sample Information from the *OOH*

graduates of 2-year programs, and people with less than a 2-year degree or its equivalent in work experience, should face stronger competition for programming jobs. Competition for entry-level positions, however, can even affect applicants with a bachelor's degree. Although demand fluctuates as employer's needs change with technology, prospects should be best for college graduates with knowledge of and experience working with a variety of programming languages and tools, particularly C++ and other object oriented languages—such as Smalltalk, Visual Basic, Ada, and Java—as well as newer, domain-specific languages that apply to computer networking, data base management, and Internet applications. In order to remain competitive, college graduates should keep up to date with the latest skills and technologies.

Many employers prefer to hire applicants with previous experience in the field. Employers are increasingly interested in programmers who can combine areas of technical expertise or who are adaptable and able to learn and incorporate new skills. Therefore, individuals who want to become programmers can enhance their chances of doing so by combining the appropriate formal training with practical work experience. Students should try to gain experience by participating in a college work-study program, or undertaking an internship. Students also can greatly improve their employment prospects by taking courses such as accounting, management, engineering, or science—allied fields in which applications programmers are in demand.

With the expansion of client/server environments, employers will continue to look for programmers with strong technical skills who understand their business and its programming needs. Businesses also look for programmers who develop a technical specialization in areas such as client/server programming, multimedia technology, graphic user interface (GUI), and 4th and 5th generation programming tools. Programmers will be creating and maintaining expert systems and embedding these technologies in more and more products. Other areas of progress include data communications and the business application of Internet technologies. Networking computers so they can communicate with each other is necessary to achieve the greater efficiency organizations require to remain competitive. Demand for programmers with strong object-oriented programming capabilities and experience should arise from the expansion of Intranets, extranets and World Wide Web applications.

Earnings

Median earnings of programmers who worked full time in 1996 were about $40,100 a year. The middle 50 percent earned between about $30,700 and $52,000 a year. The lowest 10 percent earned less than $22,700; the highest 10 percent earned more than $65,200. Starting salary offersfor graduates with a bachelor's degree in the area of computer programming averaged about $35,167 a year in private industry in 1997, according to the National Association of Colleges and Employers. Programmers working in the West and Northeast earned somewhat more than those working in the South and Midwest. On average, systems programmers earn more than applications programmers.

A survey of workplaces in 160 metropolitan areas reported that beginning programmers had median annual earnings of about $27,000 in 1995. Experienced mid-level programmers with some supervisory responsibilities had median annual earnings of about $40,000. Median annual earnings for programmers at the supervisory or team leader level were about $55,000.

According to Robert Half International Inc., starting salaries ranged from $32,500 to $39,000 for programmers and $47,500 to $60,000 for systems programmers in large establishments in 1997. Starting salaries for programmers in small establishments ranged from $28,000 to $37,000.

In the Federal Government, the entrance salary for programmers with a college degree or qualifying experience was about $19,520 a year in early 1997; for those with a superior academic record, $24,180.

Related Occupations

Programmers must pay great attention to detail as they write and "debug" programs. Other professional workers who must be detail-oriented include computer scientists, computer engineers, and systems analysts, statisticians, mathematicians, engineers, financial analysts, accountants, auditors, actuaries, and operations research analysts.

Sources of Additional Information

State employment service offices can provide information about job openings for computer programmers. Also check with your city's chamber of commerce for information on the area's largest employers.

For information about certification as a computing professional, contact:

- Institute for Certification of Computing Professionals (ICCP), 2200 East Devon Ave., Suite 268, Des Plaines, IL 60018. Homepage: http://www.iccp.org

Further information about computer careers is available from:

- The Association for Computing (ACM), 1515 Broadway, New York, NY 10036.
- IEEE Computer Society, Headquarters Office, 1730 Massachusetts Ave., NW., Washington, DC 20036-1992.

Computer Scientists, Computer Engineers, and Systems Analysts

(D.O.T. 030.062-010, .162-014, .167-014; 031; 032; 033; 039; and 109.067-010)

Significant Points

- Expected to be the top 3 fastest growing occupations and among the top 20 in the number of new jobs as computer applications continue to expand throughout the economy.
- A bachelor's degree is virtually a prerequisite for most employers. Relevant work experience also is very important. For some of the more complex jobs, persons with graduate degrees are preferred.

Nature of the Work

The rapid spread of computers has generated a need for highly trained workers to design and develop new hardware and software systems and to incorporate technological advances into new or existing systems. The *Handbook* refers to this group of professionals as computer scientists, computer engineers, and systems analysts, but in reality this group includes a wide range of professional computer-related occupations. Job titles used to describe this broad category of workers evolve rapidly, reflecting new areas of specialization or changes in technology as well as the preferences and practices of employers. Although many narrow specializations exist, the professional specialty group is commonly referred to as computer scientists, computer engineers, and systems analysts.

The title *computer scientist* can be applied to a wide range computer professionals who generally design computers and the software that runs them, develop information technologies, and develop and adapt principles for applying computers to new uses. Computer scientists perform many of the same duties as other computer professionals throughout a normal workday, but their jobs are distinguished by the higher level of theoretical expertise and innovation they apply to complex problems and the creation or application of new technology.

Computer scientists can work as theorists, researchers, or inventors. Those employed by academic institutions work in areas ranging from complexity theory, to hardware, to programming language design. Some work on multi-discipline projects, such as developing and advancing uses of virtual reality in robotics. Their counterparts in private industry work in areas such as applying theory, developing specialized languages or information technolo-

DICTIONARY OF OCCUPATIONAL TITLES (DOT)

Another source of information is the *Dictionary of Occupational Titles* **(DOT).** This book contains occupational descriptions. It assigns a number to each job title. Many career resource centers and libraries use these numbers to organize all of their career information. If you know the *DOT* number, you can usually find more sources of information.

There are over 20,000 different kinds of jobs listed in the *DOT.* The government does not revise this book as often as it does the *OOH.* Updates are published once in a while. Ask your librarian about these updates if you want to see them.

When you use the *Dictionary of Occupational Titles,* you will learn about jobs you didn't even know existed. The way you use the *DOT* is to identify and explore groups of occupations that are about the same. You do this by looking at the first three numbers in each of the numbered codes. Occupations that have the same first three numbers are similar. There are fifteen career clusters developed by the U.S. Department of Education. In Chapters 6 through 20 you will have an opportunity to study each of these fifteen clusters.

Your best bet is to read the instructions in the *DOT* before you use it. Then ask your librarian or guidance counselor to make sure you are using it correctly.

DOT
Dictionary of Occupational Titles—a guide containing descriptions of jobs organized by numbered code into related groups.

GOE
Guide for Occupational Exploration—book giving information on career areas.

online
connected to the Internet.

GUIDE FOR OCCUPATIONAL EXPLORATION (GOE)

Remember in Chapter 2, when we talked about interests—the things that interested you the most? The *Guide for Occupational Exploration* **(GOE)** divides careers into groups according to interests. There are twelve groups, called *interest areas.* The *GOE* gives you a definition of each interest area. Then it explains it in more detail. The information tells you the following:

1. The kind of work done.
2. The skills and abilities needed.
3. How to decide if you could learn to do this kind of work.
4. How to prepare for entry into the job area.
5. Other factors to take into account when you are thinking about a particular job.

The *GOE* can be very helpful if you know your strongest interests. Ask your guidance counselor or librarian about getting a copy of the *GOE.*

THE ONLINE WORLD

The word **online** has become part of our everyday work vocabulary. Working online means simply connecting to the Internet, which is a vast collection of about 100,000 major computers throughout the world. Much of the communication among employees and businesses is now done over the Internet. Sometimes the Internet is simply referred to as the Net. Sometimes it is even referred to as cyberspace.

OTHER READING RESOURCES

Your library at school and the local community college or university library contain many more books with career information.

Attitude makes a difference

Taking Advantage of the Computer

Miranda and Juanita are identical twins. When they were little, their mother dressed them alike. Today they still look alike, but they are as different as night and day.

Miranda is captain of the girls' basketball team. She has done her best work in drafting. She is thinking about becoming an architect who will design big houses. She is also fascinated with computers. She started playing with her family's home computer when she was in the fourth grade.

Juanita says she doesn't like computers. Her best class, so far, has been social studies. She likes to discover why things happen. She also likes history. But Juanita doesn't really know what she wants to do.

Miranda found out that the school guidance counselor had a new computer program in career choices. Because she was already familiar with computers, she wasn't afraid to make an appointment to use the new program. When she opened up the program the first screen showed the following:

Select one:

1. Identifying your values.
2. Self-assessment.
3. Information on occupations.
4. Educational requirements for different occupations.
5. Job-seeking preparations.
6. Skill building in decision making and problem solving.

Using the computer (and with a little help from the counselor), Miranda found out that she really did have an interest in becoming an architect. She started dreaming about designing beautiful houses for other people.

She told Juanita about the new program. Juanita said she wasn't interested. Although she was, she didn't want to show how little she knew about computers. Juanita still doesn't know what she wants to do.

What Do YOU Think?

What's the difference between Miranda's and Juanita's attitudes? Can you think of a way Miranda might have helped Juanita change her attitude?

Don't be like Juanita. Whenever you have a chance to use a computer, go ahead and do it. Almost all computer programs are "user friendly" these days. That means you can use them even if you don't know anything at all about how a computer works. Most computer programs are made so you can use them alone, on your own. You don't have to worry about someone standing over your shoulder. No one will criticize you.

You can find whole books devoted to some careers. And the U.S. government, through the Department of Labor, prints pamphlets and articles about the job market every couple of weeks. Your state government may also publish career information. Many companies publish brief descriptions called *Career Briefs.*

There are also many magazines that you can read to find career information. Two interesting magazines are *Real World* and *Career World.* They tell you about getting and keeping a job. Even magazines such as *Seventeen* and *Motor Trend* have articles about careers. If you look for them, you can find career stories in many reading resources.

O*NET—THE OCCUPATIONAL INFORMATION NETWORK

The newest source on careers and job characteristics is O*NET, the online occupational information network. By the time you read this book, O*NET will probably be available to you online (through the Internet) at home, at school, at community libraries, at shopping malls, at career centers, or on the job.

O*NET is the result of a partnership between government and private businesses. It is already linked to the online job-matching system called America's Job Bank.

Occupations are changing rapidly in America because of rapid changes in technology. O*NET was designed to react quickly to the changing job needs in the marketplace. If your home, school, or library is already hooked up to the Internet, you can access O*NET now. Ask your teacher, guidance counselor, or librarian about it. At the same time, you can ask about the other online information sources for your career research.

AUDIOVISUAL MATERIALS

Libraries contain lots of resources in addition to books, other reading materials, and online sources. You can also find videos, films, and audiotapes about careers. For example, your school and local libraries probably have a wide assortment of videotapes that will help you choose a career. These videos can do something books can't do—they can show you people in actual work settings. They can also show you close-ups of a variety of working conditions in different jobs. If you think you've found a career you'd really like through your reading, ask your librarian for audiovisual materials on that career.

Career Decision-Making Activities

1. Go to your school or public library. Find three books on careers that are *not* mentioned in this chapter. Using a separate sheet of paper for each book, write down the title, author, copyright date (found on the page after the title page), and publisher. Also write two sentences describing the kind of information found in the book. Bring your information to class. Contribute it to a class list of career resources, which everyone can use.
2. Career resource books are organized in different ways. Obtain copies of the three books mentioned in this chapter as the main government sources of career information. Make three columns on a sheet of paper. At the top of each column write the name of one of the three books. Then, in the appropriate column, list the main career areas for each book. (Clue: One book is divided into nine categories; one is divided into twelve; and one is divided into twenty categories.) Now look at the different ways of grouping jobs. Does one way seem better than another to you? Can you suggest a better method? Discuss this in class.
3. Use one of the three career reference books discussed in this chapter to find names of occupations of which you've never heard. Find five such job titles. On a sheet of paper, write down the job titles and a brief description of the duties for each. Then bring your notes to class. Take turns reading the name of each occupation and seeing if anyone else can guess what a worker in that job does.

ASKING PEOPLE ABOUT THEIR WORK

Reading about careers is a good idea. Finding computer programs and online sources to help you learn about yourself and careers is another good idea. But you have all around you perhaps the greatest source of information—people who work.

FAMILY AND FRIENDS

First, there is your family. Someone in your family is probably working. Other family members may have worked in the past. You can start asking them about the different jobs they now have or have had in the past.

Ask them more than simple questions such as, "Do you like your work?" Find out what they do or did in different jobs. Ask what a typical workday is like. Ask how much each job involves working with other people. Ask what kind of education is best for each job.

Other relatives and friends can help you, too. Each of their experiences will give you a unique view of different jobs and careers. Talk to as many different relatives and friends as you can about their jobs. See how many careers you can learn about.

Suppose you want to find out more about two or three certain careers. The problem is that you don't know anyone who works in these careers. To whom can you talk? Should you just give up on this type of research?

The answer is no, you shouldn't give up. Ask your teachers, guidance counselors, friends, and relatives to help you identify people who work in those careers. A friend or relative might happen to know just the right person with whom you could talk. That friend or relative can then set up an appointment for you to meet the person.

THE YELLOW PAGES

If no one turns up a lead, don't give up. One idea is to obtain addresses out of the Yellow Pages of your phone book. If, for example, you think you might enjoy a career in nursing, look in the Yellow Pages under that heading. Write a few letters to registered nurses who advertise in the Yellow Pages. Chances are one of them might be willing to talk to you.

When you do find someone to interview about his or her job, schedule an appointment. Then be prepared. Have your questions ready. Know what you want to ask. And either have a pencil and paper ready to write down what you want to remember or have a tape recorder ready to record your interview.

You will probably think of many of your own questions. Listed below are some general questions to get you started. Pick from this list the questions that are most important to you. Try to organize your questions into groups such as the ones below.

A. Questions about What Goes on at Work

1. What are your duties?
2. Do your duties change much from day to day?
3. What do you like about your work?
4. What do you dislike about your work?
5. What are your regular hours?
6. Have you learned to use any special equipment or tools on your job? If so, what are they?
7. Do you have to work many extra hours?
8. Do you ever have to work nights, weekends, or holidays?
9. Describe your work environment. Is it clean or dirty? Noisy or quiet? Hot, cold, or air-conditioned?
10. Are any parts of your job dangerous? If so, please describe them.
11. Do you have a boss? If so, how much supervision does your boss give you?

B. Questions about Decision Making

1. Why did you choose this occupation?
2. Did you ever have any hobbies related to the kind of work you do?
3. How long have you worked at the job you have now?
4. If you could change one thing about your job, what would it be?
5. In your opinion, can both men and women do this kind of work? What percentage of people who do this kind of work would you estimate to be men? Women?

C. **Questions about Education and Training**
   1. What did you learn in junior high and high school that helped you in your work?
   2. Are there any subjects that you wish you had studied *more* while you were in school?
   3. What special training and education, if any, is necessary to enter this career area?

D. **Questions about People on the Job**
   1. How much of your job involves working with other people?
   2. Describe the people you work with on a day-to-day basis. What are they like?
   3. Do you have much contact with people outside your company?

E. **Questions about Earnings, Advancement, and Outlook**
   1. How much money can a person expect to earn starting out in this career field?
   2. How much can a person expect to make with five years of experience?
   3. What do you think is the top pay for someone in this career field?
   4. Do most employers in this field provide *fringe benefits* (health insurance, sick pay, vacation pay, and so on)? If so, which benefits?
   5. Are there many opportunities for advancement in your career?
   6. What personal qualities and skills do you think are the most important for success in your career area?
   7. What other types of work could a person get with these same qualities and skills?
   8. What changes, if any, do you see coming in the years ahead for this occupation?

F. **Questions about Finding a Job**
   1. What does a company like yours look for in a new employee?
   2. What advice would you give someone like me, who is thinking of pursuing a career in this field?

Career Decision-Making Activities

1. Interview a parent, guardian, or adult friend or relative about his or her job. From the list of questions in this section, pick the fifteen you want most to ask. Tape your interview or make notes. Review the interview or your notes several times as you think about whether or not you would enjoy this occupation. Write a paragraph telling why you would or would not enjoy it. If you want to, share your interview and paragraph with the class.

WORKING—THE REAL THING

There is no better way to research a career than by actually working at a job in that career area. You may not even need the money. That's okay. The job will still be helpful. An after-school job in a field that interests you can sometimes tell you more in a few days than reading all the books in the library will ever tell you. Of course, you're probably not going to be doing exactly the kind of work you might do with more education and more training. But at least you will be getting a feel for what that particular kind of work is all about. And you will get paid!

While you are researching a career by having a job, you gain experience. No matter what kind of work you do, you gain experience in the career area. **Experience,** which is having done something in the past, is very important to employers. In the future, an employer will pick you over someone with equal skills and training if you have had more experience than the other people applying for the job.

experience
duties or jobs you have done that will help your performance in future jobs.

Remember that research, not experience, is your main goal at this point. You want to try these jobs to find out if you might enjoy this career area. If it turns out you don't like the work, that's all right. You can try something else.

There are at least three types of jobs you might consider in doing your research: volunteer, temporary, and part-time. In addition, there are at least two other ways—school work programs and creating your own job—you can explore careers.

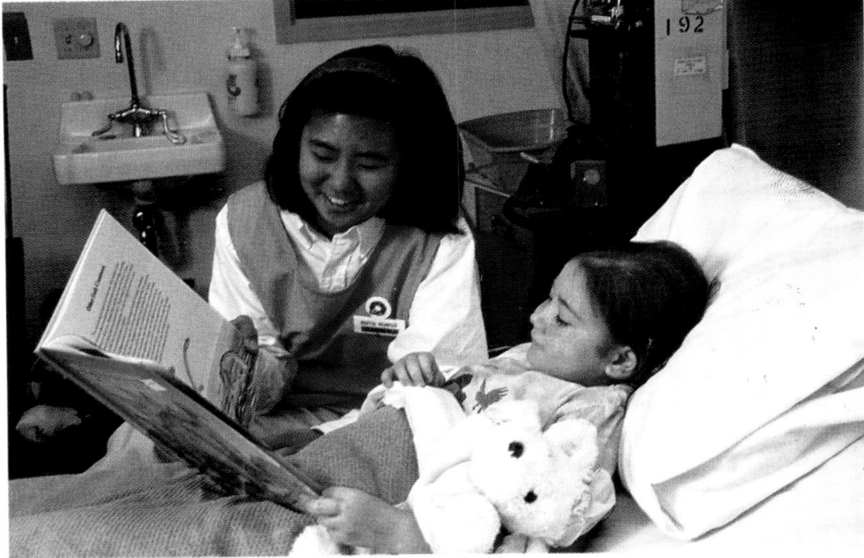

◀ Part of your job research could include volunteer work in a field that interests you.

volunteering
doing a job, which you are not paid for, to gain the experience.

VOLUNTEER WORK

Even though you might prefer to be paid for your work, consider **volunteering.** In a volunteer job you work without pay. For example, if you are interested in the health-care field, you might want to volunteer as an aide in a hospital.

If you think you want to work with people in the sports area, you could volunteer at your local YWCA or YMCA. Or you could help children by working with various sports leagues. It's usually easy to find a volunteer job.

In many school districts today, some volunteering is a requirement for graduation. If you must volunteer in order to graduate, you might as well volunteer in an area in which you are interested, one that might become part of your career path.

temporary job
a job obtained for the summer or any other time period that is limited.

part-time job
a job less than 40 hours per week, such as an after-school or weekend job.

work-study program
jobs that give students a chance to explore careers while earning school credit.

TEMPORARY JOBS

During holidays there are lots of **temporary jobs.** These are jobs that last only a short time. Lots of stores need extra help because of the holiday rush. There are also temporary jobs during the summer—in construction and farming, for example. A temporary job is an excellent way to get work experience. You don't have to work during regular school days.

PART-TIME JOBS

In a **part-time job,** you work only a portion of a full workweek, but you do it regularly. You might, for example, get a job at a local restaurant for an hour or two after school each day. You might get a job helping a local lawn-care company and work five hours every Saturday.

SCHOOL WORK PROGRAMS

Some schools have **work-study programs.** These programs give students a chance to explore careers while earning school credit and a chance to earn some money at the same time. These programs have many different names. Talk to your guidance counselor about the types of programs available. Who knows? There may be a job opening in the very career area in which you are most interested.

▼ Many teens find part-time jobs that fit their school schedules.

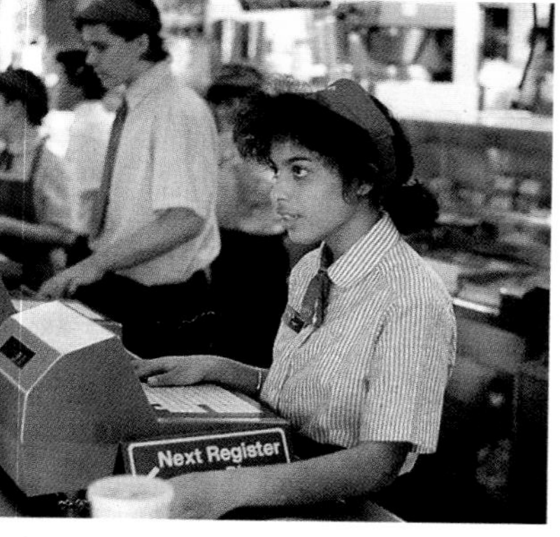

CREATING A JOB

More and more young people are creating their own jobs. Some even manage to make quite a bit of money. Could you start your own business in a career area you'd like to explore?

Starting and running a business is called *entrepreneurship.* You will learn more about this in Chapter 23. There are also books in the libraries and bookstores that focus on jobs that teenagers can create for themselves.

Career Decision-Making Activities

1. Think of five kinds of occupations you would like to explore. Flipping through the pages of Chapters 6 through 20 might help you get some ideas. The Yellow Pages of the phone book could also give you ideas. For each of the five occupations, list at least three possible sources in your community for part-time, temporary, or volunteer jobs that would give you a chance to explore the career area. Read and compare lists in class. Does anyone else have ideas that you can use?
2. Contact at least three employers who might have jobs like those you listed in Activity 1. Ask them about their policies regarding part-time, temporary, and volunteer help. How old would you need to be to get such a job? Compare your results in class.

A CAREER RESEARCH CHECKLIST

Any time you are trying to get information on a career, you need a checklist. It doesn't have to be long, but it should be specific. Here is a sample checklist:

1. **What is the nature of the work, and what will my duties be?** Every job has a set of job duties. These are the tasks that make up the job. In doing your research, make sure you find out the duties of each job. More than anything else, these duties will determine whether or not you enjoy the work. In career resources such as the *OOH,* duties are described under headings like "Nature of the Work."
2. **What are the working conditions?** Working conditions include how many hours you are expected to work and when those hours are. Working conditions also include the job location—indoors or outdoors, for example. In addition, you need to know whether you are going to work in an office or a warehouse. Some people can work around dirt and dust without a problem. Others can't.
3. **What personal and physical qualities do I need for the job?** Some jobs require you to wear a business suit. Others require scuba diving gear. Your personal qualities might make you suitable for one type of dress but not the other. Your physical qualities are also important. You may not have the strength or stamina to run a jackhammer all day, for example.
4. **How much will I earn?** How much a job pays is clearly an important question. We haven't listed it as the first item on our checklist because money earned should never be the most important aspect of a job choice. It is just one of many things you need to know about different jobs within different career areas.

   You should always find out, though, what you are going to get paid. You don't want to be surprised.

entry-level job
a job for a beginner to start with to train for higher-level jobs.

5. **Are there any advancement possibilities?** Is the job you are looking at a "dead-end" one (a job with no chance of advancement to other duties and levels)? Or can you be promoted to a better-paying position with more responsibility? Usually when you start in any career you start at an **entry-level job.** This is a job requiring the minimum skills and experience. Most people do not stay in such a position. They advance up the ladder. You need to know how many rungs there are in that ladder.

   It is okay to take entry-level jobs with no future for temporary work or part-time work while you are in school. You are gaining experience and trying out different careers to find out what you're good at and what you like. That's important.
6. **What training and education will be required?** How much education do you need? A high school diploma? A community college or technical school diploma? Or more? Will you be able to obtain training while in school or on the job? Will you need more training in order to take a particular job within a particular career? You may decide that you don't want to go to college. If so, make sure the careers you are interested in don't require a college education.

   You also need to know about required education and training because they're expensive. Sometimes you can't afford as much education as a particular job might require. You will need to be realistic about what's possible for you. You might need to get your education a little bit at a time, while you're working. You will learn more about paying for education in Chapter 24.
7. **What is the career outlook?** Are there many jobs available in the area in which you are interested? What are the job trends? Will the industry get bigger? Will it get smaller? You don't want to choose a career if it's not going to be there when you finish school.
8. **What are some related jobs?** Just because you have done research on one job doesn't mean you should ignore other possibilities. For example, if you are interested in working with animals, you may have done some research on becoming a veterinarian—an animal doctor. At the same time, you might want to look at related jobs that require less education and less expense. You could become an assistant in a veterinarian's office. Or you could work your way up the career ladder in a large pet store.
9. **What are other sources of information?** Many career resources give names, addresses, phone numbers, and other information for further research. When you are looking up information on the Internet, virtually every site has links to other related sites. Whenever you have time, explore those related sites.

   Remember—knowledge is power. The more information you have, the more likely you are to choose a career in which you will be happy and successful.

Career Decision-Making Activities

By the time you have worked your way to this point in the book, you will probably have thought of some jobs that could interest you.

1. Think back through all that you've read in this book so far. Many careers have been mentioned. List three jobs about which you would like to know more. Then select one of the three to research.
2. List all of the sources of career information you have learned about in this book.
3. Using the career research checklist as a guide, write a career research report on the job you have selected.
4. On the day your report is due, bring it to class. Along with your class members, place your report on a table in the classroom. Choose one person from the class to write all of the jobs the class has researched on the board.
5. Pick the classmate's report that interests you the most, and read it. Then discuss the job reported on with the student who wrote the report.

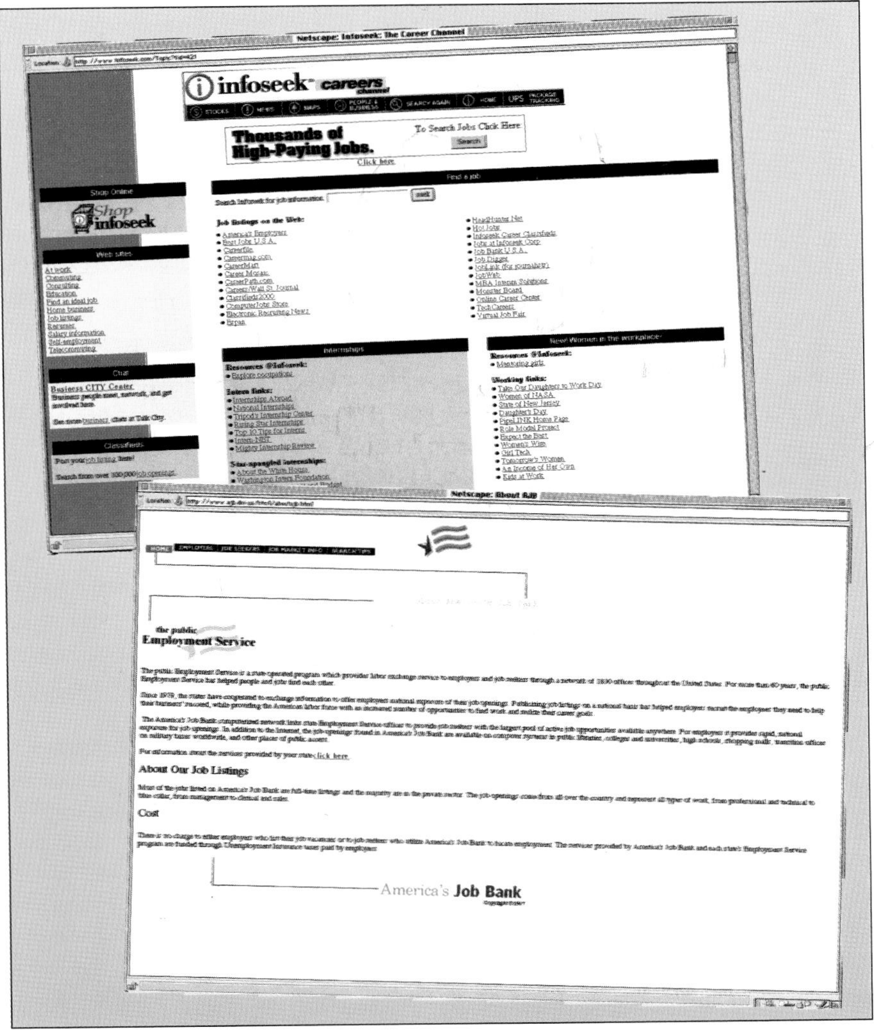

◀ There are thousands of Internet sites to explore in your career research. Use "career" as your initial search key word.

Review and Enrichment

Summarizing the Chapter

Summarizing information is a critical thinking skill that will help you succeed in the world of work. Write a summary of what you learned in Chapter 5. Focus on the main points of the chapter. Then in a class discussion, compare your summary with the summaries done by your classmates. Can you improve your summary?

Improving Your Career Vocabulary

Learning to use new vocabulary terms will improve your communication skills, which are important in almost all areas of work. Write definitions for the terms listed below. Then for each term, write an original sentence about yourself in which you use the term correctly.

- research
- *OOH*
- job duties
- *DOT*
- online
- *GOE*
- experience
- volunteering
- temporary job
- part-time job
- work-study programs
- entry-level job

Finding the Facts

Finding exact information is a frequently used skill in many careers. Find the answers to the exercises below, and write the answers on a separate sheet of paper.

1. List the eight kinds of information the *OOH* gives on jobs.
2. What kind of code is used in the *DOT* for groups of occupations?
3. What five kinds of information about an interest area can you find in the *GOE?*
4. What types of jobs can you apply for now, while you're in school?
5. What is the best way to research a career?

Thinking for Yourself

To complete the exercise below you will need to use critical thinking and communication skills, which are skills valued by all employers. Write out your answers or be prepared to discuss them in class, depending on your teacher's instructions.

1. Tell in your own words why you think researching a career is important.
2. Which family members and friends will you consult for career information? What kinds of questions do you plan to ask?
3. What kind of work experience do you plan to try? What do you hope to learn from it?
4. What kind of working conditions are important to you? Why?
5. Think of a career area in which you might be interested. What kinds of jobs can you think of that might be related to the career area in which you are *most* interested?

Practicing Your Basic Skills

Your career success depends greatly on your basic math and communication skills. Work hard at improving in the areas where you have trouble with the following exercises.

Math

1. Last summer Mark worked at a temporary job for twelve weeks. He earned $5.75 an hour and worked forty hours a week. After school Monday and Friday he works at another job from 4:00 to 6:30. He earns $5.00 an hour. He's done this for sixteen weeks. How much has Mark earned altogether?
2. Lynette talked to three friends and family members and learned eighteen facts about jobs. How many people must she talk to if she wants to learn seventy-two facts?
3. You are going to meet a friend at the library at 9:00 to do job research. The usual driving time is twelve minutes. You need to stop at the drugstore on the way, which will take fifteen minutes. The library lot is usually crowded, and you'll need ten minutes to find a parking space. The road you'll be taking has a lot of traffic, so you want to allow five extra minutes. What time should you leave for the library?

Review and Enrichment, continued

Reading and Writing

1. Have you ever volunteered to do a job for which you received no pay? Perhaps you helped your parents around the house or worked on a school dance committee. Describe your volunteer experience in a couple of paragraphs, and tell what you gained from it.
2. Get a copy of the classified section of your local newspaper. Look under the headings for part-time and temporary jobs for any occupations that interest you. Make a list of the jobs.
3. Your friend Gary wants to make some career decisions, but he knows nothing about the *OOH, DOT,* or *GOE.* Write him a letter telling him about these resources.

Speaking and Listening

1. Talk to several people about their own work experiences. Tell the class about the most interesting interview. Use notes if you need to do so.
2. Listen to other class members talk about the interviews they had. Why do you think they found those particular interviews interesting? Did they learn anything you too could use?

Activities Working with Others

In almost all careers you must be able to get along well with other people to be successful. Work with your classmates to do the following activities. As you work together, pay attention to how well you get along. If necessary, work hard at improving your ability to do your part and to cooperate.

1. As a class, break into groups interested in related careers. Each group should draft a letter to a company, trade association (a group organized with people who do the same kind of work), or other organization asking for information on that career area. Send the letters.
2. Divide the class into four or five teams. Each team should make a list of as many jobs as it can think of under each letter of the alphabet. The team with the most jobs listed after 15 minutes wins.

Decision Making and Problem Solving

You will be a big help to your employer if you can make decisions and solve problems. List all the possible ways of resolving the situations described below. Then pick the best alternative (possible choice), and tell why you chose it. If you need help, you might want to refer to Chapter 3.

1. You have a choice of two jobs. One is in a factory near your home. It pays $6 an hour, requires about 3 hours of overtime each week, and allows you to wear jeans and other casual clothes to work. The second job is in an office. It pays $7 an hour. There is no overtime, but the drive to and from work takes 30 minutes. You will need to buy new clothes to wear to work. Which job will you choose?
2. You have a choice of two jobs. Both are entry level. One pays well, and there is a chance for advancement within one year. However, you're not sure you and the boss will get along. The second job pays a little less. The job is a dead end as far as advancement is concerned. However, the company is large, and the interviewer told you that you could transfer to another department if you wanted to later on. Which job will you choose?

CHAPTER 6 AGRIBUSINESS AND NATURAL RESOURCES CAREERS

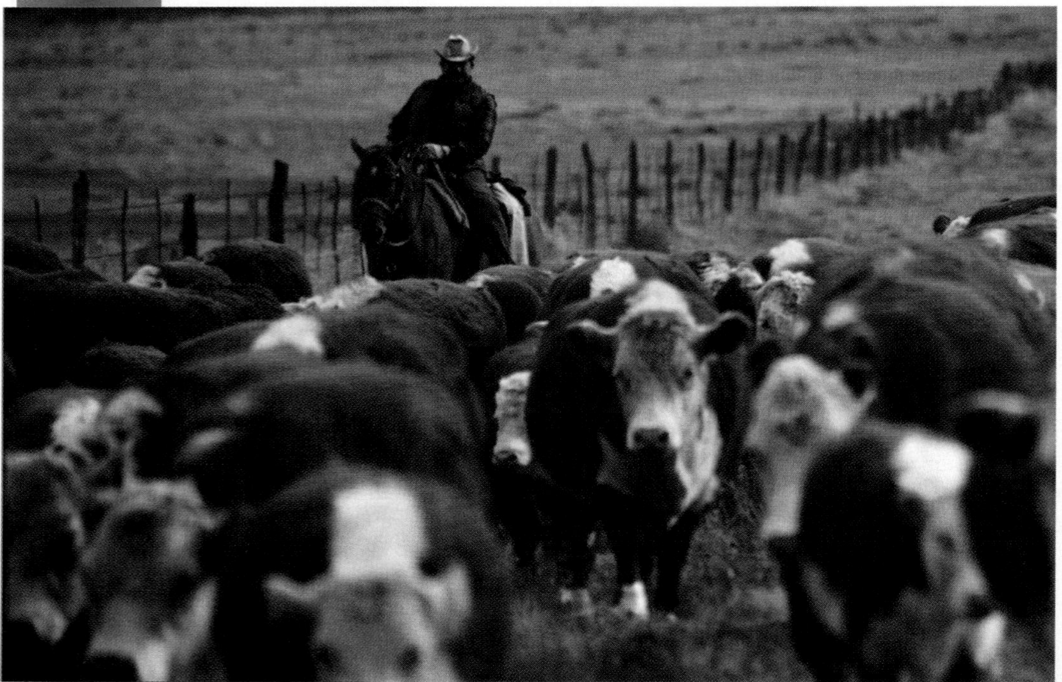

◆ Chapter Objectives ◆

After completing this chapter you will be able to do the following:

- ◆ Define the terms listed under "New Career Terms."
- ◆ List and describe the ten job families in the Agribusiness and Natural Resources Cluster.
- ◆ Identify several careers included in this cluster.
- ◆ Name several slow-growing and fast-growing jobs in this cluster.
- ◆ Explain what it would be like to work at a career in this cluster.
- ◆ Evaluate your own interest in this cluster.
- ◆ Identify skills common to many careers in this cluster.

◆ New Career Terms ◆

In this chapter you will learn the meanings of the following career terms:

- ✔ Agriculture
- ✔ Natural resources
- ✔ Agribusiness
- ✔ Career cluster
- ✔ Agribusiness and Natural Resources Cluster
- ✔ Job families
- ✔ Quarry
- ✔ Petroleum

Over two hundred years ago, when America first became a nation, almost everybody worked in **agriculture** or dealt with **natural resources.** You probably know that agriculture has to do with farming and producing crops, such as corn, soybeans, and vegetables. Natural resources are the useful materials provided by nature. Some natural resources are soil, gold, trees, water, and minerals in the earth.

The term **agribusiness** comes from two words: *agriculture* and *business.* Agribusiness combines the producing operations of a farm with the rest of the business of farming. Today's successful farmers must be as knowledgeable about how to run a business as they are about how to grow crops.

Today only about 2 to 3 percent of Americans work in agriculture. But this 2 to 3 percent (numbering in the millions) provides the critical raw materials that we need to produce food and shelter. These are important jobs, don't you think?

As you explore this **career cluster,** you'll find that it includes much more than just being a farmer. After all, the word *cluster* means a collection or group of similar things. A career cluster, then, is a group of similar careers.

The **Agribusiness and Natural Resources Cluster** is a group of occupations involved in producing, regulating, conserving, and guaranteeing the quality of the raw materials used for food, shelter, energy, and comfort. In this cluster are jobs for nursery laborers, beekeepers, cattle ranchers, forest firefighters, and park superintendents. Crop dusters are also part of this cluster. They are airplane pilots

agriculture
the science of cultivating the soil and producing crops (farming) and raising livestock.

natural resource
a useful material provided by nature; natural resources include soil, gold, trees, water, and minerals.

agribusiness
the entire process or business of producing, processing, and distributing agricultural products.

career cluster
a group of similar occupations.

Agribusiness and Natural Resources Cluster
a group of occupations involved in producing, regulating, conserving, and guaranteeing the quality of the raw materials used for food, shelter, energy, and comfort.

◀ Are you interested in agriculture?

who fly dangerously low to spray fields with chemicals to help control pests that can ruin crops. (All career clusters in the chapters that follow will be defined in the same manner as we just did for agribusiness and natural resources.)

To get an idea of how important the agricultural and natural resources industry is, think about a typical day in your life. When you have breakfast in the morning, lunch in the afternoon, and dinner at night, you're eating food provided by farmers. Those farmers had to use the services of harvest workers, irrigation specialists (to supervise the watering of the crops), and soil scientists. Soil scientists are men and women who study the ground. They determine the best way to treat it for whatever crops a farmer wants to grow.

If you had any fish for one of your meals, it might have been provided by a fish farmer. Or it could have been provided by a commercial fisher who caught the fish on the open seas.

The house you eat your meals in and the school you go to were built with natural resources such as lumber. Some of the people who

Attitude makes a difference

Settling Down

Daryl Mangels could never sit still. When he was in class, he was always fidgeting with his pencil, papers, or books. His teacher never stopped telling him the same thing: "Daryl, please be quiet and sit still."

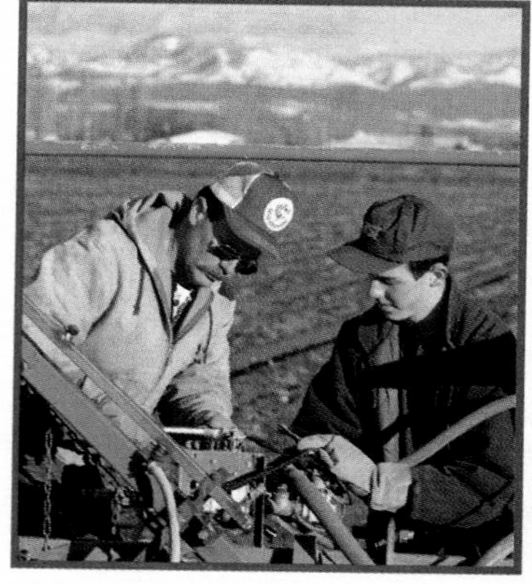

Daryl's grades weren't the greatest. He just never seemed to be able to concentrate—to focus his attention on anything for very long.

One day he had an interview with his guidance counselor. She asked him what he wanted to do. His answer was, "I don't know. I'm too young to think about it." The counselor gave Daryl some tests to find out what his interests were. She discovered, along with Daryl, that he loved cars, engines, and anything mechanical. She told him about a friend of hers who worked on a big farm nearby. The friend's job was to keep all the farm equipment in good working order.

Daryl liked that idea. He decided that's what he wanted to be. After school he helped his dad repair a lawn mower engine. In school he became interested in how physical things worked. He learned how engines actually produce power.

Daryl's teachers still tell him to be quiet and settle down. But his attitude has changed. He has a goal.

What Do YOU Think?

Can you think of anybody you know who is like Daryl? Did Daryl necessarily have the wrong attitude in school? Do you think Daryl is making the right choices?

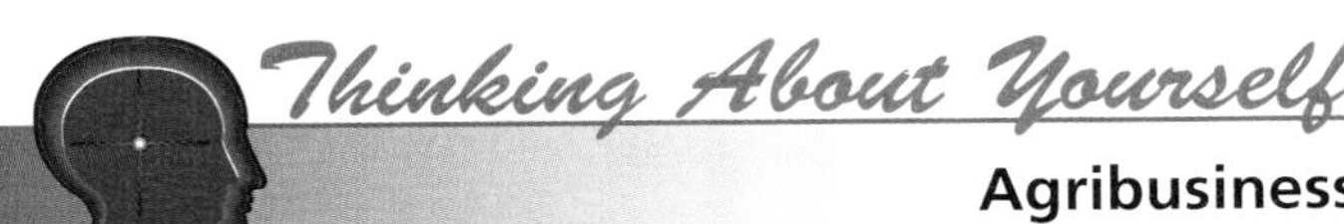

Agribusiness and Natural Resources Careers

Take your time reading and thinking about the following questions. You might even want to make notes on a sheet of paper and write out your answers.

- ▲ Have you ever helped your mother or father plant flowers, shrubs, or trees around your house or in the window boxes or on the patio of your apartment? Did you enjoy this work? Would you like to do it again?
- ▲ Do you have a pet? Do you enjoy taking care of your pet even if some of the chores are dirty, messy, or time consuming? Would you like spending more time with animals?
- ▲ Think about what you usually do after school, on weekends, and after your chores and homework are finished. Do you spend most of your free time indoors or outdoors?
- ▲ Do you prefer life in the city or the country?

If you answered yes to the first two questions, there's a good chance you might enjoy a career in agribusiness and natural resources.

work in the forest industry are foresters, who manage forested lands. Foresters try to make sure that there will be trees for lumber in the future. Of course, there were loggers, who had to cut the trees. Sawmill workers prepared logs for cutting into lumber and storing it.

Many of the other natural resources that go into the buildings in which you live, eat, and go to school came from the mining industry. In that industry there are quarry workers, who work with some of the stones that go into buildings. There are miners, who go down into the ground to take out coal and other ores.

If you heated your house or rode in a car, you used the products of people who work in the oil industry. There are workers in oil fields who help with the drilling into the ground. There are well-pullers, who control the power equipment needed to repair oil and natural gas wells.

You benefit from the efforts of workers in the agribusiness and natural resources field every day and in many ways. You may want to become a part of that field.

WHAT WOULD IT BE LIKE?

When you think of agribusiness and natural resources, you obviously think of the outdoors. Indeed, much of the work in this career cluster is done outdoors. That doesn't mean there aren't jobs done in laboratories and offices, however. If you became any type of engineer within this field, you would work inside much of the time. A petroleum engineer, for example, analyzes (looks at carefully) a lot of information he or she might have obtained in the field (at the site

As a logger, you might drive the truck that takes the logs to where they are processed.

of the natural resource). But the analyzing of the information would occur in an air-conditioned office environment. If you became a biologist you would be studying the basic principles of plant and animal life. You would probably be doing this in a laboratory.

Would you enjoy working in this career cluster? Do some daydreaming as you "listen" to the following conversation. Several people who enjoy working in the Agribusiness and Natural Resources Cluster are talking about why they enjoy their jobs. As you listen to what they say, imagine yourself doing their jobs.

Farmer: You know what I like most about farming? I like those early morning hours when I'm outside doing my chores—feeding the livestock, getting the machinery ready. It's quiet, the sun's coming up, and I'm thinking about the day ahead. I like being outdoors, and I like being my own boss.

Logger: I know exactly what you mean. I love it in the forest surrounded by all those trees. The fresh air, the smell of pine. It's great. And at the end of the day, I really feel like I've accomplished something. That's why I like the physical labor. It sounds crazy, but I actually like it sometimes when my muscles are sore from a really hard day.

Animal Breeder: That's how I feel about cleaning all those animal cages, and washing the animals, and doing all the other jobs most people would hate. I love doing it because I care so much about the animals.

Landscape Architect: That's the way I feel about the plants. I feel like I'm giving them a home when I plant them. I think that's why I've been successful. When I'm planning the landscaping for someone's home, I find myself thinking about how each bush, or flower, or tree will feel in a particular spot. Of course, the real thrill of the job is actually handling the plants, putting them in the ground, and covering them with the soil.

Geologist: I'm interested in just about everything all of you have mentioned, but I like the scientific side of things. I like to study the why and the how of soil and rocks and plants. I spend more time inside—in the lab—than I like, but that's okay. The excitement of making a new discovery or solving a problem more than makes up for it.

What do you think? Do any of these careers sound appealing? Can you see yourself doing one of these jobs—or a similar job? Would you like to learn more about agribusiness and natural resource careers?

Career Decision-Making Activities

1. Try to arrange a class trip for your classmates and yourself to a work setting for agribusiness and natural resources. Talk to your parents, guardians, or adult friends. Ask if they know someone who works at a nearby farm, fish hatchery, mine, oil field, lumber camp, or other setting in this cluster. Other possibilities are game preserves, city reservoirs, national and state parks, agricultural laboratories, and zoos. Ask if it would be possible for members of your class to visit. See how many trips you and your classmates can arrange. Keep track of your observations on each trip. Did you feel comfortable in that setting? Did you like the people you met? Discuss your reactions in class.
2. If it is not possible to actually visit a work setting for this cluster, identify television programs and movies that take place in such settings. Watch these programs, and imagine yourself working in those conditions. What was your reaction? Do you think you would enjoy working in that setting? Why or why not?
3. Participate in as many recreational activities as possible that are related to the jobs in this cluster. For example, you could go fishing, go on a hike, go boating, or go horseback riding. A camping trip to a park where you could do many of these activities would be a good way to find out how you feel about the outdoors. Did you enjoy the activity? Report back to the class.

JOB FAMILIES IN THE AGRIBUSINESS AND NATURAL RESOURCES CLUSTER

The Agribusiness and Natural Resources Cluster is divided into ten **job families**, groups of jobs with similar characteristics. You can see all of the job families in this cluster in the figure on page 96. Looking at the different families will help you decide which kinds of careers in this cluster you might enjoy the most.

job family
groups of jobs with similar characteristics.

- **Fisheries and wildlife.** All the jobs concerned with the development of fish and wildlife are in the fisheries and

Job Families in the Agribusiness and Natural Resources Cluster

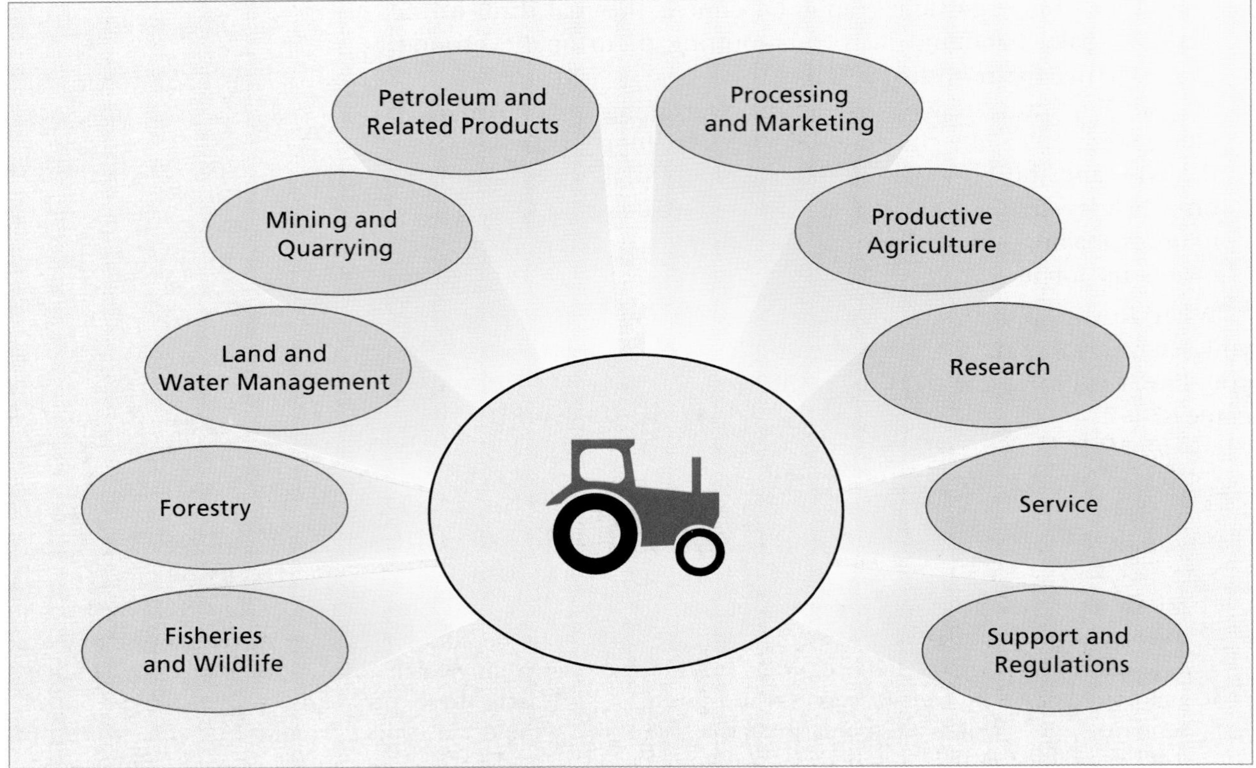

wildlife job family. Animal trappers are, too. The number of wildlife jobs is limited, but the people who work in this area enjoy it very much because of their love of animals.

- **Forestry.** Anybody who works with growing trees or cutting them is in forestry. You could do a range of jobs, from estimating the amount of timber in a forest to stacking logs in a sawmill. Forest firefighters make sure that living trees don't burn up.
- **Land and water management.** Another job category concerns the use of land and water resources. Irrigation engineers plan and design irrigation projects. Irrigation is the movement of water to where it is needed for growing purposes. Surveyors plan and direct surveys of land areas. (Surveys are studies that measure land to map out its area, elevation, boundaries, and so on.)
- **Mining and quarrying.** Workers who are involved in locating and taking raw materials from the land are in the mining and quarrying job family. Miners, such as coal miners, are the largest group. A mine machinery mechanic repairs and maintains the cranes and motors around

mines. Quarry workers work in rock quarries. A **quarry** is a big pit from which limestone and other kinds of stone are removed.

> ***quarry***
> a big pit from which limestone and other kinds of stone are removed.
>
> ***petroleum***
> an oily, flammable liquid obtained from wells drilled in the ground, which is refined into gasoline, fuel oils, and other products.

- **Petroleum and related products. Petroleum** is another word for oil. All people in jobs concerned with taking oil out of the ground are in the petroleum and related products job family. In the oil fields there are drillers, who operate drills on oil and gas wells. There are oil pumpers, who operate the equipment to make oil flow from wells. There are also roustabouts, who assemble and repair the machines in oil fields.
- **Processing and marketing.** In the agricultural business some people purchase and process products before they are sent to the customer. These people are the people who turn the raw materials into products we can use. An egg candler inspects eggs to make sure their quality is acceptable. A fruit-buying grader examines and sorts sample fruit according to the grade (a standard for measuring food quality). An auctioneer sells livestock at an auction to the highest bidders.
- **Productive agriculture.** The productive agriculture job family includes all the occupations involved in growing farm crops and plants, and in breeding and raising animals. Farmers are in this family. So are cattle ranchers, poultry breeders, and harvest workers.
- **Research.** Many scientists conduct studies and experiments to find ways to increase productivity (the amount of a product that is grown or otherwise produced) and

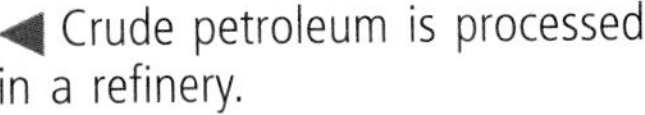
◀ Crude petroleum is processed in a refinery.

solve problems. Soil scientists study soil characteristics. Entomologists study insects to prevent them from destroying crops and trees. And geneticists are those scientists who study how different traits are transmitted from one generation to the next. They understand genetics, which is the science of dealing with genes (units in cells that are involved in passing on inherited characteristics).

- **Service.** Any job involving technical assistance and supplies in this industry is in the service category. For example, a farm equipment mechanic helps keep farm equipment in good repair. A soil tester performs tests in the laboratory. He or she tries to figure out what qualities soils have so that the soils can be used in the most productive ways. A poultry vaccinator gives medicine to different birds, such as chickens, ducks, and turkeys. He or she makes sure that the birds get shots so they remain disease-free.
- **Support and regulations.** The production of agricultural products and the materials taken from the ground are regulated by state and federal laws. Many inspectors make sure that these laws are followed. These jobs are important for the health and safety of consumers. A food and drug inspector inspects places where foods are manufactured and stored. A mine inspector inspects mines to make sure that they are safe places to work.

CAREER OUTLOOK

The agricultural part of the Agribusiness and Natural Resources Cluster has seen a reduction in the number of jobs over the past

Careers for Tomorrow

FISH AND GAME FARMERS

Americans are demanding diets with less fat. More Americans are eating fish and meat with less fat. We can now buy hot dogs made with turkey, which we couldn't do in years past. And many fashionable restaurants are serving venison (deer meat) and ostrich for the first time. All of these meats have less fat than beef or pork.

It is not surprising that fish farmers and game farmers are in higher demand. These are people who raise fish, such as trout, and game, such as ducks and deer.

Sometimes these jobs are messy, but they can be rewarding. If you are interested in working outdoors and helping Americans have better diets, you might consider becoming a fish or game farmer.

◀ Soil conditions must be monitored to insure the best growing conditions.

several decades. The natural resources part of the cluster has seen an increase.

FASTEST-GROWING JOBS

In agribusiness and natural resources the following jobs are among those that are growing the fastest:

- Animal caretakers.
- Nursery laborer.
- Geneticist.

SLOWEST-GROWING JOBS

These are among the slowest-growing jobs in the Agribusiness and Natural Resources Cluster:

- Harvest worker.
- Orchard pruner.
- Miner.
- Agricultural park superintendent.

AT THE HEART OF THE AGRIBUSINESS AND NATURAL RESOURCES CLUSTER

What makes the Agribusiness and Natural Resources Cluster different from the other fourteen clusters you'll be exploring? What would it really be like to work in this cluster? Let's try to get at the heart of agribusiness and natural resources.

Sending and Receiving E-Mail

One of the major uses of the Internet is the sending of communications, or electronic messages. These are typically called e-mail. Many billions of e-mail messages are sent every year just in the United States. Communication among workers, between businesses and customers, and between companies is now done through e-mail.

Most people who use e-mail also keep an e-mail address book on their computers.

The essence of this cluster is being outdoors and working with nature. It means getting your hands dirty, sweating in the hot sun, and having cold feet in the winter. It means working outside on beautiful, sunny days and on cold, damp, windy days. It means sloshing through mud in hip boots and trying to break ground that's been baked solid by the sun.

It also means having the patience and knowledge or skill to fix a broken machine or figure out a way to replace a missing part. It means working hard with your muscles and back and legs in all kinds of weather conditions. It means working with soil, rocks, trees, animals, oil, and coal. It's usually working outdoors with nature.

Figure 6.1 lists just a few examples of occupations from this cluster. Think about the job title, the work activities, and the work settings. Figure 6.1 just gives examples to help you get at the heart of this cluster. You don't need to read for details. Scan the entries to get a feel for the cluster as a whole.

Would you like a career in this cluster? Ask yourself the following questions:

- Do you like the sound of the occupations listed under "Who"? Would you feel good about having an identity like one of these?
- Would you enjoy doing activities like those described under "What"?
- Picture yourself working in the settings described under "Where." Would you be comfortable in these settings?

Figure 6.1 Sample Occupations in Agribusiness and Natural Resources Cluster

WHO You Would Be	WHAT You Would Do	WHERE You Would Do It
Farm Worker	Plow fields, tend livestock, mend fences	Cornfields, feedlots, machine sheds
Logger	Cut down trees, trim trees, cut logs	Forests
Roustabout	Dig ditches, unload trucks, repair machinery	Oil and gas fields, offshore drilling rigs
Fisher	Throw out and pull in nets, clean equipment	Fishing boats, harbors
Animal caretaker	Feed, water, groom, and exercise animals	Zoos, kennels, stables
Gardener, groundskeeper	Mow, trim, plant, and water lawns and shrubs	Grounds around public and private properties

SKILLS, TRAINING, AND EXPERIENCE

Even if you don't now have the right skills for a career in agribusiness and natural resources, you can develop them. Just look at a few of the skills that people in nature-related careers have:

- Can operate heavy equipment.
- Can work with their hands.
- Can fix machines.
- Can withstand a variety of weather conditions.
- Can work with animals.
- Can lift heavy objects repeatedly.

Some jobs require more skills than others. If you pursue a career in this field, you might begin with the jobs needing fewer skills. You could then move on to the jobs requiring more skills.

Every career cluster in this book involves jobs demanding few skills and jobs demanding lots of skills. No job is better or worse than any other. Every job carries with it its own rewards.

People who work in offices are jealous of people who work outside. They say that the people who work outside are lucky. They get to work with their hands and bodies and stay in shape without having to go to a gym.

People who work outside are jealous of people who work inside in offices. Outdoor workers say that they would love not to have to be outside in bad weather so much.

▼ A plant geneticist might spend most of her time inside analyzing data while a harvest worker would spend all of his time outside. Both jobs fall in the Agribusiness and Natural Resources job cluster.

▲ Did you ever think that farms grow and harvest other crops besides food crops?

The fact is that every job has pluses and minuses. But all jobs are good. They are good in the sense that when you work you can feel better about yourself.

Many different skill levels are required for the different jobs in the Agribusiness and Natural Resources Cluster. The following are three categories of jobs.

JOBS REQUIRING LESS-THAN-AVERAGE TRAINING AND EXPERIENCE

- Feed mixer.
- Logger.
- Sawmill worker.
- Seed cone picker.
- Roustabout.
- Miner.
- Quarry worker.
- Driller.
- Egg candler.
- Ginner.
- Harvest worker.
- Orchard pruner.
- Coal washer.
- Rotary-driller helper.

JOBS REQUIRING AVERAGE TRAINING AND EXPERIENCE

- Fish and game farmers.
- Hunting and fishing guides.
- Forest firefighter.
- Forester.
- Farm equipment mechanic.
- Soil tester.
- Log grader.
- Log scaler.
- Watershed tender.
- Seismic prospector.
- Fruit-buying grader.
- Meat grader.
- Beekeeper.
- Cattle rancher.
- Irrigation supervisor.

JOBS REQUIRING MORE-THAN-AVERAGE TRAINING AND EXPERIENCE

- Predatory animal hunter.
- Biologist.
- Entomologist.
- Geneticist.
- Geologist.
- Zoologist.
- Veterinarian.
- Petroleum engineer.
- Agronomist.
- Biochemist.

See Figure 6.2 for a list of some of the jobs in the Agribusiness and Natural Resources Cluster, along with their *DOT* numbers. You will recall from Chapter 5 that a job's *DOT* number can help you find more information about it.

Career Decision-Making Activities

1. If you are interested in getting into agribusiness and natural resources work, the first place you can start is a summer job. There are jobs on farms, in parks, and in food-processing plants. You can get some experience in this field during the summer. Start now to identify possible summer jobs.
2. If possible, grow your own garden. If you don't have a location for a garden, grow flowers in a window box, or pot some houseplants. Keep a diary of your activities. Evaluate your interest in the project from time to time.
3. Tell your science teacher you are interested in learning more about agribusiness and natural resources. Ask if you could do any extra-credit experiments working with soil, rocks, or plants. Report your findings to the class.
4. Volunteer for school, community, and home jobs that require physical labor. Work as hard as you can without overdoing it. Did you feel good about the work you accomplished?

Occupations in Agribusiness and Natural Resources

Here is a list of occupations mentioned in this chapter. Next to the name of each occupation is its *DOT* number. You can use the *DOT* number to locate further information about the occupation in your school or public library. For the broad occupational terms mentioned in this chapter, only one or two examples of that occupation are listed below. You can easily find more examples of the occupation in the *DOT.*

Agriculture Airplane Pilot (196.263-010)
Agronomist (040.061-010)
Animal Breeder (410.161-010)
Animal Caretaker (410.674-010)
Animal Trapper (461.684-014)
Auctioneer, Livestock (294.257-010)
Beekeeper (413.161-010)
Biochemist (041.061-026)
Biologist (041.061-030)
Cattle Rancher (410.161-018)
Coal Washer (541.382-010)
Commercial Fisher (see Fisher)
Crop Duster (see Agriculture Airplane Pilot)
Driller (930.382-026)
Egg Candler (529.687-074)
Entomologist (041.061-046)
Farm Equipment Mechanic (624.281-010)
Farmer, Cash Grain (401.161-010)
Farmer, Vine Fruit Crops (403.161-010)
Farmworker, Field Crop (404.663-010)
Farmworker, Machine (409.686-010)
Feed Mixer (520.685-098)
Fish Farmer (446.161-010)
Fisher (441.684-010)
Food and Drug Inspector (168.267-042)
Forest Firefighter (452.687-014)
Forester (040.061-034)
Fruit-Buying Grader (529.387-018)
Game Farm, Supervisor (412.131.010)
Game Farmer (412.131-010)
Game-Bird Farmer (412.161.010)
Game Farm Helper (412.684.010)
Gardener (406.684-014)
Geneticist (041.061-050)
Geologist (024.061-018)
Ginner (429.685-010)
Groundskeeper (406.687-010)
Harvest Worker (403.687-018)
Hunting and Fishing Guide (353.161-010)
Irrigation Engineer (005.061-022)
Irrigation Specialist (see Irrigation Engineer)
Irrigation Supervisor (409.137-010)
Landscape Architect (001.061-018)
Log Grader (455.367-010)
Log Scaler (455.487-010)
Logger (454.684-018)
Meat Grader (525.387-010)
Mine Inspector (168.267-074)
Mine Machinery Mechanic (620.261-022)
Miner (939.281-010)
Nursery Laborer (405.687-014)
Oil Pumper (914.382-010)
Orchard Pruner (408.684-018)
Park Superintendent (188.167-062)
Petroleum Engineer (010.061-018)
Poultry Breeder (411.161-014)
Poultry Vaccinator (411.684-014)
Predatory Animal Hunter (461.661-010)
Quarry Worker (939.667-014)
Rotary-Driller Helper (930.684-026)
Roustabout (869.684-046)
Sawmill Worker (667.686-014)
Seed Cone Picker (453.687-010)
Seismic Prospector (024.061-026)
Soil Scientist (040.061-058)
Soil Tester (029.261-010)
Surveyor (018.167-038)
Veterinarian (073.101-010)
Watershed Tender (954.382-018)
Well-Puller (930.382-030)
Zoologist (041.061-090)

Review and Enrichment

Summarizing the Chapter

Summarizing information is a critical thinking skill that will help you succeed in the world of work. Write a summary of what you learned in Chapter 6. Focus on the main points of the chapter. Then in a class discussion, compare your summary with the summaries done by your classmates. Can you improve your summary?

Improving Your Career Vocabulary

1. Learning to use new vocabulary terms will improve your communication skills, which are important in almost all areas of work. Write definitions for the terms listed below. Then for each term, write an original sentence about yourself in which you use the term correctly.
   - agriculture
   - natural resource
   - agribusiness
   - career cluster
   - Agribusiness and Natural Resources Cluster
   - job families
   - quarry
   - petroleum
2. List the job families in the Agribusiness and Natural Resources Cluster. Write a one-sentence description of each.

Finding the Facts

Finding exact information is a frequently used skill in many careers. Find the answers to the exercises below, and write the answers on a separate sheet of paper.

1. What kinds of workers cut down trees?
2. Which kind of worker designs the way the lawn and trees look in someone's yard?
3. Which kind of worker studies rocks?
4. Name at least three job families in the Agribusiness and Natural Resources Cluster.
5. Name at least three skills people in nature-related careers usually have.

Thinking for Yourself

To complete the exercise below you will need to use critical thinking and communication skills, which are skills valued by all employers. Write out your answers or be prepared to discuss them in class, depending on your teacher's instructions.

1. In your own words, describe someone who would enjoy working in agribusiness.
2. Of all the occupations mentioned in this chapter, which seems most interesting to you? Why?
3. What parts of the country do you think would attract people interested in agribusiness?
4. What values do you think would be important to people in agribusiness?
5. In your own words, describe someone who would not enjoy working in this career area.

Practicing Your Basic Skills

Your career success depends greatly on your basic math and communication skills. Work hard at improving in the areas where you have trouble with the following exercises.

Math

1. Wally was a farmer who raised crops. Last year he planted 3 acres of soybeans. He paid $100 for the seed and $200 for fertilizer. A part-time worker helped him plant and harvest. The man's labor cost a total of $500. The crop yielded 700 bushels of soybeans, and Wally sold them for $2.03 a bushel. How much did Wally earn on soybeans last year?
2. Linda is a geologist who studies valuable mineral deposits. Below are five sets of numbers. The numbers represent, in order, the weight of the rock when mined, the weight after any minerals were removed, and the profit from selling those minerals. How much was each of the minerals worth per pound?
   a. 100-65-$30
   b. 56-55-$25
   c. 97-13-$27
   d. 33-30-$10
   e. 17-12-$2
3. Mei Chen raised rabbits for sale. In April she owned thirty-six rabbits. In May, after all the litters of baby rabbits were born, the rabbits numbered fifty-seven. She sold half the adult rabbits and gave her brother one-third of the babies to start his own business. How many did she have remaining?

Review and Enrichment, continued

Reading and Writing

1. Look through the job section of your local newspaper. Find and circle as many jobs in the agribusiness and natural resources area as you can find.
2. Write a two-page short story about someone in an agribusiness or natural resources occupation.
3. Exchange stories written for Problem 2 with a classmate. Read that person's story. Did the story make you think about agribusiness in a new way?
4. Pick at least one occupation mentioned in this chapter that you think would be interesting. Research the occupation thoroughly, and write a report. Use the career research checklist in Chapter 5 as a guide for your report. Conclude your report with an explanation of your interest in that occupation based on your findings.

Speaking and Listening

1. Select one of the agribusiness and natural resources occupations. Read about it in the *OOH.* Give a one-minute speech to the class about job duties and advancement possibilities in that occupation.
2. Listen to your classmates' speeches. After each, note those facts that sounded interesting to you.

Activities Working with Others

In almost all careers you must be able to get along well with other people to be successful. Work with your classmates to do the following activities. As you work together, pay attention to how well you get along. If necessary, work hard at improving your ability to do your part and to cooperate.

1. With a classmate, design and create a bulletin board collage of pictures and drawings representing different occupations in the agribusiness and natural resources career area.
2. As a class, collect a number of common everyday items that represent work done by people in agribusiness and natural resources. (For example, an empty egg carton could represent a chicken farm.) Label the items and make a display.

Decision Making and Problem Solving

You will be a big help to your employer if you can make decisions and solve problems. List all the possible ways of resolving the situations described below. Then pick the best alternative (possible choice), and tell why you chose it. If you need help, you might want to refer to Chapter 3.

1. When you were a child, your family spent many summers at your grandparents' farm in Wisconsin. You loved it and would like to be a farmer yourself. Your parents are against it. They say it is a hard life and not very profitable. Besides, you live in a large city, and your chances to get experience are limited. What will you do to get experience?
2. You are female and not very big. You want to be an animal caretaker and work with horses at a nearby racetrack. Your friends say you will never get a job there because you're too small to handle big animals, and the track probably won't hire women. What will you do?

CHAPTER 7

BUSINESS AND OFFICE TECHNOLOGY CAREERS

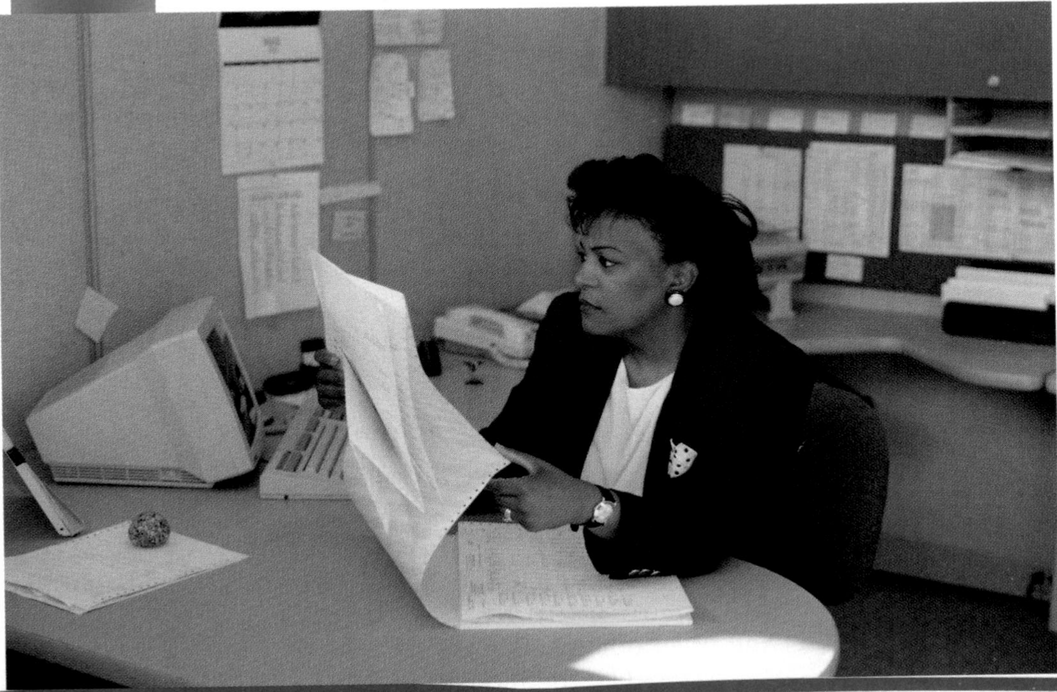

◆ CHAPTER OBJECTIVES ◆

After completing this chapter you will be able to do the following:

- ◆ Define the terms listed under "New Career Terms."
- ◆ List and describe the nine job families in the Business and Office Technology Cluster.
- ◆ Identify several careers included in this cluster.
- ◆ Name several slow-growing and fast-growing jobs in this cluster.
- ◆ Explain what it would be like to work at a career in this cluster.
- ◆ Evaluate your own interest in this cluster.
- ◆ Identify skills common to many careers in this cluster.

◆ NEW CAREER TERMS ◆

In this chapter you will learn the meanings of the following career terms:

- ✔ Business and Office Technology Cluster
- ✔ Ergonomics
- ✔ Data
- ✔ Processing
- ✔ Commission

At every school you attend there is somebody in an office keeping track of what you are doing. Have you ever noticed the file cabinets or computers in the main office of your school? That's where your records are kept. These records include information about what classes you took and what grades you got. They also include comments from your teachers. The school office contains all this information for every student in the school.

Part or all of the records about your activities may be put into the school computer system. Certainly much, if not all, of the financial information in the school is kept in the computer. This computer contains millions of facts.

If your parents ever had a fender bender, they had to deal with the people who work for insurance companies. Maybe you had a bike stolen once and had to fill out a report for your parents' insurance company. Insurance companies gather and store information on all their customers.

Do you have a checking or savings account at a local bank? Have you visited the bank with your parents? Think about all the facts and numbers the bank must keep track of to handle your account. Multiply that times all the bank's customers.

Every day you deal with people who are involved in the **Business and Office Technology Cluster** *of careers. This is a group of occupations involved in managing and organizing the daily operations of businesses and offices. The people working in these occupations handle all the information that our society creates and uses.*

Business and Office Technology Cluster a group of occupations involved in managing and organizing businesses and offices.

WHAT WOULD IT BE LIKE?

Most jobs in the Business and Office Technology Cluster are done inside buildings. If you work in business, you will probably be working in an office building.

Do you like the thought of going to work every day in an office? If so, the business world might be for you. You might go into a small office in which only three or four people work. Or you might end up working for a big corporation that is housed in a fifty-story building with hundreds of people working on each floor.

One of the basic conditions of almost all jobs in business and offices is attention to details. Most workers spend a lot of time recording, sorting, and checking details. That means that you might be doing work that repeats itself. If you are a bank teller, for example, you are inside a bank most of the day. You do the same activity over and over.

If you become a computer operator, you will be working inside most of the time. Your attention to detail has to be at its greatest. Any type of clerical job will involve the details of filing letters, receipts, and the like.

Some types of business jobs involve getting outside and traveling. If you become an insurance claims adjuster, for example, you might have to drive to different body shops. You might drive to people's homes to look at wrecked cars and burned houses.

Careers for Tomorrow

DESIGNING OFFICE ENVIRONMENTS

Office planners make good money and do interesting work. An office planner is sometimes called an office designer. He or she designs the layout of a new office. The office planner decides where to put the desk, where the computer should be, and where the receptionist should sit. A good office planner can make an office seem like a nicer place to work. Then each worker in the office can get more work done.

The study of office environments and how to improve them is **ergonomics.** You don't have to have a college degree to be an office planner. But you should learn about interior design. That means you have to learn about the different types of materials that go inside a house or office. You should also know design principles so that you can coordinate colors and textures.

You also have to learn about how to use simple interior design computer programs. These allow you to easily plan a layout or redesign of any office space. You may need to learn a little bit about architecture, or how things are actually built in an office or home.

ergonomics the study of office environments and how to improve them.

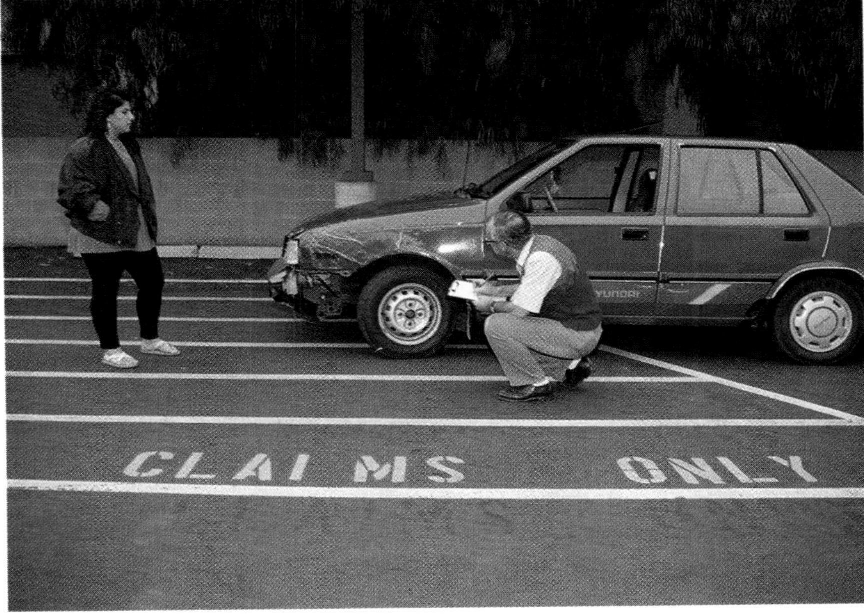

◀ An insurance adjuster works both outside and inside and may have to drive some on the job.

Transmitting Files

Many people work for companies that have more than one physical location. Sometimes important files should be seen by employees working in another location.

Enter the online world. It is now possible to transmit even very large files with graphics over the Internet, using a simple e-mail program. Sometimes when the files are really big, they have to be broken up into several smaller files. Transmitting files online is much cheaper than using expensive delivery services or even a fax machine.

The amount of time you spend dealing with other people depends, of course, on the particular job. If you become a computer operator, you might not talk with many people. If you become a real estate agent, however, that's most of what you do—talk, talk, and then talk some more.

Would you enjoy working in this cluster? Do some daydreaming as you "listen" to the following conversation. Several workers who enjoy working in the Business and Office Technology Cluster are talking about why they enjoy their jobs. As you listen to what they say, imagine yourself doing their jobs.

Receptionist: It's fun being with and working with people. I love being around people. I like talking to them, I like making friends, and I learn something from everyone. I couldn't imagine working at a job where I never talked to others. The day goes by so quickly.

Accountant: I like people, too, but the thing about my job that I really enjoy is working with numbers. Ever since I can remember, as far back as third grade, I've loved adding and subtracting—doing anything with numbers. Now I'm using more complicated math and computers, but it's really still the same. Getting the numbers to come out right is what it's all about.

Word Processor: I love computers. I can do anything with them. And there's a great deal of satisfaction in turning out that final document. They always come out perfect. And I can do it so fast. I really enjoy my job.

Secretary: I like my job because I get to do a little bit of everything. I like people. I like writing and producing neat, well-written letters. I like working with numbers. I guess I'm one of those people who never got really excited about one certain thing, but seemed to like doing just about anything—a jack-of-all-trades, I guess. And as a secretary I do anything and everything. I answer the phone, word process letters, set up meetings, work with numbers—so many different things. It's great.

What do you think? Do any of these jobs sound appealing? Can you see yourself doing one of these jobs—or a similar one? Would you like to learn more about business and office technology careers?

Career Decision-Making Activities

1. Write a letter using a word-processing program. Either use your computer at home or schedule a time when you can use a computer at school. Write a letter to yourself, telling yourself why you think you might enjoy or not enjoy a business and office technology career. Write at least one-half page. Count all your errors. When your letter is perfect, save it and print it. Ask a teacher for help if you don't know how to use the computer. After you've completed this chapter, reread

your letter. Are your opinions the same, or do you need to revise your letter? Revise it if necessary to reflect your current attitude about this cluster.

2. Set up a filing system at home for all your school papers. Keep all your papers in your files for six weeks. Evaluate the experience. Did you lose any papers? Did you enjoy the feeling of being organized and knowing exactly where each paper was located? Do you think you would enjoy and be good at organizing a complex filing system in a business office? Discuss your filing experience in class.

3. On a separate sheet of paper, make a list of thirty six-digit numbers. Pass the list to the person behind you, while receiving a similar list from the person in front of you. Write each of the thirty numbers on that person's list in reverse (for example, write *725431* as *134527*), taking no more than two minutes. Check your work, and return it to the person in front of you. Then check that the person behind you copied all the numbers on your list correctly. How did that person do? How did you do? Have a class discussion about attention to detail. Are you good at it or not so good?

JOB FAMILIES IN THE BUSINESS AND OFFICE TECHNOLOGY CLUSTER

Within the Business and Office Technology Cluster of careers there are nine job families. They are shown in the diagram on page 112. Looking at the different families will help you decide which kinds of careers in this cluster you would enjoy the most.

- **Accounting.** All the occupations that deal with keeping and explaining records about money are in the accounting field. Accountants are the people who keep track of how much money is being spent and how much is being collected. There are also accounting clerks, who do less complicated jobs. Bookkeepers keep sets of records.
- **Clerical.** Any type of activity that is involved in supporting an ongoing office operation can be clerical in nature. If you ever helped sort mail for delivery, for example, you were involved in clerical work. A receptionist at the front of an office who answers the phone and greets people as they come in the door is in a clerical or office position. Also within this job family are messengers, word processors, and general office clerks.
- **Computer.** Nothing runs without computers these days, at least not in the business world. This family of jobs deals with electronic data processing. **Data** is a term you should know if you work in offices. Data are facts and numbers, the bits of information that are so important in business. **Processing** data means entering, storing, sorting, retrieving, and editing the data. Within this job family are computer operators and programmers—the ones who run and write programs to make computers work.

data
information (facts, numbers, measurements, etc.) used as a basis for reasoning, discussion or calculation important to business.

processing
a series of actions or operations as a means to conclusion (for example, processing data would involve entering, storing, sorting, retrieving and editing the data).

▼ Some people prefer to work in an organized, routine job with regular hours.

Job Families in the Business and Office Technology Cluster

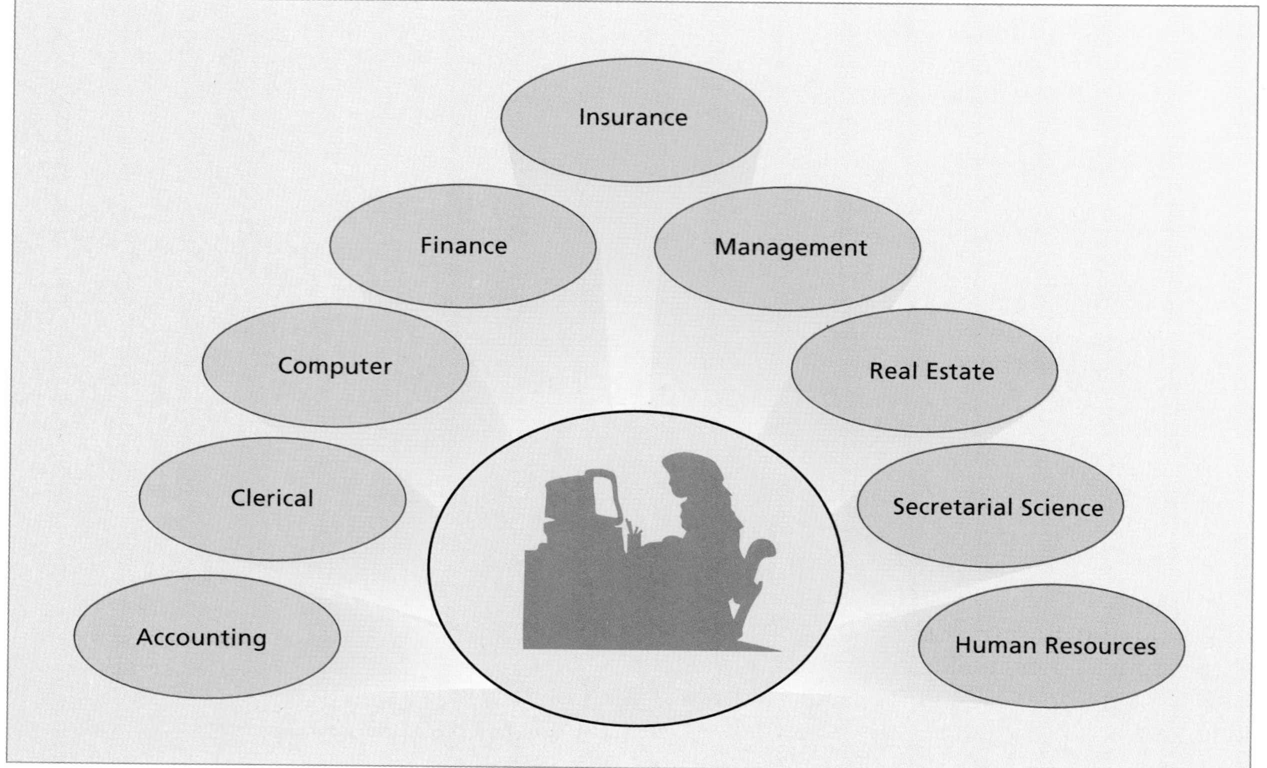

- **Finance.** Like the accounting family, the finance job family has to do with money. It involves jobs dealing with money management. In the finance job family, lots of the occupations have to do with banks and savings and loans.

  You might want to be a teller who receives and pays out money at your local bank. Tellers can sometimes get promoted to become loan officers in the bank. Loan officers recommend whether the bank should loan money to somebody who wants it for a new car or a boat, for example.

  Another job in the finance field is selling stocks and bonds. These are types of investments that your parents might have.
- **Insurance.** You probably know that insurance is protection you buy against possible loss. People insure their cars, houses, and lives, for example. The insurance family of jobs has to do with occupations involving insurance. If your parents have ever had a car accident, a claims adjuster might have come to the house to look at your wrecked car. A claims adjuster tries to see if what you claimed

actually happened. Do you need a complete repainting job on the wrecked car, or could something less do?

The insurance industry also has lots of sales agents. They sell many types of insurance, such as insurance on a person's life or on a house, boat, or car. The biggest portion of most agents' income is based on **commission.** A commission is a percentage of what the agent sells, which he or she receives as income.

How high did you value *security* when you looked at your values in Chapter 2? If you value security, you might *not* want a job like insurance sales representative, where your earnings can vary a great deal. You may prefer a steady, secure income to the *possibility* of making a lot, or nothing.

- **Management.** Every business and office has to have managers. Within the management job family there are general managers, who plan and organize just about everything in a business. There are assistant managers, too. Usually when you have a problem at your local grocery store, you talk to the assistant manager. Another type of manager is called a supervisor. This is a person who works with people to get things done in an office.
- **Real estate.** Anybody involved in renting, buying, and selling houses, land, and office buildings is in real estate. Like insurance salespeople, real estate sales agents usually work on a commission basis. For example, if you are a real estate agent who is working on a 5 percent commission, you can

WORKING ONLINE

Human Resources Work on the Web

A human resources officer now has to be aware that employment information can be posted online on the World Wide Web. Also, human resources officers know that they can obtain information on numerous potential candidates for job openings by going online.

There are literally dozens of online employment sites already. Many more will follow. They are a quick and inexpensive way to match job openings with job hunters.

commission
a percentage of what an agent sells, which is received by the agent as income.

Careers for Tomorrow

CREATING BROCHURES AND ADS WITH YOUR COMPUTER

It used to be that only advertising agencies could figure out how to create brochures and ads. Today, that has all changed because of simple computer application programs that are easy to learn.

Anybody who works in a modern office uses a word-processing program to enter information. It is just one simple step more to word-process a document in order to make it come out ready to send to the printer as an ad or flier. Of course, it is essential that you be comfortable with the keyboard. You also have to know the basic rules of grammar and punctuation. A beginning class in graphic design is a help as well.

You do not have to know a lot about computers (but it never hurts). Training videos are usually available to teach you how to use the so-called page makeup programs that allow you to create beautiful documents ready for printing.

FROM SCHOOL TO CAREERS

Removing a Mental Block

David Saunders loved baseball from the time he was six years old. His grandfather took him to a baseball game and tried to explain to him what was happening. David didn't understand too much, but he was hooked. When David was nine he was keeping statistics—numerical information—on his favorite teams and players. By the time David reached junior high he had memorized the "stats" on all the great pitchers and hitters for the last ten years.

When David played baseball, he was just average. But that didn't make any difference. He still loved watching the games and keeping the statistics.

David's grades were average or better in all his subjects except one. David said he didn't like mathematics. His teacher thought he had a mental block against the subject, that he didn't want to learn mathematics because he couldn't see how it would ever make a difference in his life. One day David's teacher showed him how much mathematics is used in coming up with baseball statistics.

David decided to play a game with himself in math class. He tried to see how many things he was learning that could be applied to baseball statistics.

David still doesn't get perfect scores on his math exams. But he learns more quickly than before.

What Do YOU Think?

Are there any subjects against which you have a mental block, just like David? If so, can you think of a way to make those subjects more interesting in your mind?

expect to get 5 percent of whatever you sell. If you sell a house that costs $100,000, you will get 5 percent of $100,000, or $5,000.

There are lots of different clerks in the real estate field who maintain the records for the rental and sale of houses and apartments. There are also agents who specialize in showing and renting apartments. They are called residence leasing agents. (The term *leasing* is a different way of saying *renting.*)

- **Secretarial science.** Secretaries are involved in just about all the different kinds of activities that go on in offices. Most secretaries are involved in writing and correcting the words that somebody else wants word processed. They also set up meetings, do filing, and handle phone calls.

  Many secretaries specialize in certain fields. A legal secretary, for example, prepares legal papers and letters for lawyers who work in law firms. A medical secretary does many of the same duties for doctors.
- **Human resources.** The human resources family of jobs contains occupations involved in recruiting, interviewing, and hiring workers. Large companies have human resources departments (which used to be called personnel depart-

ments). The workers in these departments are responsible for all hiring and the handling of employee records.

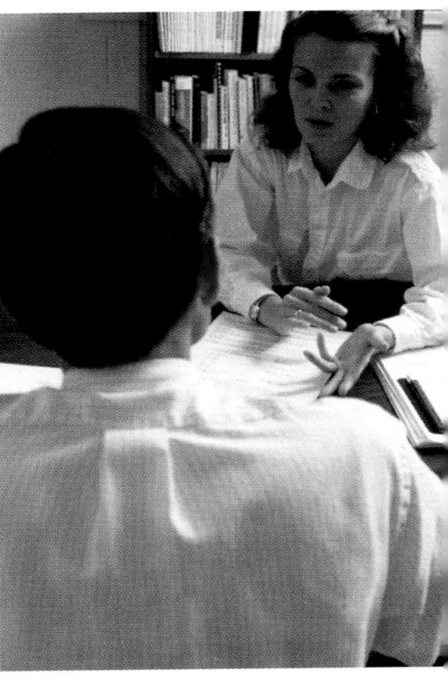

▲ Human Resources workers not only hire other employees, they also maintain records and file reports.

CAREER OUTLOOK

The United States has entered the Information Age. And where is this information? It's in all the offices throughout the country, being processed. It's all over the Internet, too.

The amount of information and the demand for it continue to increase. As you might guess, this explosion of information has enlarged greatly the number of office jobs. Although the field is expanding rapidly, some jobs are not growing as fast as others.

FASTEST-GROWING JOBS

Among the fastest-growing jobs in the Business and Office Technology Cluster are these:

- Paralegal.
- Data processing equipment repairer.
- Network control operator.
- Management analyst.
- Receptionist and information clerk.

SLOWEST-GROWING JOBS

Some jobs in the Business and Office Technology Cluster are growing slowly, or not at all:

- Bookkeeping, accounting, and auditing clerks.
- Word processor.
- Statistical clerk.

AT THE HEART OF THE BUSINESS AND OFFICE TECHNOLOGY CLUSTER

What makes the Business and Office Technology Cluster different from the other fourteen clusters you'll be exploring? What would it really be like to work in this cluster? Let's try to get at the heart of business technology careers.

The essence of the Business and Office Technology Cluster is the office environment. It's all the people, machines, computers, furniture, and activities of the office. It means working closely with other people, following orders, and asking others for help. It's the combined sound of the different noises made by telephones, computers, copiers, printers, fax machines, and people talking and hurrying from one place to the next. It's being in the same space, with the same people, doing much the same thing, day after day.

What are the people doing? They're working with words and numbers. They're reading them and entering them into their computers.

Business and Office Technology Careers

Take your time, and think about how you would answer each of the following questions. You may want to keep notes about your thoughts and write out your answers.

- ▲ Have you ever been in charge of the records for a club? Did you like it? Did you manage the records well, without making many mistakes?
- ▲ Have you started balancing a checking account? Is it easy?
- ▲ Have you written many personal letters? Can you write using proper grammar, spelling, and punctuation? Have you received good grades in language arts?
- ▲ Do you like to plan your work schedule carefully?
- ▲ Have you learned to keyboard? If so, do you like it?
- ▲ Do you enjoy computer games?
- ▲ Do you like to use hand calculators?
- ▲ Do numbers interest you?

If you answered yes to most of these questions, and you think you'd like working indoors, in an office, there's a good chance you might enjoy a career in the Business and Office Technology Cluster.

They're correcting, checking, changing, adding, subtracting, and checking again a constant stream of facts and figures. Details, details, details. Everybody has his or her job. There's an organized routine. Everything must be in its place.

The workers are turning out hundreds and thousands and millions of documents: letters, memos, electronic messages, faxes, reports, invoices, checks, and statements. They do and redo the documents until they're perfect. Then the workers copy the documents, file them, mail them, distribute them, and store them in their computers. They're constantly working together to perfect and process the endless stream of numbers and words.

Listed in Figure 7.1 are just a few examples of occupations from this cluster. Think about the job title, the work activities, and the work settings. These are just examples to help you get at the heart of this cluster. You don't need to read for details. Scan the entries to get a feel for the cluster as a whole.

Would you like a career in this cluster? Ask yourself the following questions:

- ◆ Do you like the sound of the occupations listed under "Who"? Would you feel good about having an identity like one of these?
- ◆ Would you enjoy doing activities like those described under "What"?
- ◆ Picture yourself working in the settings described under "Where." Would you be comfortable in these settings?

Figure 7.1 Sample Occupations in Business and Office Technology Cluster

WHO You Would Be	WHAT You Would Do	WHERE You Would Do It
Secretary	Schedule appointments, fill out forms, organize files, answer phone calls	At a desk and throughout an office
Word processor	Record, edit, store, revise, and print documents	At a computer terminal in an office
Bank teller	Cash checks, take and record deposits, pay and record withdrawals	In banks and savings and loans
Office clerk	File, keyboard, photocopy, answer phones, deliver messages	In a variety of areas inside an office
Bookkeeper	Maintain records of business transactions, prepare financial statements	At a desk in an office
Clerical supervisor	Plan work schedules and assignments, train new workers, solve problems	In an office

SKILLS, TRAINING, AND EXPERIENCE

The Business and Office Technology Cluster is like all others when it comes to skills. There are jobs requiring a wide range of skills. Some require no specialized skills or training, others require average skills, and yet other jobs require quite a bit of experience and training. There are some common skills that people in business and office jobs must have. See how many of the following you think you have:

- I can write well.
- I can plan to get my work done on time.
- I know how to keyboard.
- I can work a hand calculator easily.
- Computers don't scare me.
- I've taken math courses and done fairly well.

The following are examples of business and office jobs requiring different amounts of skills.

JOBS REQUIRING LESS-THAN-AVERAGE TRAINING AND EXPERIENCE

- Clerk or teller.
- Bookkeeper.
- Machine operator.
- Debt collector.
- File, mail, and office clerks.
- Messenger.
- Office machine servicer.
- Receptionist.
- Keyboarder.

JOBS REQUIRING AVERAGE TRAINING AND EXPERIENCE

- Claims adjuster.
- Computer operator or programmer.
- Secretary.

JOBS REQUIRING MORE-THAN-AVERAGE TRAINING AND EXPERIENCE

- Accountant.
- Bank officer.
- Financial planner.
- Credit official.
- Stockbroker or bond broker.

The figure at the end of the chapter lists some of the jobs in the Business and Office Technology Cluster, along with their *DOT* numbers.

Career Decision-Making Activities

Do you think this career cluster might hold a job for you? Then the first thing you should do is make sure that you learn how to use a keyboard. You must also perfect your basic skills in math, speaking, and writing. As you know, these skills are important in all careers. They are especially important in many of the business and offfice technology careers. Also take all the business, mathematics, and computer courses you can.

Here is a list of some activities that will help you find out more about your interest in business and office careers:

1. Help your parents balance their checking account each month. Better yet, start your own account, and balance it yourself.
2. Get a part-time job or internship in an office.
3. Save articles about office automation that appear in your newspaper.
4. Keep a detailed summary of how you spend your money. Make a budget, and see if you can stick to it.

Occupations in Business and Office Technology

Here is a list of occupations mentioned in this chapter. Next to the name of each occupation is its *DOT* number. You can use the *DOT* number to locate further information about the occupation in your school or public library. For the broad occupational terms mentioned in this chapter, only one or two examples of that occupation are listed below. You can easily find more examples of the occupation in the *DOT*.

Accountant, Budget (160.167-014)
Accountant, Cost (160.167-018)
Assistant Manager (see Manager, Employment)
Bank Officer (186.117-078)
Bookkeeper (210.382-018)
Clerical Supervisor (see Supervisor, Steno Pool)
Computer Operator (213.362-010)
Computer Programmer (020.162-014)
Computer Repairer (828.261-014)
Corporate Legal Assistant (119.267-026)
Corporate Programmer (see Computer Programmer)
Credit Official (see Manager, Credit and Collection)
Debt Collector (241.357-010)
File Clerk (206.362-010)
Financial Planner (020.167-014)
General Manager (see Manager, Credit and Collection)
General Office Clerk (219.362-010)
Insurance Claims Adjuster (241.217-010)
Insurance Sales Agent (250.257-010)
Keyboarder (203.582-066)
Legal Secretary (201.362-010)
Loan Officer (241.367-018)
Machine Operator, Duplicating (207.682-014)
Mail Clerk (209.587-026)
Manager, Credit and Collection (168.167-054)
Manager, Employment (166.167-030)
Medical Secretary (201.362-014)
Messenger (230.667-010)
Network Control Operator (031.132.010)
Office Clerk, General (219.362-010)
Office Machine Servicer (633.281-018)
Office Planner (019.261-018)
Payroll Clerk (215.482-010)
Real Estate Sales Agent (250.357-018)
Receptionist (237.367-038)
Resident Leasing Agent (250.357-014)
Secretary (201.362-030)
Stenographer (202.362-014)
Stockbroker (251.157-010)
Supervisor, Personnel Clerk (209.132-010)
Supervisor, Steno Pool (202.132-010)
Teller (211.362-018)
Word Processing Operator (203.582-054)

Review and Enrichment

Summarizing the Chapter

Summarizing information is a critical thinking skill that will help you succeed in the world of work. Write a summary of what you learned in Chapter 7. Focus on the main points of the chapter. Then in a class discussion, compare your summary with the summaries done by your classmates. Can you improve your summary?

Improving Your Career Vocabulary

1. Learning to use new vocabulary terms will improve your communication skills, which are important in almost all areas of work. Write definitions for the terms listed below. Then for each term, write an original sentence about yourself in which you use the term correctly.
   - Business and Office Technology Cluster
   - ergonomics
   - data
   - processing
   - commission
2. List the job families in Business and Office Technology Cluster. Write a one-sentence description of each.

Finding the Facts

Finding exact information is a frequently used skill in many careers. Find the answers to the exercise below, and write the answers on a separate sheet of paper.

1. What type of job supports an ongoing office operation?
2. What type of job deals with money management?
3. What is the term used for protection against possible loss?
4. What is another term for *manager?*
5. What is the career outlook for business and office technology careers?

Thinking for Yourself

To complete the exercise below you will need to use critical thinking and communication skills, which are skills valued by all employers. Write out your answers or be prepared to discuss them in class, depending on your teacher's instructions.

1. Do you think someone who likes being outdoors would ever enjoy working in an office? If so, when and why?
2. Of all the occupations mentioned in this chapter, which seems *least* interesting to you? Why?
3. Do you think a business career would be more suitable for an outgoing person or for someone who is shy? Give reasons for your answer.
4. What values do you think would be important for businesspeople to possess?
5. Some business careers involve managing other people. What do you think makes a good manager? Contrast a good manager with a poor one.

Practicing Your Basic Skills

Your career success depends greatly on your basic math and communication skills. Work hard at improving in the areas where you have trouble with the following exercises.

Math

1. Jacob had to make plane reservations for his boss, who had a number of stops to make. Her plane left Boston at 6:31 A.M. and arrived in New York at 7:50. At 10:20 A.M. she boarded another flight for Toronto that arrived at 12:15. She had a 2:00 meeting in Toronto. Then at 4 P.M. she took a flight to Chicago that arrived at 5:07. How much time did she spend in airplanes?
2. Working *across,* find the number in each row below that is unlike the others. Write that number on a sheet of paper. Then, going *down,* add the numbers in each column, and write the four totals on your paper.

56789	56789	57689	56789
23190	23091	23190	23190
59043	59043	59043	43950
20068	20680	20680	20680

3. Lou can keyboard 59 words a minute with only 3 mistakes. Tomas keyboards 96 words with 10 errors. Rosemary makes 7 errors and keyboards 43 words a minute. If you subtract 1 word for each mistake they make, how many words can each keyboard in 5 minutes?

Review and Enrichment, continued

Reading and Writing

1. Read the financial section of your local newspaper for one week. Find the stock market report, and select one stock that appears there. Keep a record of that stock's closing prices for the entire week.
2. How neat is your handwriting? Some office workers, such as accountants, use ledgers and other forms that often must be filled in by hand. Obtain a sheet of record-keeping or ledger paper, and practice writing names and numbers on it.
3. Pick at least one occupation mentioned in this chapter that you think would be interesting. Research the occupation thoroughly, and write a report. Use the career research checklist in Chapter 5 as a guide for your report. Conclude your report with an explanation of your interest in that occupation based on your findings.

Speaking and Listening

1. Some secretaries use a dictaphone. A dictaphone works like a tape recorder. The person composing the letter dictates (records by speaking) it into the machine. Later the secretary listens to the tape and word processes the letter. Obtain a tape recorder and dictate a letter. Try to speak clearly so a secretary listening to it later could understand every word.
2. Exchange tapes from Problem 1 with a classmate. Listen to the tape. Either by hand or with a keyboard, copy down the letter. When you've finished, listen to the tape again and check your work. Did you hear the letter correctly?

Activities Working with Others

In almost all careers you must be able to get along well with other people to be successful. Work with your classmates to do the following activities. As you work together, pay attention to how well you get along. If necessary, work hard at improving your ability to do your part and to cooperate.

1. With a classmate, write and perform a one-minute radio or TV commercial advertising a job in an office. Describe all the duties, and try to make the job sound appealing.
2. As a class, devise a database of information about all the jobs listed in Chapters 6 through 20 of the text. (Do Chapters 6 and 7 now; add the others as you study those chapters.) Some students can design the computer file, and others can keyboard in the basic data (such as job title and cluster). Still others can add bits of information from other sources, such as education and training, salary range, and job prospects.

Decision Making and Problem Solving

You will be a big help to your employer if you can make decisions and solve problems. List all the possible ways of resolving the situation described below. Then pick the best alternative (possible choice), and tell why you chose it. If you need help, you might want to refer to Chapter 3.

You are the boss of the data processing department. Harold, one of the programmers, is a fine worker. However, he has a problem with personal hygiene. Two of his co-workers have asked you to remedy the situation. What will you do?

CHAPTER 8

COMMUNICATIONS AND MEDIA CAREERS

◆ Chapter Objectives ◆

After completing this chapter you will be able to do the following:

- ◆ Define the terms listed under "New Career Terms."
- ◆ List and describe the six job families in the Communications and Media Cluster.
- ◆ Identify several careers included in this cluster.
- ◆ Name several slow-growing and fast-growing jobs in this cluster.
- ◆ Explain what it would be like to work at a career in this cluster.
- ◆ Evaluate your interest in this cluster.
- ◆ Identify skills common to many careers in this cluster.

◆ New Career Terms ◆

In this chapter you will learn the meanings of the following career terms:

- ✔ Communications
- ✔ Media
- ✔ Communications and Media Cluster
- ✔ Telecommunications
- ✔ Satellite dish

Think about last month. How many newspaper articles did you read? How many magazines did you look at? How often did you surf the Internet for news? Did you go to any movies? How many hours of radio did you listen to? How many hours of television did you watch? How many times did you play a compact disc or digital video disc (DVD)? And finally, how many hours did you spend on the telephone?

If you're an average American, you spent many hours last month taking advantage of the work done by the people in communications and media careers. **Communications** *involves ways that people share their ideas with others.* **Media** *is the word that usually describes the different ways or methods—such as radio, television, and newspapers—that information is presented to you. If you work in the* **Communications and Media Cluster,** *you'll be working in a group of occupations involved in designing, preparing, and sending information and messages.*

WHAT WOULD IT BE LIKE?

Many people would say that the most glamorous of all occupations are found in motion pictures and television. Movies and television occupy many hours of most Americans' time every week. The celebrities in movies and television are talked about constantly. The celebrities in the recording industry are, too. There is no doubt—communications and media work can be very exciting.

Getting to the top in all the glamorous, high-prestige jobs in the Communications and Media Cluster requires hard work, long hours, and luck. The competition for these jobs is fierce. Few people make it to the top.

If that's your dream and you think you can make it, though, give it your best effort. If you don't become the next national TV news anchorperson, you won't have been a failure. There are many other rewarding jobs in television, radio, movies, and **telecommunications** (the science or technology of communication through copper wires, cable, and wireless systems). You may not be in the limelight, but you will have a good job, and it will be satisfying.

If you decide to work on a newspaper or magazine, you will be working in an office much of the time. If you become a reporter, you will be going out in the field to interview people.

Any type of work in radio and television, and to some extent in the recording industry and motion picture industry, will probably be inside work. You will be working with other people most of the time. You will be interacting with them.

In the satellite and cable transmission industry you might get a job outside installing or repairing cables and satellite communications equipment. You could become a telephone installer and be working both outside and inside, but also having to drive a lot. In

communications
ways in which people share ideas and information (for example, conversation and the media).

media
means of communication such as newspapers, television, radio, magazines, and the Internet that influence people widely.

Communications and Media Cluster
a group of occupations involved in designing, preparing, and sending information and messages.

telecommunications
sending and receiving messages over the telephone system.

A sound mixer works with processes, methods, and machines.

the greatly expanding wireless, or cellular, communications industry, you might have a job signing people up for the new services.

Would you enjoy working in this cluster? Do some daydreaming as you listen in on the following conversation. Several workers who enjoy communications and media careers are talking about their jobs. Imagine yourself in their jobs. Do you think you'd enjoy this kind of work?

Disc Jockey: Let's face it—I'm a ham. I can't stop talking. I think I'm the funniest, smartest, most clever person who ever talked into a microphone. I can't imagine doing anything else.

Director: For me the great thing is the creativity. Taking words on a page and bringing them to life is a creative, exciting thing to do. I used to do a lot of acting and enjoyed it, but I couldn't really "let myself go" the way you have to in order to be a great actor. As a director I can communicate my understanding of the characters to the actors and let them do the actual acting. I'm more in control of the end product—the whole look and sense of the show. It's a great feeling.

Sound Engineer: I don't think of myself as being especially creative, but I do make my own contribution to the recordings we do here at the studio. I've got a good ear for music and know my equipment. I get to work with a lot of very creative, talented musicians, singers, and producers, which is really exciting. And it's nice to know that they need me. A lot of these people are not good with things—you know—setting up and adjusting all the electronic recording equipment—which is what I'm good at. It's nice to be part of a team.

"Net-Zine" Reporter

More and more sources for news and magazine articles can be found online on the Internet every day. For example, Microsoft Corporation and NBC have a magazine called *Slate* that you can view on the Internet. Many of the major television networks have Internet sites that give news all the time. They have such names as AllPolitics and others.

Although many of the news articles are taken directly from normal newspaper and TV sources, some are original to the Internet. People who use the Internet call them "Net-Zines" (*Internet* plus *magazine*). Some well-known TV personalities have even quit their jobs to become Net-Zine journalists.

Newspaper Reporter: I know what you mean about being part of a team. Do you know how many people it takes to get out a newspaper? It's very rewarding to know that you're part of a team of talented, dedicated people working hard each day to put out a product that millions of people rely on so much. Where would this country be without its newspapers? I actually consider it a privilege to do the work I do. I wouldn't want my boss to hear this, but I'd probably do this job for almost nothing. I'm able to practice my first love—writing—and at the same time be part of a massive team effort to keep people informed about what's going on in the world. Who could ask for a better job?

What do you think? Do any of these jobs sound appealing? Would you like to learn more about the Communications and Media Cluster?

Career Decision-Making Activities

1. On a separate sheet of paper, make a list of all the movies you've seen in the last month. Show on your list whether you saw the movie at the theater, on your videocassette recorder at home, or on television. Compare your list with your classmates' lists in a class discussion. Do you seem more or less interested than most of your classmates in movies? Do you think you might enjoy a career in the movie industry?
2. How much reading do you do on your own? Think about the reading you've done over the past few weeks. Estimate how much time you spend reading the following in an average week:
   a. Front page of a newspaper.
   b. Sports section of a newspaper.
   c. Entertainment section of a newspaper.
   d. Other sections of a newspaper.
   e. Magazine articles.
   f. Books (other than school assignments).
   g. News sites on the Internet.

   In class compile the results to determine the average time spent on each type of reading. How does your reading time compare with that of your classmates? Does this indicate an interest in journalism?
3. In a class discussion, tell what your favorite magazine is and why it is your favorite. Share an article from that magazine with your class. Did anyone else talk about a magazine that sounds interesting to you that you haven't read?
4. Write a one-minute news report highlighting the most interesting things that happened to you last week. Listen to national and local newscasts for ideas on how to lead in to your stories and make transitions from one story to the next. For example, you might begin by saying, "In our top story tonight . . ." "Broadcast" your report to the class as you would if you were a television newscaster.

JOB FAMILIES IN THE COMMUNICATIONS AND MEDIA CLUSTER

There are six job families in the Communications and Media Cluster. Look at the diagram of these job families on page 126. Then read on to find out what each involves. Reading about these job families will help you find out which types of careers might interest you most.

Job Families in the Communications and Media Cluster

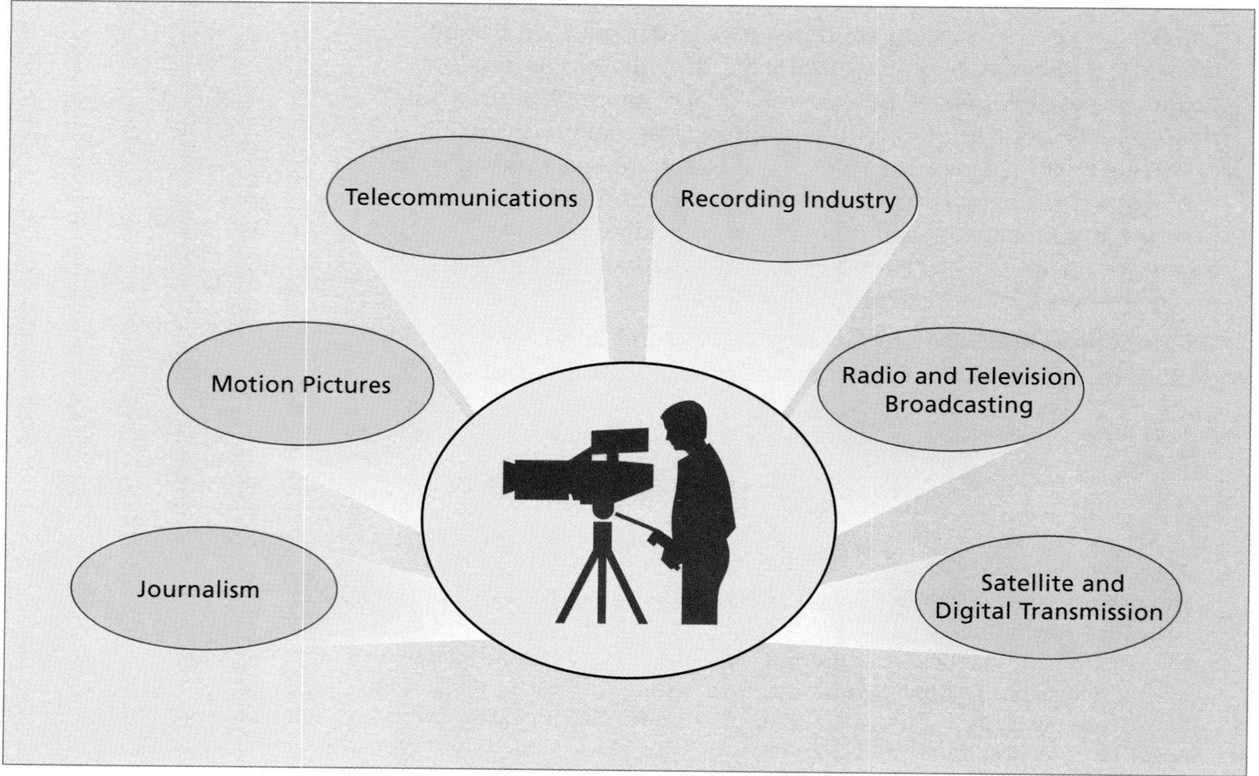

- **Journalism.** Anything that has to do with creating, producing, and printing the words and pictures that make up newspapers, print magazines, and online magazines is part of journalism. Journalists can be sent to foreign lands to report on the news there. Reporters—another name for journalists—can be required to write all sorts of stories about sports, politics, and lifestyles.

  There are also movie critics, food critics, technology critics, and art critics. These critics write reviews that carefully examine and judge movies, restaurants, computers and computer programs, and art. Some journalists work with magazines or newspapers as editors, or in other jobs that help to put the whole publication together.
- **Motion pictures.** The motion picture industry involves all the jobs people do to make movies. This job family has a wide range of jobs.

  The producer is the person who puts a movie project together. The producer hires and coordinates the writers and directors and decides how money is spent on a film.

The director tells the cast and crew members what to do during rehearsals and filming. The director also controls the artistic development of the movie.

There are many jobs in the movie industry in which you would use your hands a lot. These jobs include camera operator and light technician. Prop makers put together the sets for the scenes in movies. Painters paint those sets. Decorators are the people who decorate them.

The next time you watch a movie, wait until the credits come on at the end. You will see a long list of the different jobs that go into making a movie.

- **Telecommunications.** Any of the work that goes into sending and receiving messages over the telephone system is included in the telecommunications family of jobs. Within this industry there are, of course, telephone operators, who handle problems and place calls. There are also line inspectors and repairers, who check the lines and cables and repair them when they are broken.

  Some people sell wireless, or cellular, phones. Others help businesses set up complicated international phone networks using a combination of fiber-optic cable systems and satellites.
- **Recording industry.** Tapes, compact discs, and digital video discs (DVDs) are made in the recording industry. Some of the most important people involved, of course,

Careers for Tomorrow

MUSIC VIDEO PRODUCERS

Do you like to watch MTV? Or maybe VH-1? If you do, you are watching the results of the work of music video producers. They take charge of all aspects of putting together a music video. Some of those music videos cost a half a million dollars or more to make!

Usually music video producers are hired and paid by recording companies. But sometimes famous singers and musicians hire them, too. If you are interested, you should probably get your training in filmmaking and video. You can start as a "gofer," a person who does just about anything for a production team.

Very few people can be at the top of this field. But you might have lots of fun trying to get there. For more information, write the Association of Independent Commercial Producers, 11 East 22nd Street, Fourth Floor, New York, NY 10010.

▲ Does your family or anyone you know have a home satellite dish?

are musicians and singers. The composers are also important. They are the ones who create and write the actual music and words.

The industry also involves people who produce the music. They are responsible for the quality of the production and are often expert musicians themselves. Engineers make sure that the sound of the different microphones is just right and that the recording machines work correctly.

- **Radio and television broadcasting.** The radio and television broadcasting job family consists of the people who prepare and present radio and television programs. What you hear and see are the broadcasters and announcers. They might be disc jockeys or sportscasters.

  Behind the scenes there are many other workers. Video operators make sure that the scenes you see on television are well recorded. Radio engineers maintain the equipment that sends out the radio signals.

  For the home market in this industry there are radio and television repairers. There are also cable installers, who make sure that your system is working correctly.

- **Satellite and digital transmission.** Have you ever seen one of those 10- to 15-foot dishes sitting on the roofs of big buildings? Have you ever seen them on people's lawns? They are part of the communications industry. **Satellite dishes** are bowl-shaped receivers that gather the signals sent from satellites spinning more than 22,000 miles above the earth. The satellites are retransmitting the signals sent to them from television stations. Today, satellite dishes can be as small as 18 inches in diameter.

  In addition, there are satellites that retransmit Internet signals at a much more rapid speed than do regular copper phone lines. Finally, there are many satellite systems on the ground that are used for cellular phone systems.

  The satellite and digital transmission family of jobs also includes the cable industry. Cables have been put under the ground and above the ground throughout most cities in the United States. Cable companies take the signals from television broadcasts and retransmit them through the cables.

satellite dish
a bowl-shaped receiver that gathers signals from satellites in space.

CAREER OUTLOOK

Technology is responsible for making lots of things cheaper. Technology is responsible for making lots of things better. But also, technology causes some jobs to disappear.

FASTEST-GROWING JOBS

Many jobs are growing rapidly in communications and media. They are the following:

- Production designer.
- Digital satellite dish installers.
- Public relations worker.

SLOWEST-GROWING JOBS

In communications and media there are at least four job categories that are growing very slowly. They are as follows:

Attitude makes a difference

Overcoming a Language Barrier

Gloria Gonzalez came to the United States from Mexico when she was ten. She lived with her grandmother and grandfather while she was going to school. At first she had difficulty because her English wasn't very good. She wanted to go back to Mexico, where nobody made fun of her accent. Her grandparents convinced her to stay.

Gloria didn't do well at first because of the language barrier. It wasn't easy for Gloria to understand her teachers and books. By the time she finished junior high, however, she was a B student.

She never lost interest in her native language, Spanish. She never lost interest in the music she loved from Mexico. She watched Spanish-language television shows whenever her grandparents would let her. She listened to Spanish-language radio, too.

When she graduated from high school she applied for a job at the local Spanish-language television station. She started at the bottom. Gloria would do anything that needed to get done. She worked long hours and didn't get paid very much. Some nights she was discouraged. She didn't like her job.

Gloria stayed on, though. She watched carefully how all the announcers acted. She practiced saying the news herself in front of a mirror at home. She also read a lot about world events. She remained enthusiastic most of the time when she was working.

One day the weather announcer got sick just before he was to tell about that night's weather. Gloria said she could do it, and she did. She was scared to death. But she did it anyway.

Today Gloria still works for the same Spanish-language television station. Gloria has her own show. She interviews high school kids about their problems. Gloria still works long hours, but she loves her job. She knows her hard work was worth it.

What Do YOU Think?

How did Gloria channel her Spanish-language roots into a career? How did Gloria project her positive attitude about work?

- **Telephone long-distance operator.** In the good old days, every long-distance call required a long-distance operator. Today you can direct dial anywhere in the world. Just about the only time you use the services of a long-distance operator is when you have a problem. Only rarely do you have to use the operator to make a collect call, for even that activity is computerized. New technology is eliminating the need for such workers.
- **Telephone information operator.** Most telephone companies charge for calls to obtain information and telephone numbers. Sometimes they let you make five or six such calls without charge each month. But after that you might have to pay as much as $1.00 per call.

  Not surprisingly, people use these information services less often now. They don't want to pay the extra money. They look in the telephone book. In some countries, such as France, you can use a little computer hooked up to your phone line to find out information from the Yellow Pages. No information operators are required.

  In the United States, through the use of voice-recognition systems within the telephone companies' computers, much of the time you can find out someone's phone number without ever talking to a human. Also, you can usually find out most people's phone numbers anywhere in the United States for free on the Internet.

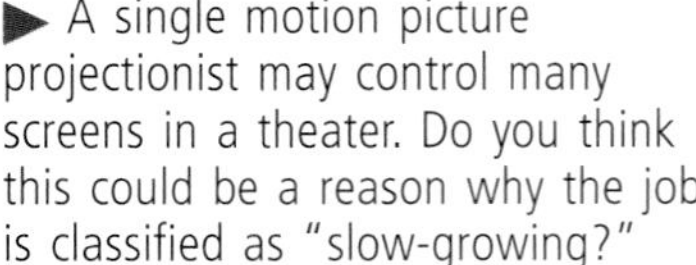

▶ A single motion picture projectionist may control many screens in a theater. Do you think this could be a reason why the job is classified as "slow-growing?"

- **Telephone central office technician.** When the telephone industry was beginning, there were often breakdowns at the central office. That's where all the equipment for switching calls is located. Today, in contrast, the equipment is more sophisticated and faster. It doesn't break down very often. That means fewer jobs for technicians located at the central office.
- **Motion picture projectionist.** Technology again is making another job less and less important. Showing movies used to require a lot of people. Today movie theaters may have as many as ten separate screens operating at once. Projection booth technology has made it possible for one person to operate all ten different projectors. You can guess the effect on the number of jobs.

As with all the career clusters, there are many types of jobs to aim for in communications and media. To decide whether you should be thinking about this career cluster, look at the checklist in the "Thinking about Yourself" box.

AT THE HEART OF THE COMMUNICATIONS AND MEDIA CLUSTER

At the heart of the Communications and Media Cluster is the communication of ideas and emotions. It's all about people sending messages to other people. It means working closely with other people to gather information. It means analyzing and sifting through lots of information and then summarizing the key facts so that people can get the main points quickly. It also means creating characters and scenes that will communicate ideas and feelings in an entertaining way. If you are interested in current events, ideas, and emotions, as well as in discussing these ideas with other people, this career cluster could be one for you.

Figure 8.1 lists just a few examples of occupations from this cluster. Think about the job titles, the work activities, and the work settings. These are just examples to help you get at the heart of this cluster. You don't need to read for details. Scan the entries to get a feel for the cluster as a whole.

Would you enjoy a career in this cluster? Ask yourself the following questions:

- Do you like the sound of the occupations listed under "Who"? Would you feel good about having an identity like one of these?
- Would you enjoy doing the activities listed under "What"?
- Would you like working in the settings described under "Where"?

Figure 8.1 Sample Occupations in Communications and Media Cluster

WHO You Would Be	WHAT You Would Do	WHERE You Would Do It
Writer, editor	Write original stories, reports, plays, ads, books; edit and rewrite material and decide what to publish or broadcast	Home; newspaper, magazine, and book publishing offices
Newscaster	Read news stories during public broadcasts; write news stories and edit material to fit time restrictions	Television and radio studios; on actual locations
Musician	Play musical instruments, sing, write musical arrangements, conduct musical groups	In a variety of settings, such as recording studios, concert halls, nightclubs
Photographer, camera operator	Use cameras to photograph people, places, and events for publication and broadcasting	Broadcasting studios, on-site locations of events (all of which require travel)
Digital satellite dish installer	Install satellite dishes, put wires and cables in place and connect them	Outdoors in all kinds of weather, often high above the ground

Thinking About Yourself

Communications and Media Careers

Read the following questions. Think carefully about your answers. You may want to make notes for yourself as you read.

- ▲ Do you enjoy writing? Have you received good grades in English?
- ▲ Do you do a good job of editing and proofreading your writing assignments? Do you work at these assignments until they are perfect or nearly perfect?
- ▲ Are you a curious person? Do you ask lots of questions? Do you always want to know why and how something happened?
- ▲ Have you participated in class plays or the school band? Have you enjoyed these activities?
- ▲ Have you ever made a speech in front of a large audience? Do you feel comfortable speaking and performing in front of groups?
- ▲ Have you ever used a video camera to record an event? How did the film turn out? Would you enjoy doing this type of activity on a regular basis?

If you answered yes to most of these questions, you may want to find out more about careers in the Communications and Media Cluster.

SKILLS, TRAINING, AND EXPERIENCE

Within the Communications and Media Cluster of careers there are a number of jobs that require little specialized training. There are others that require more training.

Listed here are some skills common to many of the occupations in this cluster:

- Thinking logically.
- Analyzing written materials.
- Speaking clearly.
- Identifying the important elements of an event.
- Organizing facts.
- Being creative.

JOBS REQUIRING LESS-THAN-AVERAGE TRAINING AND EXPERIENCE

- Film librarian.
- Film loader.
- Tree trimmer for communications lines' rights-of-way.
- Stagehand.
- Telephone central office technician.
- Telephone service representative.
- Telephone service worker.

◀ Musicians are included in the Communications and Media Cluster. Think about why music would be included in this cluster.

JOBS REQUIRING AVERAGE TRAINING AND EXPERIENCE

- Actor or announcer.
- Camera operator.
- Proofreader.
- Film editor.
- Set electrician.
- Lighting technician.
- Sound technician.

JOBS REQUIRING MORE-THAN-AVERAGE TRAINING AND EXPERIENCE

- Director or producer.
- Book editor.
- Composer.
- Journalist or reporter.
- Magazine or newspaper editor.
- Musician.
- Script writer and technical writer.
- Production designer.
- Telephone maintenance engineer.

Refer to the occupations list at the end of the chapter to identify some of the jobs in the Communications and Media Cluster, along with their *DOT* numbers.

Career Decision-Making Activities

1. Get a job on the school newspaper. Do whatever job is assigned, even if it's not the type of job you want. Many people who become successful in the most prestigious jobs in this cluster start out running errands or doing whatever needs to be done.
2. Write a movie review of the next movie you attend. Ask your English teacher to critique it. Offer it to the local newspaper as a review by a local critic.
3. Keep a daily journal. Write down anything and everything that you notice or think about. If an especially interesting idea occurs to you, develop it into a short story, poem, or play.
4. Photograph a school event. Use your own camera or video recorder. Display your pictures or show your video to the class.

Occupations in Communications and Media

Here is a list of occupations mentioned in this chapter. Next to the name of each occupation is its *DOT* number. You can use the *DOT* number to locate further information about the occupation in your school or public library. For the broad occupational terms mentioned in this chapter, only one or two examples of that occupation are listed below. You can easily find more examples of the occupation in the *DOT*.

Actor (150.047-010)
Announcer (159.147-010)
Art Critic (see Critic)
Book Editor (132.067-014)
Broadcaster (see Announcer)
Camera Operator (143.062-022)
Composer (152.067-014)
Critic (131.067-018)
Decorator, Set (142.061-042)
Digital satellite dish installer (823.261.022)
Director (159.067-010)
Disc Jockey (159.147-014)
Editor, Managing, Newspaper (132.017-010)
Engineer, Video Recording (194.362-010)
Film Editor (962.264-010)
Film Librarian (222.367-026)
Film Loader (962.687-014)
Food Critic (131.067-010)
Journalist (see Reporter)
Light Technician (962.362-014)
Line Inspector (822.267-010)
Line Repairer (822.381-014)
Magazine Editor (132.037-022)
Motion Picture Projectionist (960.362-010)
Movie Critic (see Critic)
Music Video Producer (see Producer, Recording Industry)
Musician, Instrumental (152.041-010)
Newscaster (see Reporter and Announcer)
Newspaper Editor (132.017-014)
Newspaper Reporter (see Reporter)
Painter, Animated Cartoons (970.681-026)
Painter, Stage Settings (840.681-010)
Photographer, Motion Picture (143.062-022)
Producer, Motion Pictures (187.167-174)
Producer, Recording Industry (159.117-010)
Production Designer (142.031-010)
Proofreader (209.387-030)
Prop Maker (962.281-010)
Public Relations Worker (165.067-010)
Radio Engineer (193.262-026)
Radio Repairer (720.281-010)
Reporter (131.267-018)
Scriptwriter (131.087-018)
Set Electrician (824.137-010)
Singer (152.047-022)
Sound Engineer (194.262-010)
Sportscaster (see Announcer)
Stagehand (962.684-014)
Technical Writer (131.267-026)
Telephone Central Office Technician (822.281-014)
Telephone Information Operator (235.662-022)
Telephone Long-Distance Operator (235.462-010)
Telephone Maintenance Engineer (822.261-018)
Telephone Operator (235.462-010)
Telephone Service Representative (299.357-014)
Telephone Service Worker (822.261-022)
Television Installer (823.361-010)
Television Repairer (720.281-018)
Tree Trimmer (408.664-010)
Video Operator (194.282-010)
Weather Announcer (see Announcer)
Writer, Editorial (131.067-022)
Writer, Gag (131.087-018)

Review and Enrichment

Summarizing the Chapter

Summarizing information is a critical thinking skill that will help you succeed in the world of work. Write a summary of what you learned in Chapter 8. Focus on the main points of the chapter. Then in a class discussion, compare your summary with the summaries done by your classmates. Can you improve your summary?

Improving Your Career Vocabulary

1. Learning to use new vocabulary terms will improve your communication skills, which are important in almost all areas of work. Write definitions for the terms listed below. Then for each term, write an original sentence about yourself in which you use the term correctly.
   - communications
   - media
   - Communications and Media Cluster
   - telecommunications
   - satellite dish
2. List the job families in the Communications and Media Cluster. Write a one-sentence description of each.

Finding the Facts

Finding exact information is a frequently used skill in many careers. Find the answers to the exercise below, and write the answers on a separate sheet of paper.

1. Name three different news media you use every day.
2. What is the name of the job family having to do with newspapers and magazines?
3. Who takes care of the electronic sound equipment at a recording studio?
4. How many miles above the earth do communications satellites orbit?
5. Name three fast-growing jobs in communications and media.

Thinking for Yourself

To complete the exercise below you will need to use critical thinking and communication skills, which are skills valued by all employers. Write out your answers or be prepared to discuss them in class, depending on your teacher's instructions.

1. Review what you learned about jobs and personalities. Do you think someone could enjoy being both a writer and an actor? Why or why not?
2. Competition is fierce for jobs in communications and media. How do you feel about competition? Do you think that in competitive situations, only the best people make it or only the pushiest? Give reasons for your opinion.
3. What sort of things do you think an actor would value? A reporter? A composer?
4. Most of the top jobs in communications and media occur in large cities like New York and Los Angeles. Why do you think this is so? How do you feel about living in a large city?
5. Define creativity. How would you describe a creative person?

Practicing Your Basic Skills

Your career success depends greatly on your basic math and communication skills. Work hard at improving in the areas where you have trouble with the following exercises.

Math

1. The *Journal-Record* had a circulation of 1,728,916 readers. When a new TV station that stressed news came to town, the *Journal-Record* lost 115,676 subscriptions. What is the new circulation total? The *Journal-Record* wants to increase its circulation to a level 10 percent above its *original* circulation. How many subscribers must the newspaper add?
2. A local telephone company charges 5¢ a call for local calls. For long distance it charges 13¢ a minute on weekends, 16¢ a minute in the evenings, and 20¢ a minute during weekdays. Ramon made thirteen local calls. He also talked long distance for twenty-four minutes on the weekend, one and one half hours in the evening, and sixteen minutes during a weekday. What was Ramon's total bill?
3. Judy was a "gofer" for a TV studio. Her boss asked her to inventory the equipment. In each set of

Review and Enrichment, continued

equipment listed below, tell what fraction of the total items are red.

a. 4 red microphones, 2 yellow, 4 green
b. 1 orange TV camera, 1 red, 1 green
c. 3 blue lights, 2 orange, 1 green, 2 red
d. 4 red video cables
e. 5 blue headsets, 2 red

Reading and Writing

1. Write a one-minute script for a radio or TV show. It can be serious, as for a news show, or silly, as for a comedy.
2. Write a one-page magazine or news article on a subject that interests you. Research your facts. Be sure your work is accurate.
3. Read about how a TV program is actually produced.
4. Pick at least one occupation mentioned in this chapter that you think would be interesting. Research the occupation thoroughly, and write a report. Use the career research checklist in Chapter 5 as a guide for your report. Conclude your report with an explanation of your interest in that occupation based on your findings.

Speaking and Listening

1. Read aloud to the class the one-page article you wrote for the previous "Reading and Writing" section. Speak clearly. Be sure everyone can hear and understand you.
2. Listen as your classmates read their articles. Pretend you are a talent scout looking for a radio announcer. Which qualities will you listen for?

Activities Working with Others

In almost all careers you must be able to get along well with other people to be successful. Work with your classmates to do the following activities. As you work together, pay attention to how well you get along. If necessary, work hard at improving your ability to do your part and to cooperate.

1. Obtain a video camera and tape. With a few classmates, perform one of the one-minute scripts you wrote for the previous "Reading and Writing" section. Not everyone has to be an actor. Some can direct—advise the actors how a scene should be played. Others can set up the "props," work the camera, and so on. If possible, show the tape to the class.
2. Take this test for creativity. With a classmate, see how many uses you can think of for a brick. Do this for five minutes and keep a list. Compare your results with others in the class.
3. Add the careers mentioned in this chapter to your database.

Decision Making and Problem Solving

You will be a big help to your employer if you can make decisions and solve problems. List all the possible ways of resolving the situations described below. Then pick the best alternative (possible choice), and tell why you chose it. If you need help, you might want to refer to Chapter 3.

1. You are the editor of your local newspaper. A reporter has written a good story about a car accident in which a friend of yours was involved. It sounds like your friend was drinking while driving. Your friend asks you not to include the information about drinking in the story. What will you do?

CHAPTER 9

CONSTRUCTION TECHNOLOGY CAREERS

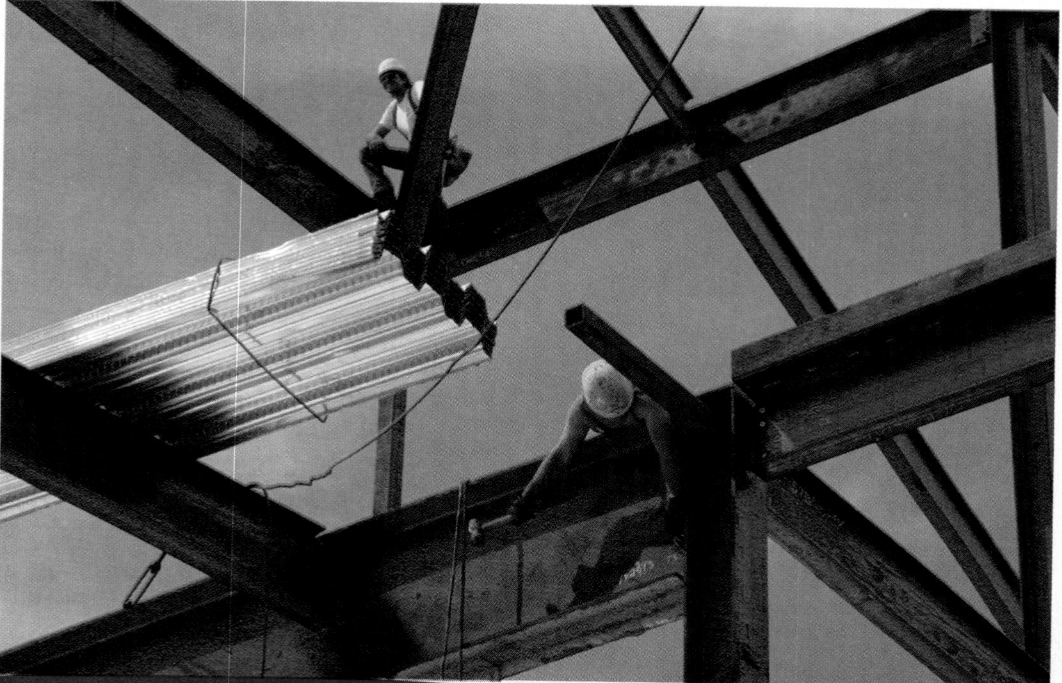

◆ Chapter Objectives ◆

After completing this chapter you will be able to do the following:

- ◆ Define the terms listed under "New Career Terms."
- ◆ List and describe the seven job families in the Construction Technology Cluster.
- ◆ Identify several careers included in this cluster.
- ◆ Name several slow-growing and fast-growing jobs in this cluster.
- ◆ Explain what it would be like to work at a career in this cluster.
- ◆ Evaluate your own interest in this cluster.
- ◆ Identify skills common to many careers in this cluster.

◆ New Career Terms ◆

In this chapter you will learn the meanings of the following career terms:

- ✔ Construction Technology Cluster
- ✔ Subcontractors
- ✔ Computer-Aided Design (CAD)
- ✔ Module

Have you been across a bridge during the last few weeks? You might have been walking, riding your bike, or riding in a car or bus. Chances are you have been across at least one. You may even cross one or two bridges every day.

Did you ever think about how difficult it would be to build a bridge—especially a big one across a river, or a freeway, or a bay? Think of the know-how, hard work, and money that must go into such a project. Would you enjoy being part of such an undertaking?

A project just as demanding would be that of building a skyscraper. Picture in your mind the tallest building in your city or a nearby city. Or maybe you don't have to imagine it—maybe you can just look out your window and see a skyscraper.

How would you like to be in charge of constructing that building? You'd be in charge of a lot of workers. You'd have command of cranes, hoists, generators, and other kinds of powerful equipment. And think of the millions of dollars' worth of materials made of steel, wood, concrete, glass, aluminum, copper, and plastic—all your responsibility for putting together. That would be quite a project to be in charge of—or even work on at all—wouldn't you say?

▲ Have you taken any technology or woodworking courses? If you enjoyed these courses and did well in them, you might like working in the construction industry someday.

Building a single-family home in a quiet neighborhood sounds easy compared with building a twenty- or thirty-story office building in the heart of the city, doesn't it? But think about it. Could you build a house? Even with some help? Would you know where to put the walls, how many two-by-fours you'd need, and how far apart to put them? How much would you slope the roof, and how would you go about building a stairway? When you think about it, building even a small house—much less a skyscraper or a bridge—would be quite an accomplishment.

Everywhere that you see buildings and bridges—and that's almost everywhere—you see the work output of people in the **Construction Technology Cluster** of jobs. The Construction Technology Cluster is a group of occupations involved in planning, designing, building, and repairing structures of all kinds.

Construction Technology Cluster a group of occupations involved in planning, designing, building, and repairing structures of all kinds

The construction technology industry is enormous. More than a million new houses are started each year. The average selling price of each of those new houses is over $150,000. What does some simple multiplication tell you about the total size of the home construction business?

People have been involved in construction ever since men and women wanted to be protected from the cold, heat, rain, and snow. Designs have changed. They will continue to change as people use new materials and prefer different looks. But people will always need

Ann Pursues Her Dream

Ann Stern did well in most of her classes. She especially liked English. But she also loved drafting. When her parents' friends asked her what she wanted to become, she knew the answer: a drafter.

Because Ann did well in other courses, her guidance counselor and her parents suggested she think more about becoming a journalist. Actually, Ann's dad, who owned an advertising agency, wanted Ann to get into advertising.

Ann wasn't sure what to do. On the one hand, she wanted to take more industrial education courses, such as advanced computerized design, because that's what had interested her most. On the other hand, she didn't want to disappoint her parents or her guidance counselor.

Ann solved her problem by taking more shop courses as extra credit. She didn't have as much free time as some of her friends, but she didn't mind.

During high school she would be able to make a decision. She'd also be in a position to choose.

What Do YOU Think?

What would you have done if you were in Ann's situation? Why would Ann be in a position to choose later on in high school because of the decisions she made earlier?

shelter. They will always need ways to conveniently cross bodies of water and other transportation rights-of-way.

WHAT WOULD IT BE LIKE?

Certain types of construction technology work can be backbreaking, with lots of bending over and lifting heavy objects. And the weather can add to the difficulty, because you'll usually be out in the hot sun or the cold winter. There are many exceptions, though. Architects work in an office. And if you become skilled at a craft such as cabinetmaking, you will work inside most of the time.

In almost all jobs in the construction technology industry, you have to interact with many other people. If you start out as a helper on a job site, you'll have to take directions from your supervisor. You will have to be able to ask him or her questions about things you don't understand.

If you decide to become an equipment operator, you will have lots of responsibilities. You might learn how to work a bulldozer that costs over $200,000!

If you choose to go into electrical work, you might face some risk. Sometimes electricians who aren't careful get shocked. All jobs require being careful, but some are more dangerous than others.

Would you like to run your own business someday? Lots of construction technology workers become **subcontractors.** Subcontractors are people who agree to supervise part of a construction job for a certain amount of money. After learning a trade, such as carpentry or bricklaying, you might become a subcontractor and have your own business.

subcontractor
people who agree to supervise part of a construction job for an agreed-upon amount of money.

Would you enjoy working in this cluster? Do some daydreaming as you "listen" to the following conversation. Several people who enjoy working in the Construction Technology Cluster are talking about their jobs. As you listen to what they say, imagine yourself doing their jobs.

Carpenter: I build houses. I'm very proud of that. Most people would not know where to begin. It's taken me twenty years to learn all that I know, and I'm still learning. It may sound like I'm bragging, but I'm really proud of my skills and my knowledge. I feel like I could build just about anything if I had to. That's a great feeling to have.

Electrician: I have that same feeling. Do you have any idea how many people are afraid of electricity? Some people are even afraid to change a lightbulb. When you think about being able to wire a whole building so that every light, machine, appliance, and utility works as it's supposed to—it gives you a really good feeling about yourself.

Bricklayer: My work's not so specialized, but I do get a lot of satisfaction from it. I really enjoy my work. You know what I enjoy most? It's the companionship. I almost always work with a team of bricklayers. We're outside, we're laying brick, and we're talking to one another. A lot of the talk is about the job, but a lot of it isn't. We talk about everything under the sun while we're working. And then before you know it, there's a wall there that wasn't there when we started. A bricklayer's life is hard to beat, in my opinion.

Steelworker: I'm the same way. I like being outdoors, and I like working with my friends. We work together. We work hard, but we have a good time doing it—possibly because there's a lot of communication and sharing going back and forth while we work. I do a lot of high-rise work, which I suppose most people wouldn't like, but I do. I like that little element of danger—it makes the work just that much more interesting. And it may sound crazy, but I even like working with steel. It's hard and solid, and when you bolt pieces of steel together, you really feel like you're making something that's going to last forever.

What do you think? Do any of these jobs sound appealing? Can you see yourself doing one of these jobs—or a similar job? Would you like to learn more about construction technology careers?

▼ Can you imagine a day without electricity? Electrician is a stable occupation in this cluster.

Career Decision-Making Activities

1. Some households have a complete workshop in the garage or basement. Others have a toolbox somewhere with lots of tools. Still others have only a hammer or screwdriver in a kitchen drawer. On a separate sheet of paper, make a list of all the tools in your household. Next to each tool tell whether or not you have ever used it. If you have used a tool, describe what you did with it on one or two occasions. Discuss your lists in class. Have you spent less time, about the same time, or more time than your classmates using tools? Do you come from a tool-oriented family?
2. Design and build something that you can use or that you can give to someone as a present. You could use materials such as wood, ceramic tiles, glass, or metal. If someone in your family is handy with tools, ask this person to help you. If no family member can help, ask an industrial arts teacher at your school to help you. Some things you could build are a bookshelf, a picture frame, a serving tray, or a toolbox. The possibilities are endless. Keep track of the tools and materials you use and your reaction to the experience. Did you enjoy the project? Will you do a similar project in the future?
3. Visit construction sites. Try to visit a site where a large building is being constructed and one where a single-family house is being built. What differences do you see? Would you prefer working at one or the other, or at neither? Discuss your reactions in class.

JOB FAMILIES IN THE CONSTRUCTION TECHNOLOGY CLUSTER

There are seven different job families within the Construction Technology Cluster. They include jobs that range from keeping the construction site clean and safe to designing buildings and roads. These job families are shown in the diagram on page 143. Reading about the job families will help you decide which careers in this cluster you might enjoy most.

- **Electrical installation.** The electrical installation job family involves building with electrical materials and parts. Today all buildings have some sort of electrical system. That means that electricians have to be on the job. They install and repair wiring in electrical fixtures, such as light outlets that go bad. There are also air-conditioning installers, who put wall units and central air units in houses and office buildings.
- **Engineering and support services.** The engineering and support services occupations provide technical assistance to the building industry. One typical job is that of an architect, who designs buildings. Surveyors are also included. They're the people who determine the exact location and measurements of the building. Sometimes you see surveyors in the street or in an open area looking through an instrument on three legs (a theodolite).

Job Families in the Construction Technology Cluster

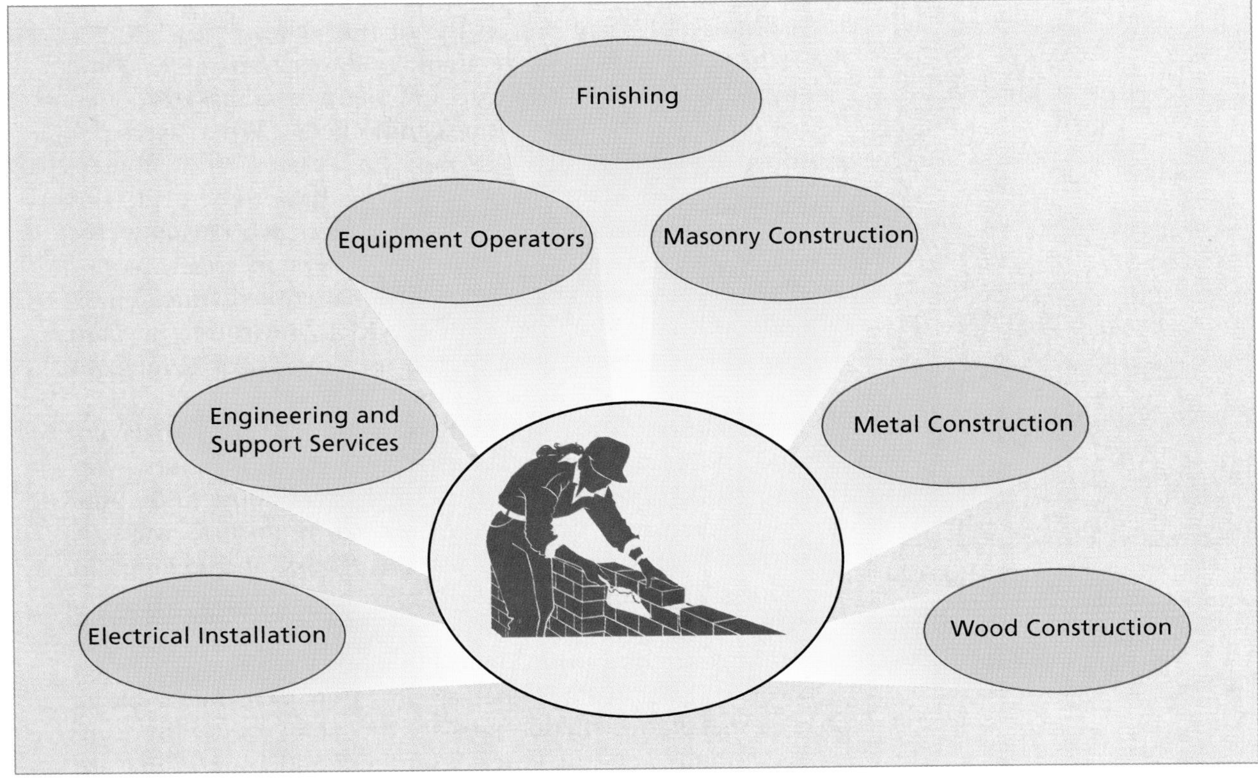

Drafters are another kind of worker in this family. They make up maps, specification sheets, and construction drawings for highways and bridge improvement projects.

Much of the work of architects and drafters is done on computers today. The process is known as **computer-aided design,** or **CAD** (using the computer and special software to create designs).

computer-aided design (CAD) using a computer and special software to create designs.

- **Equipment operators.** Just about every construction technology job requires heavy equipment to be operated by somebody. The equipment operator job family includes the workers who use and maintain this equipment.

There are bulldozer operators, who operate the tractors that push out, level, and distribute earth and rock. When driveways have to be put in, paving machine operators are called in.

Sometimes concrete has to be dug up. Then a jackhammer operator uses a noisy piece of equipment that goes up and down to break the concrete. These workers must have strong arms.

▲ Most construction jobs require learning to read blueprints.

- **Finishing.** Every job has to be finished, and usually finished well. Workers in the finishing category do all the finishing work. They put on the final touches.

  In the construction technology industry, painters come in after a building is put up. Cabinetmakers make wooden or plastic cabinets for homes and offices. Carpet layers put down the rugs and carpets in offices and homes. Windows, skylights, and display cases have to be made and installed. These jobs are done by glaziers, who install glass.
- **Masonry construction.** The workers in the masonry construction job family build with natural or artificial mineral products such as stones, bricks, and tiles. They are called masons. Usually a mason uses mortar or cement to keep the stones and bricks together.

  Within the masonry family of jobs there are bricklayers and chimney builders. There are also marble setters, who use tools to cut and set marble slabs in floors and counters. Stonemasons build stone structures such as walls.

  Tile setters apply tile to walls, floors, and ceilings in homes and offices. A stucco mason applies waterproof, decorative types of plaster to the outside walls of buildings.
- **Metal construction.** Some buildings are made of metal. Even those buildings that aren't often have metal parts. The metal construction jobs are those involved with using metal and metal materials. Plumbers and pipe fitters are in this group.

  There are also sheet metal workers, who might make control boxes for air conditioning units. The ducts used for air-conditioners are put in by duct installers. Welders join metal parts together in houses and factories.
- **Wood construction.** All the occupations involved in building with wood and wood parts are included in the wood construction family. For example, one of the most familiar jobs on a construction site involves the use of wood by carpenters. Rough carpenters come in and build the frame ("skeleton") for wooden structures according to the plans given to them by an architect. Finish carpenters come in and do the more detailed work. There are also carpenters who specialize in bridges, walk-in refrigerators, and packing containers. Carpenters all have assistants, who are sometimes called helpers or laborers.

As with all career clusters, the number of possible jobs in the Construction Technology Cluster is great. Your interests will be different if you want to become an engineer than if you want to become a bricklayer. To find out whether you have sufficient interest for getting a job in any part of the Construction Technology Cluster, use the checklist in the "Thinking about Yourself" feature.

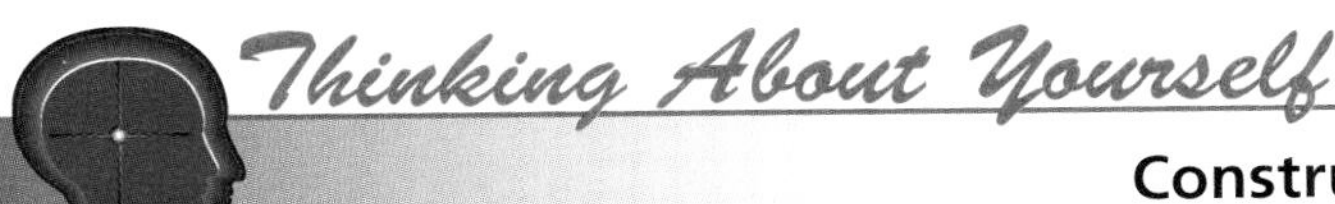

Construction Technology Careers

Take your time reading and thinking about the questions below. You might even want to make notes on a sheet of paper and write out your answers.

- ▲ Do you build model cars, model airplanes, or any other kinds of models? Do you usually finish the models you start to build?
- ▲ Do you ever help an adult fix things around the house? Do you help repair electrical cords, lamps, or fixtures? Do you enjoy this work?
- ▲ Do you enjoy arts and crafts projects at school? If given a choice between writing a report or building some sort of model, do you usually choose the model?
- ▲ Do you like fixing things, such as bikes? Do you spend much time with tools?
- ▲ Do you regularly read any craft or mechanical magazines? Do you seem to understand what you read?
- ▲ Did you ever design and build something on your own, such as a bookshelf?

If you answered yes to most of these questions, there's a good chance you'd enjoy a construction technology career.

CAREER OUTLOOK

The construction technology industry is going to grow about as fast as the rest of the economy. But within it, some jobs will become more important while others become much less so.

FASTEST-GROWING JOBS

The following jobs are among the fastest growing in construction technology:

- ◆ **Glazier.** A glazier installs glass. The reason this is a growing job is because more decorative glass is being used in new home construction and in new office buildings. Also, when people decide to redo part of their houses, they often want to install more glass.
- ◆ **Landscape architect.** Did you ever drive by an office complex that has trees, vines, and flowers and notice how beautiful it is? Did you ever drive by a big house surrounded by gardens?

  Chances are that the person who decided where all the plants should go was a landscape architect. This person prepares the plans for the land development—where things should be grown, where the walks and roadways should be placed, and where the fences should be.

Landscape architects might work for local and federal government agencies. Many have their own businesses. Landscape architects have to know about engineering and business, but more important, about design and plants.

Landscape architecture is a fairly new field. More and more people are recognizing its importance, though. By the year 2005 there will be more than double the number of landscape architects that there were in 1985.

- **CAD operator.** Using now well-developed computer-aided design (CAD) programs, CAD operators can do design projects in days that might have taken months before. Virtually all major construction projects require people familiar with the latest CAD programs.

SLOWEST-GROWING JOBS

Among the slowest-growing jobs in the Construction Technology Cluster are these:

- **Painters.** You would think that with all the building that goes on, the outlook for house and building painters would be rosy. The reason that there won't be much growth in the demand for painters is because of technology. Quicker, easier methods of applying paint to surfaces have been developed.

  For example, instead of using brushes, spray systems can apply more paint, more evenly, more quickly. Also, the paint itself lasts longer. That means that houses do not need to be repainted as often.
- **Paperhangers.** In some houses wallpaper is applied to the walls. This is done by a paperhanger. Fewer and fewer homeowners, and certainly fewer office building designers, seem to want wallpaper. This means that the outlook is not very good for paperhangers.

▼ Residential construction provides jobs in all seven job families in the diagram on page 143.

AT THE HEART OF THE CONSTRUCTION TECHNOLOGY CLUSTER

What makes the Construction Technology Cluster different from the other fourteen clusters? What would it really be like to work in this cluster? Let's try to get at the heart of the Construction Technology Cluster.

The essence of this cluster is building things. Bridges, roads, houses, office buildings, department stores, apartment complexes, airports—any structure that needs to be built is built by people working at jobs in this cluster.

These jobs often mean working with your hands. Strong hands are needed to lift, squeeze, pull, stretch, and twist materials. The hands

Careers for Tomorrow

PREBUILT HOME ASSEMBLERS

As houses get more expensive to build, some people have figured out less expensive ways to build them. One of those cheaper ways is to build different parts of the house in a factory. These different **modules** (units that fit or work together) are then shipped to the home site and put together. This is called premade, prefabricated, or manufactured home building.

All the pieces have to be installed and assembled. Workers have to do this. Most of these jobs do not require more than a high school education.

These jobs should become more numerous in the next couple of decades as people buy more pre-made homes and want them assembled.

Workers who do well and can talk with other people often get promoted to supervisor. For more information, write the Manufactured Housing Institute, 2101 Wilson Blvd., Suite 610, Arlington, VA 22201-3062.

module
units that fit or work together (for example, prefabricated houses are made from separate factory-made modules put together on the home site).

are toughened by the weather and by working day after day with bricks, boards, aluminum, pipes, and steel beams.

Construction means putting things together and pulling them apart. It means working with tools—saws, hammers, screwdrivers, wrenches, trowels, wheelbarrows, shovels, picks, jackhammers, pliers, and many more. There's constant pounding and hammering.

Much of the work is done outdoors in all kinds of weather—hot summers as well as cold winters. The work is done at locations that don't yet have sidewalks, running water, or heat. The air is often filled with swirling dirt and dust and the loud noises of different machines, such as bulldozers and cement mixers.

Construction usually means working with other people—it's a team effort. Each job needs carpenters, concrete workers, plumbers, electricians, bricklayers, painters—all kinds of construction workers. They work together to build the whole structure.

Figure 9.1 lists just a few examples of occupations from this cluster. Think about the job title, the work activities, and the work settings. These are just a few examples to help you get at the heart of the cluster. You don't need to read for details. Scan the entries to get a feel for the cluster as a whole.

Would you like a career in this cluster? Ask yourself the following questions:

- Do you like the sound of the occupations listed under "Who"? Would you feel good about having an identity like one of these?

Figure 9.1 Sample Occupations in Construction Technology Cluster

WHO You Would Be	WHAT You Would Do	WHERE You Would Do It
Carpenter	Build forms and frameworks; frame roofs; install doors, windows, cabinets, floors, and trim	Outdoors and indoors, sometimes in dangerous positions
Electrician	Assemble, install, and maintain electrical systems, following blueprints	Outdoors and indoors, sometimes in potentially dangerous situations
Painter, paperhanger	Prepare surfaces and then apply paints, varnishes, and decorative papers to the walls of buildings	Painters work both indoors and outdoors; paperhangers work indoors; most stand, often in uncomfortable positions, for long periods
Plumber, pipe fitter	Install, maintain, and repair pipe systems for water and waste systems	Outdoors and indoors, often in cramped positions
Bricklayer, stonemason	Build walls, floors, partitions, fireplaces, and other structures with bricks and stones; spread mortar and set bricks and stones in place	Mostly outdoors, often in bad weather; often in dangerous positions

- Would you enjoy doing the activities described under "What"?
- Picture yourself working in the settings described under "Where." Would you be comfortable in those settings?

SKILLS, TRAINING, AND EXPERIENCE

Although the Construction Technology Cluster contains a wide range of careers, some skills are common to all of them. Most workers in the construction technology industry are able to do the following:

- Use hand tools or machines skillfully.
- Read blueprints or drawings.
- Measure, cut, and work on materials with great precision.
- Use basic arithmetic to figure amounts of materials needed.
- Form a mental picture of a product not yet built.

Do you have these skills? Do you think you can develop them?

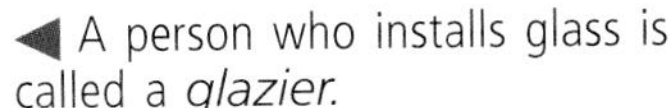

◀ A person who installs glass is called a *glazier.*

There are many levels of skills required for the different jobs in the construction technology industry. Below are listed three categories of jobs.

JOBS REQUIRING LESS-THAN-AVERAGE TRAINING AND EXPERIENCE

- Air-conditioning and heating mechanics.
- Insulation worker.
- Bricklayer.
- Carpenter.
- Cement mason.
- Construction laborer or helper.
- Roofer.
- Elevator repair worker.
- Marble and tile worker.
- Painter and paperhanger.
- Glazier.
- Plasterer.
- Plumber and pipe fitter.
- Welder.
- Stonemason.
- Surveyor's helper.

JOBS REQUIRING AVERAGE TRAINING AND EXPERIENCE

- Architectural drafter.
- Architectural model maker.

- Highway contractor.
- Construction equipment dealer.

JOBS REQUIRING MORE-THAN-AVERAGE TRAINING AND EXPERIENCE

- Construction supervisor.
- Architect.
- Computer-aided design (CAD) specialist.
- Building inspector.
- Highway engineer.
- Surveyor.
- Landscape architect.

See the box on page 151 for a list of some of the jobs in the Construction Technology Cluster, along with their *DOT* numbers.

Career Decision-Making Activities

1. If you think you might like the construction technology industry, you can probably start doing something in the summer. There are usually helper jobs on construction sites during busy summer months. Summer is a busy time for the construction industry because the weather is so good in most parts of the country. There is no snow to stop outside work. Because lots of people want these jobs, they usually go to those who apply first. Don't wait until mid-June to look for these jobs.
2. If you are interested in using your hands in a craft, such as cabinetmaking, now is the time to start in school. Take as many shop courses as you can, and develop your skills early. You can use them in a job as a helper in a cabinetmaking shop locally, for example.
3. If you want to become an architect or engineer in the construction technology industry, you will need to prepare yourself with a lot of education. That means that when you are in junior high and high school you need to take many courses in mathematics and the sciences. You also should take vocational courses in drafting.
4. Here is a list of some other things you might consider doing:
   - Start learning how to use computers now. You might be able to get into computer-aided design (CAD) later on.
   - Start looking at how things are built in your own house. See where the supports are. Try to notice the difference between good and bad workmanship around you.
   - Ask people you know who work in construction technology what their jobs are like.
   - Watch what a repairperson does when he or she comes to your house to fix the electricity or plumbing.

Occupations in Construction Technology

Here is a list of occupations mentioned in this chapter. Next to the name of each occupation is its *DOT* number. You can use the *DOT* number to locate further information about the occupation in your school or public library. For the broad occupational terms mentioned in this chapter, only one or two examples of that occupation are listed below. You can easily find more examples of the occupation in the *DOT*.

Air-conditioning and Heating Mechanic (637.261-014)
Air-conditioning Installer, Domestic (827.464-010)
Architect (001.061-010)
Architectural Drafter (001.261-010)
Architectural Model Maker (777.261-010)
Bricklayer (861.381-018)
Bulldozer Operator (850.683-010)
Cabinetmaker (660.280-010)
Carpenter, Form (860.381-046)
Carpenter, Maintenance (860.281-010)
Carpenter, Rough (860.381-042)
Carpenter Helper, Hardwood Flooring (869.687-026)
Carpentry Laborer (869.664-014)
Carpet Layer (864.381-010)
Cement Mason (844.364-010)
Chimney Builder (861.381-018)
Concrete Worker (see Cement Mason)
Construction Equipment Dealer (185.167.042)
Contractor (182.167-010)
Duct Installer (869.664-014)
Electrician (824.261-010)
Elevator Repair Worker (825.281-030)
Engineer, Civil (005.061-014)
Engineer, Electrical (003.061-010)
Finish Carpenter (see Carpenter, Maintenance)
Glazier (865.381-010)
Highway Contractor (see Contractor)
Insulation Installer (869.664-014)
Jackhammer Operator (930.684-018)
Landscape Architect (001.061-018)
Marble Setter (861.381-030)
Painter (840.381-010)
Paperhanger (841.381-010)
Paving Machine Operator (853.663-014)
Pipe Fitter (862.381-018)
Plasterer (842.361-018)
Plumber (862.381-030)
Prebuilt Home Assemblers (860.681-010)
Roofer (866.381-010)
Sheet Metal Worker (804.281-010)
Steelworker, Structural (801.361-014)
Stonemason (861.381-038)
Stucco Mason (842.381-014)
Supervisor, Cofferdam Construction (860.131-018)
Supervisor, Form Building (860.131-018)
Surveyor (018.167-018)
Surveyor's Helper (869.567-010)
Tile Setter (861.381-054)
Welder, Gas (811.684-014)
Welder-Fitter (819.361-010)

Review and Enrichment

Summarizing the Chapter

Summarizing information is a critical thinking skill that will help you succeed in the world of work. Write a summary of what you learned in Chapter 9. Focus on the main points of the chapter. Then in a class discussion, compare your summary with the summaries done by your classmates. Can you improve your summary?

Improving Your Career Vocabulary

1. Learning to use new vocabulary terms will improve your communication skills, which are important in almost all areas of work. Write definitions for the terms listed below. Then for each term, write an original sentence about yourself in which you use the term correctly.
   - Construction Technology Cluster
   - subcontractor
   - computer-aided design (CAD)
   - module
2. List the job families in the Construction Technology Cluster. Write a one-sentence description of each.

Finding the Facts

Finding exact information is a frequently used skill in many careers. Find the answers to the exercise below, and write the answers on a separate sheet of paper.

1. Name four materials used in the construction of a skyscraper.
2. Name one type of worker in the Construction Technology Cluster who works in an office.
3. Name four job families within the Construction Technology Cluster.
4. What type of work does a glazier do?
5. How many more landscape architects will there be in the year 2005 than there were in 1985?

Thinking for Yourself

To complete the exercise below you will need to use critical thinking and communication skills, which are skills valued by all employers. Write out your answers or be prepared to discuss them in class, depending on your teacher's instructions.

1. A lot of construction work is seasonal—done during good weather. What effect do you think this has on job openings in different parts of the country? Why?
2. Which position do you think would be more suitable for someone who valued perfection: steelworker or bricklayer? Why?
3. There is a certain level of accuracy needed when building a house or a bridge. Why do you think this accuracy is necessary?
4. In your own words, describe someone who would probably not enjoy working in construction technology.

Practicing Your Basic Skills

Your career success depends greatly on your basic math and communication skills. Work hard at improving in the areas where you have trouble with the following exercises.

Math

1. Scott Nakamura was a carpenter. He cut the following wood for a house. How much wood (in length) did he cut altogether?
   - 16 pieces 8 feet long
   - 17 pieces 7 feet 4 inches long
   - 12 pieces 4 feet 6 inches long
   - 2 pieces 2 feet 9 inches long
   - 13 pieces 6¾ inches long
   - 1 piece 9 feet 3 inches long
2. The construction technology industry is gradually converting to metric measurements. Convert the following measures to their metric equivalents. Use your problem-solving skills to find the metric conversions you need.
   a. a 100-lb. sack of cement (1 lb = 0.454 kg)
   b. a 4 × 8 feet board (1 feet = 0.3 m)
   c. 4 gal. water (1g = 0.951)
   d. insulation that must work in temperatures down to 20° below zero [°C = 5⁄9 (°F − 32)]
   e. a nail 3½ inches long (1 inch = 2.54 cm)
   f. 3 oz of glue powder (1 oz = 28.35 g)

Review and Enrichment, continued

3. Plywood is sold by the square foot. At $1.23 per square foot, how much would the following sizes cost?
   a. 1 × 3 feet
   b. 12 × 12 inches
   c. 4 × 8 feet
   d. 5½ × 6 feet

Reading and Writing

1. Technology is changing the construction world. Research a current technology as it applies to construction. Topics might include electron beam machining, use of plastics in pipe, or the machinery used to dig the "Chunnel" under the English Channel in England.
2. Pretend you are a building subcontractor. Go for a walk around your neighborhood or school. Select a building that appeals to you, and write a one-page description of it as if you were describing it to other subcontractors.
3. Words are symbols we use to represent ideas, actions, and things. The "language" of the construction technology industry is used on the project plans. Obtain the blueprint of a building or other project, and try to read it.
4. Pick at least one occupation mentioned in this chapter that you think would be interesting. Research the occupation thoroughly, and write a report. Use the career research checklist in Chapter 5 as a guide for your report. Conclude your report with an explanation of your interest in that occupation based on your findings.

Speaking and Listening

1. In construction technology you often have to tell others how you did something so they can add their work to it. Select an object you have made, and give a one-minute speech to the class describing how it was done so others can do it, too. The object can be simple, such as a paper airplane, or more complex. Try not to leave out any steps.

Activities Working with Others

In almost all careers you must be able to get along well with other people to be successful. Work with your classmates to do the following activities. As you work together, pay attention to how well you get along. If necessary, work hard at improving your ability to do your part and to cooperate.

1. With a classmate, buy a kit for a model of some kind, such as a model airplane, or design your own "kit." Put the model together.
2. With a classmate, design the "perfect" classroom. Your design does not have to be serious, but it should resemble the plans for a real room.
3. Add the careers mentioned in this chapter to your database.

Decision Making and Problem Solving

You will be a big help to your employer if you can make decisions and solve problems. List all the possible ways of resolving the situations described below. Then pick the best alternative (possible choice), and tell why you chose it. If you need help, you might want to refer to Chapter 3.

1. You are the boss of electricians on the construction site for a house. One of your workers comes to you saying that the electric wiring put in the house by another worker has been done all wrong and might give the future owners trouble. However, no one but another electrician would notice it now, and the wiring will soon be hidden behind the walls. You are already behind schedule, and if you're late you'll have to pay the main contractor (the person who agrees to perform the work) a penalty. What will you do?
2. You are a helper on a construction site. You enjoy the work and like being outside. But one of the workers doesn't like you and teases you constantly. Sometimes his teasing interferes with your job. Another worker says you should tell the boss, but you don't want to sound like a complainer. What will you do?

CHAPTER 10

FAMILY AND CONSUMER SCIENCES CAREERS

◆ Chapter Objectives ◆

After completing this chapter you will be able to do the following:

- ◆ Define the terms listed under "New Career Terms."
- ◆ List and describe the six job families in the Family and Consumer Sciences Cluster.
- ◆ Identify several careers included in this cluster.
- ◆ Name several slow-growing and fast-growing jobs in this cluster.
- ◆ Explain what it would be like to work at a career in this cluster.
- ◆ Evaluate your own interest in this cluster.
- ◆ Identify skills common to many careers in this cluster.

◆ New Career Terms ◆

In this chapter you will learn the meanings of the following career terms:

- ✔ Family and Consumer Sciences Cluster
- ✔ Consumer
- ✔ Interrelate
- ✔ Family interactions
- ✔ Budget
- ✔ Advocate
- ✔ Dietitian
- ✔ Nutritionist

Seventy-five years ago, in most families, the man worked outside the house and the woman worked in the house. Times have changed. In many families today both the woman and the man work outside the home. This means that there isn't always somebody home. Without an adult present, who takes care of the kids, and the household chores, and the problems that come up? It's not surprising that the **Family and Consumer Sciences Cluster** is a growing one. It is a group of occupations involved in developing, producing, and managing goods and services that improve the quality of home life.

Just think about a typical Monday morning. Imagine a family with a mother, a father, and two preschool children. Dad agrees to drop the kids off at the day-care center. Mom agrees to pick them up. The clothes dryer is broken. Mom calls somebody to come and fix it the following Saturday.

Family and Consumer Sciences Cluster a group of occupations involved in developing, producing, and managing goods and services that improve the quality of home life.

The kids need two separate bedrooms. Mom and Dad have decided to convert a basement into one bedroom. Dad calls an interior designer and makes an appointment. That person will help plan and lay out the converted basement.

This family is going to have to borrow money from the local bank to pay for the remodeling. When Dad goes to the bank, the loan officer may introduce him to someone else. That person might be a budget consultant, otherwise known as a family finance specialist. He or she will advise Dad on how to handle any family financial problems.

◀ Have you ever prepared and served a meal for your family and friends?

Both Mom and Dad want to make sure that they and their children eat the right kind of foods. They might watch a weekly program on television presented by a nutritionist—someone who knows what the best kinds of foods are and how to eat a balanced diet.

WHAT WOULD IT BE LIKE?

Family and consumer sciences careers involve what used to be called *home economics.* Home economics jobs used to be thought of as dressmaking and teaching home economics in school. Today, in contrast, family and consumer sciences specialists can be researchers, dietitians, extension service workers, and writers.

One of the main concerns of family and consumer sciences specialists is to educate the individual for family living. That means teaching individuals about food, clothing, and how to raise children. These specialists also try to help improve the goods and services used by a family. And finally, they conduct research.

For the most part, anybody in family and consumer sciences—in interior design, fashion, child care, and so on—will be working indoors. In this career cluster you will be expected to know about the latest developments in the care of fabrics and about the best food at the lowest cost. That means that you will be reading a lot and maybe watching special television shows on **consumer** problems. (Consumers are people who buy goods or services.)

People in the family and consumer sciences field usually have to **interrelate** (communicate closely) with others. Anybody who gives advice relates with others. Those who try to teach others about con-

consumer
one who buys and uses goods and services.

interrelate
to communicate with and get along with other people.

Thinking About Yourself

Family and Consumer Sciences Careers

Take your time reading and thinking about the questions below. You might want to make notes on a sheet of paper and write out your answers.

- ▲ Have you ever had to take care of children or sick people? Were you patient with these people? Did you enjoy helping them?
- ▲ Have you ever planned or organized a party or event? Do you like to be the leader for party games and group activities?
- ▲ Do you often cook or bake? Do you measure ingredients accurately?
- ▲ Do you ever mend your own clothes? Do you take good care of your clothes?
- ▲ Do you often help with the family housecleaning? Does it matter to you how the inside of your home looks?

If you answered yes to most of these questions, there's a good chance you might enjoy a family and consumer sciences career.

sumer issues and homemaking spend a lot of time talking to groups of people.

Men as well as women work in this cluster. Family and consumer sciences, like the words *homemaking* and *home economics,* used to be associated with female interests. That is not true today, however. The number of males who are getting degrees in family and consumer sciences has more than tripled in the last twenty-five years. Also, men and women in two-worker families have to share the responsibilities for homemaking. They both have to be interested.

Would you enjoy working in this cluster? Do some daydreaming as you "listen" to the following conversation. Several people who enjoy working in the Family and Consumer Sciences Cluster are talking about their jobs. As you listen to what they say, imagine yourself doing their jobs.

Food Service Supervisor: Don't you just love hot apple pie? Or a stuffed turkey with all the trimmings? Or a really great Caesar salad? I've always loved to eat. It's no surprise to anyone in my family that I ended up in food service. Now that I'm a manager, I have less time actually to cook or even supervise the cooking myself. I have to order and inspect supplies, arrange schedules, monitor the budgets—the list goes on and on. But it still comes down to serving a "dynamite" meal—one that the customer won't forget. It's a great challenge, and I love it. Would you like some fresh strawberry shortcake?

Drapery and Upholstery Estimator: No thanks, I'm on a diet. But I will give you an estimate on a nice set of drapes for your dining room. I'm sure you realize how important the decor is to a positive dining experience. And I get as excited about fabrics as you do about food. Just tell me your budget, and I'll come up with several options from which you can choose. I'll even get the drapes installed for you. I seem to have a sixth sense for colors and textures—just as you probably do for food tastes.

▲ Do you have a good eye for matching colors and fabrics?

Preschool Teacher: I couldn't help but overhear. Could I get you to make some suggestions for decorating my new preschool? I'm so excited. My dream is about to come true. I'll have my very own nursery school. I love little children, and I especially enjoy helping them learn. We haven't even opened the school yet, and I've already planned about fifteen years' worth of activities. It's hard for me to worry about clothes, furniture, or even food when I think of all those precious children with those open, creative minds just waiting for a chance to express themselves in my classes. I love working with kids.

Extension Service Specialist: Kids are wonderful, aren't they? Indirectly I help them by training others in the latest child care techniques. I work with teachers, health-care workers, and parents from all over our county. Every day I'm helping people improve their lives in some way. It could be helping them plan more balanced meals, or helping them get along better with family members, or showing them how to stretch their dollars—and believe me, there are a lot of people out there who don't have enough dollars. And many of them don't have a hint about how much more they could get for their money. You should see their faces light up when I show them how to put three meals a day on the table and have money to spare.

What do you think? Do any of these careers sound appealing? Can you see yourself in one of these jobs—or a similar job? Would you like to learn more about the Family and Consumer Sciences Cluster?

Career Decision-Making Activities

1. Tell your family you will be responsible for the evening meal on a certain night. Give yourself a couple of weeks to plan. Choose a menu from the food section of your daily newspaper or a magazine. Pick something that you think the people you are cooking for will like. Make a list of the ingredients you need, and shop for them. Go through the recipe steps several times, and write questions about everything you don't understand. Ask someone who knows a lot about cooking to answer your questions. Think about how you will set the table and serve the meal. You might want a brother, sister, or friend to help you serve. Evaluate the experience. Did you enjoy it? Which part did you enjoy the most: planning, shopping, cooking, or serving? Discuss your experience in class.
2. Carefully study two or three homes. Choose from your own home and the homes of your relatives, friends, and neighbors. For each home, develop a room-by-room list of things you would suggest changing or adding to improve the home's overall appearance. You could suggest anything from simply rearranging the furniture to replacing all the furniture. Cost is always a key issue, so try to give cost estimates for each of your suggestions. You can obtain estimates from local furniture and home furnishing dealers. Do you think you might have a flair for home decorating? Discuss your experiences in class. If someone takes your advice and uses your suggestion, bring "before" and "after" photos.
3. Volunteer to take care of a friend's, relative's, or neighbor's small children for a day. At three or four points during the day, write down your feelings about your experiences with the children. At the end of the day, summarize the experience. Do you enjoy taking care of children? Given a choice, do you think you would prefer working with children or adults? Discuss this in class.

JOB FAMILIES IN THE FAMILY AND CONSUMER SCIENCES CLUSTER

There are six categories of jobs within this career cluster. Look at them on the diagram below. Reading the following descriptions of the job families will help you decide which kinds of careers in this cluster you might enjoy the most.

- **Extension services.** Government agencies, such as the federal Department of Agriculture, offer services called *extension services.* The people who work in these services help educate groups of homemakers and young people. They cover such subjects as how to select and care for clothing and household equipment. They give information on food preparation and child care. The people who deal in this education are often called extension service specialists.

In rural communities—away from the cities—there are county home-demonstration agents. These people give lectures and demonstrate the techniques for home management and child care. They are there to improve farm and family life.

- **Family economics and home management.** The family economics and home management family of jobs involves helping people manage their homes and **budgets.** We already talked about a budget consultant who works for a bank. This person helps people sort out their family financial problems.

  Another worker in this category is a journalist who specializes in home management and family economics subjects. He or she might write on how to take care of a problem with washing machines or dryers.

- **Family relations and child development.** Another group of jobs includes all those involved in studying and improving family relations and child growth. One of the

budget
a plan for spending and saving money over a specific period of time.

Careers for Tomorrow

BEING A CONSUMER ADVOCATE

Advocate means to speak or write in favor of something. A consumer advocate is a person who does things in support of consumer causes. One consumer cause might be cleaner kitchen conditions in local restaurants.

Sometimes consumer advocates help individual consumers. For example, if a consumer doesn't get what he or she ordered through the mail, a consumer advocate will help solve the problem.

Some consumer advocates go to the state capital or to Washington, D.C. There they try to get lawmakers to pass laws that protect the consumer.

If you are interested in becoming a consumer advocate, you can volunteer to work for a consumer organization. That's one good way to explore this career. For more information, write the Consumer Federation of America, 1424 16th Street N.W., Suite 604, Washington, D.C. 20036.

advocate
to speak or write in favor of a cause or causes.

Job Families in the Family and Consumer Sciences Cluster

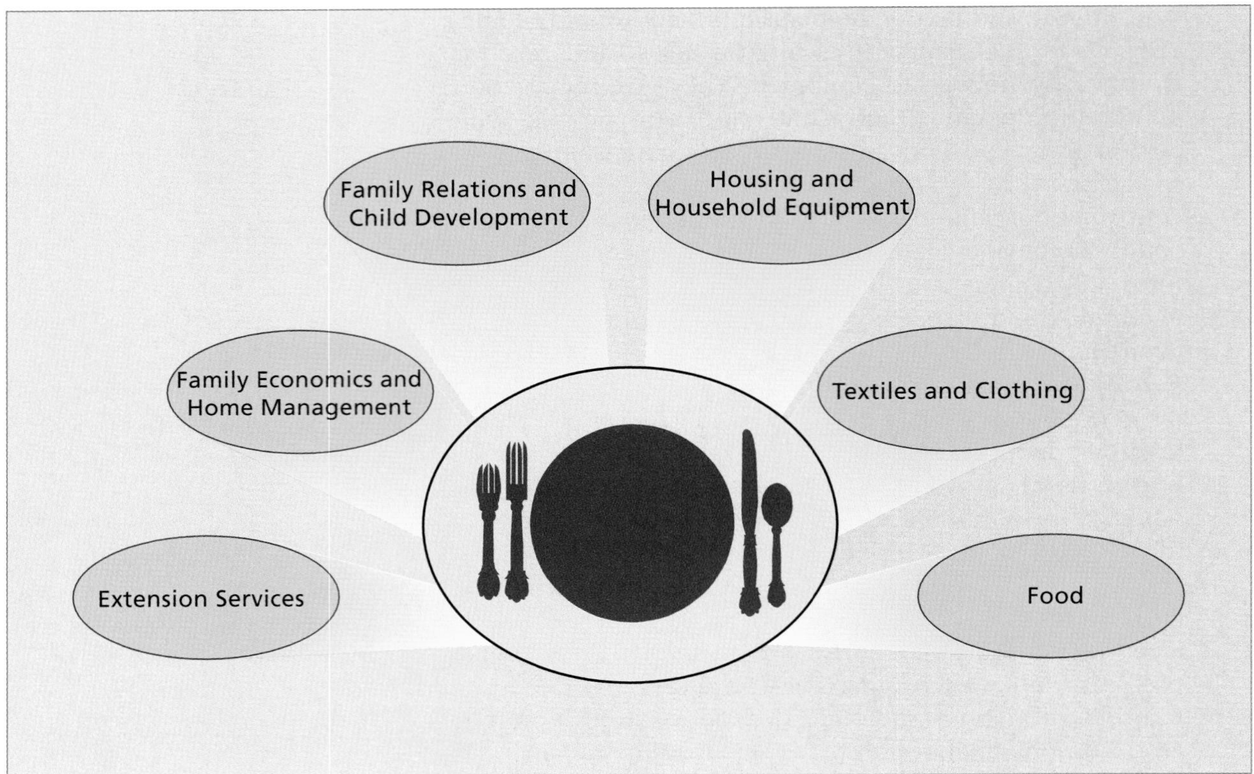

family interaction
the experiences that take place involving family members.

jobs within this category is a researcher in child development and family relations. This person studies those things that might affect how people get along within a family. One of the things he or she might study are the **family interactions** that occur. Family interactions are the experiences that take place involving family members. They occur between the mother and father, among children, and between each of the parents and each of the children. Nursery school teachers and day-care specialists are other jobs within this category.

- **Housing and household equipment.** One job family deals with designing and developing home interiors and equipment. Sometimes people aren't sure about which colors they should pick for their walls, their draperies, and other parts of their houses. They might go to a color expert. Or they might go to an interior designer, who also

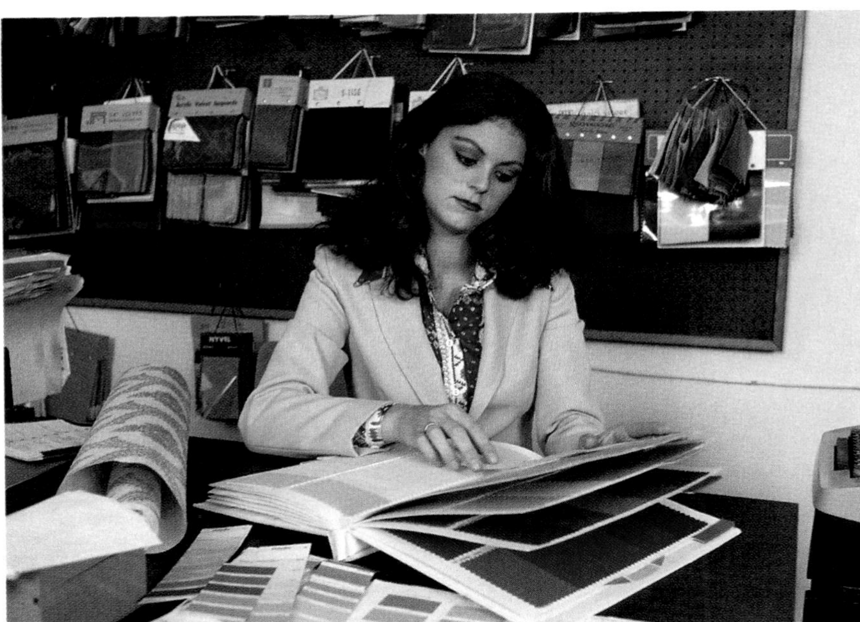

◀ Interior designers must use their knowledge of textiles to advise their clients.

plans the space and the layout for where furniture goes. Within this category of jobs there is also a household appliance installer. This person installs washing machines, stoves, and refrigerators.

- **Textiles and clothing.** Fabrics have designs. Clothes have designs. The people who are involved in designing fabrics and clothing are working in the textiles and clothing category of jobs. Also included is the wedding consultant. This person recommends the kind of clothes the bride and the attendants should wear at a wedding. Writers for magazines and newspapers sometimes specialize in fashion. These fashion journalists also are part of this job family.
- **Food.** The food family of jobs involves all those occupations in which people provide food and food information to consumers. For example, a **dietitian** plans and directs food service (involving the final preparation and delivery of food products) programs in hospitals and cafeterias. There may even be a dietitian who works in your school cafeteria.

  Food testers mix, cook, and bake experimental food products for big food-producing companies. Food journalists are writers for magazines and newspapers. They may test and write about recipes.

dietitian
a person who plans and directs food service programs, including preparation and delivery in hospitals and cafeterias.

nutritionist

a person who studies the effects of food on the human body.

Careers for Tomorrow

BECOMING A NUTRITIONIST OR DIETITIAN

Americans are more interested in proper diet and proper nutrition (food, nourishment) than ever before. Enter nutritionists and dietitians. Both are health professionals who study nutrition and food management. Then they apply them to specific settings. Your school probably has an administrative dietitian, who manages the food services. He or she directs the purchase and preparation of the food. Clinical dietitians plan meals for hospital patients and others who need special diets.

Nutritionists, in contrast, usually study the use of food in the human body. They deal with the principles of nutrition and try to teach them. To pass on their information, they write articles in newspapers and magazines. They also appear on radio and television shows to tell us how we can eat better to improve our health.

For more information, write the American Dietetic Association, 216 W. Jackson Blvd., Suite 800, Chicago, IL 60606, and the American Institute of Nutrition, 9650 Rockville Pike, Bethesda, MD 20814.

AT THE HEART OF THE FAMILY AND CONSUMER SCIENCES CLUSTER

What makes the Family and Consumer Sciences Cluster different from the other fourteen clusters you'll be exploring? What would it really be like working in this cluster? Let's try to get at the heart of the Family and Consumer Sciences Cluster.

The essence of this cluster is the family home. It involves all the people who live in the home. It involves the physical building itself and all the objects in it. And it involves all the activities that go on in the home: cooking, caring for children, shopping for groceries and household supplies, cleaning, repairing, decorating, managing the money needed to keep the household running smoothly, and the relationships among the family members.

Food, children, clothing, homes, family relationships, and management are the main areas of this cluster. Many workers specialize in one or the other of these areas. Many workers deal almost daily with all the areas.

Making up this cluster is everything that goes on in the family home. It's the smells, utensils, heat, and foods of the kitchen. It's the noise, activity, questions, requests, and needs of children. It's finding enough money to buy the new piece of furniture, the groceries, two pairs of new shoes, and school supplies—and then doing it again the

Figure 10.1 Sample Occupations in Family and Consumer Sciences Cluster

WHO You Would Be	WHAT You Would Do	WHERE You Would Do It
Chef, cook	Prepare dishes by measuring, mixing, and cooking according to recipes; also plan meals	Kitchens of restaurants, schools, hospitals, nursing homes, hotels
Child-care worker	Look after young children; feed, bathe, diaper, comfort, and play with children	Mostly at home, sometimes in child-care centers
Restaurant and food service manager	Select and price menu items, use food efficiently, recruit and train workers, buy food supplies, control quality, keep records	Restaurants and other eating and drinking establishments; also in institutions, such as hospitals and schools
Fashion designer	Design coats, suits, dresses, hats, handbags, shoes, and other apparel; adapt original designs for the mass market	Own home or office studio; also in the design area of a clothing manufacturer
High school family and consumer sciences teacher	Teach high school students about food, child development, consumer issues, and clothing; plan lessons, give tests, maintain class discipline	High school classrooms and labs
Homemaker	Manage the home, including caring for children, preparing meals, shopping, budgeting, and decorating the home	In the home

next week. And it's managing time to get everything that needs to be accomplished done in twenty-four hours each day.

In Figure 10.1 are just a few examples of occupations in this cluster. Think about the job title, the work activities, and the work settings. These are just a few examples to help you get at the heart of the cluster. You don't need to read for details. Scan the entries to get a feel for the cluster as a whole.

Would you like a career in this cluster? Ask yourself the following questions:

- Do you like the sound of the occupations listed under "Who"? Would you feel good about having an identity like one of these?
- Would you enjoy doing activities like those described under "What"?

◆ Picture yourself working in the settings described under "Where." Would you be comfortable in these settings?

CAREER OUTLOOK

The employment outlook for the Family and Consumer Sciences Cluster is as follows.

FASTEST-GROWING JOBS

Among the fastest-growing jobs are these:

- Preschool teacher.
- Child-care worker (wage earning).
- Food service manager.

SLOWEST-GROWING JOBS

Among the slowest-growing jobs are these:

- Child-care worker (private household).
- Vocational family and consumer sciences teacher.
- Budget analyst.

SKILLS, TRAINING, AND EXPERIENCE

Listed below are some skills common to many of the occupations in the Family and Consumer Sciences Cluster:

- Work with precise measurements.
- Use arithmetic to measure and figure the amount of materials needed.
- Plan and carry out activities.
- Patiently deal with children and others needing help.
- Use arms, hands, eyes, and fingers with skill.

▼ Nutritionists must complete advanced training before employment.

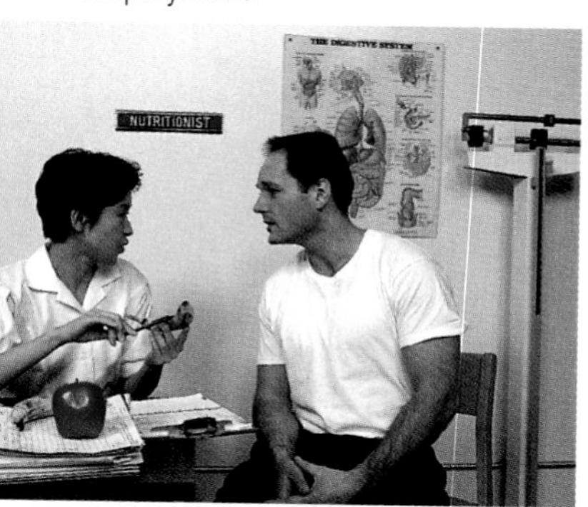

Of course, you need a different set of skills if you want to work in a day-care center than if you want to teach about nutrition to working mothers in a rural community. The best way to think about the skills you will need is to look at the different jobs and different categories and see what's required. Below are three categories of jobs in this cluster.

JOBS REQUIRING LESS-THAN-AVERAGE TRAINING AND EXPERIENCE

- Day-care center assistant.
- Household appliance installer.
- Food services assistant.

Attitude makes a difference

Only One Thing Seems to Count

Derrick Kulminski had only one thing on his mind every day: sports. He played football with the football team. He ran track with the track team.

He was good, but not great. His coaches could always count on him, though. He always showed up for practice. He was always lending spirit to the team.

Derrick thought he didn't like most of his teachers. He ignored many homework assignments. He told his parents he was too tired after team practice to study. Actually, sometimes it was true.

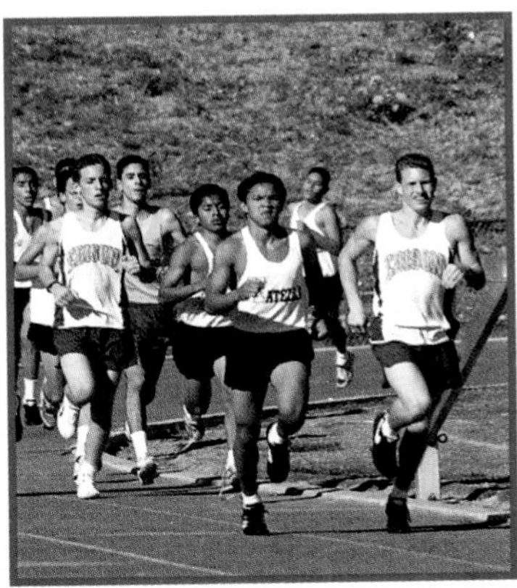

What Do YOU Think?

Is it possible to have a positive attitude toward one aspect of school and a negative attitude toward others? Is Derrick putting all his eggs in one basket? If you were going to advise Derrick what to do, what would you say?

JOBS REQUIRING AVERAGE TRAINING AND EXPERIENCE

- Budget consultant (family finance specialist).
- Sewing machine operator.
- Drapery and upholstery estimator.
- Preschool teacher.
- Color expert.
- Interior decorator.
- Dietetic technician.
- Food service supervisor.

JOBS REQUIRING MORE-THAN-AVERAGE TRAINING AND EXPERIENCE

- Dietitian.
- Nutritionist.
- Family and consumer sciences teacher.
- Consumer sciences writer.
- Food chemist.
- Fashion journalist.
- Researcher in child development and family relations.

See the Occupations Box for a list of some of the jobs in the Family and Consumer Sciences Cluster, along with their *DOT* numbers.

Career Decision-Making Activities

Usually if you follow your interests within any field you will find a way to get into it. The same is true with family and consumer sciences. In some cases you can just follow your nose—when you are interested in food. But don't specialize in eating. Start reading about the nutritional qualities of the food you eat. If you want to become a dietitian or a nutritionist, think about doing the following:

1. Check your television guide to make sure you see all the programs about nutrition and cooking. You will find many of these programs on your local public television station.
2. Make an appointment with the dietitian or nutritionist for your school cafeteria. Discuss what he or she does.
3. Take more courses in family and consumer sciences, psychology, biology, and the other sciences.
4. Try to get a summer job in an area of interest. A hospital's kitchen, a day-care center, and a clothing store are just a few possibilities. You could also try the local cooperative extension service of the U.S. Department of Agriculture.

Occupations in Family and Consumer Sciences

Here is a list of occupations mentioned in this chapter. Next to the name of each occupation is its *DOT* number. You can use the *DOT* number to locate further information about the occupation in your school or public library. For the broad occupational terms mentioned in this chapter, only one or two examples of that occupation are listed below. You can easily find more examples of the occupation in the *DOT*.

Budget Consultant (160.207-010)
Chef (313.131-014)
Child-care Worker (359.677-018)
Color Expert (141.051-010)
Consumer Advocate (see Home Economist)
County Home-Demonstration Agent (096.121-010)
Day-Care Assistant (see Child-care Worker)
Day-Care Specialist (355.674-010)
Dietetic Technician (077.121-010)
Dietitian (077.117-010)
Dietitian, Administrative (see Dietitian)
Dietitian, Clinical (077.127-014)
Dietitian, Research (077.061-010)
Drapery and Upholstery Estimator (298.387-010)
Dressmaker (782.684-058)
Extension Service Specialist (096.127-014)
Fashion Designer (142.061-018)
Fashion Journalist (131.067-010)
Food Chemist (022.261-014)
Food Journalist (131.067-010)
Food Service Supervisor (319.137-010)
Home Economist (096.121-014)
Home Management and Family Economics Journalist (131.067-010)
Homemaker (309.354-010)
Household Appliance Installer (827.661-010)
Interior Decorator (142.051-014)
Loan Officer (241.367-018)
Nursery School Teacher (092.227-018)
Nutritionist (096.121-014)
Researcher (054.067-014)
Restaurant and Food Service Manager (185.137-010)
Sewing Machine Operator (787.682-046)
Teacher, Home Economics (091.227-010)
Wedding Consultant (299.357-018)
Writer, Consumer Science (131.067-022)

Review and Enrichment

Summarizing the Chapter

Summarizing information is a critical thinking skill that will help you succeed in the world of work. Write a summary of what you learned in Chapter 10. Focus on the main points of the chapter. Then in a class discussion, compare your summary with the summaries done by your classmates. Can you improve your summary?

Improving Your Career Vocabulary

1. Learning to use new vocabulary terms will improve your communication skills, which are important in almost all areas of work. Write definitions for the terms listed below. Then for each term, write an original sentence about yourself in which you use the term correctly.
   - Family and Consumer Sciences Cluster
   - consumer
   - interrelate
   - family interactions
   - budget
   - advocate
   - dietitian
   - nutritionist
2. List the job families discussed in this chapter. Write a one-sentence description of each.

Finding the Facts

Finding exact information is a frequently used skill in many careers. Find the answers to the exercise below, and write the answers on a separate sheet of paper.

1. How many more men get a degree in family and consumer sciences today than did twenty-five years ago?
2. What is the purpose of extension services?
3. How might a consumer advocate get involved with a local restaurant?
4. What is the difference between a clinical dietitian and a nutritionist?
5. Name three skills needed by workers in the Family and Consumer Sciences Cluster.

Thinking for Yourself

To complete the exercise below you will need to use critical thinking and communication skills, which are skills valued by all employers. Write out your answers or be prepared to discuss them in class, depending on your teacher's instructions.

1. In your own words, describe someone who would enjoy working in a family and consumer sciences career.
2. Today, being a househusband—a man who stays home and does what was formerly done by a housewife—is not uncommon. Do you think this is a positive change or a negative one? Give your reasons.
3. Consumer advocates have helped make products safer and customers happier. In some cases the extra work required has forced manufacturers to raise prices. Has the cost been worth it? Explain.
4. Many of today's preschool children spend most of the day in the care of people other than their parents. Do you think this is a good idea? Why or why not?
5. Do you think a creative person would be happy in a family and consumer sciences career? Why or why not?

Practicing Your Basic Skills

Your career success depends greatly on your basic math and communication skills. Work hard at improving in the areas where you have trouble with the following exercises.

Math

1. Yolanda is a family finance specialist. She advises a family to spend 25 percent of its income on housing, 10 percent on food, and 10 percent on clothing. The following is a list of monthly incomes. Figure out the amounts of each that Yolanda would advise being spent on housing, food, and clothing.
   a. $1,100
   b. $2,750
   c. $5,692
   d. $986
2. Mark is a day-care worker. In the morning he started with sixteen children. At noon some par-

Review and Enrichment, continued

ents came and picked up their children. The first group to arrive picked up twice as many children as the second. At the end of the day Mark had only ten children left. How many were picked up by the first group at noon?

3. Alice needs to estimate how many yards of fabric she'll need to make curtains. The window measures 108 inches long by 84 inches high. Alice will need twice as much fabric as there is window width. The fabric is 36 inches wide. How many yards will she need altogether?

Reading and Writing

1. Obtain a copy of a proconsumer magazine, such as *Consumer Reports.* Read an article in the magazine. Then write a paragraph summarizing what was said.
2. Obtain a clothing pattern. Read through the instructions. Then write a step-by-step description of how the pattern should be made.
3. Pretend you write a food and nutrition column for your local newspaper. A teenager has written you a letter asking you what her daily nutritional needs are. Do some research. Then write to the teenager making your recommendations.
4. Pick one occupation mentioned in this chapter that you think would be interesting. Research the occupation and write a report. Use the career research checklist in Chapter 5 as a guide. Conclude your report with an explanation of your interest in that occupation based on your findings.

Speaking and Listening

1. Read some children's stories, choose one, and tell it to a child you know. Be careful to use words and ideas the child understands.
2. Listen to a children's TV show. What methods does the program use to hold children's attention? Do the actors or narrators speak differently than they would to adults?

Activities Working with Others

In almost all careers you must be able to get along well with other people to be successful. Work with your classmates to do the following activities. As you work together, pay attention to how well you get along. If necessary, work hard at improving your ability to do your part and to cooperate.

1. With a classmate, obtain three different brands of the same common item, such as toothpaste or breakfast cereal. Conduct your own product test. Do the items do what they promise to do? Why or why not? Compare sizes and prices. Which is the best buy?
2. Several authors and color specialists have developed color "systems" by which people can choose clothing in colors that flatter them the most. With a classmate, learn about one of these color systems. Then design a poster or display for the class illustrating the system.
3. Add the careers mentioned in this chapter to your database.

Decision Making and Problem Solving

You will be a big help to your employer if you can make decisions and solve problems. List all the possible ways of resolving the situations described below. Then pick the best alternative (possible choice), and tell why you chose it. If you need help, you might want to refer to Chapter 3.

1. You are a child-care worker in charge of a group of preschool children. One of the children is so shy she plays by herself all day. Her parents have asked you to help her learn to be more confident. What will you do?
2. You are a family relations consultant. A family has come to you for help. Both parents work. The two male children are in junior high and high school. The house is not large, but it has a big yard. The problem is the grandfather, who is no longer able to live alone. The parents don't want to put him in a nursing home. What will you recommend?

CHAPTER 11 ENVIRONMENTAL SCIENCES CAREERS

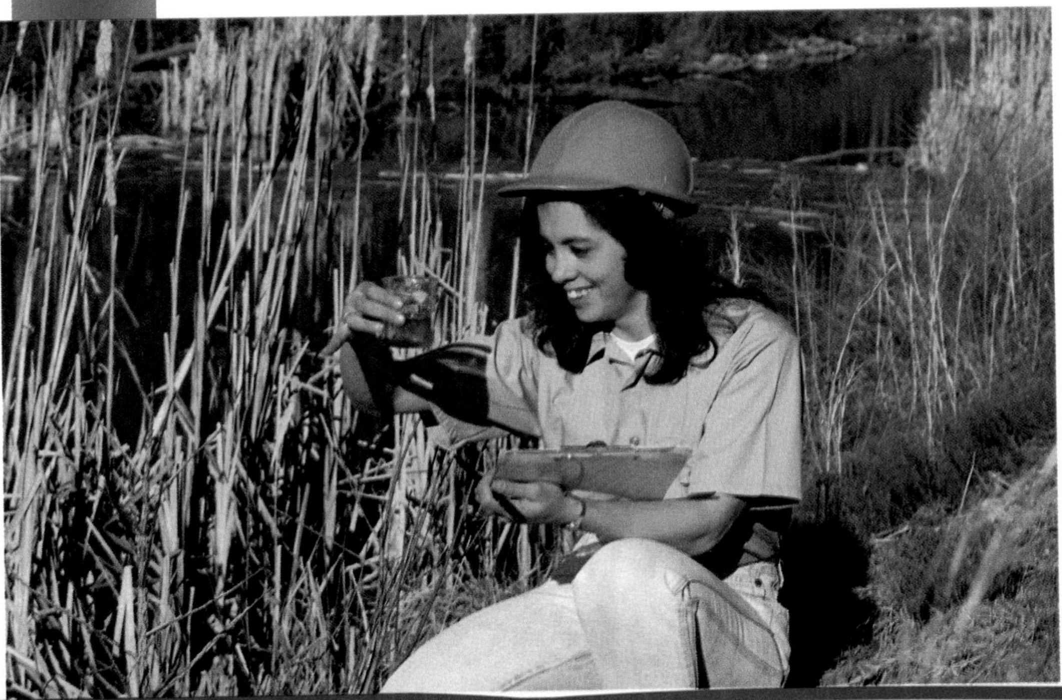

◆ Chapter Objectives ◆

After completing this chapter you will be able to do the following:

- ◆ Define the terms listed under "New Career Terms."
- ◆ List and describe the four job families in the Environmental Sciences Cluster.
- ◆ Identify several careers included in this cluster.
- ◆ Name several slow-growing and fast-growing jobs in this cluster.
- ◆ Explain what it would be like to work at a career in this cluster.
- ◆ Evaluate your own interest in this cluster.
- ◆ Identify skills common to many careers in this cluster.

◆ New Career Terms ◆

In this chapter you will learn the meanings of the following career terms:

- ✔ Environment
- ✔ Environmental scientist
- ✔ Pollution
- ✔ Environmental Sciences Cluster
- ✔ Organism
- ✔ Microorganism
- ✔ Bacteria
- ✔ Radiation

The **environment** *is everything around you. It's air, water, minerals, plants, animals, and insects. People involved with the environment are usually called* **environmental scientists.** *Environmental scientists help to protect the air, water, animals, plants, and other natural resources from pollution or its effects.* **Pollution** *usually means the introduction of harmful things into the environment.*

In 1989 a huge oil tanker, carrying millions of gallons of oil, went aground in Alaska. The waters and seashores for hundreds of miles became polluted with sticky, gooey crude oil. Many birds and fish died. This was a case of pollution on a grand scale.

Pollution also occurs at a smaller, but more steady, rate. Anything you buy that has already been made may be a cause of pollution. Just think of the steel that went into making something as common as a stapler. The steel had to be made somewhere. When making the steel, the steel company probably put smoke into the air. That pollutes the air.

Think about one of the biggest pollution problems everywhere—garbage. Just about everything we do creates some garbage. When you eat, you throw out leftovers. When you write on paper and throw it away, that's garbage, too. When restaurants clean out their trash baskets, that's garbage. You, as an average American, create more than five hundred pounds of garbage a year!

Somebody has to make sure that the garbage is removed to a safe location. Sometimes garbage has to be sprayed with chemicals so it doesn't harm the environment. And of course, there are always problems with sewage control (removing garbage from sewers and drains) and disposal.

In this chapter you will explore the **Environmental Sciences Cluster.** *This cluster is a group of occupations involved in the conservation and protection of our environment. It also involves occupations in which workers try to ensure the safe and healthful use of products made from our natural resources.*

environment
everything around us including air, water, minerals, plants, animals, and insects.

environmental scientist
a person involved in helping to protect our air, water, animals, plants, and other natural resources from pollution or its effects

pollution
the introduction of harmful elements (such as man-made waste) into the environ-ment.

Environmental Sciences Cluster
a group of occupations involved in the conservation and protection of our environment and also the safe and healthful use of products made from our natural resources.

WHAT WOULD IT BE LIKE?

Occupations within the Environmental Sciences Cluster almost all involve working outdoors at least part of the time. Some of them involve long hours with no contact with other humans. For example, the fire lookout in the forest may be alone most of the summer. A fire patroller may drive around most of the summer alone. A forest ecologist may study outdoors and in the laboratory alone.

Sometimes jobs in this cluster involve a higher degree of risk than jobs in other clusters. Anybody who works with sewage or sanitation problems may be exposed to bacteria that can cause disease.

There is something else to think about, too. If you become involved with sanitation and sewage work, you may have to adjust to disagreeable smells in your work environment. An industrial waste inspector, for example, inspects the way waste is disposed of throughout the city. These inspectors have to take samples of the waste from sewer systems and storm drains. Then they have to carry out tests on the samples.

Technicians in the environmental sciences often perform tests on samples taken by themselves or other workers.

Some jobs will be inside, though. Water purification chemists may have water samples brought to them in their laboratories. These chemists may never go outside.

Many types of inspectors in the Environmental Sciences Cluster have contact with other people on a daily basis. Many of the other inspecting jobs, however, are not people oriented.

Would you enjoy working in this cluster? Do some daydreaming as you "listen" to the following conversation. Several people who enjoy working in this cluster are talking about their jobs. As you listen to what they say, imagine yourself doing their jobs.

Industrial Waste Inspector: It's my job to make sure manufacturing companies dispose of their waste materials in the required ways. They're in business to make money, and the best waste disposal procedures are often costly. So the temptation to cut corners is always great. Most companies, though, are just as concerned as we are about keeping the environment clean. In ninety-nine cases out of a hundred I take my samples, do my tests in the lab, and give them an okay. My job is very rewarding because I know I'm helping everyone in this country—even the world—live a healthier life. I also like the job because I get to meet a lot of different people as I travel from one place to the next.

Microbiologist: I share your concern about healthy living, but I'm not too keen on meeting new people. I've always been kind of shy. That's why my job is perfect for me. I study **organisms** in contaminated and spoiled food to determine the source of the problem. Organisms are living things that can cause disease. My

Video Conferencing

"Let's have a meeting." When people working in different cities meet day after day in the work world, they do not need to get on a plane. Often, they can have a video conference. Through standard computers and telecommunications it is possible to transmit both voice and moving video pictures of individuals at the same time. Because of this technology, many people can actually have a "meeting" but not be in the same room or even the same country.

organism
an individual living thing, such as a person, animal, or plant.

findings often result in procedures that decrease the chances of future contamination, which helps everyone. And I do most of my work alone in the laboratory. For the most part it's me, my microscope, and my specimens, in a quiet lab where I can observe and analyze. I'm much better at observing and analyzing than I am at socializing.

Exterminator: I make my contribution to the environment in a different way. I get rid of undesirable rodents and insects. Talk about rewarding work—you should see the looks of appreciation and relief when I tell my customers there are no more rats in their attics. Or when I tell them the termites who were eating the foundations of their beautiful new homes have been eliminated. I suppose a lot of people wouldn't want my job, but I really like it. I like helping people, and I like solving problems.

Urban Planner: My job is certainly different from yours, but I think we're after the same goal—better living conditions for all people. You achieve this by eliminating some pretty undesirable pests. I achieve it by trying to foresee problems and recommend solutions before the problems ever exist. I spend most of my time in offices. But I also get out and about the community, inspecting new building sites and future developments. It's my job to see the "big picture" and do a lot of imagining—how much water will be needed, how many cars the highways will have to handle, and so on. It's a big job, but I love it. If you've ever lived in some of our older cities and then in some of the newer, planned communities, you know how far we've come in urban planning. And how far we've come in improving the quality of life in the cities of tomorrow.

What do you think? Do any of these careers sound appealing? Can you see yourself doing one of these jobs—or a similar one? Would you like to learn more about environmental sciences careers?

Career Decision-Making Activities

1. What is the condition of the environment in your area? Survey people in your neighborhood. Try to find people who have lived in other communities, especially in different regions of the country. Ask five people to rate your community's environment on a scale of 1 to 10, with 10 being the best and 1 the worst, in the following areas. Then give an overall rating. Rate these areas:
   - Air quality.
   - Water quality.
   - Insect and rodent control.
   - Garbage and waste removal.
   - Presence of waste dumps.

   Compile your ratings in class. What is the general opinion of your community's environment? Make a list of the most interesting comments made by the people you surveyed. Share the list with your class.
2. Visit the local water purification plant, and have the plant supervisor describe the water purification process. Notice the working conditions

and the activities in which workers are engaged. Would you enjoy work in this setting? Discuss your reactions with your classmates.

3. Have a class debate. Suppose that a manufacturer has proposed building a new plant in your community. The plant will employ one thousand people and create additional jobs in the community. Because unemployment is much higher than usual, this would be a big help to many people. The plant will, however, produce large quantities of waste materials. It will need to be built on the site of what is now the nicest park in your community. This location will create considerable traffic problems and require the expansion of your highway system. As members of the community council, you must decide how to vote on the matter of whether or not to allow the manufacturer to build the plant. Divide into two groups—for and against allowing the plant to be built. Develop your arguments, and then debate the issue.

JOB FAMILIES IN THE ENVIRONMENTAL SCIENCES CLUSTER

Within the cluster of environmental sciences jobs, there are four major job families. Looking at the different families will help you decide which kinds of careers in this cluster you might enjoy the most.

- **Disease prevention.** Any occupation involved with controlling organisms is part of the disease prevention job family. Most of the occupations within this job family require technical training.

  For example, some people study insects in order to find out how to prevent them from ruining crops. Harmful pests, such as fruit flies and moths, have destroyed billions of dollars' worth of crops and forests. The people who study insects are called entomologists.

  Recently, scientists have discovered ways to genetically reengineer (alter the genetic makeup of) certain crops so that they are more resistant to harmful pests. This field is sometimes called bioengineering.

  People who look into how food rots examine **microorganisms**—extremely small living things that have to be looked at under a microscope. These people are called food microbiologists.

  Other people in this field examine harmful **bacteria.** Bacteria are special types of microorganisms that have only one cell. Did you ever have a cut that got infected? The bacteria caused the infection. People who check for bacteria in water and food are called public health bacteriologists.

  Within the disease prevention family of jobs there are lots of inspectors. There are food and drug inspectors, who

microorganism
extremely small living things that are only visible under a microscope.

bacteria
special types of microorganisms that have only one cell.

Job Families in the Environmental Sciences Cluster

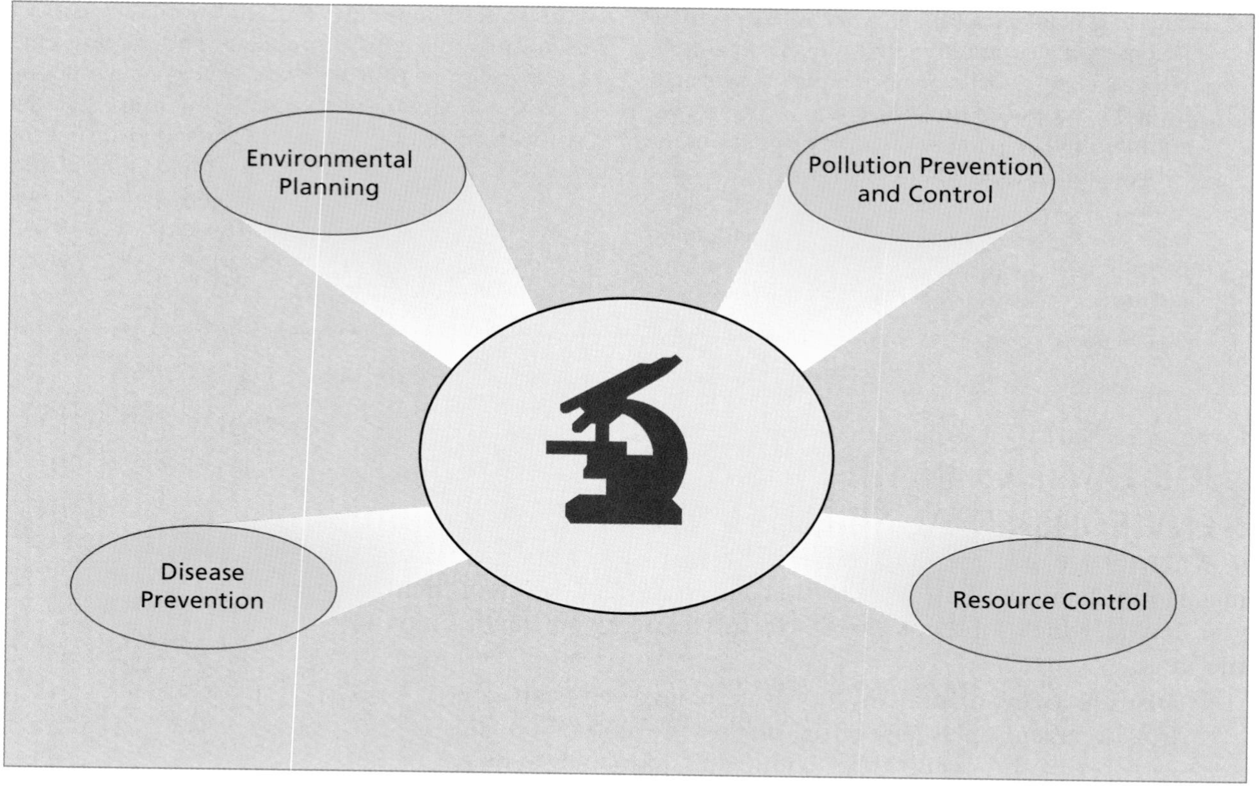

probably work for a city or a federal government agency. These people help to make sure that the food you eat is clean and pure. Sanitary inspectors go around to restaurants, hotels, and other public places to make sure that they are clean enough.

In many parts of the country bugs, rats, and mice are a problem. Exterminators help control these kinds of living things. Exterminators may use chemical poisons. Or they may use mechanical traps that have bait inside to attract the undesirable mice or rats.

- **Environmental planning.** As the United States grows in both population and its use of resources, there are increased demands on all natural resources. Workers in the environmental planning family of jobs look at the present environment and try to plan for future needs and uses.

Urban planners try to draw up plans for how land, buildings, and trees should be developed both in a city and outside of it. Urban planners have a big impact on the quality of life for people living in cities.

Sanitary engineers take charge of major garbage and trash disposal plants. They sometimes help design recycling systems. They also have to design sewage systems. Sanitary engineers often direct workers at places where sewage is turned into usable water.

- **Pollution prevention and control.** Pollution can affect water, the ground, and the air. Many individuals are involved in dealing with this problem. Workers in the pollution prevention and control job family try to control the spread of undesirable materials in the environment.

Within sewage plants themselves there are sewage disposal workers, who clean and adjust the equipment. There are sewage plant attendants, who make sure the pumps and other equipment are working.

Radiation (particles of energy) is another pollution problem. You can't see radiation. You can only measure it. Certain natural elements give off radiation. Radiation is also created by X-ray machines. Nuclear power plants that make electricity produce waste that gives off radiation.

Many individuals are hired as radiation monitors. Their job is to see if there is too much radiation. Too much radiation can cause cancer and other diseases.

Technicians measure the quality of the air we breathe in different parts of cities. They are often called air analysts. People doing the same job, involving water, are called water purification chemists.

▲ If you were a sanitary engineer, you might find a job at a waste water treatment facility.

radiation
particles of energy (given off by certain natural elements in nature; also produced by X-ray machines; and present in nuclear power plant waste).

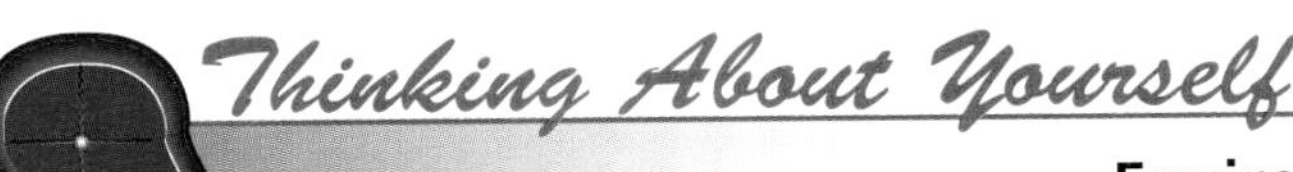

Environmental Sciences Careers

Many of the same interests are necessary for the Environmental Sciences Cluster as were necessary for the Agribusiness and Natural Resources Cluster. Look back to Chapter 6 to see how you felt about the careers in that cluster. Then read and think about the questions below. You might even want to write out your answers.

- ▲ Do you prefer being outdoors to being indoors?
- ▲ Have you taken courses in biology or zoology? Do you like conducting experiments involving plants or animals?
- ▲ Have you been a member of a scouting organization? Have you taken part in efforts to preserve forests, parks, and campgrounds?
- ▲ Can you recognize and identify different kinds of plants?
- ▲ Did you ever have a butterfly or bug collection?
- ▲ Are you concerned about pollution? Does it bother you to see smoke coming from automobile exhaust systems?

If you answered yes to many of these questions, there's a good chance you might enjoy an environmental sciences career.

- **Resource control.** In the resource control job family, people regulate the use and care of our natural resources. Some of the occupations in this job family overlap with similar occupations in the Agribusiness and Natural Resources Cluster.

  People who are interested in how animals are affected by changes in the environment are called zoologists. Those who study the same thing for fish and other animals that live in water are called aquatic biologists.

  Ecologists are people who study both plants and animals. They see how rainfall, temperature, and food differences affect the lives of plants and animals.

  There are lots of jobs within the resource control job family for people who want to work in forests. Fire is a severe problem. There are fire lookouts, fire patrollers, forest firefighters, and fire wardens to prevent and manage fires. Within forests there are also forest ecologists and forest engineers, who study forest conditions.

  People who specialize in studying wild animals are called wildlife biologists.

CAREER OUTLOOK

The employment outlook for environmental sciences careers is as follows.

FASTEST-GROWING JOBS

Among the fastest-growing jobs are these:

- Biological scientist.
- Bioengineer.
- Pest controller.
- Inspector.

SLOWEST-GROWING JOBS

Among the slowest-growing jobs are the following:

- Garbage collector.
- Forest and conservation workers.

AT THE HEART OF THE ENVIRONMENTAL SCIENCES CLUSTER

What makes the Environmental Sciences Cluster different from the other fourteen clusters? What would it really be like to work in this cluster? Let's try to get at the heart of the Environmental Sciences Cluster.

The essence of this cluster is a concern for the world in which we live. The goal for all work in this cluster is a clean, healthy and healthful, beautiful environment for all people.

An environmental sciences career means inspecting and checking up on others. It means asking strangers if you can watch them work, evaluate their equipment, look at their end products, and analyze their methods. It means being a watchdog—making sure that large companies, and small ones, follow rules established by the government for the good of our environment and all of our citizens. It means looking for wrongdoing, ignorance, and other things such as errors that can harm our environment.

The Environmental Sciences Cluster also involves science and technology. With science we develop the tests and materials that identify and combat undesirable elements in the environment. With the equipment and methods of technology we develop processes to rid our environment of harmful pollutants.

Figure 11.1 lists just a few examples of occupations from this cluster. Think about the job title, the work activities, and the work settings. You don't need to read for details. Scan the entries to get a feel for the cluster as a whole.

Would you like a career in this cluster? Ask yourself these questions:

- Do you like the sound of the occupations listed under "Who"? Would you feel good about having an identity like one of these?
- Would you enjoy doing activities like those described under "What"?
- Picture yourself working in the settings described under "Where." Would you be comfortable in these settings?

SKILLS, TRAINING, AND EXPERIENCE

Listed here are some skills common to many of the occupations in this cluster:

- Work outside for long periods in all kinds of weather while performing tasks that require physical strength and endurance.
- Use logic and scientific methods to study living things.
- Understand and use instructions that have numbers, diagrams, and chemical formulas.
- Recognize differences in size, form, shape, color, and texture.
- Make decisions using your own judgment.
- Do things that require you to be careful and accurate.

In the Environmental Sciences Cluster, jobs are available at many different skill levels. The following are three categories of jobs.

▼ Many occupations in this cluster require using sophisticated electronic equipment.

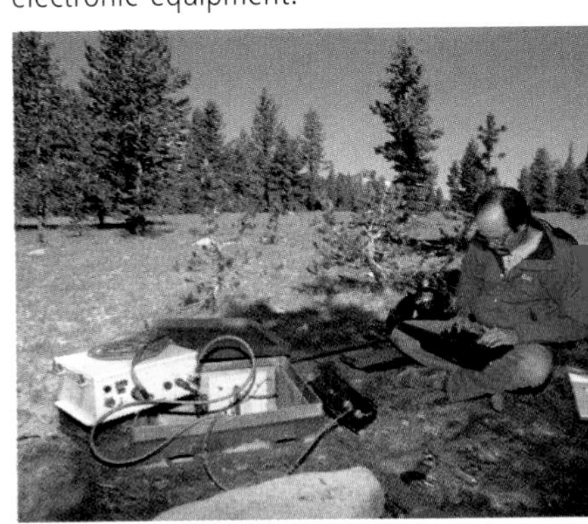

Figure 11.1 Sample Occupations in the Environmental Sciences Cluster

WHO You Would Be	WHAT You Would Do	WHERE You Would Do It
Environmental health inspector	Check cleanliness and safety of food and beverages; examine production plants, test for pollutants, collect samples	Variety of places; lots of work outside home base at manufacturing and processing sites; lots of travel for many
Zoologist	Study animals, experiment with live animals, dissect dead animals; may specialize in certain animal groups	Offices, labs, and classrooms; some field trips
Ecologist	Study the relationship between organisms and their environments and the effects of pollutants, rainfall, temperature, and altitude on organisms	Offices, labs, and classrooms; some field trips
Water and wastewater treatment plant operators	Operate and maintain pumps, control processes and equipment to remove solid materials from water, read and interpret meters and gauges, perform tests, keep records	Local treatment plants, both indoors and outdoors
Range manager	Manage, improve, and protect the more than one billion acres of rangeland (open land where livestock graze) in the United States; try to conserve the soil and vegetation for wildlife and recreation	Outdoors in all kinds of weather, frequently in remote areas

JOBS REQUIRING LESS-THAN-AVERAGE TRAINING AND EXPERIENCE

- Exterminator.
- Campground caretaker.
- Fire lookout.
- Fire patroller.
- Forest firefighter.
- Forester aide.
- Water tender.
- Sewage disposal worker.
- Sewage plant attendant.
- Sewage plant operator.

JOBS REQUIRING AVERAGE TRAINING AND EXPERIENCE

- Radiation monitor.
- Federal aid coordinator.
- Garbage collection supervisor.
- Fire warden.
- Industrial hygienist.
- Park naturalist.
- Park ranger.
- Food and drug inspector.
- Safety and sanitary inspector.
- Supervisor of water and sewer systems.

JOBS REQUIRING MORE-THAN-AVERAGE TRAINING AND EXPERIENCE

Many jobs in this cluster require more education and training than usual:

- Aquatic biologist.
- Entomologist.
- Forest engineer.
- Ecologist.
- Microbiologist.
- Public health bacteriologist.
- Water purification chemist.
- Sanitary engineer.
- Urban planner.
- Zoologist.
- Soils engineer.
- Bioengineer.

See the box on page 180 for a list of some of the jobs in the Environmental Sciences Cluster, along with their *DOT* numbers.

Career Decision-Making Activities

1. Take extra science courses, especially in biology and zoology. Ask if you can do extra-credit projects.
2. Check the television listings, especially public broadcast programs, and watch some shows about the environment. Did you see anyone working in an occupation described in this chapter? What was your reaction to that person and that person's activities?
3. Get a summer job working in a park or forest.

Occupations in Environmental Sciences

Here is a list of occupations mentioned in this chapter. Next to the name of each occupation is its *DOT* number. You can use the *DOT* number to locate further information about the occupation in your school or public library. For the broad occupational terms mentioned in this chapter, only one or two examples of that occupation are listed below. You can easily find more examples of the occupation in the *DOT.*

Air Analyst (012.261.010)
Aquatic Biologist (041.061-022)
Biologist (041.061-030)
Campground Caretaker (406.687-010)
Ecologist (see Environmental Scientist)
Entomologist (041.061-046)
Environmental Health Inspector (see Sanitarian)
Environmental Scientist (029.081-010)
Exterminator (389.684-010)
Federal Aid Coordinator (188.167-054)
Fire Lookout (452.367-010)
Fire Patroller (372.667-034)
Fire Warden (452.167-010)
Food and Drug Inspector (168.267-042)
Forest Ecologist (040.061-050)
Forest Engineer (005.167-018)
Forest Firefighter (452.687-014)
Forester Aide (452.364-010)
Garbage Collection Supervisor (909.137-014)
Industrial Hygienist (079.161-010)
Industrial Waste Inspector (168.267-054)
Landscape Architect (001.061-018)
Microbiologist (Food) (041.061-058)
Park Naturalist (049.127-010)
Park Ranger (169.167-042)
Public Health Bacteriologist (041.261-010)
Radiation Monitor (199.167-010)
Range Manager (040.061-046)
Safety and Sanitary Inspector (168.264-014)
Sanitarian (079.117-018)
Sanitary Engineer (005.061-030)
Sanitary Inspector (168.267-042)
Sewage Disposal Worker (955.687-010)
Sewage Plant Attendant (955.585-010)
Sewage Plant Operator (955.362-010)
Soils Engineer (024.161-010)
Supervisor, Water and Sewer Systems (184.167-014)
Urban Planner (199.167-014)
Water and Wastewater Treatment Plant Operator (954.382-010)
Water Purification Chemist (022.281-014)
Water Tender (599.685-122)
Wildlife Biologist (see Biologist)
Zoologist (041.061-090)

Review and Enrichment

Summarizing the Chapter

Summarizing information is a critical thinking skill that will help you succeed in the world of work. Write a summary of what you learned in Chapter 11. Focus on the main points of the chapter. Then in a class discussion, compare your summary with the summaries done by your classmates. Can you improve your summary?

Improving Your Career Vocabulary

1. Learning to use new vocabulary terms will improve your communication skills, which are important in almost all areas of work. Write definitions for the terms listed below. Then for each term, write an original sentence about yourself in which you use the term correctly.
   - environment
   - environmental scientist
   - pollution
   - Environmental Sciences Cluster
   - organism
   - microorganism
   - bacteria
   - radiation
2. List the job families discussed in this chapter. Write a one-sentence description of each.

Finding the Facts

Finding exact information is a frequently used skill in many careers. Find the answers to the exercise below, and write the answers on a separate sheet of paper.

1. What things do environmental scientists help protect?
2. How many pounds of garbage does each American create every year?
3. What danger is involved in sanitation jobs?
4. What do entomologists study?
5. What type of work do zoologists do?

Thinking for Yourself

To complete the exercise below you will need to use critical thinking and communication skills, which are skills valued by all employers. Write out your answers or be prepared to discuss them in class, depending on your teacher's instructions.

1. Of all the occupations in this chapter, which seems most interesting? Why?
2. What values are common among people interested in environmental sciences? Explain.
3. What type of environmental concern do you think would be important in a big city? In a national park? In the Great Plains?
4. Urban planners try to help cities avoid sprawling, uncontrolled growth. Does your area have an example of urban sprawl? Why do you think it should be avoided?
5. What environmental problems are common in your state? What do you think should be done about them?

Practicing Your Basic Skills

Your career success depends greatly on your basic math and communication skills. Work hard at improving in the areas where you have trouble with the following exercises.

Math

1. Every year the average American creates sixty pounds of plastic garbage. If this amounts to 30 percent of the weight of all the garbage the average person creates, how many pounds does he or she create altogether?
2. In the forest near Leslie's town, 129 acres were destroyed by fires. The next year 20 acres were reseeded and were growing, but insects destroyed 14 acres. The year after that, 20 percent of the acreage was damaged by a blizzard. How many acres remained healthy?
3. Convert the following fractions to decimals.
   a. 4¼
   b. 7⅜
   c. ⅔
   d. 201⅗
   e. 7/16
   f. 4/10

Reading and Writing

1. Research one of the following environmental sciences subjects. Then write a one-page report on it.
   a. orbital debris from the space program circling our planet

Review and Enrichment, continued

b. biodegradable plastics
c. the recycling of paper or aluminum
d. the Black Plague in Europe during the Middle Ages
e. the China Syndrome
f. the destruction of trees in Brazilian rain forests
g. fossil fuel resources in the United States
h. hog waste
i. water pollution

2. Read about the history of one of the national parks. Write a paragraph describing the park.
3. Obtain a copy of your community's environmental laws. Read them and write a brief description of each.
4. Pick at least one occupation mentioned in this chapter that you think would be interesting. Research the occupation thoroughly, and write a report. Use the career research checklist in Chapter 5 as a guide for your report. Conclude your report with an explanation of your interest in that occupation based on your findings.

Speaking and Listening

1. Give a one-minute speech to the class on an environmental problem. Research your subject, and be sure your facts are accurate.
2. Listen to your classmates' speeches. Take notes. Circle the three bits of information that surprised you the most.

Activities Working with Others

In almost all careers you must be able to get along well with other people to be successful. Work with your classmates to do the following activities. As you work together, pay attention to how well you get along. If necessary, work hard at improving your ability to do your part and to cooperate.

1. With a classmate, make a display showing some aspect of an environmental problem. Next to the display list recommendations as to what you think should be done about the problem.
2. Pretend your town is about to add two neighborhoods totaling a thousand homes and a giant shopping center. Where do you think the additions should be located? Consider natural areas that may be destroyed, increased traffic on existing roads, appearance, and so on. Working with a classmate and using a map of your town, work out the best locations for the additions. Give your reasons.
3. Add the careers mentioned in this chapter to your database.

Decision Making and Problem Solving

You will be a big help to your employer if you can make decisions and solve problems. List all the possible ways of resolving the situations described below. Then pick the best alternative (possible choice), and tell why you chose it. If you need help, you might want to refer to Chapter 3.

1. You are a garbage collection supervisor. One of the customers on the routes you supervise calls you complaining that your workers leave the garbage cans overturned and lying in the street. You talk to your workers. They deny it, saying that dogs turned the cans over and the customer is a troublemaker. You have to call the customer back, and you know you'll get an argument. What will you do?
2. You are a public health specialist. You learn that two people in your town have died of a contagious illness. The doctor who treated the people wants you to warn the town. The mayor, who is afraid of a panic, disagrees. He thinks people will leave the area and spread the disease further. What will you do?

CHAPTER 12

FINE ARTS AND HUMANITIES CAREERS

◆ Chapter Objectives ◆

After completing this chapter you will be able to do the following:

- ◆ Define the terms listed under "New Career Terms."
- ◆ List and describe the six job families in the Fine Arts and Humanities Cluster.
- ◆ Identify several careers included in this cluster.
- ◆ Name several slow-growing and fast-growing jobs in this cluster.
- ◆ Explain what it would be like to work at a career in this cluster.
- ◆ Evaluate your own interest in this cluster.
- ◆ Identify skills common to many careers in this cluster.

◆ New Career Terms ◆

In this chapter you will learn the meanings of the following career terms:

- ✔ Fine arts
- ✔ Humanities
- ✔ Fine Arts and Humanities Cluster
- ✔ Drive
- ✔ Curator
- ✔ Linguistics
- ✔ Theology

Little kids like to draw. Even preschoolers try to copy images. Cave dwellers carved and painted art images on the walls of caves. Let's face it: Many people like to express themselves by drawing and painting. They like to produce art images.

Another type of art expression is writing. Every book of fiction that you read has been written by someone who wants to present his or her view of our world. Writers also express themselves through their poems, plays, and essays. All these writers are artists.

Performing artists work in the theater. They dance in ballets. They play violins in an orchestra. They act out the plays written by writers.

All of us, at one time or another, enjoy the **fine arts** *and* **humanities.** *The fine arts are concerned mostly with the creation of beautiful objects. Symphonies, ballets, paintings, and sculptures are some examples of fine art creations. And all of us, at one time or another, have at least thought about being a great painter, or a writer, or a dancer, or an actor.*

The humanities involve the study of subjects having to do with people. Philosophy, psychology, and literature are examples.

In this chapter you will explore careers in the **Fine Arts and Humanities Cluster.** *These careers are grouped together because they all involve developing, promoting, and preserving the social and moral values of a culture and the value of art and beauty.*

fine arts
activities concerned with the creation of beautiful performances or objects such as symphonies, ballets, paintings, and sculptures.

humanities
the study of subjects having to do with people.

Fine Arts and Humanities Cluster
careers that are grouped together because they all involve developing, promoting, and preserving the social and moral values of a culture and the value of art and beauty.

drive
motivation, the ambition and energy to do something productive.

WHAT WOULD IT BE LIKE?

Almost all jobs within the Fine Arts and Humanities Cluster involve work indoors. Much of the work is creative. Artistic work also requires repetition. If you become a dancer or a musician, you have to repeat the same steps or phrases over and over and over until you get them right. Many jobs in this field require attention to detail.

Beauty is in the eye of the beholder. What that famous saying means is that some people may consider what an artist does ugly. Others may find it beautiful. You may like a particular musical piece. Your friends may think it is terrible. Does that mean you can become a painter because *somebody* will like your work? Not necessarily.

Even though beauty may be in the eye of the beholder, there are millions of people trying to sell their own ideas of beauty. Only a small portion or percentage of people who want to become painters actually can make a living at it.

Certainly people who want to go into the arts have to expect lots of competition. That means hard work for low pay. Your dream may be to become a superstar ballet dancer. Lots of other young dancers are dreaming the same way. You should dare to dream at all times. But you have to be realistic, too. In the Fine Arts and Humanities Cluster, success may have to mean just getting a job and keeping it.

To be successful in many occupations in this cluster, you have to have a lot of **drive.** Drive is motivation. It's what you have when

Attitude makes a difference

Never Giving Up

Heinz Heckman had an older sister. She was taking dance lessons and practiced in the hallway of their apartment. Heinz used to watch her from behind the door. He started imitating her moves.

One day Heinz's sister announced at the family dinner table that she was quitting dancing lessons. She didn't like them. Heinz asked if he could go in her place. Everybody at the table laughed. Heinz insisted.

Heinz found himself in a dance class with eleven girls. They giggled when he made mistakes.

His teacher was nice. She encouraged him and showed him pictures of famous male ballet dancers.

When Heinz was in high school he was afraid to tell people that he liked to dance. When he was in the gym working out with weights to become stronger, his friends asked him why he didn't go out for after-school sports. He didn't want to tell them it was because he was practicing dance.

Heinz is going to graduate from high school next year. He doesn't know what to do. He loves to dance but is still ashamed of it.

What Do YOU Think?

When the other dance students laughed at Heinz, he kept trying. What does this show about his attitude? Do you think that Heinz has drive (motivation to reach his goals)? What would you recommend that Heinz do?

---

you want something very badly, and are willing to give up many other things that you like in order to get what you want. You do so willingly, because you are driven to succeed in something that is important for you. You have to take the arts seriously if you are going to be a serious artist of any kind. Most famous fiction writers, painters, musicians, and dancers have been driven.

Would you enjoy working in this cluster? Do some daydreaming as you "listen" to the following conversation. Several people who enjoy working in the Fine Arts and Humanities Cluster are talking about their jobs. As you listen to what they say, imagine yourself doing their jobs.

Dancer: It hasn't been easy. In fact, it's been a real struggle. Working at lots of part-time jobs I couldn't stand, practicing every day, going to auditions. And the rejection. You hear "no" over and over. And then lots of times they don't even bother to tell you. They just ignore you. But it's all been worth it. I've got a part in a long-running musical play. I've made enough contacts and I've got enough experience that I should be able to keep working for

▼ An interest in school productions might lead to your pursuing further education in the fine arts.

Fine Arts and Humanities

Take your time reading and thinking about the questions below. You might even want to write out your answers.

- ▲ Do you enjoy writing creative stories for English class? Are you good at creating original characters or situations?
- ▲ Do you enjoy creating designs with clay?
- ▲ Do you like to draw?
- ▲ Do you like performing in front of an audience?
- ▲ Have you ever sung in a chorus? Did you enjoy this?
- ▲ Do you play any musical instruments? Do you like to practice?
- ▲ Have you taken ballet or tap dancing lessons? If so, would you like to continue dancing lessons?
- ▲ Have you been active in church or community goups? Do you enjoy volunteering your time for a common cause?
- ▲ Do you like to visit museums?
- ▲ Do you take lots of pictures with a camera? Have you ever submitted your photos to a contest?

If you answered yes to any of these questions, you might enjoy a career in fine arts and humanities.

some time. And when I'm working, it's wonderful. I've always loved dancing—any kind of dancing. I think the only time I'm truly happy is when I'm dancing. It's my whole life.

Writer: I can't walk across a room without falling down, but I like to think I can do with words what you can do with your body. Writing a perfect sentence is very difficult, you know. And just as you practice your dancing for hours on end, I write and rewrite every sentence, striving for that perfect combination of words. It's very frustrating, and it takes a great deal of dedication and commitment. In my opinion, this is all that separates the good writers from the bad. It's not some talent you're born with—it's hard work and being able to hang in there, doing it over and over. It sounds crazy, but I love it.

Interpreter: I like words, too. I've always been good with words. But I wasn't good at creating stories. I liked the spoken word. I liked hearing the different sounds of words. And learning languages came easily. Most of my friends would spend hours and hours studying for the French exam, and I'd just walk in and ace it. And as a result of this special talent, I've been able to travel all over the world as part of my job. It's exciting to meet people from different countries and learn how they live and think.

Illustrator: I'm not good with words in any language, and I can't dance. What I can do is draw. I can draw anything. I've been doing it since I was a kid. Just seemed to have a talent for it. And now I get paid for it—and paid pretty well. I have my own business. I draw illustrations for advertisers, book publishers, political groups—anybody who needs pictures.

What do you think? Do any of these careers sound appealing? Can you see yourself doing one of these jobs—or a similar job? Would you like to learn more about fine arts and humanities careers?

Career Decision-Making Activities

1. Give a dramatic reading in class. Find a piece of literature that you like. Choose one passage that you especially like. This passage should be short enough to be read aloud in about two minutes. Briefly tell your classmates anything they need to know to understand the passage, and then read it. Read the passage with feeling. Try to communicate to your classmates the emotions you feel as you read.
2. Create a work of art that represents one of your career goals at the present time. You could paint a realistic scene showing a work setting in which you hope to work someday. You could do a clay model that symbolizes an occupation that interests you. You could write a poem about your dream career. Present your work of art to the class. Tell the class whether creating this work has increased or decreased your interest in fine arts and humanities. Explain why.
3. Pick a place and period in world history that interests you. You can pick anything from ancient Rome to modern-day Central America. Do some research in your school or public library. Then write a two-page report on the art of that period and place. In your report you could write about topics such as the following:
   - Which art form (dance, visual art [fine art, paintings], literature, or sculpture) was most popular.
   - What features were unique to the art of that time and place.
   - Who the most well known artists were.
   - The importance or lack of importance of art in that culture.

   Bring books or pictures to class showing examples of the art from that period. When you've finished your report, ask yourself whether or not you would enjoy doing lots of research like this as your occupation.

JOB FAMILIES IN THE FINE ARTS AND HUMANITIES CLUSTER

Fine arts and humanities careers are divided into six job families. These are shown in the Job Cluster diagram that follows. Learning more about each family will help you decide which careers in this cluster you would enjoy most.

- **History and museums.** All the occupations that involve preserving and studying the records from the past are in the history and museums job family. Most of these jobs require much specialized study and training. If you really enjoy reading about the past, you might like a career in this job family.

Figure 12.1 Job Families in the Fine Arts and Humanities Cluster

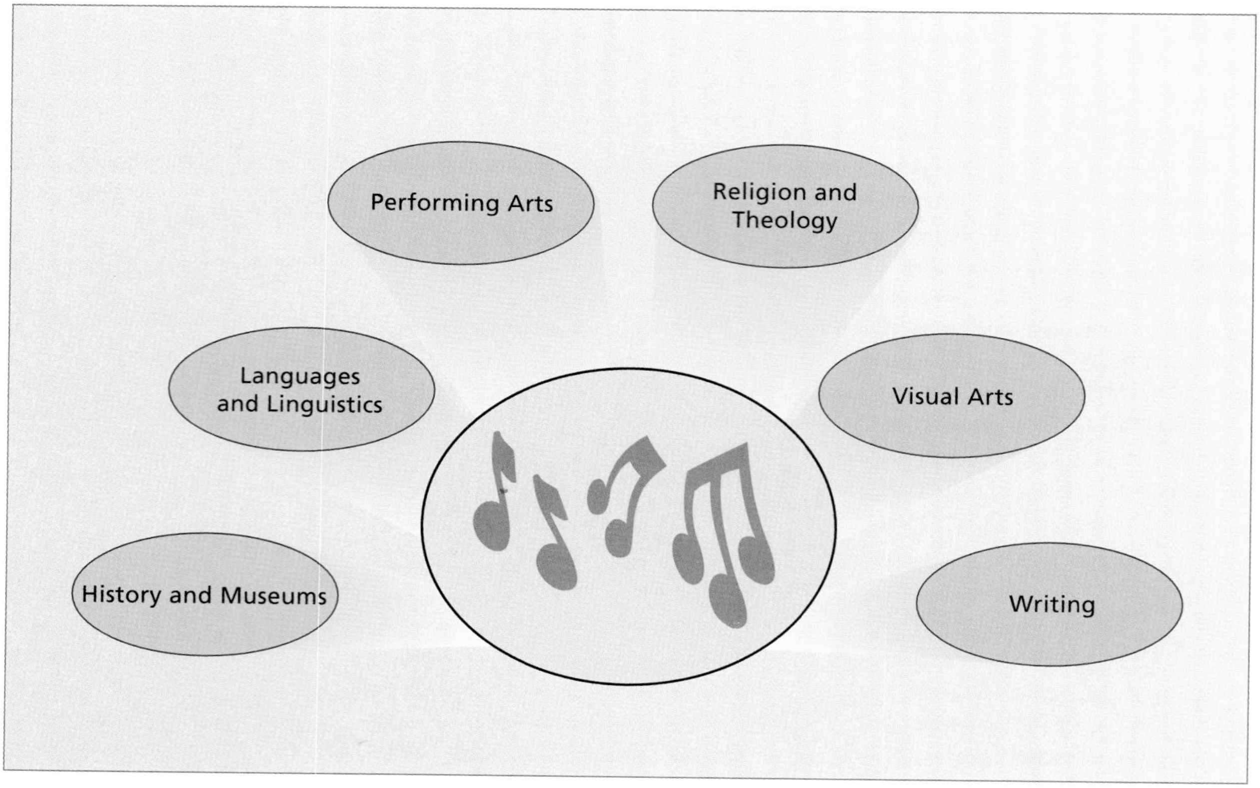

curator
a person who is in charge of the whole museum and its research.

For example, a **curator** of a museum is the person who is in charge of the whole museum and all of its research programs. The curator develops and organizes the collections within a museum. If you have ever been to a museum show, the curator was the person in charge of it. Museum curators usually have a clerical staff to help them.

Art appraisers are in this job family, also. They study artworks and make judgments about their value. Sometimes they do this for insurance companies. Then, if the art is stolen, the person who paid for the insurance will get the full value repaid from the insurance company.

- **Language and linguistics.** The language and linguistics job family includes occupations involved in studying written and oral languages. Many people enjoy studying the structure of speech. This kind of study is called **linguistics.** A linguist is a person who is skilled in foreign languages. Linguists might work for the government or for group tour providers.

linguistics
the structure of speech.

When linguists become good at understanding several languages, they may become translators. Translators use

◀ Museum curators can often share their love of history or art with their patrons.

their language skills to change a document from Spanish into English, for example.

People who do oral translation on the spot are called interpreters. Being an interpreter is difficult. You have to be able to think in two languages almost at the same time.

◆ **Performing arts.** Any job that has to do with producing music, theater, and dance is in the performing arts job family. The most visible people who do these things are dancers, actors, and vocalists. Vocalists sing classical, church, and opera music. They may also sing folk and popular music. In the music field there are conductors of orchestras and directors of choirs, who are called choral directors.

In theater work, dramatic coaches coach (train or teach) the actors. Property coordinators provide the stage properties (props) necessary for plays. On the stage there are stage electricians. They install electrical equipment and lights used for theater work. There are also stage managers, set designers, and stage directors.

In the world of dance there is a person called a choreographer. This person creates the dances for musical shows and ballet performances. He or she then teaches the steps and movements to the dancers. Sometimes this person does the same thing for dances in motion pictures and nightclubs.

▶ Today's illustrator must have strong computer skills as well as artistic ability.

theology
the study of different religions

- **Religion and theology.** Occupations involved in providing religious services are in the religion and theology family of jobs. The main job holders in this job family are clergy (church officials) in different religions. Some of the people in this job family have studied **theology** in college. Theology is the study of different religions.

  There are also missionaries in this job family. They carry religious messages to other lands and to people with other faiths. Missionaries often try to establish churches in other countries.
- **Visual arts.** Anybody involved in the production of art images is included in the visual arts job family. In the graphics and printing arts, there are layout artists, who design the way pictures, words, and photographs go together on a page. Pasteup artists work with the design and the pictures and words that will be used in a publication. Using a paper printout and a cutter or working at the computer, pasteup artists then arrange each element on a page in the exact location that it will later be printed.

  There are many types of artists. Some illustrate medical journals. Some design the covers of magazines and books. Some draw clothes for newspaper advertisements. These are just a few examples.

  Of course, painters are also within the visual arts. This is one of the most difficult ways to make a living. Very few painters make a living from their painting. Here we're not talking about the kind of painter who paints your house. We're talking about the painters who paint the works of art in your local art museums and galleries.

Within the field of photography there are commercial photographers, who take pictures for businesses. There are also portrait photographers. They take pictures of people. Increasingly, there are digital photographers who use the latest digital cameras. They can easily transmit their pictures to others over the Internet.

- **Writing.** The writing job family includes the occupations involved in artistic communication through written forms. When an artist wishes to communicate in a written form, he or she is called a writer. Writers who write plays are called playwrights. Those who write poems are called poets.

  There are also technical writers. Have you ever read an instruction manual for a new computer game? A technical writer probably wrote it.

CAREER OUTLOOK

The employment outlook for fine arts and humanities careers is as follows.

Careers for Tomorrow

COMPUTER ARTISTS

The world is filled with computers. We all know that now. In the future computers will be used more and more to create art. Many things that were drawn by artists in the past are now drawn by computer artists. This field is sometimes called computer graphics.

On the computer, the computer artist can instantly see different possibilities. He or she can also create a three-dimensional image almost as good as a real one.

Many computer artists are using their talents to design fashions, cars, and new product images. Most book illustrations are now done by computer artists. In fact, much of the art in this book was created on the computer.

What can you do to become a computer artist? First, you need to finish high school and then take some commercial art training at a special art school or community college.

If you have some natural artistic talent and you are not afraid of computers, this could be the job for you. For more information, write the National Computer Graphics Association, P.O. Box 660, Dunkirk, MD 20754-0660.

WORKING ONLINE

Web Page Designers

Just as there are layout artists who put pictures, words, and photographs together to design a printed page, there are designers who develop the look and feel of "pages" on the Internet. These are often called Web page designers, because the part of the Internet they use is called the World Wide Web.

The same talents needed for normal page layout are needed for Web page design. Obviously, though, more experience is required in the use of computers.

In addition, any type of design or layout (not just those for Web pages) can be transmitted online from one location in the world to another. Layout artists can immediately show their clients what they are doing over the Internet. Their clients can tell them if it is right.

FASTEST-GROWING JOBS

Among the fastest-growing jobs are these:

- Producer, director, and actor.
- Commercial artist.
- Designer.
- Web page designer.

SLOWEST-GROWING JOBS

Among the slowest-growing jobs are these:

- Musician.
- Photographer.

AT THE HEART OF THE FINE ARTS AND HUMANITIES CLUSTER

What makes the Fine Arts and Humanities Cluster different from the other fourteen clusters you'll be exploring? What would it really be like to work in this cluster? Let's try to get at the heart of the Fine Arts and Humanities Cluster.

The essence of this cluster is beauty. It can be the beauty of a colorful painting, or an inspirational sculpture in the park. It can be the beauty of the opening page you first see when you check out a company's Internet site. It can be the beauty of the free-flowing movements of a graceful dancer, or an emotional scene between two actors that brings tears to the eyes of the audience. It can be the rhymes and rhythm of a poem, or the breathtaking landscape of a photograph.

▼ A nature photographer uses many "tricks" to keep nature beautiful.

This cluster is not about the practical, business side of life. It's not about the things that have to be done today. Instead, it's about the beautiful things that have no practical value. It's about beauty for beauty's sake. It's about beauty that lasts forever.

The people who work in this cluster are especially sensitive to beauty. Many can create it. They create beauty with their spoken and written words; with their brush strokes as they blend color, line, and texture; and with the movements and expressions of their bodies as they glide across a dance floor or stage.

Others do not create beauty, but are especially sensitive to it. They look for and judge the beauty created by artists. Then they present that beauty in museums and theaters for millions of people to see and appreciate.

Listed in Figure 12.2 are just a few examples of occupations from this cluster. Think about the job title, the work activities, and the work settings. These are just examples to help you get at the heart of this cluster. You don't need to read for details. Scan the entries to get a feel for the cluster as a whole.

Figure 12.2 Sample Occupations in Fine Arts and Humanities Cluster

WHO You Would Be	WHAT You Would Do	WHERE You Would Do It
Graphic designer	Design displays and logos	Art studio in a company office or at home
Cartoonist	Draw cartoons for newspapers and comic books	Home art studio or newspaper office
Medical illustrator	Make sketches and draw final illustrations of parts of the body	Home studio or book publishing office
Choreographer	Interpret an idea or story or express rhythm and sound with body movements	Theaters, dance studios
Dancer	Perform dances in ballets, stage musicals, movies, variety acts	Theaters, auditoriums, nightclubs; changing locations
Archivist	Analyze, catalog, and store items of lasting value, such as historical documents	Library or museum
Curator	Search for, acquire, and exhibit artworks such as paintings and sculptures	Museums and some travel to locations of artworks
Actor	Entertain audiences using facial and verbal expressions to bring characters to life	Theaters, television studios, auditoriums
Producer	Select plays or scripts, hire directors and actors, and coordinate all aspects of theatrical production	Theater, television, and movie offices; travel to locations of production

Do you think you would like a career in this cluster? Ask yourself the following questions:

- Do you like the sound of the occupations listed under "Who"? Would you feel good about having an identity like one of these?
- Would you enjoy doing activities like those described under "What"?
- Try to picture yourself working in settings such as those described under "Where." Would you be comfortable in these settings?

SKILLS, TRAINING, AND EXPERIENCE

Listed here are some skills common to many of the careers in this cluster:

- Make decisions based on personal judgment.
- Spend long hours developing and perfecting your talent, and practice daily.
- Influence other people's opinions through words.
- Visualize final products from rough sketches.
- Perform in front of an audience with poise and self-confidence.
- Select tools, materials, and methods that are best for each purpose.

Many different skill levels are needed for various jobs in this cluster. The following are three categories of jobs.

JOBS REQUIRING LESS-THAN-AVERAGE TRAINING AND EXPERIENCE

- Darkroom technician.
- Model.
- Photo engraver.
- Stagehand.

JOBS REQUIRING AVERAGE TRAINING AND EXPERIENCE

- Camera operator.
- Cartoonist.
- Actor.
- Commercial artist.
- Singer.
- Dancer.
- Photographer.

JOBS REQUIRING MORE-THAN-AVERAGE TRAINING AND EXPERIENCE

- Art director.
- Literary and theatrical agent.
- Clergy member.
- Composer.
- Fiction writer.
- Musician.
- Scriptwriter.
- Technical writer.

- Production designer.
- Translator or interpreter.

See the occupations diagram on the next page for a list of some of the jobs in the Fine Arts and Humanities Cluster, along with their *DOT* numbers.

Career Decision-Making Activities

1. Take school courses in drawing, music, drama, literature, speech, and art history. Also sign up for after-school activities such as chorus, a school or community play, the school band or orchestra, or the school newspaper.
2. Check your local television guide for plays. Watch them and take notes on them. You can also rent videos of famous musicals, possibly from your local library. Discuss the plays and musicals with your parents and friends.
3. Buy or borrow a camera. Take pictures. Decide which ones are good, and why. Submit your best photos to local contests.
4. Visit as many galleries and museums in your city as possible. Go on the guided tours. Do you enjoy looking at art?
5. Compose your own dance routine for an imaginary show.

Occupations in Fine Arts and Humanities

Here is a list of occupations mentioned in this chapter. Next to the name of each occupation is its *DOT* number. You can use the *DOT* number to locate further information about the occupation in your school or public library. For the broad occupational terms mentioned in this chapter, only one or two examples of that occupation are listed below. You can easily find more examples of the occupation in the *DOT*.

Actor (150.047-010)
Archivist (101.167-010)
Art Appraiser (102.167-010)
Art Director, Motion Pictures (142.031-010)
Art Director, Retail Trade (141.031-018)
Ballet Dancer (151.047-010)
Camera Operator, Animation (143.382-010)
Camera Operator, Special Effects (143.062-022)
Cartoonist (141.081-010)
Choral Director (152.047-010)
Choreographer (151.027-010)
Clergy Member (120.007-010)
Commercial Artist (see Graphic Designer)
Commercial Photographer (143.062-030)
Composer (152.067-014)
Computer Artist (141.061-018)
Conductor, Orchestra (152.047-014)
Curator (102.017-010)
Dancer (151.047-010)
Darkroom Technician (976.681-010)
Dramatic Coach (150.027-010)
Fiction Writer (131.067-046)
Graphic Designer (141.061-018)
Grip (962.684-014)
Illustrator (141.061-022)
Interpreter (137.267-010)
Layout Artist (141.061-018)
Linguist (059.067-014)
Literary and Theatrical Agent (191.117-034)
Medical Illustrator (141.061-026)
Missionary (120.007-010)
Model, Artist's (961.667-010)
Model, Photographer's (961.367-010)
Musician, Instrumental (152.041-010)
Painter (144.061-010)
Pasteup Artist (979.381-018)
Photo Engraver (971.381-022)
Photographer, Motion Picture (143.062-022)
Photographer, Still (143.062-030)
Playwright (131.067-038)
Poet (131.067-042)
Portrait Photographer (143.062-030)
Producer, Motion Picture (187.167-174)
Producer, Radio and TV (159.117-010)
Production Designer (see Set Designer)
Property Coordinator (962.167-018)
Screenwriter (131.087-018)
Scriptwriter (see Screenwriter)
Set Designer (142.061-050)
Singer (152.047-022)
Stage Director (150.067-010)
Stage Electrician (962.362-014)
Stage Manager (962.167-014)
Stagehand (see Grip)
Technical Writer (131.267-026)
Translator (137.267-018)
Vocalist (152.047-022)
Writer, Copy (132.067-014)
Writer, Literary (131.067-046)

Review and Enrichment

Summarizing the Chapter

Summarizing information is a critical thinking skill that will help you succeed in the world of work. Write a summary of what you learned in Chapter 12. Focus on the main points of the chapter. Then in a class discussion, compare your summary with the summaries done by your classmates. Can you improve your summary?

Improving Your Career Vocabulary

1. Learning to use new vocabulary terms will improve your communication skills, which are important in almost all areas of work. Write definitions for the terms listed below. Then for each term, write an original sentence about yourself in which you use the term correctly.
   - fine arts
   - humanities
   - Fine Arts and Humanities Cluster
   - drive
   - curator
   - linguistics
   - theology
2. List the job families in the Fine Arts and Humanities Cluster. Write a one-sentence description of each.

Finding the Facts

Finding exact information is a frequently used skill in many careers. Find the answers to the exercise below, and write the answers on a separate sheet of paper.

1. For which job would you do oral translations on the spot?
2. Name three jobs in the performing arts.
3. Define theology.
4. What kind of work does a technical writer do?
5. Name the fastest-growing jobs in the Fine Arts and Humanities Cluster.

Thinking for Yourself

To complete the exercise below you will need to use critical thinking and communication skills, which are skills valued by all employers. Write out your answers or be prepared to discuss them in class, depending on your teacher's instructions.

1. People in the arts, especially those who are performers, need confidence. Why do you think this is so?
2. Think of a painting, book, or piece of music you like. Describe in your own words why you like it.
3. Technology has affected the humanities and fine arts as it has other areas of our lives. Drawings can now be made using computers. Do you think this is a good change or a bad one? Explain.
4. Many people think that artists and writers get their ideas quickly and easily. Much of the job is often hard work. Some of it, like any job, is boring. Knowing this, would you do anything special to prepare yourself for an artist's career?

Practicing Your Basic Skills

Your career success depends greatly on your basic math and communication skills. Work hard at improving in the areas where you have trouble with the following exercises.

Math

1. Nirad took a job to paint a mural for his community's city hall. It was agreed he would do the job for $5,000. Nirad wanted the mural to be good, so he put in a lot of hours. In October he worked 40 hours a week for 2 weeks. In November he worked 35 hours the first week, 23 the second, and 55 the third. In December he worked 61 hours the first week and 70 the second. If Nirad had been paid by the hour, how much per hour would he have earned?
2. Greta was an assistant minister and was in charge of buying choir robes for the church. The robes cost $76 each. They needed 12 robes for women and 8 for men. There was enough in the choir fund to cover one-third of the cost. Donations would cover one-fourth. How much money would Greta still need?
3. Tony worked for a museum. He was being sent to Japan to buy art objects and wanted to take $2,500 with him for travel expenses. A friend advised him to exchange his money for yen (Japanese currency). Tony learned that on that

Review and Enrichment, continued

day, $1 was worth 144 yen. How many yen would Tony take with him?

Reading and Writing

1. Obtain a book from the library on learning a foreign language. Look over the book, and learn several phrases.
2. Music, too, has a language—a language of symbols. Get a book on reading music from the library, or ask a music teacher to explain what the notes and other symbols mean.
3. Write a one- or two-minute skit for three actors about one of the following:
   a. a robbery of an interpreter who works at the United Nations
   b. a missionary who discovers a lost city in the Brazilian jungle
   c. an art appraiser who discovers his clients have been sold a worthless painting
4. Pick at least one occupation mentioned in this chapter that you think would be interesting. Research the occupation thoroughly, and write a report. Use the career research checklist in Chapter 5 as a guide for your report. Conclude your report with an explanation of your interest in that occupation based on your findings.

Speaking and Listening

1. Using one of the skits written by you or another classmate in the "Reading and Writing" section, memorize one of the actor's parts. Practice saying the lines so they sound natural. Perform the skit for the class.
2. Listen to the skits performed by your classmates. Note which performers seemed most "real." Why was this so?

Activities Working with Others

In almost all careers you must be able to get along well with other people to be successful. Work with your classmates to do the following activities. As you work together, pay attention to how well you get along. If necessary, work hard at improving your ability to do your part and to cooperate.

1. Choose one of the following to do with a classmate. Don't choose an activity you already know how to do or do frequently. Pick one that interests you but that you haven't already explored.
   a. Learn the words and music to a song that you will perform for the class.
   b. Design and make a poster on one of the career families.
   c. Visit a local museum or historical society, and pretend you have been asked to create a display. Make a drawing of the display and label it.
   d. Write a list of instructions for an appliance or tool telling how to use it.
   e. Use a camera to take pictures for a photo "essay" on how it feels to be a young person preparing for the world of work.
2. As a class, write a short story. One person should start by writing a sentence and then passing it on to the next person. As you write you must try to extend what the people before you have done so the story makes sense.
3. Add the careers mentioned in this chapter to your database.

Decision Making and Problem Solving

You will be a big help to your employer if you can make decisions and solve problems. List all the possible ways of resolving the situations described below. Then pick the best alternative (possible choice), and tell why you chose it. If you need help, you might want to refer to Chapter 3.

1. You have been asked to paint a picture that will hang in the school library. You are interested in the subject and think the job will be a good experience and will show others what you can do. However, the principal doesn't like your first sketches. She wants something different. You feel that as an artist, you have the right to paint what you believe in. What will you do?
2. You are the director of a ballet company. You are considering two performers for the lead in a new ballet. Performer A is very talented and has a chance to be a top ballerina. However, she is hard to work with and causes trouble with the other dancers. Performer B is less talented but does everything just as she is told. Your time is limited, and the ballet must be ready in a few weeks. What will you do?

CHAPTER 13

HEALTH AND MEDICAL CAREERS

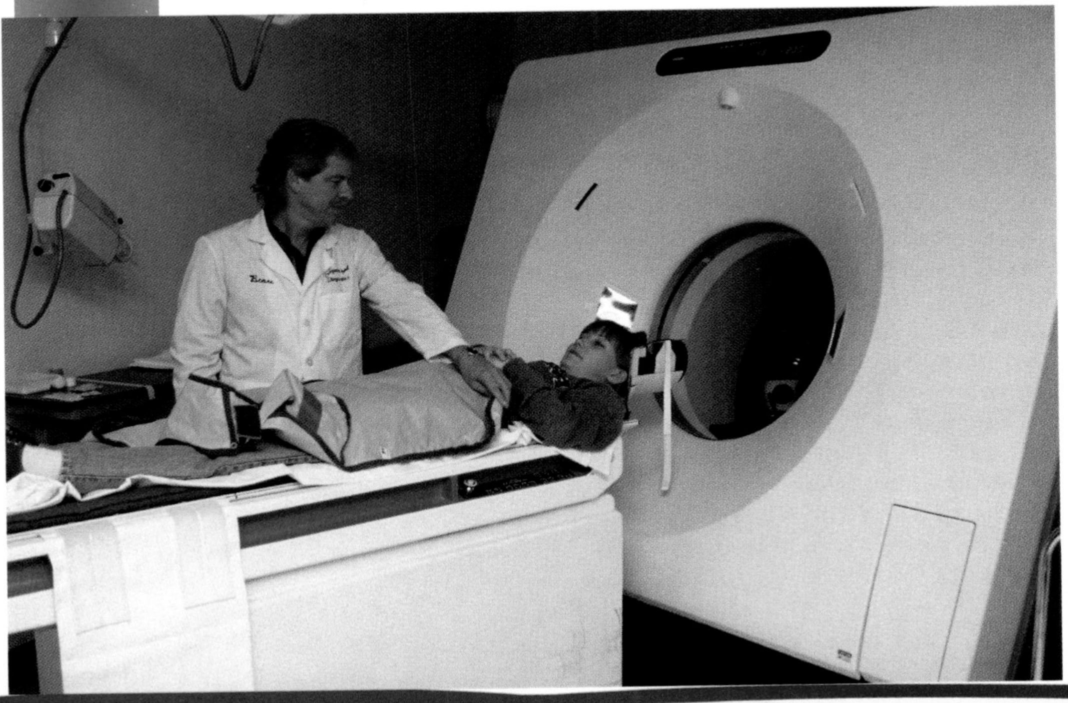

◆ Chapter Objectives ◆

After completing this chapter you will be able to do the following:

- ◆ Define the terms listed under "New Career Terms."
- ◆ List and describe the ten job families in the Health and Medical Cluster.
- ◆ Identify several careers included in this cluster.
- ◆ Name several slow-growing and fast-growing jobs in this cluster.
- ◆ Explain what it would be like to work at a career in this cluster.
- ◆ Evaluate your own interest in this cluster.
- ◆ Identify skills common to many careers in this cluster.

◆ New Career Terms ◆

In this chapter you will learn the meanings of the following career terms:

- ✔ Health and Medical Cluster
- ✔ Pharmacy
- ✔ Profession
- ✔ Professional

Millions of people work at taking care of the health of Americans. The health care industry in America is a giant business. It includes everything from physicians (doctors) with many years of training to medical clerks just out of high school. There are even high school students working as nurse's aides, orderlies, or volunteers in hospitals. The **Health and Medical Cluster** *is the group of all occupations involved in providing the services necessary to meet people's physical and mental health needs.*

The health care field employs over seven million people and is growing fast. About 14 percent of all yearly economic activity in the United States involves health and medical care spending.

Let's try to get a better idea of how large the health care industry is. Think about how many different health care professionals you would see if you had a bicycle accident and couldn't move your arm.

First, you might be picked up by an ambulance driver and cared for on the way to the hospital by an emergency medical technician. At the hospital you would be admitted by an admitting clerk and taken to see a physician.

The physician would want to check for broken bones, so he or she would call for a radiologic technician to take X-ray images. An orthopedist (a doctor who specializes in bones) might be brought in to look at your arm if it were broken.

Lab technicians would take samples of your blood to examine them. A registered nurse would check your blood pressure and temperature. If your arm required an operation, you would need a surgeon, an anesthesiologist (the doctor who puts you to sleep), and an assistant surgeon or nurse.

After your operation you might need a physical therapist to help you use and exercise your arm again. During your stay in the hospital you would have dozens of hospital orderlies and nurse's aides to help you with meals and clean your room. Other people you wouldn't see would be planning your meals and taking care of your records. There would be dozens of health care workers around you, all because you went too fast on your bicycle.

Health and Medical Cluster the group of all occupations involved in providing the services necessary to meet people's physical and mental health needs.

▶ We depend on Health and Medical Cluster workers every day.

Attitude makes a difference

Dreaming about Nursing

Sue Chin didn't move to the United States until she was twelve. She didn't speak English, and it was difficult for her to catch up with the other students. She had the most trouble with her English classes and with learning science in the English language. In her native country she had been a straight A student in science. She had dreamed of being a nurse someday.

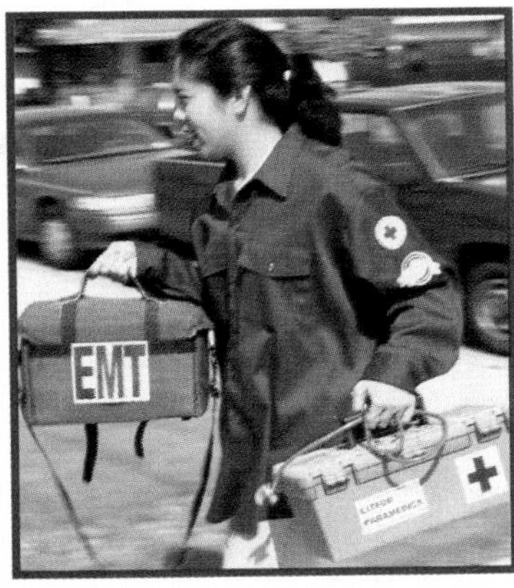

Her grades were poor in science and math all through junior high school. She tried not to be discouraged. She kept a positive attitude and got special help through her school counselor in both subjects. Her grades improved in high school. She took a first-aid course and started watching all the medical programs about health that she could find on cable TV. She also started regularly reading a magazine on health.

One day on her way to school, Sue saw an automobile accident. One person was hurt, and the other three involved were too upset to do anything. Sue was the only one who stayed calm. She called an ambulance and used what she had learned in her first-aid course to keep the injured person safe.

When the ambulance got there, Sue stepped back and let the emergency medical technicians (EMTs) take over. She watched them carefully. They worked quickly and calmly, and Sue later found out they probably saved the person's life.

Sue never got As in math and science, but she kept trying. She kept up her first-aid and other studies. She kept a positive attitude, and she believed in herself. When she graduated, Sue completed a training program to be an EMT, which she finished in one year. She is now an ambulance EMT and helps accident victims every day. She is still taking extra training courses and is working hard to advance to the paramedic level, which is the most highly trained level.

What Do YOU Think?

What would you have done if you had seen the same automobile accident that Sue saw? Would you like to be an ambulance emergency medical technician? Why or why not?

WHAT WOULD IT BE LIKE?

In health care you could choose from many different work settings. Most of the health and medical jobs are inside hospitals. Many others are in clinics, nursing homes, doctors' offices, and laboratories. Some are in schools, day-care centers, and private homes. Almost all jobs are indoors.

There are many different kinds of jobs in the health and medical industry. You could perform surgery. You could oversee all the activities at a hospital. You could give medications to patients. Most jobs involve caring for and treating people who are sick or injured. You would probably have to deal with extreme illnesses, serious injuries, and even death. Some jobs involve research about illnesses. Some involve preventing people from getting sick or injured. Many other jobs are available for those who want to provide support services for physicians and nurses.

Many careers in the Health and Medical Cluster require special training beyond high school. Some require two-year programs and some, four-year college programs. To become a physician requires many more years of even more advanced study.

Would you enjoy working in this cluster? Do some daydreaming as you "listen" to the following conversation. Several people who enjoy working in the Health and Medical Cluster are talking about their jobs. As you listen to what they say, imagine yourself doing their jobs.

Nurse: I always knew I'd be a nurse. No one else in the family had been in nursing or medicine, but I knew I was going to be a nurse. I couldn't imagine a better job. Helping people who really need it. Even the little things like bringing them drinks, fluffing their pillows, and helping them turn over in the bed. The job has been a lot tougher than I imagined. And dealing with the pain and suffering of others takes a lot out of you. I used to cry a lot. But I love people, and I love making them comfortable and happy. They need me. Sometimes their faces just light up when I walk in the room.

Dental Hygienist: I get a lot of the same satisfaction as you do from my job. Basically, I'm helping people. I clean their teeth and take X rays. I don't have to deal with life-threatening situations like you do in the hospital, which is good, because I'm not sure I could handle that kind of pressure. But my patients do need help, and they are often a little scared. It makes me feel good about myself when I can reassure them and help them relax.

Emergency Medical Technician: See, I'm just the opposite. I like excitement, and I like testing myself under pressure. Of course I hate seeing anyone seriously injured or ill, but it happens. People have car accidents and heart attacks, and they always will. And as long as they do, someone will have to try to save their lives as best he or she can. And that's where I come in. I'm often the first medical person on the scene. I'm in constant contact with the dispatcher at the hospital. Everything happens so fast. You never know what you'll need to do next. And before you know it, the doctor is taking over, and you're on to the next case. It's exciting and rewarding—to know that you're helping save lives. I only wish I could do more.

General Practitioner: I wouldn't describe my job as exciting, but it is rewarding. I'm one of the most respected people in our com-

The Doctor May Be Miles Away

Because of the possibility of connecting to the Internet via a wireless or cellular phone, emergency medical technicians (EMTs) arriving at the scene of an accident can now work with a physician in a hospital miles away.

The EMT connects a portable body-monitoring device to the accident victim. The EMT then connects to the Internet or directly to the hospital via a cell phone. The accident victim's vital signs (pulse rate, body temperature, and so on) can be monitored by a doctor. The doctor can talk to the EMT using a separate cell phone number and tell him or her what to do.

munity, and that feels good. It took a lot of hard work and long hours in college, medical school, and residency to get here, but it was worth it. I'm the person most responsible for the general health of all my patients. I can take care of most of their problems. I prescribe medicine, and I do minor surgery. And if something really serious comes along, I recommend a specialist. There are long hours, but the pay is good. And as I said—people really look up to me. I think I like that best of all.

What do you think? Do any of these careers sound appealing? Can you see yourself doing one of these jobs—or a similar job? Would you like to learn more about health and medical careers?

Career Decision-Making Activities

1. People in the health-care industry must know the meanings of, be able to pronounce, and be able to tell differences between many medical terms that often sound alike. Contribute three medical terms to a class list. Find terms in medical dictionaries. Learn how to pronounce your three terms, and be able to give definitions for the terms. Develop a class list. How many terms are there that are not repeated? Do many sound alike? Do you think you could learn and remember all these terms, and more?
2. From a biology book, encyclopedia, medical reference book, or the Internet, find information about the heart, lungs, brain, kidneys, or liver—whichever you'd like to know more about. Do a presentation to your class about that body part. You could write a report or make a photo montage with captions. "What would it say if it could talk?" might be one way of approaching your presentation.
3. Interview three people you know who have had recent stays in hospitals or nursing homes. Ask these people to describe the health and medical careers they encountered. What did these workers do for them? What didn't the workers do that the patients would have liked to have had done? Ask the people you talk to for comments on the following groups of health and medical workers.
   - Physicians.
   - Nurses.
   - Therapists.
   - Technicians.
   - Clerical personnel.
   - Administrators.
   - Emergency workers.

JOB FAMILIES IN THE HEALTH AND MEDICAL CLUSTER

There are ten job families in the Health and Medical Cluster of careers. Look at the diagram on page 204. Then read about the job families. This will help you learn which careers in the Health and Medical Cluster you would enjoy the most.

- **Mental health and mental health services.** Mental health involves your mind and your emotions. Many people work to help others prevent or recover from mental

Job Families in the Health and Medical Cluster

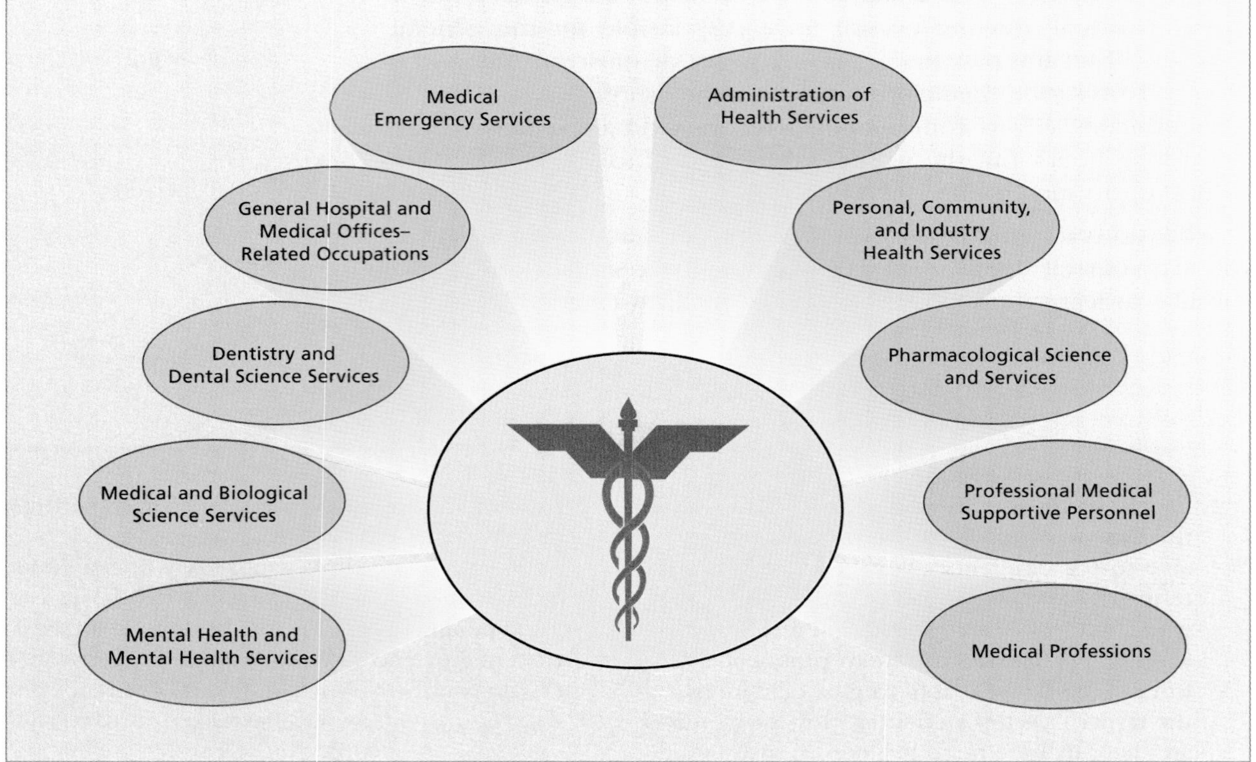

illnesses. The mental health and mental health services job family includes all the occupations involved with helping people who have mental and emotional problems.

A psychologist helps evaluate people's emotional problems. A psychiatrist does similar things. The difference between the two is that the psychiatrist has gone to medical school and can prescribe medicine.

- **Medical and biological science services.** Somebody has to find and analyze basic medical data. The people who do this are those in the medical and biological science services.

  One such job is that of a radiologic technologist. These technologists position patients in just the right ways and then take X-ray images.

  Another occupation in this job family is a pathologist. This person, usually a physician, studies diseases. He or she tries to figure out what diseases people have.

- **Dentistry and dental science services.** Any job that has to do with taking care of your teeth and gums is included in the dentistry and dental science services job family. Besides dentists, there are dental hygienists, who specialize in cleaning your teeth. A children's dentist is called a pedodontist.

- **General hospital and medical office–related occupations.** Hospitals often are big places. They need lots of people to run them. All the people who support medical services by keeping records and handling supplies are in the general hospital and medical office-related job family.

  Every hospital and doctor's office has a receptionist at the front door. This person greets patients, takes their names and other information, and directs them to the proper places. Another kind of worker is a central supervisor. In a hospital this person makes sure that everything gets cleaned. He or she makes sure there are enough clean sheets and towels, for example.
- **Medical emergency services.** Another family of jobs deals with medical needs that are immediate—that must be taken care of right away. When there is an emergency, things happen fast. Emergency medical technicians (EMTs) rush to the scene to give quick medical attention. They give first aid and move sick or injured patients in and out of ambulances, helicopters, and hospitals. Ambulance drivers bring injured people to the hospital emergency room.
- **Administration of health services.** Health care is a team effort. Lots of people work together to help each patient. When a large number of people are working closely together, managers become very important. The managers and supervisors of health-care services make up the administration of health services job family.

  A hospital administrator watches over the way a hospital is being run. This person also hires other managers to supervise different departments. A medical officer makes sure that the research programs and the medical care in a hospital are carried out properly.
- **Personal, community, and industry health services.** People in homes, schools, and factories need health services. The workers who provide services to these people are found in the personal, community, and industry health services job family.

  A community health nurse may visit homes to give nursing services to sick people. You've probably visited your school nurse, who tends to the health and safety needs of all students.
- **Pharmacological science and services.** Another job family includes occupations involved in providing medications

▶ A pharmacist dispenses the medicine your doctor prescribes for you. He or she must learn how each medication does its job to get you well.

pharmacy
a store for dispensing medical drugs, a drugstore.

and health supplies. The term *pharmacological* is related to *pharmacy.* **Pharmacy** is another term for *drugstore.* Pharmacological science refers to the science of medicines that you take to help you get better when you are sick. Or you might take certain prescription medicines to prevent you from getting sick. At a drugstore there is usually a pharmacist, who measures out the right kind of medicine for your prescription. A pharmacist often has a pharmacist's assistant.

- **Professional medical supportive personnel.** The people who work at providing patient care and treatment under the direction of medical professionals work in the professional medical supportive personnel job family. Physicians have many people who help them. For example, nurses help them. There are many kinds of nurses.

  A physical therapist may work under the direction of a doctor. Such people help injured patients regain the proper use of their arms and legs, for example. Respiratory therapists help people with breathing problems.
- **Medical professions.** The medical professions job family involves workers, such as physicians, who give highly skilled medical care. A **profession** is a career that requires special knowledge and usually many years of schooling. People who work in the different professions are called **professionals.** Lawyers, for example, are professionals working in the legal profession.

profession
a career that requires specialized training and academic preparation.

professional
a person who works in a profession (a career that requires special knowledge and usually many years of schooling).

Physicians usually specialize. There are many types of physicians. The one you might see most often is called a general practitioner. Or you might still see the pediatrician you saw when you were younger. If you break your leg, you see an orthopedist. If you need an operation, you see a surgeon. And if something goes wrong with your heart, you see a cardiologist. All of these people are special kinds of doctors. All have gone to school and been trained for many years after going to college.

CAREER OUTLOOK

Most jobs in the Health and Medical Cluster are growing, but some aren't.

FASTEST-GROWING JOBS

The following are among the fastest-growing jobs in the Health and Medical Cluster:

- Medical assistant.
- Home health aide.
- Radiologic technologist.
- Psychologist.
- Physical therapist.
- Physical and corrective therapy assistants and aides.

Careers for Tomorrow

BECOMING A RECREATION THERAPIST

Are you interested in both sports and exercise? Do you like helping people? Recreation therapists help people who have had accidents or diseases that have left them with a disability. These therapists use special exercises, games, sports, and crafts to help people with disabilities. They are also known as play therapists. Some specialize in certain types of recreation such as music, art, dance, drama, or sports.

The job outlook for recreation therapists in the twenty-first century is excellent. You would probably get a job in a hospital, rehabilitation center, training center, or camp. You need a college education to be a recreation therapist. You could get some experience by volunteering to work in the physical therapy department of a hospital or by finding out about special camps or training centers that offer recreation therapy.

For more information, write the American Therapeutic Recreation Association, P.O. Box 15215, Hattiesburg, MS 39402-5215.

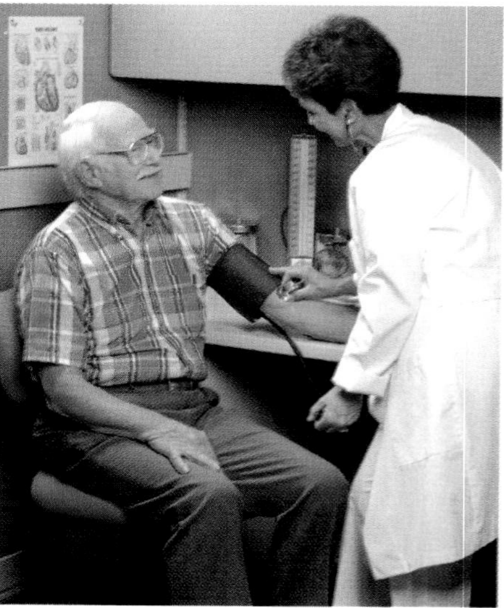

▲ Think about going to the doctor. The important first step in your visit is checking your blood pressure.

SLOWEST-GROWING JOBS

Other jobs in the Health and Medical Cluster are growing more slowly, if at all:

- Dentist.
- Optometrist.
- Electrocardiogram technician.

AT THE HEART OF THE HEALTH AND MEDICAL CLUSTER

What makes the Health and Medical Cluster different from the other fourteen career clusters you'll be exploring? What would it really be like to work in this cluster? Let's try to get at the heart of health and medical careers.

The essence of this cluster is helping people who are sick or injured. It means caring for the well-being of others. It means enduring personal hardships and emotionally painful situations for the benefit of others.

Working in the Health and Medical Cluster means putting the well-being of others before your own comfort. You must often take care of patients who can do little for themselves. You will need to bathe them, feed them, shave them, turn them over in bed—take care of many personal things for them. You'll be on your feet all day.

The patients may not be grateful. Instead, they may be critical of the way you are trying to help them. They will feel bad both physically and mentally. They might be scared or angry. And still, you must be kind and helpful and comforting to the patients. You will need to rise above the situation, and you will need to do this time and time again.

Another important part of this cluster is science and precision. So much needs to be done scientifically and with great accuracy. Medications must be measured exactly and given at exact intervals. Temperatures, blood pressures, and heart rates must be measured and recorded, and then measured and recorded again and again. Mistakes can be fatal. Everything must be exact. Scientific names for medicines, diseases, parts of the body, and procedures all must be learned and memorized. A scientific understanding of the human body is essential.

Listed in Figure 13.1 are just a few examples of occupations from this cluster. Think about the job title, the work activities, and the work settings. These are just examples to help you get at the heart of this cluster. You don't need to read for details. Scan the entries to get a feel for the cluster as a whole.

Would you like a career in this cluster? Ask yourself the following questions:

Figure 13.1 Sample Occupations in Health and Medical Cluster

WHO You Would Be	WHAT You Would Do	WHERE You Would Do It
Licensed practical nurse (LPN)	Provide bedside care, take and record temperatures, change dressings, bathe patients	Hospitals, nursing homes
Radiologic technologist (also called radiographer or X-ray technician)	Take X rays, prepare patients for X rays, position patients, use instruments and equipment, develop film	Hospitals
Surgical technician	Set up the operating room, including instruments, equipment, solutions, and sterile linens; prepare patients by washing and shaving them; assist surgeons and nurses	Hospital surgery rooms
Dental assistant	Assist dentist, hand instruments to dentist, sterilize instruments, make patients comfortable	Dental offices
Nurse's aide	Assist nurses; answer patient calls, serve meals, and feed patients; make beds, give massages, take temperatures	Hospitals
Health services manager	Plan, organize, and coordinate delivery of health and medical care; communicate with the community	Hospitals, health maintenance organizations (HMOs), nursing homes, community health centers
Pharmacist	Advise health and medical professionals about medicines, dispense drugs, manage business	Pharmacies
Physical therapist	Plan, organize, and give treatment to relieve pain and limit disabilities	Hospitals, clinics, private homes
Physician	Perform medical exams, diagnose illnesses, and treat people who are suffering; also advise patients	Hospitals, physicians' offices, clinics

- Do you like the sound of the occupations listed under "Who"? Would you feel good about an identity like one of these?
- Would you enjoy doing activities like those described under "What"?

Health and Medicine

Take your time reading and thinking about the questions below. You might want to write out your answers.

- ▲ Have you owned a chemistry set or microscope and learned how to use it? Was it interesting?
- ▲ Have you had first-aid training? Did you find it interesting?
- ▲ Are you calm in emergencies?
- ▲ Do you like helping people who are sick or injured?
- ▲ Do you like doing science experiments?
- ▲ Can you read charts and graphs?
- ▲ Have you ever cared for a sick pet until it got better?
- ▲ Do you like teaching other people skills such as arts or crafts?
- ▲ Do you like shows on television that present and talk about medical facts?
- ▲ Do you like looking at the instruments in your doctor's or dentist's office and asking him or her questions about them?
- ▲ When someone at your school has an accident, do you run to help them? (Or do you run the other way?)

If you answered yes to most of these questions, there's a good chance you would enjoy a health and medical career.

- Picture yourself working in the settings described under "Where." Would you be comfortable in these settings?

SKILLS, TRAINING, AND EXPERIENCE

Do you have, or can you develop, the right skills and abilities to look for a career in the health and medical field? Listed below are a few of the skills common to careers in this cluster:

- Skills in working with people, facts, and things.
- Math and science skills.
- Skill in using eyes, hands, and fingers.
- Understanding of human or animal anatomy, or how the body is put together and how it works.
- Ability to work under stress with people who are sick or injured; ability to stay calm when other people are not.
- Ability to follow instructions exactly and record information well.
- Ability to make important decisions.
- Good concentration and alertness for a long time.
- A desire to help and care for other people.
- Communication skills to work well with people who have illnesses, disabilities, or both.

The jobs in the Health and Medical Cluster require many different skill levels. Here are three job categories.

JOBS REQUIRING LESS-THAN-AVERAGE TRAINING AND EXPERIENCE

- Ambulance driver.
- Dental assistant.
- Home health-care aide.
- Nurse's aide or orderly.
- Electrocardiogram technician.
- Operating room technician.

JOBS REQUIRING AVERAGE TRAINING AND EXPERIENCE

- Dental or medical secretary.
- Dental hygienist.
- Licensed practical nurse.
- Medical laboratory worker.
- Optician.
- Physical therapy assistant.

JOBS REQUIRING MORE-THAN-AVERAGE TRAINING AND EXPERIENCE

- Dentist.
- All types of physicians.
- Hospital administrator.
- Occupational therapist.
- Optometrist.
- Pharmacist.
- Podiatrist.
- Psychiatrist.
- Psychologist.

See the following list of some of the jobs in the Health and Medical Cluster diagram on the next page, along with their *DOT* numbers.

Career Decision-Making Activities

1. Take classes in science, biology, math, advanced math, and chemistry.
2. Sign up for a first-aid course if you haven't already taken one. Evaluate your reaction to the course. Did you like it? Did it seem worthwhile? Did it make you curious about the human body and how it works? Discuss your reactions in class.
3. Volunteer to work in a hospital or nursing home near you. If you can't do this, help care for someone in your family who is ill, such as your grandmother or your younger sister when she has the flu. Keep notes about your responses to the experience.
4. Watch television shows about hospitals and shows presenting medical facts. Do you think you'd like working in these situations? Talk to people in your community who are in the health and medical field about what they do. Do they think the television shows are realistic?

Occupations in Health and Medical

Here is a list of occupations mentioned in this chapter. Next to the name of each occupation is its *DOT* number. You can use the *DOT* number to locate further information about the occupation in your school or public library. For the broad occupational terms mentioned in this chapter, only one or two examples of that occupation are listed below. You can easily find more examples of the occupation in the *DOT.*

Admitting Clerk (see Hospital Admitting Clerk)
Ambulance Driver (913.683-010)
Anesthesiologist (070.101-010)
Assistant Surgeon (079.364-018)
Cardiologist (070.101-014)
Central Supervisor (see Supervisor, Central Supply)
Community Health Nurse (075.124-014)
Dental Assistant (079.371-010)
Dental Hygienist (078.361-010)
Dental Secretary (see Secretary)
Dentist (072.101-010)
Electrocardiogram Technician (078.362-018)
Emergency Medical Technician (079.374-010)
Family Practitioner (070.101-026)
General Practitioner (070.101-022)
Health Services Manager (see Hospital Administrator)
Home Health-Care Aide (354.377-014)
Hospital Administrator (187.117-010)
Hospital Admitting Clerk (205.362-018)
Hospital Orderly (see Orderly)
Lab Technician (see Medical-Laboratory Technician)
Licensed Practical Nurse (079.374-014)
Medical Clerk (see Medical-Record Clerk)
Medical-Laboratory Technician (078.381-014)
Medical Laboratory Worker (see Medical-Laboratory Technician)
Medical Officer (070.101-046)
Medical-Record Clerk (245.362-010)
Medical Secretary (201.362-014)
Nurse, General Duty (075.374-010)
Nurse's Aide (355.674-014)
Occupational Therapist (076.121-010)
Operating Room Technician (079.374-022)
Optician (716.280-014)
Optometrist (079.101-018)
Orderly (355.674-018)
Orthopedic Surgeon (070.101-094)
Orthopedist (see Orthopedic Surgeon)
Paramedic (see Emergency Medical Technician)
Pathologist (070.061-010)
Pediatrician (070.101-066)
Pedodontist (072.101-026)
Pharmacist (074.161-010)
Pharmacist Assistant (074.381-010)
Physical Therapist (076.121-014)
Physical Therapy Assistant (076.224-010)
Physician (see Family Practitioner)
Play Therapist (see Recreation Therapist)
Podiatrist (079.101-022)
Psychiatrist (070.107-014)
Psychologist (045.107-022)
Radiographer (see Radiologic Technologist)
Radiologic Technician (see Radiologic Technologist)
Radiologic Technologist (078.362-026)
Receptionist (237.367-038)
Recreation Therapist (076.124-014)
Registered Nurse (see Nurse, General Duty)
Respiratory Therapist (079.361-010)
School Nurse (075.124-010)
Secretary (201.362-030)
Supervisor, Central Supply (079.164-010)
Surgeon (070.101-094)
Surgical Technician (079.374-022)
Volunteer (no number assigned)
X-Ray Technician (see Radiologic Technologist)

Review and Enrichment

Summarizing the Chapter

Summarizing information is a critical thinking skill that will help you succeed in the world of work. Write a summary of what you learned in Chapter 13. Focus on the main points of the chapter. Then in a class discussion, compare your summary with the summaries done by your classmates. Can you improve your summary?

Improving Your Career Vocabulary

1. Learning to use new vocabulary terms will improve your communication skills, which are important in almost all areas of work. Write definitions for the terms listed below. Then for each term, write an original sentence about yourself in which you use the term correctly.
   - Health and Medical Cluster
   - pharmacy
   - profession
   - professional
2. List the job families discussed in the Health and Medical Cluster. Write a one-sentence description of each.

Finding the Facts

Finding exact information is a frequently used skill in many careers. Find the answers to the exercise below, and write the answers on a separate sheet of paper.

1. How many people are currently employed in the health care field?
2. What is the difference between a psychologist and a psychiatrist?
3. What kind of work does a pharmacist do?
4. Name the three slowest-growing jobs in the Health and Medical Cluster.
5. Name three skills needed for jobs in this cluster.

Thinking for Yourself

To complete the exercise below you will need to use critical thinking and communication skills, which are skills valued by all employers. Write out your answers or be prepared to discuss them in class, depending on your teacher's instructions.

1. In your own words, describe a person who you think would enjoy working in a health and medical career.
2. There seems to be a general shortage of nurses. Why do you think this is so?
3. Have you ever been present at a crisis? If so, how did you behave?
4. What values do you think would be high on the lists of people in a health and medical career?
5. Some people would like to have a national medical insurance that would be paid for with tax money. Do you think this is a good idea? Why or why not?

Practicing Your Basic Skills

Your career success depends greatly on your basic math and communication skills. Work hard at improving in the areas where you have trouble with the following exercises.

Math

1. Medicines and other related items are usually measured using the metric system. Convert the following to their U.S. equivalents:
   a. 15 cc (1 cc = 0.06 cubic inches)
   b. 56 mg (1 mg = 0.000035 ounce)
   c. 4 gm (1 g = 0.035 ounce)
   d. 60 ml (1 ml = 0.001057 quart)
   e. 12.5 cm (1 cm = 0.4 inches)
2. Phyllis works as a billing clerk for a dentist. Total the following bills she has prepared:
   a. 1 filling, $40; 1 crown, $425; cleaning, $18
   b. orthodontia, $256; X rays, $78
   Both patients neglected to pay within 30 days. The next month Phyllis added a 1½ percent finance charge to each bill. What were the new totals?
3. Dr. Rivera saw sixteen patients between 8 A.M. and 12 noon. One eighth of the patients were not charged for the visits. The others were charged $40 for an office visit. If Dr. Rivera had been paid by the hour, how much per hour would she have earned?

Reading and Writing

1. Read a current book about the medical profession. Write a paragraph about at least one new

Review and Enrichment, continued

thing you learned about health care.

2. Some health and medical professionals are known for their bad handwriting. Take a look at something you have written recently. How does it look? If your handwriting needs work, practice making it better.
3. Write a one-page story about your own doctor or some other health-care worker you have contacted recently.
4. Pick at least one occupation mentioned in this chapter that you think would be interesting. Research the occupation thoroughly and write a report. Use the career research checklist in Chapter 5 as a guide for your report. Conclude your report with an explanation of your interest in that occupation based on your findings.

Speaking and Listening

1. Do research and then make a one-minute speech to the class about some health-related subject, such as AIDS, how computerized axial tomography (CAT) scans are made, or the connection between diet and illness.
2. Listen to your classmates' speeches. Pay attention to the facts. Which facts caught your attention? Why?

Activities Working with Others

In almost all careers you must be able to get along well with other people to be successful. Work with your classmates to do the following activities. As you work together, pay attention to how well you get along. If necessary, work hard at improving your ability to do your part and to cooperate.

1. As a class, research Canada's system of socialized medicine. Form two teams, and debate the truth of this statement: "The United States should adopt a system of socialized medicine similar to that used by Canada."
2. With a classmate, put together an activity kit for a hospitalized child or for an older person in a nursing home. For example, a child's kit might include finger puppets, a storybook, a puzzle, and so on. Collect the kits and deliver them to a local hospital or nursing home.
3. Add the careers mentioned in this chapter to your database.

Decision Making and Problem Solving

You will be a big help to your employer if you can make decisions and solve problems. List all the possible ways of resolving the situations described below. Then pick the best alternative (possible choice), and tell why you chose it. If you need help, you might want to refer to Chapter 3.

1. You are a female physician who has just moved into a small town. The town has no other doctor, but you have few patients. Finally one of them tells you the townspeople are reluctant to go to a female doctor. What will you do to persuade them to come to you?
2. You are a physical therapist. One of your patients is a young man who was injured in a car accident. He was driving when another car ran a red light and hit his car. A friend who was with him was killed. The young man is paralyzed from the waist down. There is a good chance he will walk again if he works with you, but he doesn't seem to care and won't try. What will you do?

CHAPTER 14

HOSPITALITY AND RECREATION CAREERS

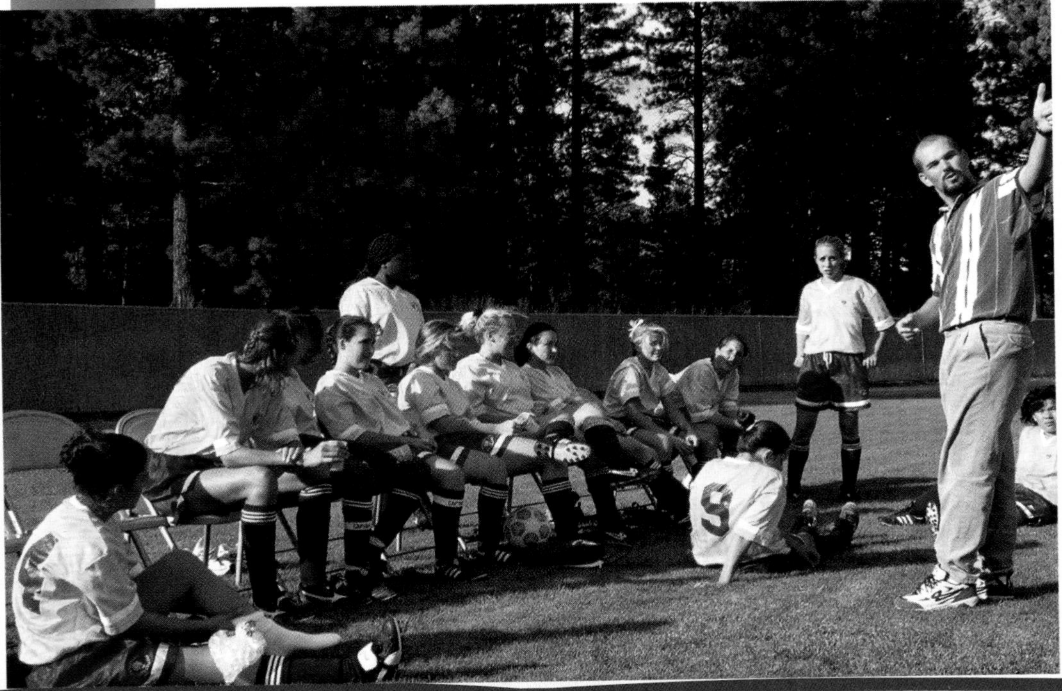

◆ Chapter Objectives ◆

After completing this chapter you will be able to do the following:

- ◆ Define the terms listed under "New Career Terms."
- ◆ List and describe the four job families in the Hospitality and Recreation Cluster.
- ◆ Identify several careers included in this cluster.
- ◆ Name several slow-growing and fast-growing jobs in this cluster.
- ◆ Explain what it would be like to work at a career in this cluster.
- ◆ Evaluate your own interest in this cluster.
- ◆ Identify skills common to many careers in this cluster.

◆ New Career Terms ◆

In this chapter you will learn the meanings of the following career terms:

- ✔ Hospitality and Recreation Cluster
- ✔ Hospitality
- ✔ Accommodate
- ✔ Recreation
- ✔ Accommodations
- ✔ Aerobics

Summer is coming up soon. Sara Fong's family is planning a trip to a Caribbean island. Sara goes with her mom to a travel agency, where a travel agent shows them brochures of different island resorts. They pick a resort right on the beach in St. Thomas, which is part of the U.S. Virgin Islands.

In the plane on the way to St. Thomas, the Fong family is served lunch by flight attendants. At the resort hotel they are greeted by a man who takes care of their luggage. At the desk a hotel clerk or assistant manager checks them in. Another person shows them to their room.

While in the resort, restaurant waiters and waitresses serve them. A scuba diving instructor teaches Sara how to dive underwater.

Throughout the resort there are many different workers. Their job is to take care of the Fong family and all other guests at the resort. The workers are there to attend to the wishes of others. The workers are providing services to the Fongs.

Hospitality and Recreation Cluster
occupations involved in providing pleasure for people involved in leisure-time activities.

hospitality
the friendly reception and treatment of guests.

accommodate
to give others something they need or want.

All of the workers just mentioned are in the **Hospitality and Recreation Cluster** of careers. **Hospitality** means the friendly reception and treatment of guests. When someone is very *hospitable,* that person is treating guests or strangers warmly and generously. You might have friends who have hospitable families. You always feel at home when you spend time with those families' or go to dinner with them.

Another word you should know has a similar meaning to *hospitality.* This word is **accommodate.** To accommodate other people means to give them something they need or want. The peo-

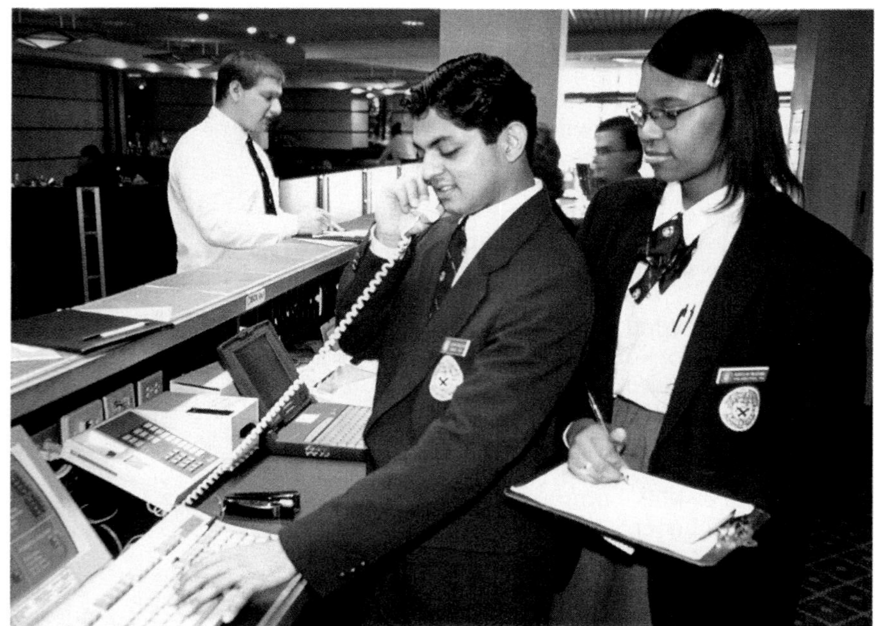

▶ Successful employees in the Hospitality and Recreation Cluster of careers genuinely wish to provide service to their customers.

ple working at the resort *accommodated* Sara Fong and her family. They brought the Fongs fresh linens, served them meals, and helped them in any other way they could. All the workers in this cluster try to accommodate others.

Recreation comes from the word *recreate.* Recreate means to refresh or make fresh again by relaxation and enjoyment. Recreation is anything that restores you physically or mentally. Recreation often involves exercise or sports—anything that gives you relaxation and enjoyment.

recreation a means of refreshing yourself by relaxation and enjoyment.

In this chapter you will explore careers in the Hospitality and Recreation Cluster. This cluster includes occupations involved in providing pleasure for people involved in leisure-time activities.

WHAT WOULD IT BE LIKE?

A job in the Hospitality and Recreation Cluster often means working inside. You have to be willing to work nights and on holidays, too.

If you get a job in the recreation industry where you teach sports, you might work outside. This would be true if you were a tennis instructor, for example.

In the Hospitality and Recreation Cluster of careers, you usually don't work a regular five-day week. Rather, you are assigned different hours for different days. You may even have to work more than forty hours a week. You will probably work on weekends and holidays.

Workers on cruise ships, for example, may work odd hours. They may work more than forty hours a week when they are on the ship.

Thinking About Yourself
Hospitality and Recreation

Read and think about the questions below. You might want to write out your answers.

- ▲ Are you good at giving directions to others?
- ▲ Have you ever served food or beverages at a party or reception? Were you able to do this without dropping or spilling things?
- ▲ Have you sold things to raise money for clubs or organizations? Did you collect money and keep accurate records of your sales?
- ▲ Do you like socializing with others?
- ▲ Do you enjoy meeting new people? Have you ever joined a community group so that you could meet and do things with people?
- ▲ Do you do any public speaking? Do you like to speak in front of groups?
- ▲ Have you ever planned or organized a party? Can you lead others in games and activities?
- ▲ Do you like to exercise? Are you athletic? Have you ever taught someone how to play a sport such as tennis?

If you answered yes to many of these questions, there's a good chance you might enjoy a hospitality and recreation career.

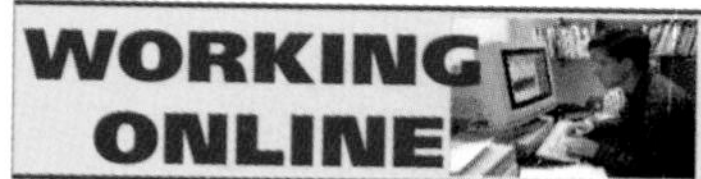

Corporate Travel Planning on the Internet

It used to be that corporate travel planners—people in charge of planning all of the travel of business executives and managers—went through travel agencies. Today, they do not have to do so. Now they can find out about all flights, hotels, and the like on the Internet. They can even make reservations and order the tickets to be sent to them. In addition, they can find out the cheapest fares on the many discount airline fare sites on the Internet.

When they are off the ship, though, they may get a number of days off in a row. This is true for flight attendants, too.

In almost all jobs in the hospitality and recreation area, the workers come in constant contact with guests. That means that the jobs in this field are *people jobs.* You have to enjoy interacting with other people.

Would you enjoy working in this career cluster? Do some daydreaming as you "listen" to the conversation below. Several people who enjoy working in the Hospitality and Recreation Cluster are talking about their jobs. As you listen to what they say, imagine yourself doing their jobs.

Travel Agent: Do you like talking on the telephone? I always did. When I was in school my parents were always telling me to get off the phone. Well, maybe all that talking paid off, because now I get paid to talk on the phone. And I love it. There's a lot more to my job than the telephone, of course, but I spend most of my time describing tours and travel arrangements and answering questions about hotels and resorts all over the world. Sometimes the customers come into the office, but lots of them just call, and we talk on the phone. I love traveling myself, of course, which makes it easier for me to give good advice. And I love helping people. All that and the telephone, too. What more could I ask for?

Physical Education Instructor: Well, I'm glad you're happy in your job, because I think I'd hate it. Talking on the phone means sitting—and I can't stand sitting. I need to be on the move. I guess

▶ If you like to travel, a career in the travel business could be exciting.

the one thing our jobs have in common is that they both involve helping people. I teach P.E. at the local high school, which means I've taught most of the kids in this community how to do exercises to keep themselves loose and in shape. I love working with kids, showing them the right way to throw a ball or swing a racquet. And in the summers I teach swimming lessons, which is my first love. I've studied the techniques of the best coaches in the country, and I think I'm pretty good at getting them across to the kids. I'm on the move constantly, keeping in shape, playing the games I love, and helping kids. Great job, huh?

Flight Attendant: Your job does sound interesting—and there are some similarities to mine. Like you, I'm on the move. My job is definitely not a sitting type of job. And although I'm not teaching people, I am helping them. I serve meals and drinks, I answer questions, and I help the passengers get comfortable. I guess I'm just

Attitude makes a difference

Flying Away

Belinda Said grew up in a family with seven brothers and sisters. Because the family was so large, her mother and father could never afford to go on a family vacation in a plane.

The Saids lived near a big airport. Belinda used to watch planes take off and land when she was little. She continued watching them even as she grew older, but she never got to fly on one.

When she was in the tenth grade, Belinda decided she wanted to become a flight attendant. She contacted several airlines in her city. They sent her information about what she would have to do to qualify for the job. She knew that she had to finish high school first.

Even before she finished, she made out her applications to several airline companies. She had her counselor check them to make sure she had filled out everything correctly.

Belinda was turned down by three of the four airlines to which she applied. The fourth one put her on a waiting list.

After graduation from high school, Belinda took a temporary job in a restaurant. At the end of the summer the fourth airline called her up and offered her a training position to become a flight attendant.

Belinda has worked for the same airline for eleven years. She is a senior flight attendant now. She has traveled to Europe and Africa.

What Do YOU Think?

How did Belinda channel her desire to fly? Should Belinda have gone into training for another career when she was turned down for flight attendants' training?

one of those people who likes to help others. Nothing gives me more of a kick than making someone feel good. And the travel part of my job isn't too bad, either. I've been in all the major cities of the United States. I've seen just about everything anyone could want to see. And I've been to Europe a few times. A chance to see the world was the main reason I decided to become a flight attendant. It wasn't until I'd been on the job awhile that I realized how much I enjoyed the "people" aspect. I guess I was lucky.

What do you think? Do any of these careers sound appealing? Can you see yourself doing one of these jobs—or a similar job? Would you like to learn more about hospitality and recreation careers?

Career Decision-Making Activities

1. Make a list on a piece of paper of all the games you know how to play. It might help to think in terms of categories, such as board games, card games, and games involving a ball. Compile lists in class. Do you know a game that several classmates don't know? Teach them how to play the game. Were you able to teach them? Could they follow your instructions? Did you enjoy teaching them?
2. Are you a person who enjoys games? Think about how many hours you spend playing games in an average month. Do not count physical education or recess time at school. *Do* count team sports associated with school. How many hours do you think you spend playing sports and other games in a typical month? Calculate the class average. Do you play games more, less, or about the same as the average?
3. You do not need to be a professional athlete to have a career in sports and athletics. On a separate sheet of paper, make a list of all the careers you can think of that are associated with sports in your community. Looking through the Yellow Pages of the telephone book and reading the sports section of the newspaper will get you started. Compile lists in class. Are there more jobs available in this area than you thought?
4. Put on a show with your classmates. Have a class discussion about circus acts that you remember seeing. Choose one type of circus entertainment you would like to try. You could include such things as doing magic tricks, performing acrobatics, dressing up like a clown, telling jokes, or walking on stilts. Pick someone to be master or mistress of ceremonies. Someone else can organize the show and direct it. Did you enjoy entertaining others?
5. Develop a travel plan for your own ideal vacation. Write out a detailed, hour-by-hour schedule for your trip, which will last two weeks. Check with airlines, hotels, and adults who travel to estimate costs. How much would your trip cost? Discuss dream vacations in class.

JOB FAMILIES IN THE HOSPITALITY AND RECREATION CLUSTER

Within the Hospitality and Recreation Cluster there are four job families. They are shown in the figure below. Reading about the job families will help you decide which careers in this cluster you might enjoy the most.

Job Families in the Hospitality and Recreation Cluster

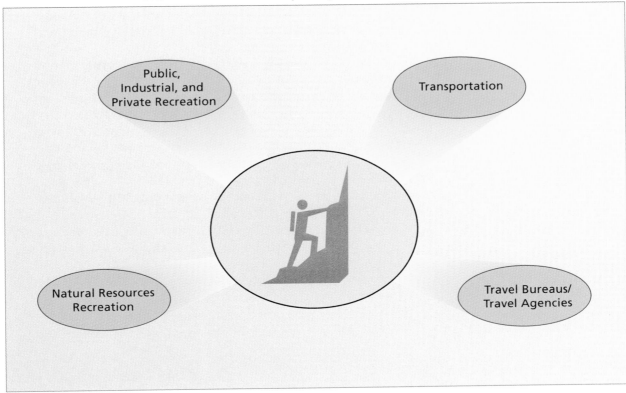

Public, Industrial, and Private Recreation

Transportation

Natural Resources Recreation

Travel Bureaus/ Travel Agencies

- **Natural resources recreation.** The people in the natural resources recreation job family help organize and preserve natural sources of recreation. At the beach, for example, there are lifeguards, who make sure that no one drowns. Lifeguards have to be trained in first aid and rescue.

  Hunting and fishing guides help people use the outdoors. Usually they have many years of experience and have learned their job as they worked with other guides.

  At the zoo there are zookeepers and attendants. They supervise the care of the animals. They also make decisions about how the animals are to be displayed to the people who go to the zoo.
- **Public, industrial, and private recreation.** Another job family includes all the occupations involved in performing and arranging public, industrial, and private recreation and entertainment activities. All of the officials at sporting events, such as the baseball umpire, are in this job family. Also included are circus workers and performers, automobile racers, fortune-tellers, magicians, mind readers, and hypnotists.

▼ Do you like the responsibility of caring for animals? Check with a zoo in your area about part-time jobs.

Anybody who teaches a sport can be classified in this job family, too. These jobs include instructors of bowling, ice skating, karate, horseback riding, skiing, swimming, and tennis.

- **Transportation.** The occupations in the transportation job family are involved in providing services for travelers' comfort. Many of the occupations in this job family are also included in the Transportation Cluster (Chapter 20).

  At the airport all the passenger agents and clerks who check you in or sell you a ticket are part of this job family. On a cruise ship, the deck steward helps passengers. He or she provides pillows, blankets, and deck chairs. Flight attendants on airplanes are, of course, part of this job family. Flight attendants are trained in safety and service.
- **Travel bureaus and travel agencies.** All of the occupations in the travel bureaus and travel agencies job family are involved in providing travel information and **accommodations.** Accommodations are the places where you stay when you go on a trip, such as a hotel or a resort.

accommodations
places to stay while on a trip, such as a hotel or resort.

At a travel bureau the main employee is a travel agent. Travel agents provide information about traveling and

Careers for Tomorrow

FITNESS INSTRUCTORS

The fitness craze is strong in America. People want to exercise because it makes them feel better, look better, and live longer.

One of the fastest-growing jobs in the Hospitality and Recreation Cluster is a fitness instructor. For example, many private gyms want aerobic exercise instructors. **Aerobics** is a type of physical conditioning. Aerobics instructors teach physical fitness programs based on lots of movement. These exercises are usually done with music in the background.

aerobics
a type of physical conditioning.

Some aerobics instructors get jobs with big companies. They then develop a fitness program for the workers in those companies.

There are also many instructors needed for bodybuilding. Bodybuilding can be done with free weights, such as barbells. Or it can be done with specialized machines.

The nice thing about being a fitness instructor is that you stay in shape while you work! If you think you might be interested in a career as a fitness instructor, contact the International Fitness Professional Association, 905 E. Martin Luther King Drive, Suite 500, Tarpan Springs, FL 34689-4830. Telephone: 1-800-785-1924.

vacations. They also sell airline and train tickets. They make reservations for hotels, resorts, camps, and anything else related to travel.

Within a travel agency there are also travel agency clerks, who answer telephone inquiries. They also do general office work. There is also a ticket clerk, who issues tickets for large travel agencies.

CAREER OUTLOOK

As our nation gets richer, more people are taking vacations. People also work fewer hours on the average than they used to. This gives them more time for recreation.

The job outlook for hospitality and recreation is good. Some jobs are going to grow faster than others.

FASTEST-GROWING JOBS

The fastest-growing jobs are the following:

- Corporate travel planner.
- Restaurant host or hostess.
- Waiter or waitress.
- Cook or chef.

SLOWEST-GROWING JOBS

Certain jobs within the industry are going to have slower growth. They include the following:

- Theater usher.
- Ticket taker.

AT THE HEART OF THE HOSPITALITY AND RECREATION CLUSTER

What makes the Hospitality and Recreation Cluster different from the other fourteen clusters you'll be exploring? What would it really be like to work in this cluster? Let's try to get at the heart of hospitality and recreation.

The essence of this cluster is helping people have a good time. Working in this cluster, you would help people plan a vacation, make them happy and comfortable while they travel, and show them how to participate in sports and other recreational activities. You could also entertain them.

Hospitality means being friendly and helpful. It means smiling a lot. Not forcing a smile—you should be genuinely happy as you do something for someone else. It means putting someone else's needs

Figure 14.1 Sample Occupations in the Hospitality and Recreation Cluster

WHO You Would Be	WHAT You Would Do	WHERE You Would Do It
Travel agent	Give advice to customers; make arrangements for transportation, hotels, car rentals, and tours	Desks in travel agency offices
Flight attendant	Instruct passengers; answer questions, distribute magazines and pillows, help care for small children, serve meals and drinks, be prepared to give first aid; assist passengers in an emergency	Airplanes
Amusement and recreation attendant	Schedule use of recreation facilities, give out equipment, collect fees	Amusement parks, sports facilities, carnivals, golf courses
Athletic director	Plan and direct athletic activities, including publicity, preparing budgets, and supervising coaches	Offices at schools and recreational facilities
Acrobat	Entertain audiences by performing difficult feats involving leaping, tumbling, and balancing	Circuses or auditoriums

before your own, and enjoying it. It means making someone else king or queen for the day, while you are his or her servant—trying to satisfy his or her every desire.

Recreation is entertainment. It's entertaining others. It can be the entertainment of a circus—clowns, acrobats, and high-wire artists. It's the entertainment of travel—seeing faraway places and meeting new people. And it's the entertainment of sports—baseball, basketball, golf, tennis, and all the others.

Figure 14.1 lists just a few examples of occupations from this cluster. Think about the job title, the work activities, and the work settings. Remember, these are just examples to help you get at the heart of this cluster. Don't read for details. Scan the entries to get a feel for the cluster as a whole.

Would you like a career in this cluster? Ask yourself the following questions:

- Do you like the sound of the occupations listed under "Who"? Would you feel good about an identity like one of these?
- Would you enjoy doing activities like those described under "What"?
- Picture yourself working in the settings described under "Where." Would you be comfortable in these settings?

SKILLS, TRAINING, AND EXPERIENCE

Listed below are some skills common to many of the careers in the Hospitality and Recreation Cluster.

- Speak clearly.
- Talk easily with all kinds of people to put them at ease.
- Perform a variety of activities, changing activities often.
- Plan and carry out activities, such as card parties or dances.
- Use arithmetic to total costs and make change.
- Stand and walk for varying lengths of time, sometimes for long periods.
- Move fingers and hands easily and quickly to handle things like dishes, money, and merchandise.
- Lift and carry things like heavy trays and sports equipment.

◀ If you like greeting and working with people, you might try getting a summer job as a host or hostess in a restaurant.

Most, if not all, of the entry-level jobs in hospitality and recreation require little or no specialized training. One exception is flight attendants. They usually have to take a special course before they can work in an airplane. Other jobs in this cluster require more advanced training. The following are three categories of jobs.

JOBS REQUIRING LESS-THAN-AVERAGE TRAINING AND EXPERIENCE

- Cafeteria attendant.
- Camp counselor.
- Dishwasher.
- Hotel doorkeeper.
- Fast-food worker.
- Hotel bellhop or porter.
- Hotel housekeeper.
- Restaurant host or hostess.
- Short-order cook.
- Football or baseball stadium worker.
- Usher.
- Waiter or waitress.

JOBS REQUIRING AVERAGE TRAINING AND EXPERIENCE

- Caterer.
- Cook or chef.
- Pastry chef.
- Headwaiter or headwaitress.
- Lifeguard.
- Theater manager.
- Travel agent.
- Swimming instructor.

JOBS REQUIRING MORE-THAN-AVERAGE TRAINING AND EXPERIENCE

- Hotel manager.
- Athletic coach.
- Zoo administrator.
- Professional athlete.
- Restaurant manager.
- Stadium manager.

See page XXX for a list of some of the jobs in the Hospitality and Recreation Cluster, along with their *DOT* numbers.

Career Decision-Making Activities

1. Most entry-level jobs in the Hospitality and Recreation Cluster don't require much training or experience. That means that if you are interested, you could probably get a summer job within this career cluster. Jobs are available for kitchen and dining room workers, dishwashers, kitchen helpers, hosts, and hostesses. You should contact local hotels, restaurants, and amusement parks. In motels and summer resorts there are jobs in room service and in social programs. In recreation, many parks and museums offer summer employment. They hope you will come back later after you graduate. Guides are always needed for parks and public monuments. You should contact tourism offices, parks, and camps in your area.
2. Take courses where you have to give speeches. It's important to be able to speak in front of others. You may even want to enter a speech-making contest. Your English or speech teacher will be able to help you.
3. Plan a party for your class. Make up lists of foods, beverages, and activities. Do your planning in an organized way. Did you enjoy the planning and organizing? Did you get excited about the party?
4. Are you going on a family vacation in the near future? If you do, talk to the workers in your hotels or resorts. Ask them what they like and don't like about their jobs. Find out what their chances for advancement are. If you travel by car, practice reading the road maps and giving directions to whoever is driving.

◀ Before you become a manager, you will need to learn all the jobs of the people you will supervise.

Occupations in Hospitality and Recreation

Here is a list of occupations mentioned in this chapter. Next to the name of each occupation is its *DOT* number. You can use the *DOT* number to locate further information about the occupation in your school or public library. For the broad occupational terms mentioned in this chapter, only one or two examples of that occupation are listed below. You can easily find more examples of the occupation in the *DOT.*

Acrobat (159.247-010)
Aerobic Exercise Instructor (see Instructor)
Animal Keeper (412.674-010)
Assistant Manager (see Hotel Manager)
Athletic Coach (153.227-010)
Athletic Director (090.117-022)
Attendant, Lodging Facilities (329.467-010)
Attendant Zookeeper (see Animal Keeper)
Automobile Racer (153.243-010)
Baggage Porter (324.477-010)
Baseball Umpire (153.267-018)
Bellhop (324.677-010)
Bowling Instructor (153.227-018)
Cafeteria Attendant (311.677-010)
Camp Counselor (159.124-020)
Caterer (187.167-106)
Chef (313.131-014)
Circus Performer (see Acrobat)
Circus Worker (969.687-010)
Cook (313.361-014)
Deck Steward (350.667-022)
Dining Room Attendant (311.677-018)
Dishwasher, Hand (318.687-010)
Fast-Food Worker (see Waiter/Waitress)
Fitness Instructor (see Instructor, Physical)
Flight Attendant (352.367-014)
Football and Baseball Stadium Worker (see Ticket Taker)
Fortune-Teller (159.647-018)
Gamekeeper (169.171-010)
Guide, Sightseeing (353.363-010)
Headwaiter/waitress (311.137-022)
Horseback Riding Instructor (153.227-018)
Hotel Clerk (329.467-010)
Hotel Doorkeeper (324.677-014)
Hotel Housekeeper (321.137-010)
Hotel Manager (187.117-038)
Hotel Porter (see Baggage Porter)
Hunting and Fishing Guide (353.161-010)
Hypnotist (159.647-010)
Ice Skating Instructor (153.227-018)
Instructor, Physical (153.227-014)
Instructor, Sports (153.227-018)
Karate Instructor (see Instructor, Sports)
Kitchen Helper and Worker (318.687-010)
Lifeguard (379.667-014)
Magician (159.041-010)
Mind Reader (159.647-018)
Park Ranger (169.167-042)
Passenger Agents and Clerks (238.367-026)
Pastry Chef (313.131-022)
Physical Education Instructor (099.224-010)
Professional Athlete (153.341-010)
Recreation-Facility Attendant (341.367-010)
Restaurant Host/Hostess (310.137-010)
Restaurant Manager (187.167-106)
Scuba Diving Instructor (153.227-018)
Short-Order Cook (313.361-022)
Skiing Instructor (153.227-018)
Stadium Manager (see Superintendent, Building)
Steward/Stewardess (350.677-022)
Superintendent, Building (187.167-190)
Swimming Instructor (153.227-018)
Tennis Instructor (153.227-018)
Theater Manager (187.167-154)
Theater Usher (344.677-014)
Ticket Clerk (238.367-026)
Ticker Taker (344.667-010)
Travel Agency Clerk (238.367-030)
Travel Agent (252.157-010)
Usher (344.677-014)
Waiter/Waitress, Informal (311.477-030)
Waiter/Waitress, Formal (311.477-026)
Zoo Administrator (see Gamekeeper)
Zookeeper (see Animal Keeper)

REVIEW AND ENRICHMENT

SUMMARIZING THE CHAPTER

Summarizing information is a critical thinking skill that will help you succeed in the world of work. Write a summary of what you learned in Chapter 14. Focus on the main points of the chapter. Then in a class discussion, compare your summary with the summaries done by your classmates. Can you improve your summary?

IMPROVING YOUR CAREER VOCABULARY

1. Learning to use new vocabulary terms will improve your communication skills, which are important in almost all areas of work. Write definitions for the terms listed below. Then for each term, write an original sentence about yourself in which you use the term correctly.
   - Hospitality and Recreation Cluster
   - hospitality
   - accommodate
   - recreation
   - accommodations
   - aerobics
2. List the job families discussed in this chapter. Write a one-sentence description of each.

FINDING THE FACTS

Finding exact information is a frequently used skill in many careers. Find the answers to the exercise below, and write the answers on a separate sheet of paper.

1. What are working hours like for jobs in this cluster?
2. Name three jobs in the transportation family.
3. Who is the main employee at a travel bureau?
4. List the slowest-growing jobs in this cluster.
5. Name a job in this cluster that requires more-than-average training and experience.

THINKING FOR YOURSELF

To complete the exercise below you will need to use critical thinking and communication skills, which are skills valued by all employers. Write out your answers or be prepared to discuss them in class, depending on your teacher's instructions.

1. In your own words describe a person you think would not enjoy working in a hospitality and recreation career.
2. Of all the occupations mentioned in this chapter, which seems most interesting to you? Why?
3. How important do you think friendliness is to success in a hospitality career? Explain.
4. Some people think the practice of tipping workers such as waiters or waitresses is wrong. They believe these workers should be paid a sufficient salary. Other people think tips encourage individualized service. What do you think?
5. Some large companies have recreation programs for their workers. Do you think this is a good idea? Why or why not?

PRACTICING YOUR BASIC SKILLS

Your career success depends greatly on your basic math and communication skills. Work hard at improving in the areas where you have trouble with the following exercises.

Math

1. Gisela is a travel agent. She has just made reservations for a customer. The man will be staying at a lodge for two weeks. The cost is $743.50 per week. The man wants to rent a car that will cost $325.67 for the two weeks. His plane ticket to the lodge will cost $249. On his return trip he will make a stop and will need a connecting flight. The plane ticket from the lodge to his first stop costs $189.32. The ticket from the stop to his home costs $99.58. Since the customer is a member of a travel club, he is entitled to a 15 percent discount on the total cost of the trip. How much did Gisela charge him for the trip?
2. Ben worked as a busboy. He was entitled to one-third of the tips the waiters collected. Waiter A collected $27.50; waiter B, $32; and waiter C, $46.25. How much did Ben earn in tips?
3. Mei-ling and the ten other people in her aerobics class were on a weight loss program. Altogether they weighed a total of 1,441 pounds. In two weeks they each lost an average of 4 pounds. How much did the average member weigh after the two weeks?

Review and Enrichment, continued

Reading and Writing

1. Pretend you own a resort hotel. Write a letter to Mr. Robert Leaphorn confirming his family's reservation for the week of December 1 to 7.
2. Obtain travel brochures from a local travel agency. As you read through them, pay attention to the words used to describe places. Which are fact and which are opinion?
3. Write a one-page story describing an occasion in which you were made to feel comfortable and welcome.
4. Pick at least one occupation mentioned in this chapter that you think would be interesting. Research the occupation thoroughly, and write a report. Use the career research checklist in Chapter 5 as a guide for your report. Conclude your report with an explanation of your interest in that occupation based on your findings.

Speaking and Listening

1. Pretend you are the social director on a cruise ship. Take one minute to explain to the class how to have fun doing something such as a dance step.
2. Listen to your classmates' instructions in Activity 1. Could you follow them? Did the person's attitude make you feel more or less like participating?

Activities Working with Others

In almost all careers you must be able to get along well with other people to be successful. Work with your classmates to do the following activities. As you work together, pay attention to how well you get along. If necessary, work hard at improving your ability to do your part and to cooperate.

1. As a class, offer to host the next meeting of your school's parent-teacher organization. Plan for the location, any decorations, refreshments, speakers, and announcements.
2. With a classmate, plan enough activities to entertain a preschool class for one hour. Activities should include some that are energetic and some that are quiet.
3. Add the careers mentioned in this chapter to your database.

Decision Making and Problem Solving

You will be a big help to your employer if you can make decisions and solve problems. List all the possible ways of resolving the situations described below. Then pick the best alternative (possible choice), and tell why you chose it. If you need help, you might want to refer to Chapter 3.

1. You are an attendant at the zoo. Some children have been feeding the animals. You explain that this is not good for the animals. One little girl refuses to listen. What will you do?
2. You are the host or hostess at a restaurant. Some people at one of the tables are being loud and disturbing the other customers. Your employer expects you to maintain a hospitable atmosphere. What will you do?

CHAPTER 15

MANUFACTURING TECHNOLOGY CAREERS

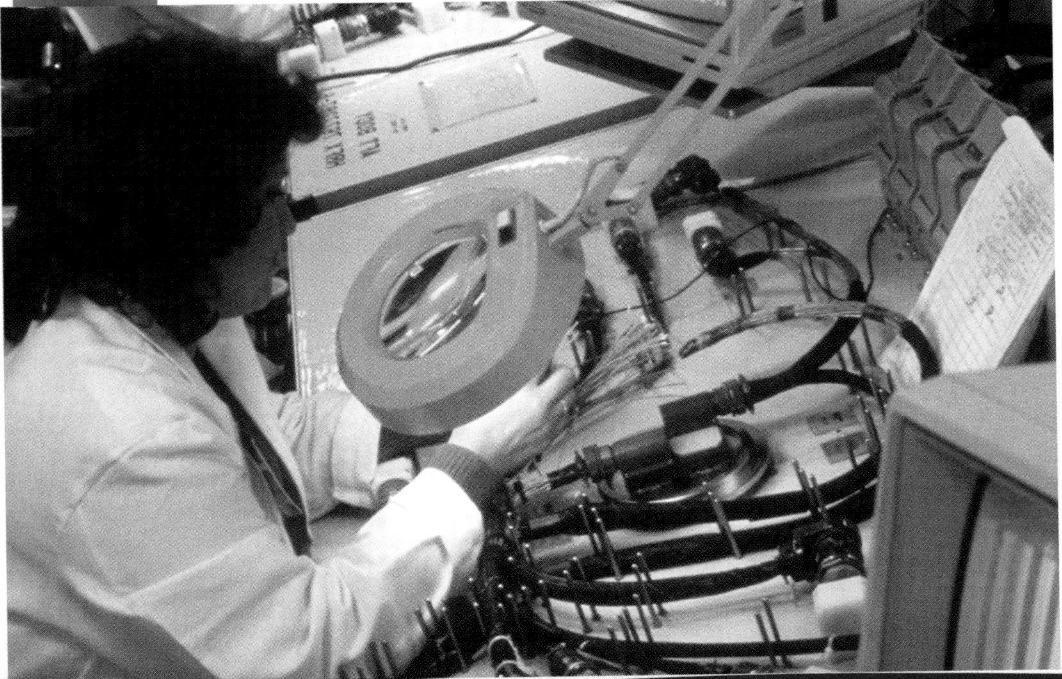

◆ CHAPTER OBJECTIVES ◆

After completing this chapter you will be able to do the following:

- ◆ Define the terms listed under "New Career Terms."
- ◆ List and describe the seven job families in the Manufacturing Technology Cluster.
- ◆ Identify several careers included in this cluster.
- ◆ Name several slow-growing and fast-growing jobs in this cluster.
- ◆ Explain what it would be like to work at a career in this cluster.
- ◆ Evaluate your own interest in this cluster.
- ◆ Identify skills common to many careers in this cluster.

◆ NEW CAREER TERMS ◆

In this chapter you will learn the meanings of the following career terms:

- ✔ Textile
- ✔ Manufacturing
- ✔ Manufacturing Technology Cluster
- ✔ Plant
- ✔ Engineering
- ✔ CAD/CAM
- ✔ Human resources
- ✔ Unskilled laborer
- ✔ Semiskilled worker
- ✔ Skilled worker
- ✔ Laser

Think about all of the goods you use in just one day. You play a radio. You watch a television set. You eat with silverware and dishes. You sit in chairs at desks. You drink out of glasses. You write on pieces of paper. You play sports with bats, balls, and nets. You wear clothes made from **textiles**—*different types of cloth.*

All of the things that you use every day are made in the **manufacturing** *part of our huge economy. Manufacturing is the process of making from raw materials products that people can use. Manufactured goods provide us with necessities, such as clothing, and conveniences, such as telephones. The* **Manufacturing Technology Cluster** *is the group of occupations involved in the design and assembly of goods.*

Most manufactured goods are made, or manufactured, in factories. Steel, for example, is made in steel factories called steel mills. Factories are also called **plants,** *such as textile plants and automobile manufacturing plants.*

Today there are about 300,000 manufacturing companies in the United States. Many of these companies have hundreds of factories. Almost 18 million people work in these factories.

textile
a woven or knit cloth.

▼ Notice the protective equipment this assembly worker wears. Safety is always important in the manufacturing cluster.

WHAT WOULD IT BE LIKE?

A wide range of jobs exists in manufacturing technology. You could do strenuous physical work all day, every day, or you could spend all day sitting at a desk. In the physical category, there are many jobs in difficult conditions. For example, work in a steel mill might be very hot. In many of these jobs you would wear work clothes and get dirty.

Work as a scientist or engineer, in contrast, might be done in an air-conditioned office. You would only have to go out into the manufacturing part of the factory from time to time.

Much of the unskilled, semiskilled, and even skilled work in this career cluster is routine. That means that you do the same thing over and over. An assembler on an assembly line in a car factory repeats the same task. As you know, your feelings about routine work are important in choosing a career. Some people like the security of doing the same tasks over and over. Other people need variety. You must know into which category you fit.

You shouldn't get the idea that a job that has lots of routine work is a bad job. All work can be good. If you work in a job on an assembly line, you'll work with many people and probably get to know them well. You also will get a regular paycheck and be able to buy many of the things you want. You may not have the worries, indecision, and lack of security that people often have in other kinds of jobs.

Would you enjoy working in this career cluster? Do some daydreaming as you "listen" to the following conversation. Several people who enjoy working in the Manufacturing Technology Cluster are

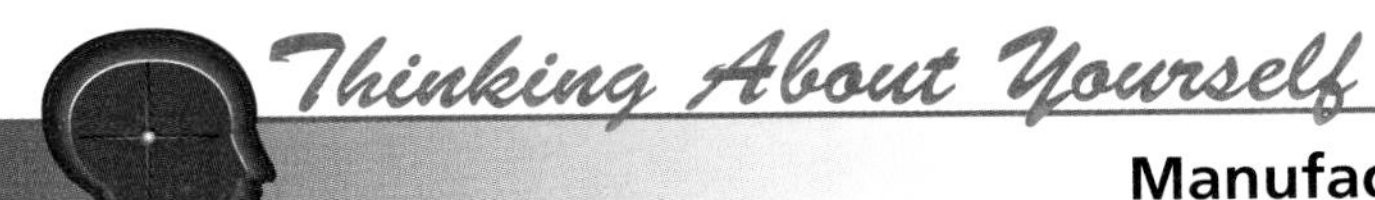

Manufacturing Technology Careers

Take your time reading and thinking about the questions below. You might even want to write out your answers.

- ▲ Have you taken any industrial technology courses (courses where you develop manual skills and become familiar with machines and tools)? Did you enjoy them?
- ▲ Do you enjoy doing projects that require math skills, such as measuring?
- ▲ Have you ever assembled a bike or toy following step-by-step directions? Did you have a fairly easy time doing this?
- ▲ Do you enjoy working with mechanical equipment?
- ▲ Have you ever helped someone install or repair something? Are you good at following directions? Do you prefer *following* directions to *giving* directions?
- ▲ Did you ever build anything, such as a model airplane, on your own?
- ▲ Do you enjoy reading magazine articles about mechanical things?
- ▲ Are you interested in knowing how a car engine works?

If you answered yes to many of the questions, and you think you would enjoy working in a factory, there is a good chance you would enjoy a manufacturing technology career.

talking about their jobs. As you listen to what they say, imagine yourself doing their jobs.

Assembler: I work on an assembly line for the manufacturer of heavy farm and construction equipment. I've worked in several different departments. Right now I'm bolting plow parts together. I've worked here for fifteen years, and I hope to stay through retirement. We've got a strong union, and the company has treated us right.

I've always been good with my hands, and I enjoy working with machinery. I like to see how fast I can put my pieces together. On some jobs we get paid piecework—you know, according to how many we do. I like the idea of racing the clock.

There are lots of other good things about the job. I work with many people, so I've made a lot of friends. I've learned how to use a lot of tools, and that's helped me with my own work around the house. And I guess one of the best things is that I know what's expected of me every day. I don't have to worry about lots of changes, and deadlines, and things like that.

Tool and Die Maker: I also like working with my hands, putting things together and taking them apart. But I need more variety. I couldn't stand doing the same thing over and over. That's why I like my job—it's a different problem every day. I get the blueprints for new tools and dies (tools for shaping, cutting, or stamping) from the engineering department, and then it's up to me to make

manufacturing
the process of making from raw materials products that people can use.

Manufacturing Technology Cluster
a group of occupations involved in the design and assembly of goods.

plant
factory (most manufactured goods are made in factories).

▶ Quality control insures that all products meet manufacturing standards before they are sold to customers.

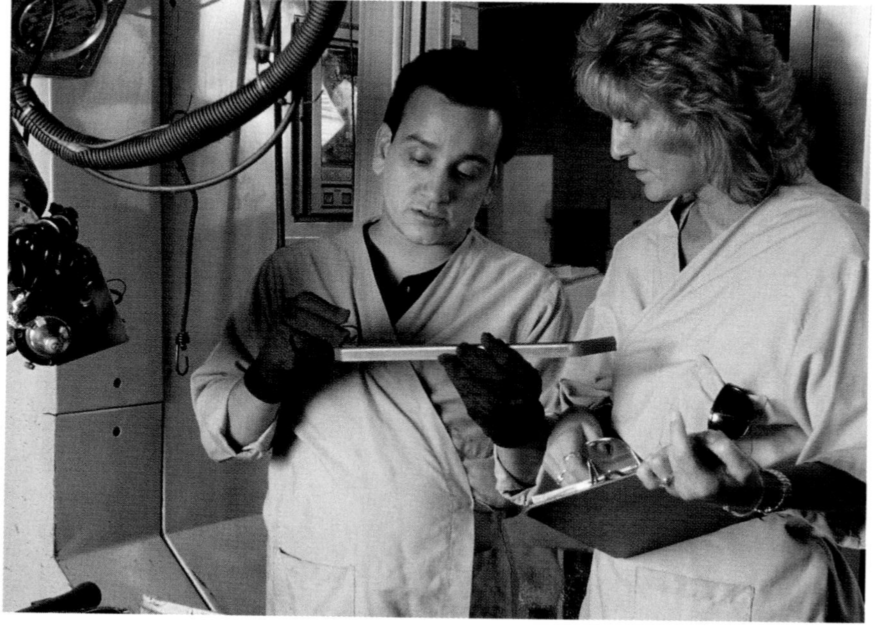

what they need. Of course, almost everything has to be sized accurately to within one- or two-thousandths of an inch. I've got my own work area with access to a lathe, drill press, grinder—just about everything you can think of. My dad could make anything under the sun with a piece of metal or a piece of wood, and I think I inherited that trait. I get a great deal of satisfaction from my work. I'd bet only about 1 out of every 400 or 500 people who work here could do this job.

Department Manager: You'll get no argument from me. Good tool and die makers are worth their weight in gold. Of course, the fact that I worked as a toolmaker for eight years prior to becoming department manager might influence my opinion some. I love my new job, though. I get to meet and work with more people around the plant. I spend a lot of time talking to managers from other departments about their needs and priorities. Then it's up to me to schedule the work according to what's most important. It's a constant juggling act trying to keep everybody happy. But I'm learning more and more about what's going on throughout the plant, and that's got to help. My goal is to be plant manager someday.

Quality Control Engineer: If you do become plant manager, I hope you realize the importance of quality control. Not everyone does, you know. Some people think all they have to worry about is quantity. They never think about quality. Well, it's my job to make sure that every nut, and bolt, and shaft—every part and final product that comes out of this plant is made to specifications. I develop and supervise all our inspections and testing. To some, I'm the bad guy. They're working hard to turn out their parts, and then one of our inspectors has to tell them it's off by a fraction. That's tough. But it has to be done. If we let quality slip, we'll be out of business before you know it. I like to think that in a way, I'm helping everybody here keep their jobs.

What do you think? Do any of these careers sound appealing? Can you see yourself doing one of these jobs—or a similar job? Would you like to learn more about manufacturing technology careers?

Career Decision-Making Activities

1. Whether you like or don't like a manufacturing career could depend on the materials you are working with and the final products you are manufacturing. On a separate sheet of paper, make a list of at least fifty products you can think of that are manufactured. Divide them into categories according to the materials from which they are made. If you were going to work in manufacturing, with which products and materials would you want to work? Compile lists in class, and discuss why you picked the products you chose.
2. Pick a manufactured product from your home or classroom. Look over the item carefully, thinking about the materials and parts that make it up. Then try to imagine how that product is manufactured. Write out the steps in the manufacturing process as you imagine it. Be as detailed as you can. Include everything from the first step to the final product leaving the factory.

   When you're finished, do some research to learn what you can about how that product is actually manufactured. What steps, if any, did you overlook? What machines did you learn about that you had never heard of? Tell your classmates what you learned.
3. Ask your parents for permission to take apart and put back together a toy belonging to a younger brother or sister. If you have no such toys in your home, see if you can borrow one from a neighbor or relative. The more parts the toy has, the better. Notice how the toy fits together as you take it apart. Then time yourself putting it back together. Repeat the process to see if you can do it still faster. Volunteer to bring the toy to class, and challenge your classmates to beat your time.

JOB FAMILIES IN THE MANUFACTURING TECHNOLOGY CLUSTER

The Manufacturing Technology Cluster spans many industries. A number of them have already been mentioned. The seven job families in this cluster are arranged by different types of work, such as scientific or technical. They are shown in the job family diagram on page 236. Reading about the different job families will help you decide what kind of career in this cluster you would enjoy most.

◆ **Engineers. Engineering** is the use of science and math to solve problems in manufacturing and other industries.

engineering
the use of science and math to solve problems in manufacturing and other industries.

Figure 15.1 Job Families in the Manufacturing Technology Cluster

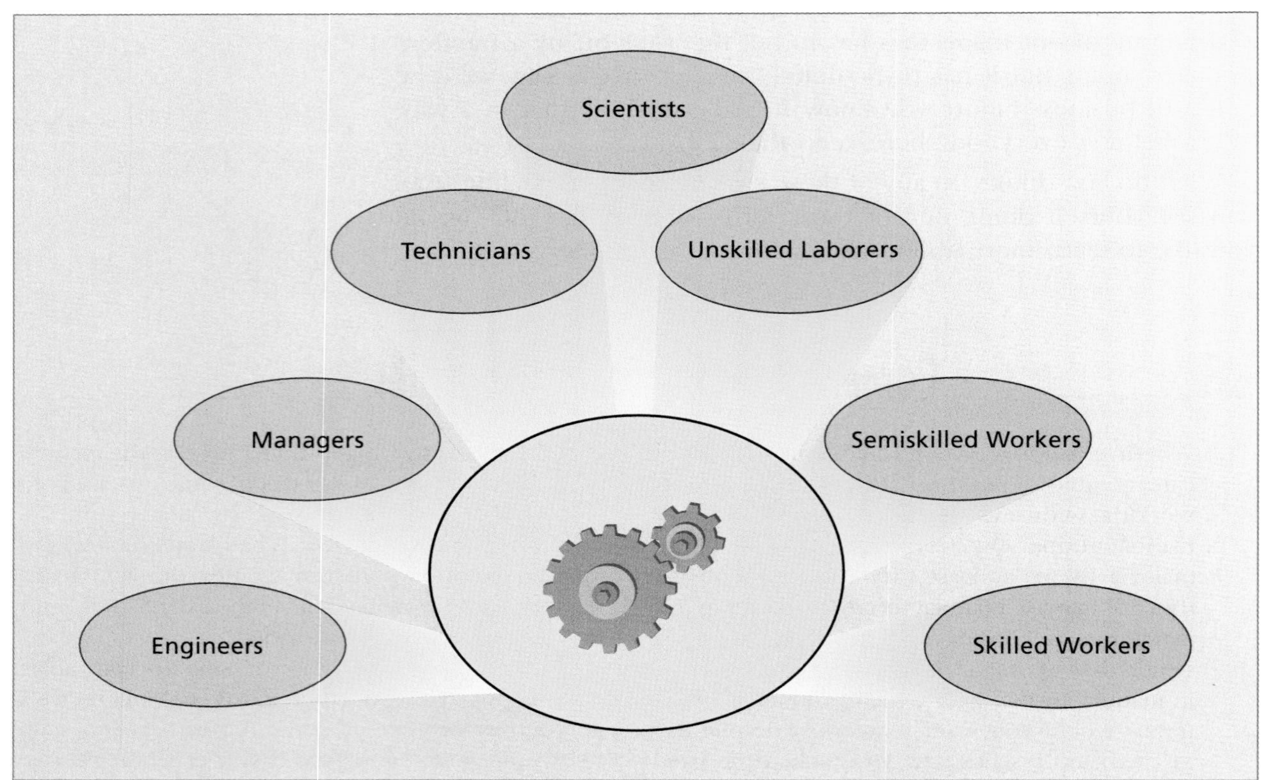

All factories and research laboratories use engineers. This job family includes the engineering occupations involved in manufacturing technology. To be an engineer you would need to go to college and take lots of math and science courses.

There are many different types of engineers. Electrical engineers work in the electricity industry. Industrial engineers work in industrial factories and plan how everything should work. Mechanical engineers design mechanical products, such as engines.

These engineers use computers for virtually all of their design work. After the design is done, computers also help translate it into a manufactured product. The design process and applying the design in a factory setting is known as **CAD/CAM,** or computer-aided design/ computer-assisted manufacturing.

Nuclear engineers help solve problems in the nuclear power industry. Nuclear power is one way to generate electricity.

CAD/CAM
Computer-Aided Design/Computer-Aided Manufacturing—translating an engineering design into a manufactured product with the use of computers.

Safety engineers start safety programs to prevent unsafe working conditions. They look at new machinery and equipment. They try to find problems with them and catch the problems before they cause harm to workers.

- **Managers.** Every factory has to have managers. These people supervise other people. They include the president, vice-president, and plant manager. This job family includes all the people involved in supervising a manufacturing plant.

  There are **human resources** managers, for example. Human resources refers to employees, or workers. A human resources manager may be in charge of hiring new workers. He or she may also be in charge of firing workers. Human resources managers establish social and recreational activities in larger companies. They are also in charge of group health insurance.

- **Technicians.** The technician job family includes the occupations involved in specialized manufacturing operations. Technicians sometimes do the work of engineers but don't need as much education and training as an engineer.

  Technicians often test equipment. An electronics tester tests electronic systems to make sure they are working correctly. An electronics tester may use an X-ray machine to look at the inside of an engine, for example.

  A math technician works closely with engineers to solve problems. Math technicians specialize in applying mathematics to manufacturing problems.

- **Scientists.** People involved in the basic research of products and manufacturing methods are in the scientist job family. Within manufacturing technology, the most common scientists are chemists and physicists.

  A chemist knows chemistry—what substances are made of and how they act and change. He or she conducts research to improve manufacturing techniques. A chemist might devise a new type of paint, for example. Physicists look at physical things—how they happen. A physicist might figure out a way to test a new material that is going to be used in a car.

- **Unskilled laborers.** Another job family, that of unskilled laborers, includes work that requires physical labor and direct supervision. Unskilled laborers do not have special skills or training to perform tasks. Every manufacturing technology industry uses a large number of unskilled laborers. In the printing industry, for example, there are bindery workers. They help bind books and magazines so that the pages all stay together. Production painters paint

human resources
employees or workers.

unskilled laborer
a person not required to have special skills or training to perform a task.

▼ If you enjoy working with information, you might consider a scientific career.

Always on the Move

Sam grew up an "army brat." Both his parents were in the armed services. They were transferred many times while Sam was growing up. Every school he went to had something different about it for Sam to get used to. He also had to make new friends.

Sometimes Sam would get to like a couple of teachers. Then his parents would be transferred to another army base. Sam would have to change schools again.

Sam's grades weren't the best. It wasn't that he didn't try. He just got discouraged.

When his dad asked him what he wanted to be, he always said he didn't know. In his heart he wanted to be a scientist or an engineer. But he was too shy to say that. Besides, his grades weren't good.

What Do YOU Think?

Can you understand why Sam seemed discouraged about school? If you were giving advice to Sam, what would you tell him? Would you mention that he needed a long-term goal? Would you give him some ideas about how to work toward that goal?

semiskilled worker
a person with partial or some skills required to perform a task

skilled worker
a person with the skills, training, and experience to perform a task.

the machines used in factories. There are assemblers in many factories. Assemblers put things together.

- **Semiskilled workers.** Workers in the semiskilled worker job family perform routine tasks with little supervision. These workers do things that are routine, and they don't have to be supervised. *Semi* means "partially" or "not completely." That means that only *some* skill is required. There are many types of occupations for semiskilled workers.

A kiln operator is one such worker. He or she works with kilns, which are large containers that get very hot. Kilns heat minerals before they are mixed with liquid metal to form steel. A kiln operator might work in a steel mill, for example.

In the paper manufacturing industry, there are digester operators. They work with a big machine, called a digester, that cooks chips of wood. These cooked chips of wood eventually are made into paper.

- **Skilled workers.** Any work in the Manufacturing Technology Cluster that requires a high level of ability without direct supervision is included in the skilled worker job family. Skilled workers have the experience, skills, and training necessary to perform tasks. A machinist is one type of skilled worker. He or she sets up and operates machines that work with metals. The metals are made into parts with these machines.

In the plastics industry there are pattern makers. They develop the patterns needed to make the parts that form the product. Pattern makers also make sure the parts are formed correctly. These formed pieces become the sides of televisions, video games, and anything else using plastic.

Toolmakers do just that—they make tools for different industries. For example, they might make the specialized tools for bending, cutting, or forming metal to make products. Toolmaking is a highly skilled occupation. Tools need to be made in exact sizes.

▲ Semiskilled workers complete tasks with little supervision.

CAREER OUTLOOK

In the United States, manufacturing is declining. U.S. manufacturers are facing stiff competition from many other countries. These countries can produce many goods more cheaply than they can be manufactured in the United States. That means American manufacturing has to get more modern. Some jobs will become more important and others less important.

FASTEST-GROWING JOBS

In manufacturing technology, the following jobs are among those that are growing the fastest:

- Engineers, including industrial, electrical, mechanical, and aerospace engineers.
- CAD/CAM specialist.
- Industrial laser machine operator.

Careers for Tomorrow

OPERATING AN INDUSTRIAL LASER MACHINE

A **laser** produces a very concentrated beam of intense light. Laser beams can pierce right through metal very quickly.

In manufacturing, laser machines are used on metal, rubber, plastic, and cloth. A laser operator might carve plastic into a special shape using a laser machine.

Not all vocational schools offer laser-related programs. If you are interested in this fast-growing job area, you can get experience first in manufacturing machinery. Then you can get on-the-job training in laser technology.

To get more information on this exciting career, write the Laser Institute of America, 12424 Research Parkway, Suite 125, Orlando, FL 32826.

laser
a device that produces a very concentrated beam of intense light that can pierce through solid objects, such as metal.

- Electrical technician.
- Numerical control machine operator.

SLOWEST-GROWING JOBS

These are among the slowest-growing jobs in the Manufacturing Technology Cluster:

- All-around machinist.
- Chemist.
- Boiler tender.
- Geologist.

AT THE HEART OF THE MANUFACTURING TECHNOLOGY CLUSTER

What makes the Manufacturing Technology Cluster different from the other fourteen clusters you'll be exploring? What would it really be like to work in this cluster? Let's try to get at the heart of manufacturing technology.

The essence of this cluster is making things. If you work in this cluster the goal of your work is a finished product, such as a television, filing cabinet, tractor, book, fork, hammer, automobile, airplane, shoe—the list goes on and on.

Manufacturing means machines—all kinds of machines. Big ones, little ones, quiet ones, noisy ones, old ones, new ones. The machines do most of the work, but the workers run the machines. They turn them on, speed them up, slow them down, and make adjustments to get parts of different shapes and sizes. When the machines break down, the workers fix them or work on other machines until someone else fixes them.

The machines grind, punch, drill holes in, cut, bend, and weld materials. They work on metal, wood, cloth, paper, plastic, and rubber. The machines often create smoke, oil, grease, heat, and lots of noise. The parts made by the machines come in all shapes and sizes. Tub after tub of parts are made, each one containing hundreds or thousands of the exact same part. Sometimes the parts are large and come one at a time, carried by a hoist.

Manufacturing also means assembly. It means working with your hands to put parts together. You bolt them together, or screw them together, or glue them, nail them, or sew them together.

Figure 15.2 lists just a few examples of occupations from this cluster. Think about the job title, the work activities, and the work settings. Remember—these are just examples to help you get at the heart of this cluster. You don't need to read for details. Scan the entries to get a feel for the cluster as a whole.

Would you like a career in this cluster? Ask yourself the following questions:

Figure 15.2 Sample Occupations in Manufacturing Technology

WHO You Would Be	WHAT You Would Do	WHERE You Would Do It
Electronics engineer	Design, develop, test, and supervise the manufacture of electrical and electronic equipment	At a desk in the office of a manufacturing company; some time spent in the manufacturing part of the plant
Tool programmer	Write computer programs to run numerically (computer-) controlled machine tools (lathes, milling machines, grinders, and so on)	At a desk or computer in the office of a manufacturer; may spend time at actual machining site
Millwright	Install and dismantle heavy machinery; prepare the foundation for the machine; fit bearings, align gears, attach motors, connect belts	In factories where heavy equipment is located
Bindery worker	Operate paper-binding machines; repair and adjust equipment; perform binding operations such as folding, gathering, gluing, stitching, and trimming	Binderies
Metalworking machine operator	Run machines that produce metal parts, set up machines according to blueprints, check tolerances (accuracy of the manufacturing) using micrometers and gauges	Factories; usually dirty, dusty, greasy conditions
Precision assembler	Put together parts, interpret detailed specifications, make independent judgments, put together prototypes (models) and subassemblies (parts of a whole product)	Factories; varying conditions

- Do you like the sound of the occupations listed under "Who"? Would you feel good about an identity like one of these?
- Would you enjoy doing activities like those described under "What"?
- Picture yourself working in the settings described under "Where." Would you be comfortable in these settings?

SKILLS, TRAINING, AND EXPERIENCE

Listed below are some skills common to many of the jobs in the Manufacturing Technology Cluster:

- Read and understand blueprints and diagrams to set up and adjust machines.
- Use eyes, hands, and fingers to do precise assembly work or to operate machines.
- Notice small differences in shape, size, and texture.
- Use math skills for measuring, computing, or record keeping.
- Pay close attention to standards and guidelines.
- Repeat tasks over and over exactly the same way each time.
- Make decisions based on standards that can be checked.
- Use high-level math.
- Solve problems of a complex nature.

There are many unskilled jobs available in manufacturing technology. Sometimes these jobs can lead to promotions. Many factory managers started out as part-time sweepers.

Many levels of skill are required for the different jobs in the Manufacturing Technology Cluster. What follows are three categories of jobs.

JOBS REQUIRING LESS-THAN-AVERAGE TRAINING AND EXPERIENCE

- Production painter.
- Assembler.
- Blacksmith.
- Machine tool operator.
- Boiler worker.
- Electroplater.
- Quality control inspector.

JOBS REQUIRING AVERAGE TRAINING AND EXPERIENCE

- Aerospace technician.
- Electrical technician.
- Electronics technician.
- All-around machinist.
- Industrial upholsterer.
- Mechanical engineering technician.
- Instrument repairer.
- Nuclear technician.
- Tool and die maker.

JOBS REQUIRING MORE-THAN-AVERAGE TRAINING AND EXPERIENCE

- Chemist.
- Electrical engineer.
- Industrial designer.
- Aerospace engineer.
- Ceramic engineer.
- Mechanical engineer.
- Nuclear engineer.
- Physicist.
- Safety engineer.
- Production manager.
- CAD/CAM specialist.

See page 244 for a list of some of the jobs in the Manufacturing Technology Cluster, along with their *DOT* numbers.

Career Decision-Making Activities

1. Take high school courses in drafting, mechanical drawing, and technology. Take as much math as you can manage successfully. Take courses in general science and physics.
2. Help one of your parents or adult relatives tune up a car, lawn mower, or other piece of equipment. Do as much of the work yourself as you can. Did you enjoy the experience? If so, try to fix your own things, such as your bicycle.
3. Factory working conditions vary a great deal, depending on the company and the type of industry. Make as many visits to as many different kinds of factories as possible in your area. Most companies will arrange tours. Work with classmates to identify surrounding factories and arrange visits.
4. Read articles in specialized manufacturing technology magazines, such as *Popular Science* and *Science Digest.* Also look for articles in the business section of your local newspaper about current events in local manufacturing companies.
5. Pursue a hobby that allows you to assemble parts and learn how objects are constructed. Putting together a model train set or a model airplane are examples.

Occupations in Manufacturing Technology

Here is a list of occupations mentioned in this chapter. Next to the name of each occupation is its *DOT* number. You can use the *DOT* number to locate further information about the occupation in your school or public library. For the broad occupational terms mentioned in this chapter, only one or two examples of that occupation are listed below. You can easily find more examples of the occupation in the *DOT.*

Aerospace Engineer (002.061-010)
Aerospace Technician (002.280-010)
Assembler, Electronic Equipment (723.684-010)
Assembler, Small Parts (706.684-022)
Bindery Worker (653.685-010)
Blacksmith (610.381-010)
Boiler Tender (805.261-010)
Boiler Worker (805.687-010)
Ceramic Engineer (006.061-014)
Chemist (022.061-010)
Department Manager (189.167-022)
Die Maker (601.281-010)
Digester Operator (532.362-010)
Electrical Engineer (003.061-010)
Electrical Technician (003.161-010)
Electronics Engineer (003.061-030)
Electronics Technician (003.161-014)
Electronics Tester (007.061-026)
Electroplater (500.380-010)
Engineer, Mechanical (007.061-014)
Engineer, Quality Control (012.167-054)
Geologist (024.061-018)
Industrial Designer (142.061-026)
Industrial Engineer (012.167-030)
Industrial Laser Machine Operator (815.682-010)
Industrial Upholsterer (780.381-014)
Instrument Repairer (722.281-010)
Kiln Operator (509.565-010)
Machine Tool Operator (600.280-034)
Machinist, All-Around (600.280-022)
Manager, Industrial Organization (189.117-022)
Manager of Personnel (166.117-018)
Math Technician (020.162-010)
Mathematician (020.067-014)
Mechanical Engineer (007.061-014)
Mechanical Engineering Technician (007.161-026)
Metalworking Machine Operator (see Machinist, All-Around)
Millwright (638.281-018)
Nuclear Engineer (015.061-014)
Nuclear Technician (710.281-030)
Numerical Control Machine Operator (609.662-010)
Pattern Maker, Plastics (754.381-014)
Personnel Manager (166.117-018)
Physicist (023.061-014)
Plant Manager (189.117-022)
Precision Assembler (see Assembler)
President (189.117-026)
Production Manager (183.117-010)
Production Painter (741.684-026)
Quality Control Engineer (012.167-054)
Quality Control Inspector (701.261-010)
Safety Engineer (012.061-014)
Scientist, Materials (029.081-014)
Sweeper (381.687-018)
Technician, Mathematical (020.162-010)
Tool Maker (601.280-042)
Tool Programmer (007.167-018)
Vice-President (189.117-034)

Review and Enrichment

Summarizing the Chapter

Summarizing information is a critical thinking skill that will help you succeed in the world of work. Write a summary of what you learned in Chapter 15. Focus on the main points of the chapter. Then in a class discussion, compare your summary with the summaries done by your classmates. Can you improve your summary?

Improving Your Career Vocabulary

1. Learning to use new vocabulary terms will improve your communication skills, which are important in almost all areas of work. Write definitions for the terms listed below. Then for each term, write an original sentence about yourself in which you use the term correctly.
   - textile
   - manufacturing
   - Manufacturing Technology Cluster
   - plant
   - engineering
   - CAD/CAM
   - human resources
   - unskilled laborer
   - semiskilled worker
   - skilled worker
   - laser
2. List the job families discussed in this chapter. Write a one-sentence description of each.

Finding the Facts

Finding exact information is a frequently used skill in many careers. Find the answers to the exercise below, and write the answers on a separate sheet of paper.

1. How many manufacturing companies are there in the United States? How many people work in factories?
2. What kind of work do engineers do?
3. What are the duties of a human resources manager?
4. What is a laser?
5. Name three jobs from the Manufacturing Technology Cluster that require average training and experience.

Thinking for Yourself

To complete the exercise below you will need to use critical thinking and communication skills, which are skills valued by all employers. Write out your answers or be prepared to discuss them in class, depending on your teacher's instructions.

1. Today, technology is replacing many workers in factories. The workers have to learn new skills. What do you think the advantages and disadvantages of this trend would be?
2. Recently products made in the United States have met a lot of competition from those made in Japan and other countries. Some people think such competition is good for everyone. Others complain that American workers lose jobs as a result. What do you think?
3. Manufacturing has often caused pollution of air and water. What do you think is the responsibility of manufacturers to the environment?

Practicing Your Basic Skills

Your career success depends greatly on your basic math and communication skills. Work hard at improving in the areas where you have trouble with the following exercises.

Math

1. Sara Bistie was an assembler at a factory and got paid for piecework. She was paid $7.50 an hour. She was also paid 55¢ apiece for every machine part she assembled over her quota (required amount). Her daily quota was 135. On Monday she made 136 parts; on Tuesday 135; on Wednesday 140; on Thursday 149; and on Friday 139. How much did she earn altogether for a forty-hour week?
2. Santiago was in charge of inventory for his company. He kept track of all materials on hand. In one bin were 3,476 screws. In another bin were 7,860 washers. Yesterday he sent out one-fourth of the screws and five-sixths of the washers. Today two dozen of each came in on a new order. How many does he now have?
3. As department manager, Yolanda has to keep track of hours and wages. Using the following figures, determine how much her department spent on labor last week:

Review and Enrichment, continued

Worker A: 40 hours at $5.45 and 6 hours at time-and-a-half.
Worker B: 40 hours at $6.88 and 10 hours at time-and-a-half.
Worker C: 40 hours at $7.76 and 2 hours at time-and-a-half.
Worker D: 40 hours at $8.12.

Reading and Writing

1. Research and write a one-page report on one of the following: (a) lasers in manufacturing; (b) water-jet cutting; (c) robots that help make cars; (d) OSHA; (e) computer-assisted manufacturing and computer-integrated manufacturing; or (f) manufacturing in outer space.
2. Read a book about the Industrial Revolution. Write a one-page report comparing the lives of factory workers then and now.
3. Write a paragraph describing a "mystery" manufactured product. Choose something common that you see or use everyday. Tell its size, the materials of which it's made, and any distinguishing details. Trade papers in class, and guess the mystery products.
4. Pick at least one occupation in this chapter that you think would be interesting. Research the occupation thoroughly, and write a report. Use the career research checklist in Chapter 5 as a guide. Conclude your report with an explanation of your interest in that occupation based on your findings.

Speaking and Listening

1. Workers in many factories belong to unions. Unions help workers bargain with company management for things the workers want, such as better working conditions or higher pay. Pretend you are running for election as a union leader. Give a one-minute speech to class members explaining why they should vote for you.
2. Listen to your classmates' speeches in Activity 1. Make notes of what is fact and what is opinion. Why would it be important to tell the difference?

Activities Working with Others

In almost all careers you must be able to get along well with other people to be successful. Work with your classmates to do the following activities. As you work together, pay attention to how well you get along. If necessary, work hard at improving your ability to do your part and to cooperate.

1. With a classmate, design a new product, an improvement on an existing product, or a robot that will perform a simple task. Your design can be serious or comic, such as a new notepad holder or a robot that squeezes out toothpaste. It should require only simple household materials like cardboard, plastic milk containers, string, and so on.
2. Make a model of the product you designed in Activity 1. If possible, it should be a working model. Demonstrate your product to the class.
3. Add the careers mentioned in this chapter to your database.

Decision Making and Problem Solving

You will be a big help to your employer if you can make decisions and solve problems. List all the possible ways of resolving the situations described below. Then pick the best alternative (possible choice), and tell why you chose it. If you need help, you might want to refer to Chapter 3.

1. You work in a factory. You know the work well, but your boss always feels as if he has to tell you how to do everything. You get tired of listening to him. Your company is installing a new process. You think you already know how it works. Your boss wants you to stay late so he can explain it to you, but your friends want you to meet them. What will you do?
2. You have just been offered a promotion. If you accept it, your monthly salary will be increased by about $90. Your new duties will include managing three other workers and filing a long report every month. You will also have to work half a day on some Saturdays. What will you do?

CHAPTER 16

MARINE SCIENCE CAREERS

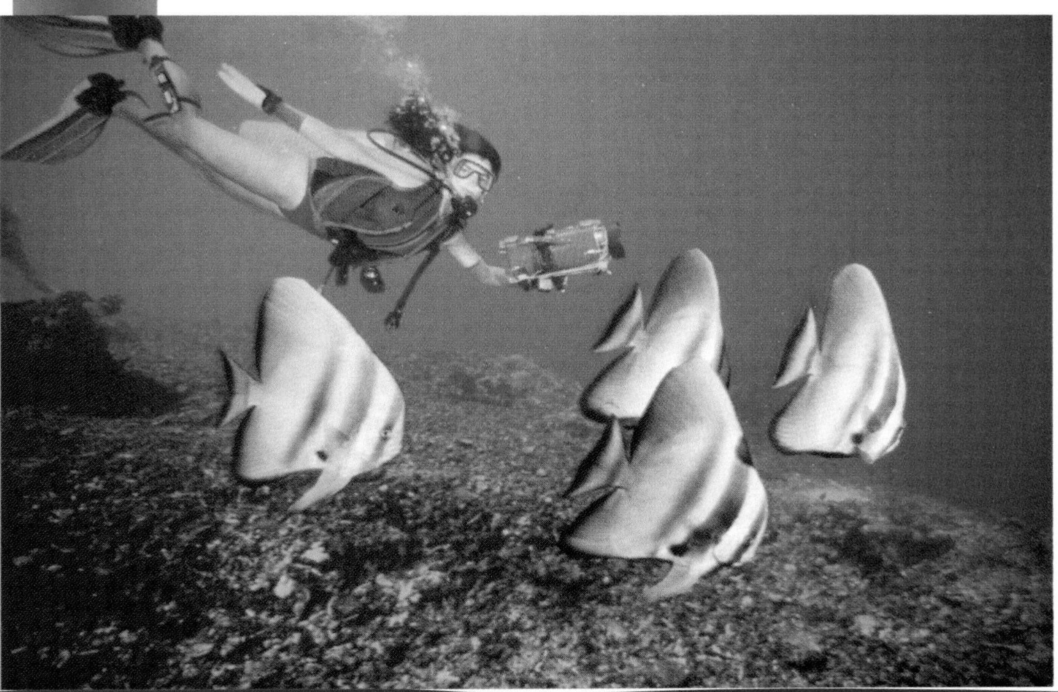

◆ Chapter Objectives ◆

After completing this chapter you will be able to do the following:

- ◆ Define the terms listed under "New Career Terms."
- ◆ List and describe the seven job families in the Marine Science Cluster.
- ◆ Identify several careers included in this cluster.
- ◆ Name several slow-growing and fast-growing jobs in this cluster.
- ◆ Explain what it would be like to work at a career in this cluster.
- ◆ Evaluate your own interest in this cluster.
- ◆ Identify skills common to many careers in this cluster.

◆ New Career Terms ◆

In this chapter you will learn the meanings of the following career terms:

- ✔ Marine
- ✔ Marine science
- ✔ Marine Science Cluster
- ✔ Seasonal
- ✔ Aquaculture
- ✔ Extraction
- ✔ Offshore drilling

***Marine** comes from a word meaning "sea." **Marine science,** then, is the study of the sea and the plants and animals that live in it. People who work in the **Marine Science Cluster** discover marine life and other things we can use from the ocean. They help develop and improve such products. If the marine products are things you eat, they help get them to you. People in marine science might be working on a fishing boat. Or they might be working as biologists for a big fish farm.*

marine
of or relating to the sea.

marine science
the study of the sea and the plants and animals that live in it.

Marine Science Cluster
jobs that discover, develop, and improve marine life and the products we can use from the ocean.

WHAT WOULD IT BE LIKE?

Many of the jobs in the Marine Science Cluster are scientific jobs. Most scientists work indoors, but marine scientists do much of their work outdoors. They work in and around the oceans, where they collect samples and do tests. They also take specimens back to their labs for more experiments and tests.

Like other scientists, marine scientists test theories and look for improved ways to do things. They use their knowledge of scientific methods, along with biology, chemistry, and other sciences.

There are also many marine science jobs that do not involve scientific methods. These are more physical kinds of jobs. For example, suppose you decided to become a crew member on a commercial fishing boat out of Alaska. You would probably be fishing for salmon. You would be working aboard a fishing boat with other fishers. You

▶ Commercial fishers have to know how to repair the nets and other equipment they depend upon.

would use a variety of different nets, depending on the sea conditions and the fish you were after.

One of your jobs might be attaching floats and weights to the nets so that the top parts stay on the surface of the water and the bottom parts sink. You might have to attach flags and lights to the nets to help the captain of the boat identify the net locations later.

In addition to putting the nets out, you would have to haul them in. This is usually done either by hand or with electric motors called *winches.* If things were going well, the nets would be full of fish.

The next step would be to empty the catch from the nets. This might be done with a small dip net or with buckets. It could also be done using big equipment with powerful motors to pull the nets up and dump the catch. You might have to sort and clean the fish. You might even repair the fishing nets.

The hours would be long and hard. The work would be **seasonal.** This means that the work would be done only during part of the year.

seasonal
work or activity done only during part of the year.

You would have to accept living on a boat for that period of time. Your room, if you had one alone, would be extremely small. Your hands and clothes would smell fishy all the time. Fussy people and those who get seasick would not enjoy this lifestyle!

If you were in the commercial fishing industry you would probably have to find another seasonal job during those months when you couldn't fish. You could take courses at a community college during those months to prepare yourself for other careers. After all, work-

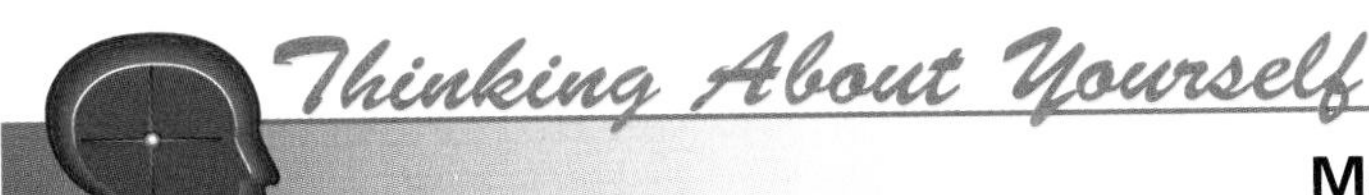

Marine Science Careers

Take your time reading and thinking about the questions below. You might even want to make notes on a sheet of paper and write out your answers.

- Have you ever raised plants or animals as a hobby?
- Have you ever owned a chemistry set or microscope? Do you enjoy using this equipment?
- Do you like to read scientific articles?
- Have you ever collected seashells?
- Do you like to go fishing?
- Are you a good swimmer? Do you enjoy water sports? Have you spent much time on boats?
- Have you ever collected rocks or minerals as a hobby?
- Do you like to watch the weather reports on television? Would you like to know more about what causes different weather conditions?
- Do you like being outdoors?

If you answered yes to many of the questions above, and you think you would like working on and around large bodies of water, there's a good chance you would enjoy a marine science career.

ing on a fishing boat in cold waters is a physical activity. Nobody stays strong enough to do that forever.

Would you enjoy working in the Marine Science Cluster? Do some daydreaming as you "listen" to the following conversation. Several people who enjoy working in this cluster are talking about their jobs. As you listen to what they say, imagine yourself doing their jobs.

Driller: I operate equipment to drill holes while trying to find oil out in the ocean. It's heavy, tough work. You have to be strong, and you've got to be able to work hard for hours at a time. I could be doing this kind of work in lots of places, but I always do offshore drilling. I like being around the sea. There's something about the sea that makes me feel alive. And I like the hard work. When the day's over I really feel like I've accomplished something.

Marine Engine Mechanic: I'm like you. I grew up on the coast, and I always spent lots of time on the beach. I've always loved the sea. I used to sit on the beach by myself for hours just listening to the waves. I learned mechanics from my dad and uncle, and I've always been good at fixing engines. I could probably make more money elsewhere, but repairing boat engines is my idea of the perfect job. I work on engines for everything from the tiniest motorboat to yachts, tugboats, and fishing trawlers. I like diagnosing a problem and figuring out how to solve it. I also like taking the engines apart and putting them back together. And being able to do all this right here in the bay is like icing on the cake.

Commercial Fisher: It's the same with me. I think I was born on a fishing boat at sea. The sea is the only place I feel at home. Sure I love my work. It's satisfying, and I earn a good living. And I work with a lot of great people. We all depend on one another. It's definitely a team effort. And on those days when you have a really big catch, it's great. But we all know the real reason we're doing this kind of work—it's a good excuse to get out there on the high seas. That's what it's all about.

What do you think? Do any of these careers sound appealing? Can you see yourself doing one of these jobs—or a similar job? Would you like to learn more about marine science careers?

Career Decision-Making Activities

1. Find a short passage from literature that describes what it's like to be at sea. Writers such as Herman Melville and Joseph Conrad, for example, are known for their stories of the sea. Your English teacher or librarian will be able to help you with suggestions. Read a passage that you like to the class. Discuss in class whether you would or would not like being at sea for long periods of time.
2. Go to your school or public library. Find books with pictures of the sea and marine life. Bring the most interesting picture to class. Tell your

classmates what you think is interesting about that picture. How does the picture make you feel about a career in marine science?

3. On a sheet of paper, make a list of all the different kinds of fish and seafood you have eaten. Compile your list with your classmates' lists to make one complete list. Ask classmates to tell about the fish they've eaten that you haven't tried. Would you like to try these fish?

4. What is your most memorable experience involving water? It could be spending a day at the beach, water-skiing at a local lake, or fishing at a vacation resort. Briefly describe your experience to the class. Tell whether or not you think you'd enjoy working on or around a body of water, and why.

JOB FAMILIES IN THE MARINE SCIENCE CLUSTER

There are seven job families in the Marine Science Cluster. They are shown in the figure below. Learning about these job families will help you decide which careers in this cluster you might enjoy most.

- **Aquaculture.** *Aqua* is another word for water. **Aquaculture** involves cultivating or growing marine life in controlled conditions. Usually this is done to sell produce or end products that people can eat, such as certain kinds of fish or clams.

  The most obvious occupation in aquaculture is that of fish farmer. Fish farmers raise trout, catfish, salmon, and other fish in ponds. Fish farmers arrange for the sale of fish. They also count and weigh the fish, load the fish into tank trucks, and pack them in ice for shipping. Fish farmers then process the fish and market them. There are also shellfish growers. They cultivate beds of shellfish, such as clams and oysters.

  A fishery bacteriologist studies ways to control bacteria and other small organisms that can harm the fish in fish farms. Bacteriologists have to study biology.

- **Chemical and mineral extraction. Extraction** means "taking out." The occupations in chemical and mineral extraction involve finding and taking chemicals and minerals from the ocean floor. Some of the jobs in this family can also be classified in the Agribusiness and Natural Resources Cluster.

  A mineralogist examines and analyzes minerals (natural substances such as coal, ore, salt, and stone). He or she does chemical tests. The mineralogist who works on the ocean uses samples from the ocean floor.

aquaculture
cultivating or growing marine life under controlled conditions, usually to be sold for consumption.

extraction
the act of removing or "taking out."

Job Families in the Marine Science Cluster

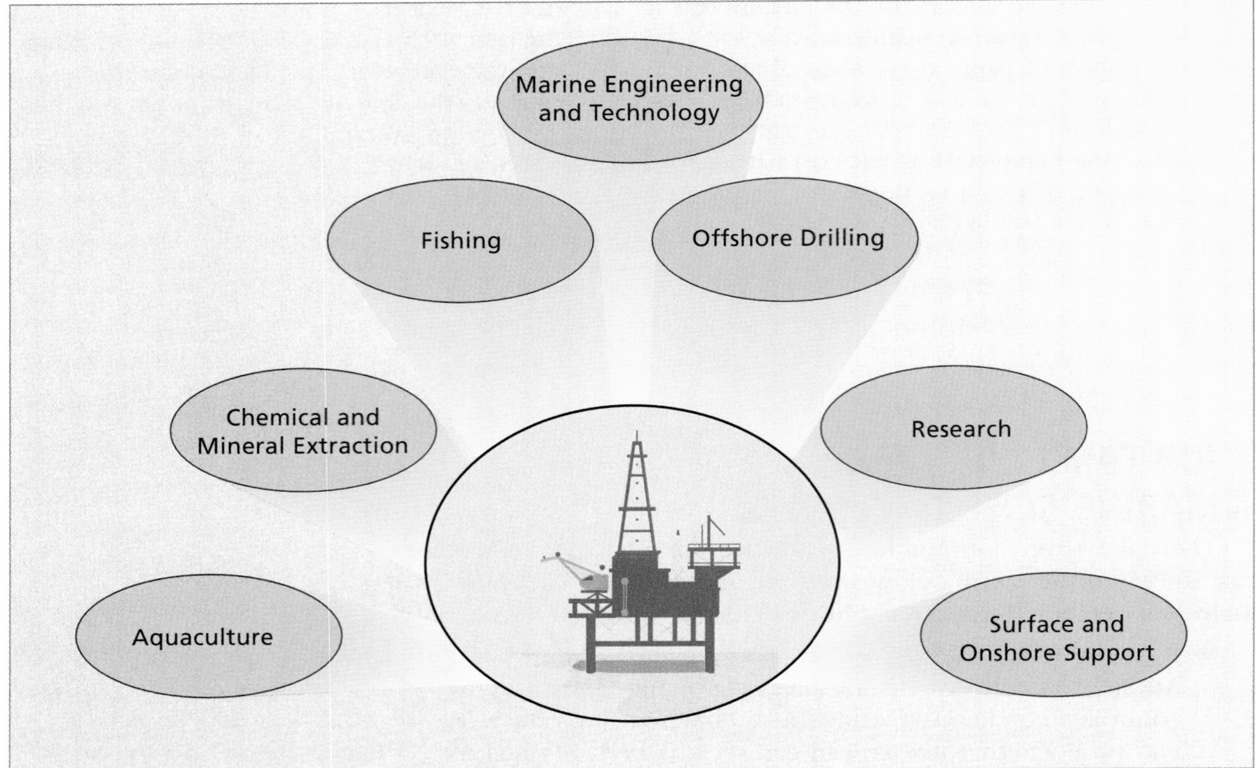

An ocean mining engineer figures out ways to extract the minerals and chemicals that are found on the ocean floor. He or she may have a more difficult job than a mining engineer in the mountains.

- **Fishing.** The fishing job family includes all the occupations involved in harvesting fish and marine produce. On a fishing boat there are line fishers. They catch fish with hooks and lines. There are spearfishers also. They catch eels, salmon, and swordfish. They don't use rods or lines. They use spears or harpoons.

  A fish cleaner cleans the fish after it's caught. Sometimes fish cleaners are called fish scalers or fish dressers.
- **Marine engineering and technology.** Boats have to be designed. So do the instruments used on the boats. Those who do the design, construction, and operation of boats and instruments are in the marine engineering and technology family of occupations.

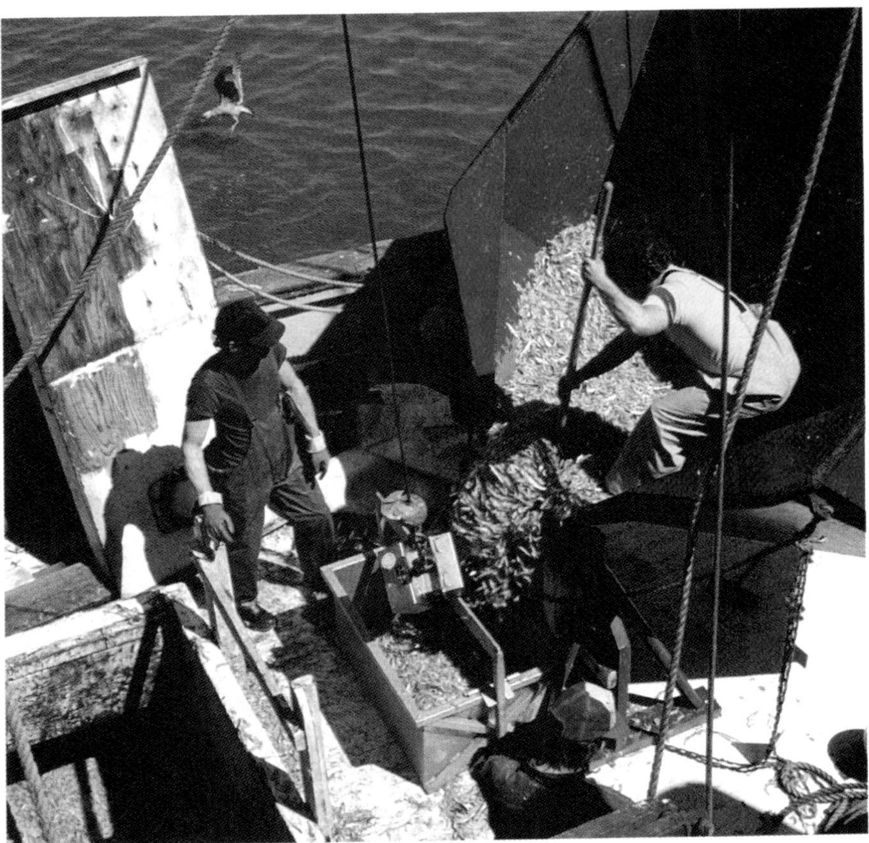

◀ The catch must be unloaded.

We have talked about architects before. A marine architect designs ships, barges, and tugs. He or she is also called a naval architect.

A diver in this job family works below the surface of the water with air lines that are connected to the surface. Divers inspect, repair, and install equipment underwater. They are usually given help by diver helpers. Also within this job family are motorboat operators and mechanics. They operate and fix boats.

◆ **Offshore drilling.** Oil and natural gas are not located only on land. They are sometimes found underneath the ocean floor. The activity of obtaining this oil and natural gas is called **offshore drilling,** because it is done off the shore of a continent or island. Occupations involved in finding and obtaining oil and gas from the ocean floor are in the offshore drilling job family.

offshore drilling
the activity of obtaining oil and natural gas off the shore of a continent or island.

▲ An offshore drilling platform provides several types of jobs requiring various skill levels.

On an offshore drilling platform there are driller helpers. They assist in operating machinery to drill oil and gas wells.

There are also drilling inspectors. They make charts of the pressures and temperatures of the oil and gas coming out of the wells.

Jobs requiring more skills are those of the petroleum geologist and the petroleum engineer. *Petroleum* is another word we use for oil. A petroleum geologist charts the structure of the earth to locate oil and gas deposits. A petroleum engineer analyzes the data to determine if the company will make money trying to drill for oil in different spots.

- **Research.** Any occupation involved in exploring and studying the marine environment is in the research job family. Almost all researchers in this field have a great deal of education and training.

  A marine meteorologist forecasts the weather. These forecasts help pilots and fishing boat operators.

  A hydrologist studies water. *Hydro* means "water." A hydrologist looks at the way water goes from land areas to oceans and into the atmosphere.
- **Surface and onshore support.** The occupations involved in helping and supporting marine science activities are in the surface and onshore support job family. Marine science activities usually involve some type of boat. These boats have to be taken care of. Sometimes they have to be taken onshore to be fixed. A dockhand, for example, helps with cleaning the exteriors of ships when they are docked at piers.

CAREER OUTLOOK

All jobs in the Marine Science Cluster will experience some growth in the future. A few of them depend a lot on how business is going in a particular industry. For example, depending on worldwide oil supplies, the oil industry may or may not be booming. When it is booming, there are lots of jobs in offshore drilling. When business is bad, there are almost no new jobs available.

FASTEST-GROWING JOBS

The following jobs are among those growing the fastest in marine science:

- Aquatic biologist.

An aquatic biologist studies the habits of marine animals.

- Fishery bacteriologist.
- Marine geologist.

SLOWEST-GROWING JOBS

Some of the slowest-growing jobs in this cluster follow:

- Marine meteorologist.
- Mining engineer.
- Sponge clipper.

AT THE HEART OF THE MARINE SCIENCE CLUSTER

What makes the Marine Science Cluster different from the other fourteen clusters you'll be exploring? What would it really be like to work in this cluster? Let's try to get at the heart of marine science.

The essence of this cluster is the ocean. All the occupations involve working around the sea. It means working on boats while they are at sea or docked. It's the rocking and rolling motion of the sea, the salt water and the breezes, and the sounds of the sea. Most people work with their feet on solid ground. Not so with those working in marine science.

Also at the heart of this cluster are the plants, rocks, minerals, and animals that live and exist in the ocean. People who work in this cluster are fascinated by these plants and fish. It's an entirely different world from the one most of us are used to. It's a world filled with strange and exciting vegetation and creatures that you don't see on land. With bright colors, unusual shapes, and strange movements, marine life sparks the curiosity of scientists. And the different fish provide a livelihood for thousands of commercial fishers.

Figure 16.1 gives just a few examples of occupations in this cluster. Think about the job title, the work activities, and the work settings. These are just examples to help you get at the heart of this cluster. You don't need to read for details. Scan the entries to get a feel for the cluster as a whole.

Would you like a career in this cluster? Ask yourself the following questions:

- Do you like the sound of the occupations listed under "Who"? Would you feel good about an identity like one of these?

Figure 16.1 Sample Occupations in the Marine Science Cluster

WHO You Would Be	WHAT You Would Do	WHERE You Would Do It
Petroleum engineer	Explore and drill for oil and gas, plan and supervise drilling operations, develop efficient production methods	Oil and gas fields in places such as Texas, Oklahoma, and California; many also work overseas
Geochemical oceanographer	Study the chemical composition, dissolved elements, and nutrients of the ocean	At sea and in the lab
Geological oceanographer	Study the ocean bottom, collect information using remote sensing devices aboard surface ships or underwater research craft	At sea and in the lab
Hydrologist	Study the distribution, circulation, and physical properties of underground and surface waters	At sea and in the lab
Line fisher	Catch marine life with hooks and lines; lay out lines and attach hooks, bait, and sinkers; chop bait; haul lines in	On boats and docks
Diver	Work below water; inspect, repair, remove, and install equipment; inspect docks, ship bottoms, and propellers	Under the water

- Would you enjoy doing activities like those described under "What"?
- Picture yourself working in the settings described under "Where." Would you be comfortable in these settings?

SKILLS, TRAINING, AND EXPERIENCE

Listed below are some skills common to many occupations in the Marine Science Cluster:

- Use logic or scientific thinking to deal with many different kinds of problems.
- Understand and express complex, technical, and scientific information.
- Make decisions based on information that can be measured or verified.
- Learn, and use knowledge about, how living things function.
- Work outside for long periods of time and in all kinds of weather.
- Perform tasks that may require physical strength and endurance.
- Work quickly and skillfully with your hands.

Different jobs require different levels of skills. You have to decide what level of skill requirement you are willing to shoot for. For example, you don't need many skills or much experience to work as a helper on a fishing boat, but you do to become a marine geologist.

JOBS REQUIRING LESS-THAN-AVERAGE TRAINING AND EXPERIENCE

- Driller helper.
- Line fisher.
- Spearfisher.
- Sponge clipper.
- Fish icer.
- Shellfish shucker.
- Fish cleaner.

JOBS REQUIRING AVERAGE TRAINING AND EXPERIENCE

- Metallurgical technician.
- Driller.
- Drilling inspector.
- Clam dredge operator.
- Fish farmer.
- Shellfish grower.

JOBS REQUIRING MORE-THAN-AVERAGE TRAINING AND EXPERIENCE

- Aquatic biologist.
- Marine geophysicist.
- Marine geologist.
- Marine meteorologist.
- Hydrologist.
- Mining engineer.
- Petroleum geologist.
- Fishery bacteriologist.
- Marine architect.

See page 259 for a list of some of the jobs in the Marine Science Cluster, along with their *DOT* numbers.

Career Decision-Making Activities

1. Take all the science and math courses you can before college. As much as possible, choose projects that involve the ocean and marine life.
2. Go fishing more often. Try to identify the different types of fish. Look for other types of marine or freshwater life.
3. Go to the aquarium, and listen to lectures by the guides. Ask questions about the areas in which you are interested. Follow up by going to the library and reading more about what you learned.
4. Learn how to scuba dive. Learn how to identify the plant and animal life you see.
5. Try to get a part-time job at a local marina, in a boating supply store, or on a fishing boat.

Occupations in Marine Science

Here is a list of occupations mentioned in this chapter. Next to the name of each occupation is its *DOT* number. You can use the *DOT* number to locate further information about the occupation in your school or public library. For the broad occupational terms mentioned in this chapter, only one or two examples of that occupation are listed below. You can easily find more examples of the occupation in the *DOT.*

Aquatic Biologist (041.061-022)
Biologist (041.061-030)
Clam Dredge Operator (446.663-010)
Commercial Fisher (see Fisher)
Crew Member (449.667-010)
Diver (899.261-010)
Diver Helper (899.664-010)
Dockhand (891.684-010)
Driller (930.382-018)
Driller Helper (930.684-026)
Drilling Inspector (930.167-010)
Fish Cleaner (525.684-030)
Fish Dresser (525.684-030)
Fish Farmer (446.161-010)
Fish Icer (922.687-046)
Fish Scaler (529.685-118)
Fisher, Line (442.684-010)
Fisher, Net (441.684-010)
Fishery Bacteriologist (041.061-058)
Geochemical Oceanographer (see Geologist)
Geological Oceanographer (see Geologist)
Geologist (024.061-018)
Hydrologist (024.061-034)
Line Fisher (442.684-010)
Marine Architect (001.061-014)
Marine Engine Mechanic (623.281-026)
Marine Geologist (024.061-018)
Marine Geophysicist (024.061-030)
Marine Meteorologist (025.062-010)
Marine Scientist (024.061-030)
Mechanic, Marine Engine (623.281-026)
Mechanic, Motorboat (623.281-038)
Metallurgical Technician (011.261.010)
Mineralogist (024.061-038)
Mining Engineer (010.061-014)
Motorboat Operator (911.663-010)
Naval Architect (001.061-014)
Petroleum Engineer (010.061-018)
Petroleum Geologist (024.061-022)
Shellfish Grower (446.161-014)
Shellfish Shucker (521.687-122)
Spearfisher (443.684-010)
Sponge Clipper (447.687-026)

Review and Enrichment

Summarizing the Chapter

Summarizing information is a critical thinking skill that will help you succeed in the world of work. Write a summary of what you learned in Chapter 16. Focus on the main points of the chapter. Then in a class discussion, compare your summary with the summaries done by your classmates. Can you improve your summary?

Improving Your Career Vocabulary

1. Learning to use new vocabulary terms will improve your communication skills, which are important in almost all areas of work. Write definitions for the terms listed below. Then for each term, write an original sentence about yourself in which you use the term correctly.
   - marine
   - marine science
   - Marine Science Cluster
   - seasonal
   - aquaculture
   - extraction
   - offshore drilling
2. List the job families discussed in this chapter. Write a one-sentence description of each.

Finding the Facts

Finding exact information is a frequently used skill in many careers. Find the answers to the exercise below, and write the answers on a separate sheet of paper.

1. What machine is used to haul in a fishing net?
2. What kind of work does a mineralogist do?
3. What does a marine architect design?
4. What is the purpose of offshore drilling?
5. What does a hydrologist study?

Thinking for Yourself

To complete the exercise below you will need to use critical thinking and communication skills, which are skills valued by all employers. Write out your answers or be prepared to discuss them in class, depending on your teacher's instructions.

1. In your own words, explain the difference between fishing and aquaculture.
2. In your own words, describe a person you think would enjoy working in the Marine Science Cluster.
3. Some environmentalists claim that fishing in certain waters should be limited. Fishers may claim they need to fish there to make a living. Who do you think is right? Why?
4. What parts of the country do you think would attract people interested in marine science?
5. Name three skills common to this cluster.

Practicing Your Basic Skills

Your career success depends greatly on your basic math and communication skills. Work hard at improving in the areas where you have trouble with the following exercises.

Math

1. Geraldo owns a fish farm. Last year he sold $730,895 worth of fish. The cost of the fish to him was $562,362. His selling expenses were $57,916. General expenses were $37,246. His taxes came to $16,578. What profit did he make?
2. Gina is a marine engineer and often uses diving gear. Each set of oxygen tanks holds enough air for four hours. Gina dove at noon with a set of full tanks and worked until 1:20. At 2:30 she went back down and at 4:00 looked at her watch. At what time will she have to resurface?
3. Jim is building his own boat. He wants to use planks to make the deck. The planks measure 8 feet long by 4½ inches wide. The deck will be 16 feet long and 6 feet wide. How many planks will he need?

Reading and Writing

1. Read a book having to do with marine science. It can be fiction or nonfiction. Write a paragraph telling whether or not those interested in marine science as a career should read the book too, and why.

Review and Enrichment, continued

2. Research one of the following pairs of sea life. Make a chart comparing them. Include such things as size, habitat, food, and commercial value.
   a. sharks and porpoises
   b. salmon and tuna
   c. catfish and trout
   d. seals and walruses
   e. eels and sea snakes
3. Ask at your local library for copies of magazines and newsletters on marine science subjects. Read any of interest, and report your findings to the class.
4. Pick at least one occupation mentioned in this chapter that you think would be interesting. Research the occupation thoroughly, and write a report. Use the career research checklist in Chapter 5 as a guide for your report. Conclude your report with an explanation of your interest in that occupation based on your findings.

Speaking and Listening

1. Talk to someone you know who enjoys fishing. Ask the person what is enjoyable about it. Compare it with your own feelings about fishing.
2. Scientists believe that whales may have a language of their own. Obtain a recording of whale songs, and listen to them. Do you think the songs have meaning?

Activities Working with Others

In almost all careers you must be able to get along well with other people to be successful. Work with your classmates to do the following activities. As you work together, pay attention to how well you get along. If necessary, work hard at improving your ability to do your part and to cooperate.

1. As a class, obtain a pair of guppies or other fish and a bowl in which to keep them. Share the task of feeding and caring for them. Keep daily records of how the fish are doing.
2. With a classmate, study some books on meteorology, and learn to tell the weather by studying the sky. Make predictions every day for two weeks. Post your predictions on the class bulletin board.
3. Add the careers in this chapter to your database.

Decision Making and Problem Solving

You will be a big help to your employer if you can make decisions and solve problems. List all the possible ways of resolving the situations described below. Then pick the best alternative (possible choice), and tell why you chose it. If you need help, you might want to refer to Chapter 3.

1. You work for a marine biologist. You are a good swimmer, but your boss warned you never to swim alone. Your co-worker was supposed to tie the boat but forgot and went inside, leaving you by yourself. The boat is drifting away and has lots of expensive equipment in it. Your boss will be mad if it's lost. What will you do?
2. You've worked on a fishing boat for two summers now, and you'd like to get a full-time job doing the same thing when you graduate. But the man you work for has never commented on your performance, and whenever anyone tries to talk to him he gets irritable because he's busy. You want to ask him about a job, but you don't want to make him mad. What will you do?

CHAPTER 17 MARKETING AND DISTRIBUTION CAREERS

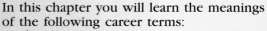

◆ Chapter Objectives ◆

After completing this chapter you will be able to do the following:

- ◆ Define the terms listed under "New Career Terms."
- ◆ List and describe the seven job families in the Marketing and Distribution Cluster.
- ◆ Identify several careers included in this cluster.
- ◆ Name several slow-growing and fast-growing jobs in this cluster.
- ◆ Explain what it would be like to work at a career in this cluster.
- ◆ Evaluate your own interest in this cluster.
- ◆ Identify skills common to many careers in this cluster.

◆ New Career Terms ◆

In this chapter you will learn the meanings of the following career terms:

- ✔ Market research
- ✔ Advertise
- ✔ Distribute
- ✔ Marketing and Distribution Cluster
- ✔ Merchandise
- ✔ Retail
- ✔ Wholesale
- ✔ Promote
- ✔ Telemarketing

Imagine that you have an idea for a new electronic game. You develop it with a friend. She's a computer specialist. You test it with students in junior high and high school. You are certain it's going to be a winner. Now what do you do?

First, you've got to do some **market research** *(a study to find out what influences someone's buying decisions). That means you have to find out whether the market (people that buy particular goods or services)—mostly young people—will want to buy your new product. You might even have to give some games away free. Then you have market researchers interview the students who have played your game.*

Let's say they loved your game. Now you have to decide what to call it and how much to charge for it. You also have to decide what kind of package to put it in. Should it be bright? Should it be big? What are the words that should go on the package?

Very few people will buy your new electronic game unless they know about it. You've got to **advertise** *your game. This means you've got to tell people about your product. You'll have to make a choice about whether to advertise it on radio, on television, on the Internet, in magazines, in newspapers, or in all of them.*

How will you **distribute** *it (get it to consumers)? Will you sell it door to door? Will you have people mail in to buy it? Will you set up a site on the Internet? Or will you sell it through local stores? If you put it in stores, what kind of stores will you put it in: computer, toy, or department stores? And how will you get it to these stores? Should you ship it by plane? By railroad? By truck?*

And what about bonuses to salespeople who sell your new electronic game successfully? How much should the salespeople be paid? Do you need to have a training program to teach salespeople about your new product?

These are just some examples of the types of questions that people in the **Marketing and Distribution Cluster** *answer. The cluster includes all the occupations involved in getting goods from the producer to the consumer and in influencing the consumer to buy the products.*

WHAT WOULD IT BE LIKE?

A wide variety of jobs are available in marketing and distribution. You could load trucks, interview people, give sales presentations, design newspaper ads, or travel to Paris to buy the latest fashions. All of these different jobs are part of marketing and distribution.

You may decide to go into retail sales. If so, you can sell **merchandise**—the many different products that are bought and sold by businesses. Depending on your interests, you can sell clothing, sporting goods, groceries, shoes, toys, electronics—whatever you like the most.

If you decide to go into sales, there are many types of sales jobs. Most retail sales involves staying inside and greeting customers. Other salespeople have to travel. For example, salespeople for textbook companies travel in cars and planes to schools and education meetings throughout the country. People who sell industrial supplies travel from one manufacturer to the next in a certain region of the country.

market research
a study to determine what influences someone's buying decisions.

advertise
to inform people about a product by means such as radio, television, the Internet, newspapers, and magazines.

distribute
the act of getting a product to consumers (distribution decisions include where to sell, how to sell, how to ship, etc.).

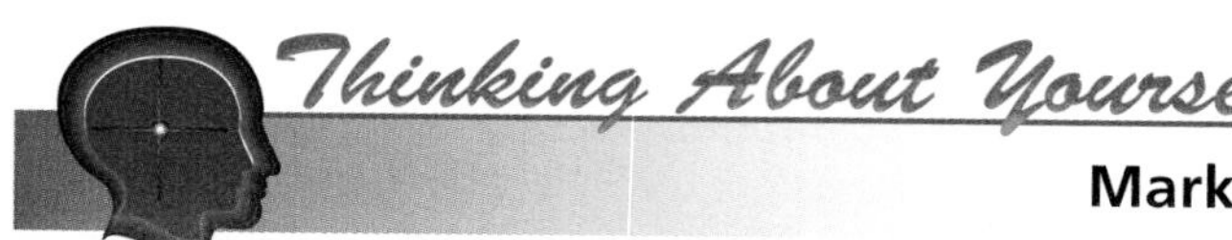

Marketing and Distribution Careers

Take your time reading and thinking about the questions below. You might even want to make notes on a sheet of paper and write out your answers.

- ▲ Do you enjoy making speeches and participating in debates in school? Are you good at these activities?
- ▲ Have you ever worked as a salesperson? Did you enjoy this work?
- ▲ Have you ever bought items for the purpose of selling them at a profit? Did this work? Did you enjoy it?
- ▲ Do you enjoy meeting and talking with strangers?
- ▲ Have you sold products to make money for a school or community project? Did you enjoy this?
- ▲ Have you ever made a poster for a school or community event? Did you enjoy this activity?
- ▲ Have you ever written anything to help advertise a product, service, or event?

If you are a persuasive person and you answered yes to many of these questions, you might enjoy a career in marketing and distribution.

Marketing and Distribution Cluster
a group of occupations involved in getting products from the producer to the consumer and in influencing the customer to buy a product.

merchandise
the vast array of products bought and sold by businesses.

If you get involved in market research, you may have to take surveys by going door to door or standing in a mall. You have to ask questions of different people and keep track of their answers.

If you are in the distribution end of this career cluster, you will probably have to do some physical activity. You might store and handle goods and products. This work might require heavy lifting and lots of bending over.

Basically, most of the jobs in this career cluster involve working inside. Selling is usually very competitive.

Would you enjoy working in this cluster? Do some daydreaming as you "listen" to the following conversation. Several people who enjoy working in the Marketing and Distribution Cluster are talking about their jobs. As you listen to what they say, imagine yourself doing their jobs.

Sales Representative: Have you ever thought about a career in sales? Don't tell me you could never sell anything, because it isn't true. You can sell anything if you know your product and you believe in it. I used to sell tires, for example. I was convinced that we had the best tires ever made, and I learned everything there was to know about tires. I sold those tires faster than they could make them. Selling is a great career. You get to make your own hours. If you work hard, you can make a lot of money. And you get to meet all those people. That's the best part. You meet new people every day. I just love meeting and talking to new people. Don't you get tired of talking to the same old people every day?

Attitude makes a difference

Raising Money for United Way

In school Anita Sinatra and Dave Wu were both members of the social service club. Anita joined because she liked helping people. Dave joined because he thought it would look good on his record.

Their school was involved in a United Way fund-raising drive. Anita and Dave were each assigned small sections of a local shopping mall.

At the end of the first weekend Anita had collected twice as much as Dave. By the end of the drive, Anita had collected three times more than Dave.

What Do YOU Think?

What was the difference in the attitudes Anita and Dave had toward their service club? How did this difference in attitude show up? Do you think it is right to do things in school just so they look good on your record?

Retail Manager: Sure I do. We all do. And you're right. One of the great things about sales is talking to new people. You know why I like meeting new people? I like it because I learn so much. Everybody has a little specialty, and if you listen, you can pick up something from just about everybody who comes in the store. Almost every night I go home with some little tidbit of information that I didn't know before. Of course, that's not the main reason I'm in retail sales. I want to have my own store someday. I'm learning how to run a business. There's also that constant challenge of trying to improve on last week's sales. I love that challenge.

Buyer: I hope to have my own store someday, too. But if I don't, that's okay too, because I love what I'm doing. Since I was in junior high my biggest interest has been clothes. I love clothes. I love to shop for them, try them on, wear them, clean them—I love everything about clothes. And that's what's so great about my job. I buy clothes—not with my own money, but with my employer's money. I can pick whatever I want and buy as much as I want. It's great. Of course, there's a lot of responsibility, and I have to make sure I buy what our customers will like, or I'll be out of a job. But it's fun. And I try to buy things I think most people will like and look good in.

Advertising Manager: That does sound like fun. And I just realized what our jobs have in common. We have to think about what other people will like. When my firm designs an ad campaign, we have to think of pictures and slogans that will appeal to most people. Those aren't always the pictures and slogans we personally like best. Our job is to get people's attention and show them why our product is so great. It's a real creative challenge. And until you've done it, you can't imagine the thrill of coming up with a really dynamite ad.

What do you think? Do any of these careers sound appealing? Can you see yourself doing one of these jobs—or a similar job? Would you like to learn more about marketing and distribution careers?

Career Decision-Making Activities

1. Notice and keep track of all the television commercials you see during a one-week period. At the end of the week, decide which commercial is the most effective and which commercial is the least effective. You're to pick the most and least *effective* commercials, not the most and least *entertaining*. On a piece of paper, write two or three sentences explaining why you picked each commercial. Discuss your picks in class.
2. Bring to class a newspaper ad that caught your attention. Discuss why the ad got your attention. Do you think the ad will cause people to buy more of the product being advertised? Why or why not? What did the advertiser do to try to get you to buy the product?
3. Think of all the objects in your home. If you had to make your living selling one of these items, which one would it be? Why? Discuss this in class.
4. Pick one item that belongs to you that you no longer want. Bring this item to class. Do a sales presentation, trying to sell this item in a classroom auction. Before the auction, think of several good *features* about the item and several ways that your classmates would *benefit* by owning it. Talk about these features and benefits as you do your sales presentation for your item. How did you do? Were you persuasive?
5. Assume you are taking a sales job. You can pick which item you will sell. Put the following ten types of products in the order you would want to sell them.
   - Insurance.
   - Houses.
   - Cars.
   - Books.
   - Cosmetics.
   - Clothes.
   - Hardware.
   - Furniture.
   - Computers.
   - Food.

   Tell why you would enjoy, and be most successful, selling the first item. Also tell why you would least enjoy, and be least successful with, the last item. How does your ordering of the items compare with your classmates' ordering of items?

JOB FAMILIES IN THE MARKETING AND DISTRIBUTION CLUSTER

There are seven job families in the Marketing and Distribution Cluster of careers. You are probably already familiar with some of them. Any time you buy something, for example, you deal with people in the selling job family. Look at the following figure that presents the job families in this career cluster. Reading about the job families will help you decide which careers in this cluster you would enjoy most.

- **Marketing management.** Those who plan and direct the work in marketing and distribution are part of the marketing management job family. Retail store owners and managers of retail stores are included in this job family. The term **retail** refers to the sale of the goods to the final consumer—you or your family, for example. **Wholesale** operations are companies that buy goods from manufacturers and then sell and deliver them to retail stores. In most cases you cannot buy directly from a wholesaler.

  In a sales operation of any size, there are retail floor managers. They coordinate the activities of workers in one department of a store. Sales managers direct the sales staff. They are responsible for training and for setting sales goals. In advertising, an advertising manager plans advertising policies.
- **Marketing research and analysis.** Every manufacturer and retailer would love to know exactly what consumers want. They use marketing research and analysis to help them find out. Workers in this job family study and then try to predict the buying practices of consumers.

  A market research analyst studies the way consumers act and think. He or she does this in different ways, with surveys, research, and interviews. An interview occurs whenever an interviewer asks questions and writes down the answers.

  There are also statisticians who work in marketing research. They help interpret the information obtained through market research.
- **Physical distribution.** Goods have to be moved from the manufacturer to wherever they are going to be sold. Sometimes they have to be stored. All the jobs involved with this physical distribution of goods are part of a job family.

  Hand and machine packagers package and wrap products before they are shipped. In both warehouses and retail stores there are markers. These people print and attach price tickets to boxes.

  In the mail order business there are mail order sorters. They fulfill mail orders from customers. These customers send in their orders by mail. Sometimes they call in their orders over the phone.
- **Purchasing.** The occupations involved in buying materials, many for resale, are in the purchasing family. Somebody in the retail store has to make a decision about what to

retail
the sale of goods to the final consumer.

wholesale
goods obtained directly from manufacturers.

Business-to-Business Purchasing

The fastest growth in online sales is occurring between businesses. Purchasing agents now use the Internet to make an increasingly large number of the purchases for the companies for which they work. Literally billions and billions of dollars' worth of goods are bought and sold between businesses every year online.

Job Families in the Marketing and Distribution Cluster

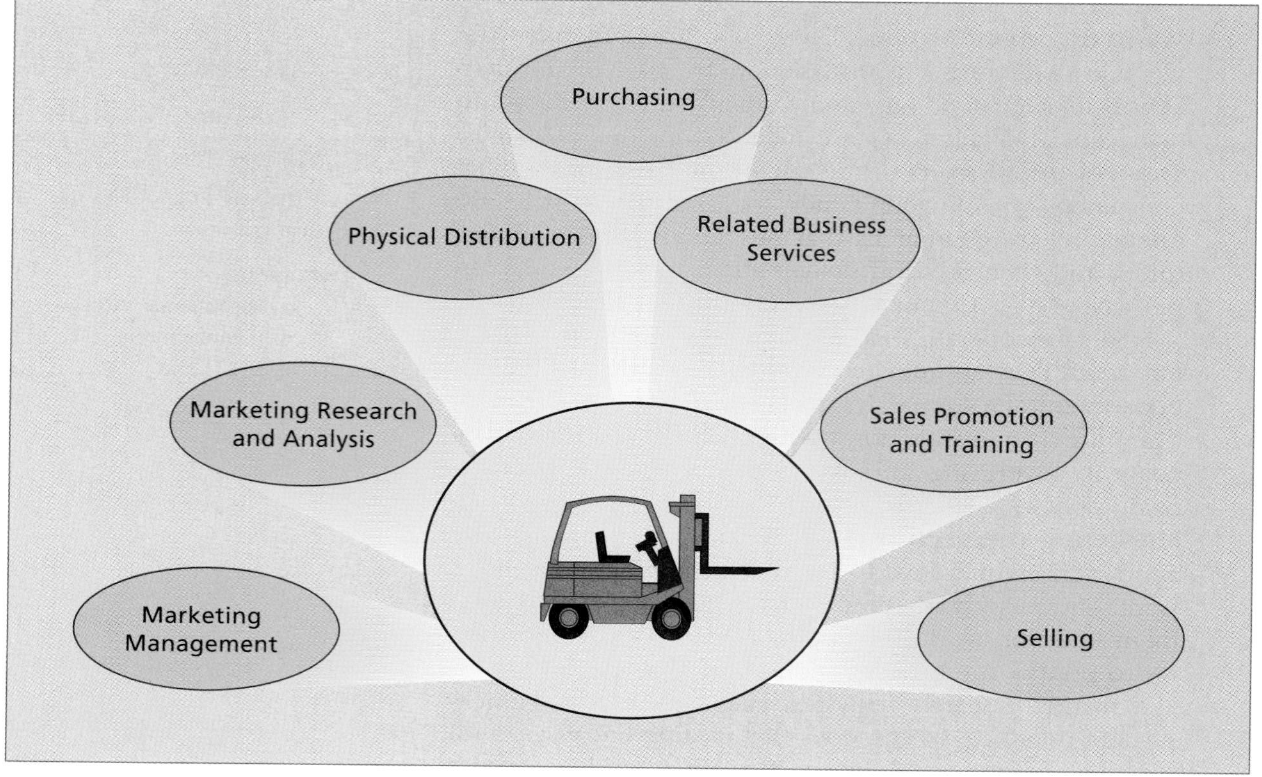

buy. The people who make these decisions are called *buyers* or purchasing agents. They try to figure out consumer wants and buying trends. Purchasing agents often go to showrooms that manufacturers set up to show off their new products.

Many retail operations have assistant buyers. They help the buyer keep records and train the sales force.

- **Related business services.** All the occupations involved in business and office activities related to marketing are included in the related business services job category. You read about these jobs in Chapter 7, "Business and Office Technology Careers." Turn back to Chapter 7 if you want to refresh your memory about these careers.
- **Sales promotion and training.** The sales promotion and training job family includes the workers who create a demand for a product. Products have to be promoted. To

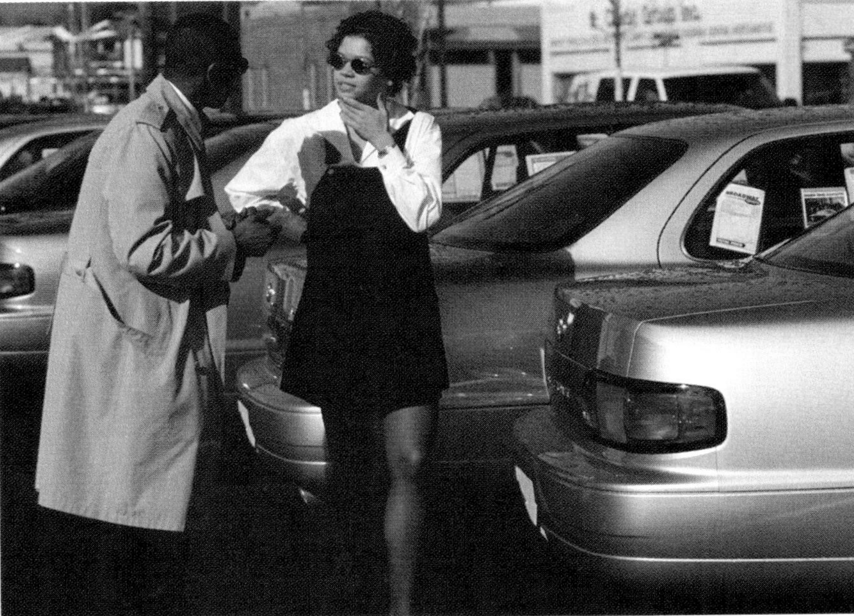

◀ If you like direct interaction with others and have a good sense for business, you could be a top salesperson.

promote a product means to advertise it and encourage people to buy it. People in sales promotion and training try to figure out ways to teach salespeople how to sell. People in sales promotion also come up with the design of products and packages. The people who do this are product and package designers.

Whenever you walk by a shop window, you are seeing the work of a window dresser. This person plans commercial displays. He or she has to know about art and design. The goal is to attract the attention of potential customers so they will come into the store.

Models are part of this job family. They wear, use, or demonstrate products in an appealing way so that people will want to buy the products.

- **Selling.** Workers who persuade people to buy products are involved in the selling job family. There are many types of salespersons. There are those in household appliances, who sell televisions, washers and dryers, and home computers. Whenever you go into a store to buy clothing, you are using the services of a clothing salesperson. Some salespersons are demonstrators. They arrange and go to house parties. At the parties they demonstrate and sell goods such as clothes, kitchenware, or makeup.

promote
to advertise and encourage people to purchase a product.

Careers for Tomorrow

TELEMARKETING SPECIALIST

One of the fastest-growing areas in sales involves **telemarketing**. That means using the telephone to sell goods. Anybody who chooses this occupation will do business only by telephone.

Many products are sold over the phone. Office supplies, books, and resort memberships are a few examples.

The nice thing about telemarketing is that no particular education is required. Training is usually given on the job. Advancement in telemarketing may involve becoming a sales manager.

Telemarketing specialists often receive commissions, such as a certain percentage of all that they sell. Those who sell a lot make a relatively high income.

If you want more information on this field, write the American Marketing Association, 250 South Wacker Drive, Suite 200, Chicago, IL 60606.

telemarketing using the telephone to sell goods (one of the fastest-growing sales areas).

CAREER OUTLOOK

As you know, our economy has become a service economy. A service economy provides a variety of consumer services. Most service jobs are growing faster than other kinds of jobs. Most of the job families in the Marketing and Distribution Cluster will grow faster than the economy. There are only a couple for which growth is going to be slow.

▼ Researchers can access much of the data they need to complete their jobs from their personal computers.

FASTEST-GROWING JOBS

The following are among the fastest-growing jobs in this cluster:

- Financial services salesperson.
- Marketing research worker.
- Advertising manager.
- Advertising salesperson.

SLOWEST-GROWING JOBS

Growth is among the slowest for these jobs:

- Insurance agent and broker.
- Shipping and receiving clerk.
- Retail butcher.

AT THE HEART OF THE MARKETING AND DISTRIBUTION CLUSTER

What makes the Marketing and Distribution Cluster different from the other fourteen clusters you'll be exploring? What would it really be like to work in this cluster? Let's try to get at the heart of marketing and distribution.

The essence of this cluster is selling. It's convincing customers to buy. It's helping customers decide what they want. It's persuading customers that one choice is better than the other choices.

A key factor in this cluster is the product or service you are marketing. It could be a book, or a vacuum cleaner, or a candy bar, or a $40,000 automobile, or a chair, or laundry service. You must believe in the product or service. You must be able to generate interest and enthusiasm about the product or service. You must believe that you are offering the customer a good value.

At the heart of marketing and distribution is communication with other people. People often have a hard time making decisions when they are about to spend their money. The more money they are spending, the more uncertain they become. Marketing workers must be able to provide information, answer questions, reassure the customer, and make the customer feel good about the decision. This involves effective communication—listening and observing, as well as talking. Communicating with people to help them make good decisions is an important part of marketing.

Figure 17.1 gives just a few examples of occupations from this cluster. Think about the job title, the work activities, and the work settings. The figure is intended to help you get at the heart of this cluster. You don't need to read for details. Scan the entries to get a feel for the cluster as a whole.

Would you like a career in the Marketing and Distribution Cluster? Ask yourself the following questions:

- Do you like the sound of the occupations listed under "Who"? Would you feel good about an identity like one of these?
- Would you enjoy doing activities like those described under "What"?
- Picture yourself working in the settings described under "Where." Would you be comfortable in these settings?

Being a Web Marketing Specialist

More and more products are being sold on the Internet, through the World Wide Web. How should these products be marketed on the Web? This is a job for Web marketing specialists. These are people who tell companies that want to sell items on the Web how to do so. They explain what types of products are most easily sold on the Web, how a Web selling page should be set up, and how the transaction should be paid for. They can tell companies how to name a site, who to hire to design online advertising, and so on.

SKILLS, TRAINING, AND EXPERIENCE

Some skills common to many of the careers in this cluster are listed below.

- Can organize your own activities to make the best use of your time and effort.

Figure 17.1 Sample Occupations in the Marketing and Distribution Cluster

WHO You Would Be	WHAT You Would Do	WHERE You Would Do It
Retail sales clerk	Interest customers in merchandise, describe and demonstrate products, receive payments, give change	Retail stores (variety of kinds and departments)
Real estate agent	Meet clients to discuss needs and resources, show appropriate homes to clients, present offers and counteroffers for clients, obtain listings, explore leads	Real estate offices; much time spent driving around the community and showing customers the houses and property for sale
Manufacturer's sales representative	Schedule appointments; visit potential buyers; present products; answer questions, make suggestions, take orders; prepare reports	Traveling from customer to customer; in customers' offices or places of business
Insurance agent	Sell policies that protect people and businesses from loss, explain policies to customers, help customers with claims, search for new customers, advise customers	Customers' homes and offices; insurance offices
Marketing manager	Develop marketing strategies, do market research, set prices, provide customer service, supervise other marketing personnel	Company offices

- Can express yourself well.
- Can use arithmetic to figure markups, markdowns, discounts, and charges.
- Can maintain accurate records of contacts, sales, and purchases.
- Can be attentive and enthusiastic at all times when dealing with customers.
- Can talk easily and persuasively to customers.
- Can create and carry out sales campaigns.
- Can work agreeably with all kinds of people.

Jobs in marketing and distribution require varying skill levels. Here are three categories of jobs.

JOBS REQUIRING LESS-THAN-AVERAGE TRAINING AND EXPERIENCE

- Display worker.
- Auto salesperson.
- Cashier.
- Door-to-door salesperson.
- Sales demonstrator.
- Retail butcher.
- Shipping and receiving clerk.
- Supermarket worker.
- Warehouse worker.
- Stocking clerk.

▲ Small-retail business owners often manage all phases of their business including inventory.

JOBS REQUIRING AVERAGE TRAINING AND EXPERIENCE

- Small-retail business owner.
- Insurance agent or broker.
- Real estate sales worker or broker.

JOBS REQUIRING MORE-THAN-AVERAGE TRAINING AND EXPERIENCE

- Purchasing agent.
- Advertising account salesperson.
- Advertising manager.
- Marketing director.
- Marketing researcher.
- Advertising buyer.
- Retail buyer.
- Store manager.
- Sales manager.

See page 274 for a list of some of the jobs in the Marketing and Distribution Cluster, along with their *DOT* numbers.

Career Decision-Making Activities

1. If you are interested in a selling career, start practicing now. Take any jobs you can find that allow you to sell. For example, sell door to door to raise money for a class project or charity. Work in the snack shack at school sporting events. It doesn't matter what you do, just as long as it involves sales.
2. Take all the marketing, sales, business management, entrepreneurship, and speech courses available at your school.
3. Volunteer your services as a market researcher to a local retailer. Ask the retailer what questions he or she would most like answered regarding products available in the store. Develop a research plan. Then interview or survey people to answer the questions.

Occupations in Marketing and Distribution

Here is a list of occupations mentioned in this chapter. Next to the name of each occupation is its *DOT* number. You can use the *DOT* number to locate further information about the occupation in your school or public library. For the broad occupational terms mentioned in this chapter, only one or two examples of that occupation are listed below. You can easily find more examples of the occupation in the *DOT.*

Advertising Buyer (164.167-010)
Advertising Manager (164.117-010)
Advertising Salesperson (254.357-014)
Assistant Buyer (162.157-022)
Auto Sales Worker (273.353-010)
Buyer (162.157-038)
Cashier (211.462-010)
Clothing Salesperson (261.357-050)
Demonstrator (297.354-010)
Display Worker (142.051-010)
Door-to-Door Sales Worker (291.357-010)
Financial Services Salesperson (251.257-010)
Hand and Machine Packager (920.587-018)
Insurance Agent (250.257-010)
Interviewer (205.362-014)
Mail Order Sorter (222.387-038)
Manager, Retail Store (185.167-046)
Manufacturer's Sales Representative (279.157-010)
Marker (209.587-034)
Market Research Analyst (050.067-014)
Market Research Worker (see Market Research Analyst)
Market Researcher (see Market Research Analyst)
Marketing Director (163.117-018)
Marketing Manager (see Marketing Director)
Model, Artists' (961.667-014)
Model, Photographers' (961.376-010)
Package Designer (142.081-018)
Product Designer (142.061-026)
Purchasing Agent (162.157-038)
Real Estate Agent (186.117-058)
Real Estate Sales Worker (250.357-018)
Receiving Clerk (248.362-010)
Retail Butcher (525.381-014)
Retail Buyer (162.157-038)
Retail Floor Manager (299.137-010)
Retail Manager (185.167-046)
Retail Sales Clerk (290.477-014)
Retail Store Owner (see Manager, Retail Store)
Sales Demonstrator (279.357-038)
Sales Manager (163.176-018)
Sales Representative, Household Appliances (270.357.034)
Sales Representative, Men's and Boy's Clothing (261.357-050)
Shipping Clerk (219.367-030)
Small-Retail Business Owner (see Manager, Retail Store)
Statistician (020.167-026)
Stocking Clerk (249.367-058)
Store Manager (see Manager, Retail Store)
Supermarket Worker (290.477-014)
Telemarketing Specialist (299.357-014)
Warehouse Worker (922.137-026)
Window Dresser (299.667-010)

Review and Enrichment

Summarizing the Chapter

Summarizing information is a critical thinking skill that will help you succeed in the world of work. Write a summary of what you learned in Chapter 17. Focus on the main points of the chapter. Then in a class discussion, compare your summary with the summaries done by your classmates. Can you improve your summary?

Improving Your Career Vocabulary

1. Learning to use new vocabulary terms will improve your communication skills, which are important in almost all areas of work. Write definitions for the terms listed below. Then for each term, write an original sentence about yourself in which you use the term correctly.
   - market research
   - advertise
   - distribute
   - Marketing and Distribution Cluster
   - merchandise
   - retail
   - wholesale
   - promote
   - telemarketing
2. List the job families discussed in this chapter. Write a one-sentence description of each.

Finding the Facts

Finding exact information is a frequently used skill in many careers. Find the answers to the exercise below, and write the answers on a separate sheet of paper.

1. Name three job families in this career cluster.
2. What type of work does a market research analyst do?
3. What is another name for a buyer?
4. Name four of the fastest-growing jobs in this cluster.
5. Name three skills common to careers in this cluster.

Thinking for Yourself

To complete the exercise below you will need to use critical thinking and communication skills, which are skills valued by all employers. Write out your answers or be prepared to discuss them in class, depending on your teacher's instructions.

1. Some people think salespeople are "phony"—that they will tell you anything to convince you to buy. Do you think this is a fair description? Explain.
2. What type of sales approach persuades you to buy a product? Give an example.
3. Has a telemarketer ever called you in your home? Did you or your family buy the product or service? Describe the transaction.
4. Confidence and enthusiasm are important to a successful sales career. Why do you think these qualities are especially valuable in sales?
5. If you were a buyer, how would you choose products for other people to buy? What standards would you use?

Practicing Your Basic Skills

Your career success depends greatly on your basic math and communication skills. Work hard at improving in the areas where you have trouble with the following exercises.

Math

1. Janice works as a car salesperson. She makes a 15 percent commission on any car she sells. Recently she sold a camper for $57,999. How much was her commission?
2. The Bisbee Baking Company sells its doughnuts to restaurants at a wholesale price. The restaurants add a 20 percent markup. If the restaurants sell the doughnuts for 35¢ apiece, for how much a dozen does Bisbee sell them?
3. Two trucks left the Bisbee Company carrying a load of doughnuts for distribution. Truck A arrived at its first stop 30 miles away in half an hour. Truck B arrived at its first stop also in half an hour, but it was only going half as fast as Truck A. How far did truck B have to drive?

Reading and Writing

1. Obtain a copy of a mail order catalog. Read through it, paying attention to how items are described. How much is fact and how much is opinion?

REVIEW AND ENRICHMENT, CONTINUED

2. Pretend you are writing entries in a catalog of merchandise for schools. Choose an item in the classroom, and write a catalog description of it. Give all important information, such as size and color.
3. Find copies of five ads in newspapers or magazines. Study each one to determine what benefit is being promised to the customer. Write a paragraph telling which ad you think communicates the benefit best, and why.
4. Pick at least one occupation mentioned in this chapter that you think would be interesting. Research the occupation thoroughly, and write a report. Use the career research checklist in Chapter 5 as a guide for your report. Conclude your report with an explanation of your interest in that occupation based on your findings.

Speaking and Listening

1. Visit a local store, and talk to a salesperson who is not busy. Ask that person what hints he or she would give to someone trying to become a salesperson.
2. The next time you shop, listen to a salesperson talk to a customer. Is the person courteous and attentive or bored and unfriendly? What effect does this attitude have on the customer?

ACTIVITIES WORKING WITH OTHERS

In almost all careers you must be able to get along well with other people to be successful. Work with your classmates to do the following activities. As you work together, pay attention to how well you get along. If necessary, work hard at improving your ability to do your part and to cooperate.

1. With the same classmate, think of a name for the product you created for Chapter 15. The name should convey what the product is or does. It should also be easy to remember.
2. With the same classmate, design a newspaper ad, store display, or billboard for the product you created.
3. Add the careers mentioned in this chapter to your database.

DECISION MAKING AND PROBLEM SOLVING

You will be a big help to your employer if you can make decisions and solve problems. List all the possible ways of resolving the situations described below. Then pick the best alternative (possible choice), and tell why you chose it. If you need help, you might want to refer to Chapter 3.

1. You are interested in sales as a career, but your friends are encouraging you to be a model. You have done some modeling in the past and been successful. But while modeling is glamorous, it is also boring. You wonder if there is some way to combine sales and modeling. How will you go about finding out?
2. You are an advertising representative. You've saved $1,500 toward a new car, which you think will impress your clients when you take them to lunch. However, a friend suggests you buy a computer with the money. A computer will help you be more organized and keep track of what your customers are interested in. What will you do?

CHAPTER 18

PERSONAL SERVICES CAREERS

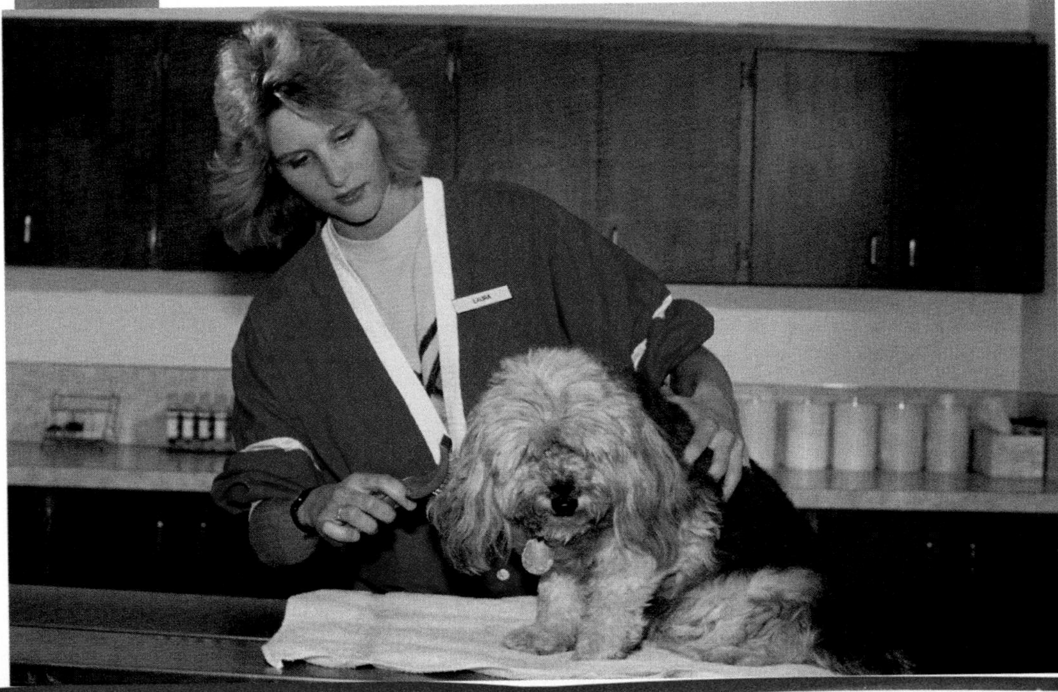

◆ Chapter Objectives ◆

After completing this chapter you will be able to do the following:

- ◆ Define the terms listed under "New Career Terms."
- ◆ List and describe the seven job families in the Personal Services Cluster.
- ◆ Identify several careers included in this cluster.
- ◆ Name several slow-growing and fast-growing jobs in this cluster.
- ◆ Explain what it would be like to work at a career in this cluster.
- ◆ Evaluate your own interest in this cluster.
- ◆ Identify skills common to many careers in this cluster.

◆ New Career Terms ◆

In this chapter you will learn the meanings of the following career terms:

- ✔ Services
- ✔ Personal Services Cluster
- ✔ Unstructured
- ✔ Initiative
- ✔ Cosmetology
- ✔ Domestic
- ✔ Lodging

The service sector of the American economy is the fastest-growing part of the economy. **Services** *are not the same as goods. You can't pick up and hold services. You can't touch them, but they are still very valuable. When someone performs a service, he or she is doing something to help someone.*

For example, when someone cleans your clothes or repairs your shoes, that person has performed a valuable personal service for you. When someone gives your dog or cat a flea bath, that person has performed a valuable personal service. The person who comes in to clean your carpets is performing a valuable personal service. The person who makes a sandwich for you in a fast-food restaurant is performing a valuable personal service.

Millions of Americans perform personal services for pay every day. These are the people working in the **Personal Services Cluster.** *This career cluster includes all the occupations that involve providing people with the services they want to make their lives more pleasurable.*

services
tasks other people or machines do that cannot be physically weighed or measured.

▼ People in personal service jobs thrive on interaction.

WHAT WOULD IT BE LIKE?

Personal services are people services. People services involve contact with people—day in and day out. People who succeed in personal services like other people. They like to talk. They like to interact. That's what personal services are all about. If you like to work alone, personal services is probably not the career cluster for you.

Many jobs in personal services are during regular hours. But there are many other jobs that require working at night and working on the weekends.

Personal services jobs are often **unstructured.** In other words, they are jobs that involve doing many different things throughout the day. A job on an assembly line is very structured. It involves repeating the same thing over and over. It is different from a personal services job.

Many personal services jobs require **initiative.** That means the ability to do something before you are told to do it. A hotel housekeeper who takes the initiative would sweep a dirty floor right away. A hotel housekeeper who doesn't take the initiative wouldn't sweep the floor unless given orders to do so. Initiative also involves making decisions about what should be done. If you are a beautician, you are often expected to tell the client what type of hairstyle you think will work best for him or her.

People who help others in times of crisis or change must be emotionally strong and stable. A funeral director, for example, performs a very personal service. He or she must help people who are in emotional pain because of the death of a loved one.

Would you enjoy working in this career cluster? Do some daydreaming as you "listen" to the following conversation. Several peo-

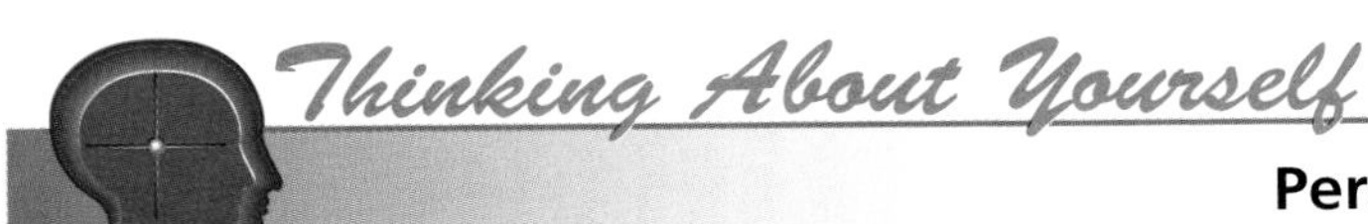

Personal Services Careers

Take your time reading and thinking about the questions below. You may even want to make notes on a sheet of paper and write out your answers.

- Have you ever cut someone else's hair? Do you style your own hair? Do you like to try new and different hairstyles?
- Do you like to read health and beauty magazines? Can you tell the differences among various skin tones and hair textures?
- Have you ever served food or drinks at a party or reception? Did you enjoy this experience?
- Can you be friendly to people even if they are rude to you?
- Do you like helping other people?
- Have you ever helped someone apply makeup? Did you enjoy this?
- Are you particular about how you look? Are you always neat and clean?
- Do you take good care of your own clothes?

If you like people and you answered yes to many of these questions, you might enjoy a career in personal services.

ple who enjoy working in the Personal Services Cluster are talking about their jobs. As you listen to what they say, imagine yourself doing their jobs.

Housekeeper: I can't stand to see anything out of place. I'm a born "tidier" and "straightener." I'm also one of those people who has to keep everything just right. I guess that's why I love my job. If I walk into a messy, dirty room, I've got to clean it and straighten it, whether I'm getting paid or not. So I might as well get paid for it. Sometimes I wish I could take "before" and "after" pictures to remind myself of what I've done.

Chauffeur: I hate cleaning house, but I love washing cars. I wonder why that is? Guess it's 'cause I enjoy cars so much. Ever since I got my driver's license when I was sixteen, my whole life has revolved around cars. I never really thought about earning my living driving. I just sort of fell into this job. I guess I was one of the lucky few who found the right job by accident. Getting this job was the luckiest break I ever got. I take care of the family cars and drive the family members wherever they want to go. It's great.

Doorkeeper: I don't drive cars, but I open lots of car doors. My job is to greet people when they arrive at our hotel. I get a kick out of it, because I'm usually the first person at the hotel they see. Their first impression of the hotel depends on me. I like making them feel like they're royalty—you know what I mean. That's my goal—to make them feel like they are the most important people in the world. It's fun!

Barber: I know exactly what you mean. I approach my customers with the same attitude. And it's not phony, either. I don't have to

Personal Services Cluster
occupations that involve providing people with the services they want to make their lives more pleasurable.

unstructured
varied; an unstructured job would involve doing many different things throughout the day.

initiative
doing something that needs to be done without having to be asked.

▶ Do you like working with people to improve their appearance?

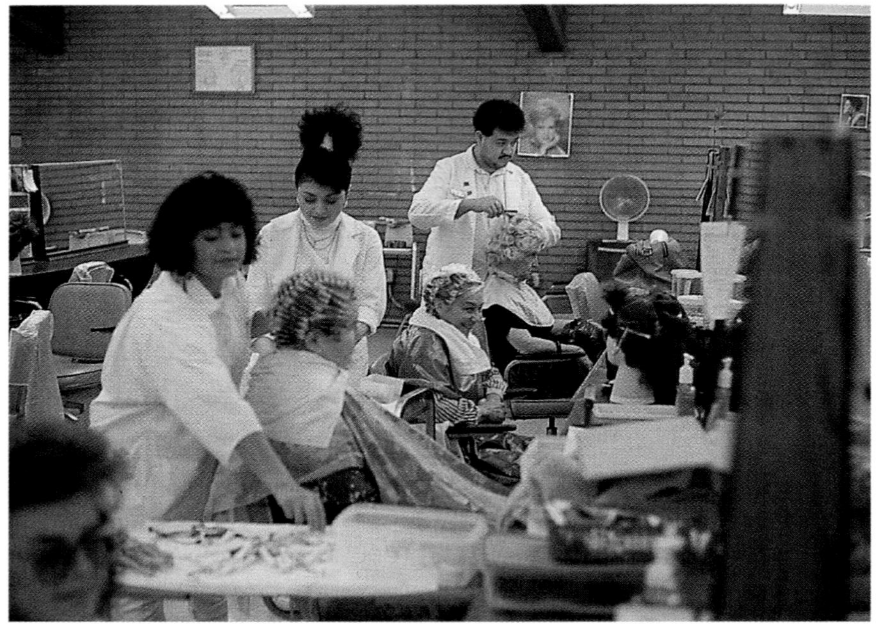

pretend. It's just my nature. I like making people feel good. And I think that's why I've been so successful. I'm good at styling and cutting hair—don't get me wrong. But so are a lot of other barbers and beauticians. I think the thing that sets me apart is the way I talk to my customers. I'm genuinely interested in them, and while they're in my chair I feel like it's my job to cater to their every wish. They like it, and I like doing it. What could be better?

What do you think? Do any of these careers sound appealing? Can you see yourself doing one of these jobs—or a similar job? Would you like to learn more about personal services careers?

Career Decision-Making Activities

1. Nominate a person from your community who you think best represents the idea of personal services. This need not be someone you know. It could be a waitress, beautician, doorkeeper, pet shop worker, rug cleaner, laundry worker—any personal services worker you've noticed doing an outstanding job. Write a one-page essay describing why you think this person is the superman or superwoman of personal services. Read your essay in class. After listening to all the essays, did you notice any common skills or abilities among the descriptions of different people? Discuss these in class. You may want to vote in class for the Personal Services Worker of the Year Award and then invite the winner to class to find out why he or she is so good at the job.
2. How good a job do you do providing personal services for yourself? On a piece of paper, rate

yourself from 1 to 10, with 10 being outstanding personal services and 1 being terrible personal services, in each of the following areas:

a. Keeping room neat and clean.
b. Keeping hair, skin, and nails neat and clean.
c. Keeping clothes neat and clean.
d. Being courteous to others—greetings, holding of doors, offers to help.
e. Preparing, serving, and cleaning up after own meals.
f. Helping pick up around home.
g. Doing chores such as taking care of pets and washing the car.

Look at your ratings. Do you think you would do a good job of providing personal services for others? Discuss this in class.

JOB FAMILIES IN THE PERSONAL SERVICES CLUSTER

There are seven job families within the Personal Services Cluster. They are shown in the diagram on page 282. Reading about these job families will help you decide which careers in this cluster you would enjoy the most.

- **Barbering, cosmetology, and related services.** Any occupation that has to do with improving someone's personal appearance fits in the barbering, cosmetology, and related services job family. Barbering has to do with cutting hair. Barbers also trim beards and give shampoos.

  Cosmetology has to do with improving the appearance of skin, hair, and nails. It is done by cosmetologists. These people are also called beauty operators or beauticians. They suggest what kind of hairstyle a man or woman should have. They apply bleaches, dyes, and tints. They provide many other beauty services, such as shaping eyebrows and giving facial massages.

  The related services part of this job family includes several different kinds of jobs. Embalmers, funeral attendants, tattoo artists, and reducing-machine operators are just a few.

- **Domestic animal care.** Animals that are **domestic** are tame and can live with people. Millions of Americans have tens of millions of pets in their houses and apartments. Almost all of these pets need some type of care. Much of the care is done by the owners, but some is paid for. The people who provide care and training for pets and other animals make up the domestic animal care job family.

  Dog groomers wash dogs and trim them. Dog trainers teach dogs to obey, to perform tricks, and to hunt.

  Horse trainers train horses to perform tricks or to compete at horse shows. Horseshoers put metal shoes on horses.

cosmetology
improving the appearance of skin, hair, and nails.

domestic
of or relating to animals that are tame and can live with people.

Job Families in the Personal Services Cluster

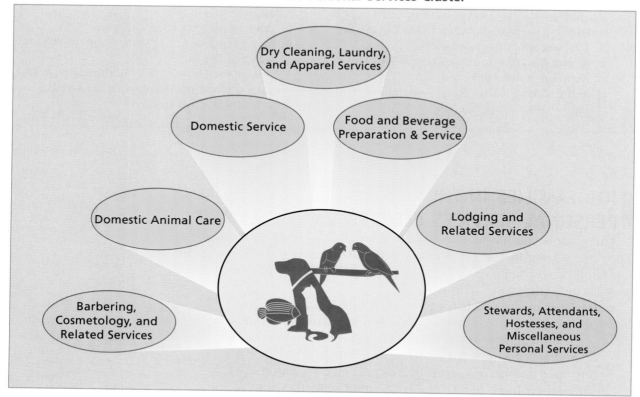

Dry Cleaning, Laundry, and Apparel Services
Domestic Service
Food and Beverage Preparation & Service
Domestic Animal Care
Lodging and Related Services
Barbering, Cosmetology, and Related Services
Stewards, Attendants, Hostesses, and Miscellaneous Personal Services

domestic
of or relating to the household or family.

▼ Service with a smile!

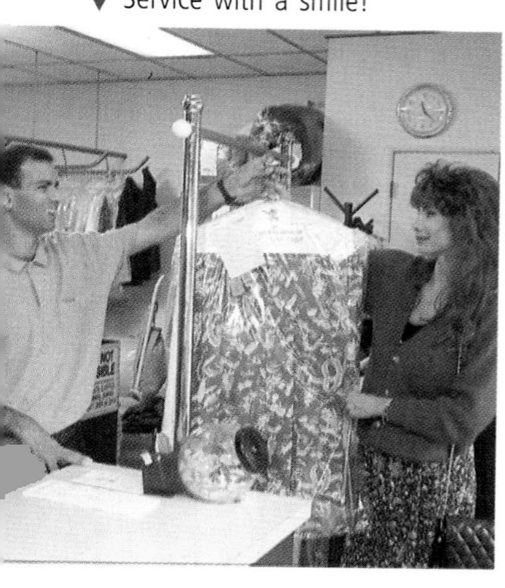

- **Domestic services.** Any job that involves providing personal services to some member of a household or a guest in the household is in the domestic services category. Here **domestic** refers to the household and family.

  Day workers who perform cleaning, cooking, and caring for a household are included. Gardeners and cooks are, too. Housekeepers and child monitors (nannies) are other workers in this field.

  Men and women who drive an automobile for an individual are called chauffeurs. They also keep the car cleaned and make minor repairs.
- **Dry cleaning, laundry, and apparel services.** Anybody working to improve the appearance of clothes and other personal items fits in the dry cleaning, laundry, and apparel services job family. Dry cleaners and silk finishers operate machines to clean and iron garments. All-around pressers use a steam pressing machine or a hand iron to press clothes. A blocker shapes clothes after they are cleaned. A flatwork finisher presses sheets, pillowcases, napkins, and tablecloths.

Among those taking care of shoes are dyers, shoe repairers, and bootblacks. Bootblacks clean and polish shoes. For furniture and carpets there are furniture cleaners and rug cleaners, who use machines. In the laundry end of the business, there are hand launderers as well as laundry attendants. Tailors and dressmakers design and sew clothing.

- **Food and beverage preparation and service.** Those who prepare and serve food and drink to customers are included in the food and beverage preparation and service job family. Some of these jobs overlap with those listed in the Hospitality and Recreation Cluster (Chapter 14).

  Chefs and bakers work in kitchens. Coffee makers work there, too. Pantry goods makers prepare salads and sandwich fillings and other cold dishes. In the kitchen there are kitchen helpers and kitchen stewards.

- **Lodging and related services. Lodging** means a place to spend the night or stay for a short time. The general services provided to people who stay in hotels and other lodgings are included in the lodging and related services job family. Many of these jobs are the same as those listed in the Hospitality and Recreation Cluster (Chapter 14).

  Bellhops and baggage porters, as well as doorkeepers, provide services to hotel guests when they come in the front door. A room service clerk usually serves food and drinks to guests in their rooms.

▲ Caterers may work inside or outside, for large or small groups. They not only prepare food but also serve it to their clients, providing a variety of jobs in this cluster.

lodging
a place to spend the night or stay for a short time.

Careers for Tomorrow

IF YOU LIKE TO SHOP

Some people are born shoppers. How would you like to shop and get paid for doing so? That's exactly what a personal shopper does.

Personal shoppers help busy people. They select and purchase clothing and other things for a person who hires them. They may buy gifts for birthdays, weddings, Christmas, or Hanukkah.

Sometimes personal shoppers buy things on their own. But some personal shoppers have to take their clients shopping to make the final selection.

This work doesn't require any particular training or education. But personal shoppers do have to get along with people. Knowledge of fashions and colors is also helpful. Having some experience in the retail business would be helpful, too.

Personal shoppers are usually self-employed. That means that sometimes they have lots to do and other times, not enough.

For more information on this occupation, make an appointment with a personal shopper at your local department store.

- **Stewards, attendants, host/hostesses, and miscellaneous personal services.** Jobs that involve greeting, serving, guiding, and otherwise helping customers are included in the stewards, attendants, hostesses, and miscellaneous personal services job family. Stewards usually work in club cars or dining cars on trains. They also work on cruise ships. They make sure that all the customers get what they want.

  Chaperons accompany minors (people who are not yet adults) on trips to educational and recreational places. The chaperons make sure that the parents' instructions are carried out.

  Some individuals help care for people who are blind. They are called blind aides or blind escorts. They drive people who are blind to where they have to go. They help type their letters and reports.

CAREER OUTLOOK

The entire field of personal services is growing rapidly in the United States. Here are some of the fastest- and slowest-growing jobs.

FASTEST-GROWING JOBS

The following are among the fastest-growing jobs in the Personal Services Cluster:

- Hairdresser.
- Cosmetologist.
- Masseur or masseuse.
- Caterer.

SLOWEST-GROWING JOBS

Some jobs are growing only slowly:

- Tailor.
- Bellhop.
- Chauffer.
- Shoe repairer.

AT THE HEART OF THE PERSONAL SERVICES CLUSTER

What makes the Personal Services Cluster different from the other fourteen clusters you'll be exploring? What would it really be like to work in this cluster? Let's try to get at the heart of personal services.

The essence of this cluster is serving other people. It's following orders, doing what you're told, putting the customer's or employer's

Figure 18.1 Sample Occupations in the Personal Services Cluster

WHO You Would Be	WHAT You Would Do	WHERE You Would Do It
Chef	Prepare meals; measure, mix, and cook ingredients according to recipes; use pots and pans; direct other kitchen workers	Kitchens of restaurants and institutions
Barber, beauty operator	Cut, trim, shampoo, and style hair	Barbershops, beauty salons
Janitor	Keep office buildings, hospitals, stores, apartment buildings, and other types of buildings clean and in good condition; fix leaky faucets; empty trash containers; paint; mop floors	Office buildings, schools, hospitals, and other buildings; often at night, after business hours
Bartender	Prepare drinks accurately and quickly, fill waiter orders, collect payments, make change, operate cash register, clean up bar area	Restaurants, hotels, and other eating and drinking establishments
Bellhop	Carry bags for travelers at transportation terminals or for guests at hotels, assist people with disabilities, run errands	Hotels, airports, train stations

needs first—above all else. And it means providing services pleasantly and enthusiastically.

If you work in this cluster you will wait on people. You will ask them what they would like—what you could get them. You will then fulfill the request as quickly and efficiently as possible. And if the customer is not satisfied, you will try again, and again if necessary. The person may be right or wrong, nice or rude, but you will put all of your effort into making that person as happy as possible. Working in this cluster means getting along with all kinds of people.

Listed in Figure 18.1 are just a few examples of occupations from this cluster. Think about the job title, the work activities, and the work settings. Figure 18.1 just gives examples to help you get at the heart of this cluster. You don't need to read for details. Scan the entries to get a feel for the cluster as a whole.

Would you like a career in this cluster? Ask yourself the following questions:

- Do you like the sound of the occupations listed under "Who"? Would you feel good about an identity like one of these?

- Would you enjoy doing activities like those described under "What"?
- Picture yourself working in the settings described under "Where." Would you be comfortable in these settings?

SKILLS, TRAINING, AND EXPERIENCE

Listed below are some skills common to many of the careers in this cluster:

- Talk with different kinds of people to find out their needs and to give them information.
- Stand or walk for long periods of time.
- Move fingers and hands easily and quickly to handle things such as dishes, money, and merchandise.
- Lift and carry things like heavy trays, sports equipment, and bundles of newspapers.
- Adapt a procedure to an individual customer's physical features.
- Add and subtract accurately so that you can mix solutions in proper proportions.
- Perform a variety of activities and change activities frequently.

Many personal services jobs require little training and education. As your skill level develops, you can get a higher-paying, more challenging job. The following are three categories of jobs.

JOBS REQUIRING LESS-THAN-AVERAGE TRAINING AND EXPERIENCE

- Chauffeur.
- Dry cleaning worker.
- Flower arranger.
- Gardener.
- Housekeeper.
- Child monitor.
- Companion.
- Shoe repairer.
- Laundry worker.
- Pet care worker.
- Carpet shampooer.

JOBS REQUIRING AVERAGE TRAINING AND EXPERIENCE

- Barber.
- Cosmetologist.
- Embalmer.

- Funeral director.
- Electrologist.

JOBS REQUIRING MORE-THAN-AVERAGE TRAINING AND EXPERIENCE

- Lodging facilities manager.
- Chef.
- Pastry chef.
- Massage therapist.

See page 288 for a list of some of the jobs in the Personal Services Cluster, along with their *DOT* numbers.

Career Decision-Making Activities

1. Try your hand at some cosmetology tasks. For example, practice shampooing and cutting the hair of someone in your family. Or practice shaving your father. Another activity you could try would be to use makeup for Halloween. Apply it to some of your friends.
2. Is a cosmetology program offered through your school? If so, you may want to sign up.
3. In most areas there are plenty of jobs available in personal services. As you get older, try various kinds of service jobs. You could try working in hotels, laundries, homes, restaurants—all kinds of different places. Keep track of which settings you prefer.

Occupations in Personal Services

Here is a list of occupations mentioned in this chapter. Next to the name of each occupation is its *DOT* number. You can use the *DOT* number to locate further information about the occupation in your school or public library. For the broad occupational terms mentioned in this chapter, only one or two examples of that occupation are listed below. You can easily find more examples of the occupation in the *DOT.*

All-Around Presser (363.684-010)
Attendant, Camp (329.467-010)
Attendant, Checkroom (358.677-010)
Attendant, Lodging Facilities (329.467-010)
Baggage Porter (324.137-010)
Baker (313.381-010)
Barber (330.371-010)
Bartender (312.474-010)
Beautician (332.271-018)
Beauty Operator (332.271-010)
Bellhop (324.677-010)
Blind Aide (359.573-010)
Blocker (363.684-010)
Bootblack (366.677-010)
Carpet Shampooer (361.682-010)
Caterer (187.167-106)
Chaperon (359.667-010)
Chauffeur (359.673-010)
Chef (313.131-014)
Child Monitor (Nanny) (301.677-010)
Coffee Maker (317.684-010)
Companion (309.677-010)
Cook (315.361-010)
Cosmetologist (332.271-010)
Day Worker (301.687-014)
Dog Groomer (418.674-010)
Dog Trainer (159.224-010)
Doorkeeper (324.677-014)
Dressmaker (785.361-010)
Dry Cleaner (362.382-010)
Dry Cleaning Worker (362.686-010)
Dyer (364.361-010)
Electrologist (339.371-010)
Embalmer (338.371-014)
Flatwork Finisher (363.686-010)
Flower Arranger (142.081-010)
Funeral Attendant (359.677-014)
Funeral Director (187.167-030)
Furniture Cleaner (362.684-022)
Gardener (301.687-018)
Hairdresser (332.271-018)
Hand Launderer (361.684-010)
Horse Trainer (159.224-010)
Horseshoer (418.381-010)
Hostess (352.667-010)
Housekeeper (301.474-010)
Janitor (382.664-010)
Kitchen Helper (318.687-010)
Kitchen Steward (318.137-010)
Launderer Attendant (369.677-010)
Laundry Worker (361.685-108)
Live-In Housekeeper (301.137-010)
Lodging Facilities Manager (320.137-014)
Massage Therapist (076.121-014)
Masseur/Masseuse (334.374-010)
Pantry Goods Maker (317.684-014)
Pastry Chef (313.131-022)
Personal Shopper (296.357-010)
Pest Exterminator (408.381-010)
Pet Care Worker (410.674-010)
Pet Shop Worker (410.674-010)
Reducing-Machine Operator (359.567-010)
Room Service Clerk (324.577-010)
Rug Cleaner (689.687-066)
Shoe Repairer (365.361-014)
Silk Finisher (363.681-010)
Steward (350.137-014)
Tailor, Alteration (785.261-010)
Tailor, Custom (785.261-014)
Tattoo Artist (339.571-010)
Veterinarian (073.101-010)
Waitress (311.477-030)

Review and Enrichment

Summarizing the Chapter

Summarizing information is a critical thinking skill that will help you succeed in the world of work. Write a summary of what you learned in Chapter 18. Focus on the main points of the chapter. Then in a class discussion, compare your summary with the summaries done by your classmates. Can you improve your summary?

Improving Your Career Vocabulary

1. Learning to use new vocabulary terms will improve your communication skills, which are important in almost all areas of work. Write definitions for the terms listed below. Then for each term, write an original sentence about yourself in which you use the term correctly.
   - services
   - Personal Services Cluster
   - unstructured
   - initiative
   - cosmetology
   - domestic
   - lodging
2. List the job families discussed in this chapter. Write a one-sentence description of each.

Finding the Facts

Finding exact information is a frequently used skill in many careers. Find the answers to the exercise below, and write the answers on a separate sheet of paper.

1. Name three job families from this cluster.
2. What is another name for beautician?
3. What type of work does a blocker do?
4. What kind of work does a personal shopper do?
5. Name three jobs in this cluster requiring less-than-average training and experience.

Thinking for Yourself

To complete the exercise below you will need to use critical thinking and communication skills, which are skills valued by all employers. Write out your answers or be prepared to discuss them in class, depending on your teacher's instructions.

1. Of all the occupations mentioned in this chapter, which seems most interesting to you? Why?
2. What do you think would be the most important aptitude (natural ability) to possess for a successful career in personal services? Why?
3. What values do you think would be most common among people interested in personal services?
4. Do you feel you are usually successful in relating to other people? Explain.
5. Of what value would the ability to communicate effectively be to someone in a personal services career?

Practicing Your Basic Skills

Your career success depends greatly on your basic math and communication skills. Work hard at improving in the areas where you have trouble with the following exercises.

Math

1. Ryan was a hair colorist at a beauty salon. He had to mix special colors for each customer. For one customer he used 4¾ ounces of formula base, 1½ ounces of tint #1 and ¾ ounce of tint #2. How much liquid did he prepare altogether?
2. Ileana is a chauffeur. The car she drives holds twenty-five gallons of gas. On Wednesday she filled the tank. On Thursday she had a quarter of a tank left. On Friday she bought ten gallons, and on Saturday she used all but ⅛ tank. How much gas did she use altogether?
3. Michelle works for a laundry. It charges $1 for a blouse or shirt, $2 for a dress, and 75¢ for every 5 pounds of general laundry. Michelle did the Riveras' laundry. In it were five dresses, three shirts, three blouses, and five pounds of general laundry. How much did she charge the Riveras altogether?

Reading and Writing

1. Pretend you are a blind aide. Ask a friend to dictate a letter that you will write.

Review and Enrichment, continued

2. Pretend someone is going to do some personal shopping for you. Write a list of what you want him or her to buy. Include sizes, colors, and other important information. Trade lists with a classmate. Could you shop from your classmate's list?
3. Read through the help-wanted section of your local paper. How many personal services jobs can you find?
4. Pick at least one occupation mentioned in this chapter that you think would be interesting. Research the occupation thoroughly, and write a report. Use the career research checklist in Chapter 5 as a guide for your report. Conclude your report with an explanation of your interest in that occupation based on your findings.

Speaking and Listening

1. Choose a classmate as a partner. Decide which of you is the employer and which is the housekeeper. The employer should give the housekeeper the day's instructions. Be clear and accurate. When the employer is finished, the housekeeper should repeat what was said. Was anything lost during communication?
2. Trade places, and repeat Activity 1.

Activities Working with Others

In almost all careers you must be able to get along well with other people to be successful. As you work with others, pay attention to how well you get along. If necessary, work hard at improving your ability to do your part and to cooperate.

1. Ask a neighbor or family member if you can take care of that person's pet for one week. Pay attention to all instructions, and take notes.
2. Volunteer to do the family laundry this week. Be sure you have adequate instructions.
3. Give your parents a treat. Serve them breakfast in bed this Sunday. Add little touches to try to make it attractive.
4. Add the careers mentioned in this chapter to your database.

Decision Making and Problem Solving

You will be a big help to your employer if you can make decisions and solve problems. List all the possible ways of resolving the situations described below. Then pick the best alternative (possible choice), and tell why you chose it. If you need help, you might want to refer to Chapter 3.

1. You are a new hairstylist, and you like your job. The only problem is that the shampoo the shop uses makes your skin break out on your hands and wrists. You'd like to tell the owner about it, but she just ordered a large supply. You're afraid she'll decide the shampoo is more important than you are. What will you do?
2. You work in a fast-food restaurant. Yesterday you got an idea for a new system of making the hamburgers, and you told your supervisor. Today you overheard him telling the owner about it, but your name wasn't mentioned. The owner loved the idea and praised your supervisor for it. You'd like to tell the owner it was your idea, but you're afraid your supervisor will be angry. What will you do?

CHAPTER 19

PUBLIC SERVICES CAREERS

◆ Chapter Objectives ◆

After completing this chapter you will be able to do the following:

- ◆ Define the terms listed under "New Career Terms."
- ◆ List and describe the eleven job families in the Public Services Cluster.
- ◆ Identify several careers included in this cluster.
- ◆ Name several slow-growing and fast-growing jobs in this cluster.
- ◆ Explain what it would be like to work at a career in this cluster.
- ◆ Evaluate your own interest in this cluster.
- ◆ Identify skills common to many careers in this cluster.

◆ New Career Terms ◆

In this chapter you will learn the meanings of the following career terms:

- ✔ Taxes
- ✔ Public
- ✔ Public Services Cluster
- ✔ White-collar jobs
- ✔ Blue-collar jobs
- ✔ Civil Service test
- ✔ Administration
- ✔ Regulatory
- ✔ Labor
- ✔ Labor union
- ✔ Utility
- ✔ Welfare

*Everyone is aware of what **taxes** are. Taxes are sums of money that people and businesses must pay to our governments. When you buy something at a store, you usually have to pay a sales tax. It might be 5¢, 6¢, 7¢, or more for every dollar you pay. When you work, you have to pay income taxes. These taxes are collected by the federal government and sometimes by state governments. If your parents own your home, they pay property tax on the value of your property. Governments take these taxes and provide many services to you, to your family, and to your friends.*

If you are going to a public school, your teachers and everybody else who works at the school are paid by tax dollars. You almost certainly use public highways and bridges. These are paid for by tax dollars, too.

The police officers and firefighters in your community are all paid with tax dollars. Postal workers are paid partly through the money you pay for stamps and partly through tax dollars.

*We use the word **public** to mean all the people living in our nation. You already know what services are. The **Public Services Cluster** includes all the jobs involved in providing services to the public. Almost all these services are paid for with tax dollars. If you are interested in any of the jobs that are paid for, in whole or in part, by tax dollars, then you are interested in public services.*

taxes
money that citizens pay to the government to provide for public services.

▼ Before obtaining a civil service job, you must pass a preemployment test.

WHAT WOULD IT BE LIKE?

The range of public services jobs is wide. Most of the jobs are involved with providing services rather than producing goods. You would probably not sell or manufacture products if you chose to be in a public services career.

Most of the public services jobs are considered **white-collar** jobs. These are jobs in offices. Less than 15 percent of the public services workers have **blue-collar** jobs. These are jobs in a factory or outdoors environment—any job requiring physical labor.

Many public services jobs require a **civil service test** (a preemployment test given by the federal government for specific government jobs). You have to pass it to get the job. But once you do get a public services job, it's very secure.

By their very nature, public services jobs usually involve people-to-people contact. If you become a teacher, you will be in contact with many people every day. If you decide to become a social worker, you will have to meet people, too. An exception would be a mail carrier.

Some public services careers are dangerous. If you become a police officer or a firefighter, you are exposed to danger some of the time.

Would you enjoy working in this career cluster? Do some daydreaming as you "listen" to the conversation below. Several people who enjoy working in the Public Services Cluster are talking about

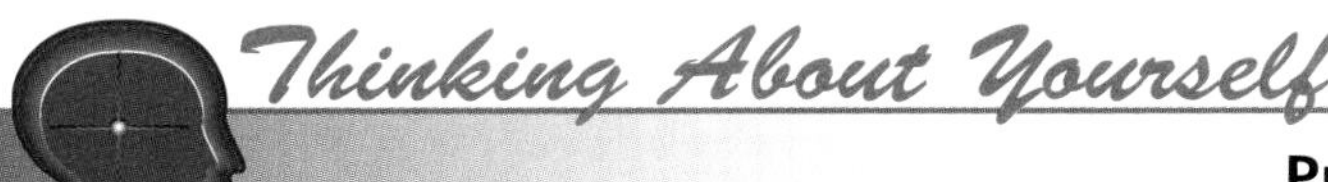

Thinking About Yourself

Public Services Careers

Take your time reading and thinking about the questions below. You might even want to make notes on a sheet of paper and write out the answers.

- ▲ Do you like to watch television programs about police officers or lawyers?
- ▲ Have you ever been to a trial or other court proceedings? Would you like working in such an atmosphere?
- ▲ Have you ever done volunteer work for a hospital or church? Did you enjoy helping people?
- ▲ Have you ever been in charge of a group or class? Can you enforce rules and regulations?
- ▲ Have you ever helped friends or relatives with their homework? Can you explain things and communicate well?
- ▲ Have you ever helped a school librarian? Do you like working in a library?
- ▲ Are you interested in current events? Do you usually read a daily newspaper?
- ▲ Do people come to you for advice when they have problems? Do you enjoy helping people solve their problems?
- ▲ Have you ever been on a school safety patrol? Do you like being responsible for others' safety?

If you answered yes to many of these questions, there's a good chance you might enjoy a career in public services.

their jobs. As you listen to what they say, imagine yourself doing their jobs.

Teacher: I was always someone who needed to know "why." I always had to understand everything. So I learned a lot, and it just makes sense that I pass on what I know and that I help kids understand "why." I like kids, and I like teaching them things they don't know. I like standing up in front of the class, explaining things. And I like figuring out clever ways of making a dull subject interesting. I guess most of all I like answering their questions. They have so many questions. It really gives me a good feeling to know that I'm helping these kids grow up and learn what the world is all about. We really have some incredible class discussions.

Police Officer: I'll bet you do. Every once in a while I speak to young people about driving safely, and I get the same good feeling—you know, that I'm making a difference, maybe even saving some lives. I do my best to get through to them. They are so young, and a lot of them don't realize how many terrible things can happen to them out there. That's why I became a police officer—to try to protect innocent people, many of whom can't protect themselves. Sometimes it's dangerous, and I think I'm crazy for doing it. But most of the time I'm helping someone who can't fight back or stopping someone from hurting someone else. It's an important job. I'm pretty proud of what I do.

Social Worker: Ditto for me. Every day I work with people who are almost helpless. Young, unwed mothers without a high school

public
the people of our nation as a whole.

Public Services Cluster
a group of occupations involved in providing services to the public (most are paid for with tax dollars).

white-collar job
a job having to do with clerical, professional, or business work.

blue-collar job
a job having to do with industrial or factory work.

civil service test
a preemployment test developed by the federal government for specific government jobs.

Attitude makes a difference

From Detective Television Shows to Real Life

Bernadette Anderson loved to watch television. What she mainly watched were cop shows. Bernie, as her friends called her, especially loved the detective shows.

One day her dad loaned her a detective novel. She read it in two days. From then on she was hooked. She read detective novels all the time.

She decided she wanted to be a detective. She asked her guidance counselor what she would have to do. Her counselor showed her the requirements for becoming a Federal Bureau of Investigation (FBI) special agent. This interested Bernie a lot.

Starting in the last year in junior high, Bernie took all the courses she could that would prepare her for college. She knew that to become an FBI special agent she had to go to college.

Right now Bernie is struggling during her last year in high school. Her grades aren't the best, but she'll pass. She knows she is going to go to college, even if she has to go to a community college for the first two years.

Bernie is determined. She wants to turn the fantasy of detective shows and books into her reality.

What Do YOU Think?

How did Bernie develop the right attitude toward school? Is Bernie being realistic? What else could she do to help prepare herself for a career as a detective?

---

education and no idea where to get a job. Children who've been abused by their parents. People with mental problems. There are so many people out there who need our help. Some days it's overwhelming, and I feel like giving up. I could get a much better paying job with a lot fewer headaches. But something inside me won't let me quit. I have to do my part. And I do help a lot of unfortunate people find jobs, get something to eat, or find a safe place to live.

Public Defender: Boy, I know what you mean about the money. I could make three or four times what I'm making now as a public defender if I worked in one of the big law firms here in town. But I think I'd hate the work they'd give me. Here I make a difference in people's lives almost every day. Most of the people I defend are really okay. They just got a bum deal somewhere along the line. Life has been pretty easy for me, so I try to help. I loved studying law, and I believe in it. It's there to help and protect people. And that's what I do. Use my knowledge of the law to help people less fortunate than most of us.

What do you think? Do any of these careers sound appealing? Can you see yourself doing one of these jobs—or a similar job? Would you like to learn more about public services careers?

Career Decision-Making Activities

1. Assume that you are in charge of driver's licenses in your state. You decide such things as what tests will be used and how many violations are allowed before someone loses his or her license. On a separate sheet of paper, write at least one regulation that you would require for all drivers. Tell how you would enforce this regulation. Discuss your regulations in class.
2. Think about ways that your community could be improved. For example, should it be safer, cleaner, or easier to get around in? Should it have better schools? If you were the mayor, what would be your number one priority? Pretend you are a candidate for mayor. Give a speech to your class emphasizing your top priority for improving your town or city. After your speech, conduct a press conference. Answer any questions from your audience.
3. Tell one of your teachers you are studying education careers and you would like to try teaching. Ask if you could prepare and teach a short lesson on a topic being studied in that class. Pick a class where the subject being studied is one of your favorite subjects. Try to come up with an interesting way to teach the topic. Report back to class on your experience. Do you think you would enjoy a career in education?
4. Try to identify at least one or two people who have worked for both public and private employers. Ask them what differences they noticed. Did they prefer working for one type of employer rather than the other? Compare your findings in class.

JOB FAMILIES IN THE PUBLIC SERVICES CLUSTER

There are eleven job families within the Public Services Cluster. All of the jobs listed are considered public services when they are paid, at least in part, by tax dollars. Many of the jobs are also done for private (nongovernment) companies. These workers are paid by their companies, not by tax dollars. That means that you have read about some of the jobs in other clusters.

First look at the cluster figure on page 296. Then read about each job family. This will help you decide which careers in this cluster you might enjoy the most.

- **Administration and regulatory services.** The word **administration** comes from the verb *to administer,* which means to manage or supervise. Thus, *administration* means management or supervision of public affairs by government officials. Administrators supervise and carry out activities of government. The

administration management or supervisory personnel.

Job Families in the Public Services Cluster

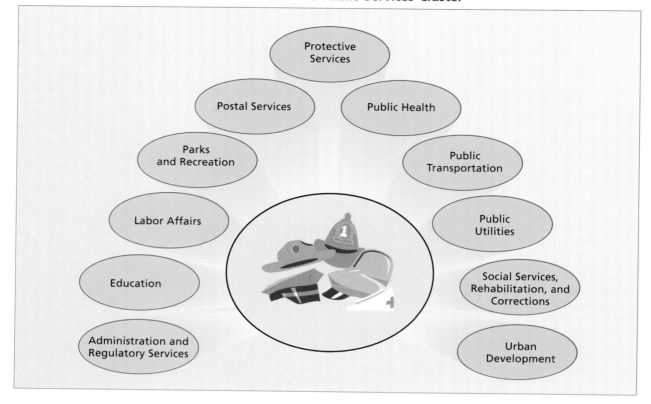

Protective Services

Postal Services

Public Health

Parks and Recreation

Public Transportation

Labor Affairs

Public Utilities

Education

Social Services, Rehabilitation, and Corrections

Administration and Regulatory Services

Urban Development

regulatory controlling how things occur; to direct according to rule.

▼ Garbage collection is usually regulated by the city in which you live.

word **regulatory** means controlling how things occur. The administration and regulatory services job family includes all the jobs involved in licensing, regulating, policymaking, and record keeping.

One type of administrator is a city manager. He or she is appointed by elected officials within a city. A city manager makes sure that tax collection is carried out. Among other things, city managers also make sure that laws are enforced and that garbage is collected.

People who work at the driver's license office are in public services, too. They take care of the testing and administration of driver's licenses.

Civil engineers help with public works projects. They design roads, harbors, and bridges. They might help with the sewage system and the water supply.

- **Education.** Anybody who trains or educates other members of society is involved in education. You probably know more about jobs in education than in any other field. After all, you've been going to school for many years now.

Careers for Tomorrow

TEACHING WHAT YOU KNOW BEST

One of the high-growth areas in public services jobs is in vocational education. *Vocational* means dealing with a trade. A trade is a job that requires manual skill (skill with the hands) or mechanical skill. Examples are a carpenter or electrician. If you really like keyboarding, plumbing, or automotive mechanics, maybe you can teach it someday.

Vocational education teachers often work in public and private high schools. They work in community colleges. They also work in privately owned trade schools.

Most "voc-ed" teachers, as they are called, specialize in one subject. The person who teaches plumbing usually doesn't also teach cosmetology (improving skin, hair, and nails), for example.

In many cases you don't need a college degree to become a voc-ed teacher. One way to start this exciting career is to agree to work as an aide to someone already teaching.

If you want more information, write the American Vocational Association, 1410 King St., Alexandria, VA 22314.

labor
the resource of employed workers.

labor union
a group of workers who have organized to increase their wages or improve their working conditions.

Most of the teachers that you have ever had are in public services careers. Most of the teachers whom you are going to have are in this career cluster, too. Your school counselor is another public servant. So are your school librarian, principal, and vice-principal.

- **Labor affairs.** The labor affairs job family includes workers who provide services to **labor.** Labor refers mainly to workers who are paid by the hour. Many of these workers are not highly skilled, do physical work, and belong to unions. Many government workers help labor get a fair deal. The government workers help labor members get a fair wage rate and make sure they have a safe place to work.

Workers in this job family also help unemployed workers get jobs. All states have employment offices. Government counselors work in many of these offices. The counselors help unemployed workers find the best career path.

Labor unions are groups of workers in a certain area or industry who join together. They combine efforts to get higher wages and better working conditions. Most unions

E-MAIL SORTER

One of the problems with e-mail is that it is so easy to use. Consequently, many people receive so many e-mail messages a day that they spend too much time reading them. If you ever become a secretary or an assistant to someone, one of your duties may be e-mail sorter. That means that you will have to read the e-mail messages first and pass on to your boss only the ones that are worth his or her time.

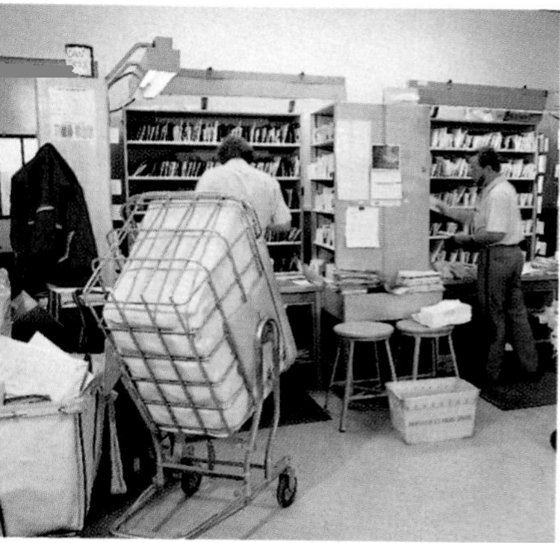

▲ Postal workers across the country sort millions of pieces of mail every day.

have a business agent. This person manages the labor union. He or she often meets with employers to talk about hours and worker safety.

Many cities and counties employ safety engineers. These engineers make sure that workplaces are safe for the workers.

- **Parks and recreation.** As our nation gets richer, people have more leisure time. They go to more parks. Anybody involved in developing and regulating public recreational areas is part of the parks and recreation job family.

  You have already read about most of the occupations in this job family. We looked at them in the Hospitality and Recreation Cluster. We also looked at them in the Agribusiness and Natural Resources Cluster and the Environmental Sciences Cluster.

- **Postal services.** The mail must go through. For this to happen, hundreds of thousands of postal workers sort and deliver the mail. All the people involved in transporting and delivering the mail are in the postal services job family.

  Mail handlers work in the larger post offices only. They load and unload mail to and from trucks. This is very physically demanding work.

  Clerical workers sell stamps and money orders in post offices. Carriers deliver the mail to your house and to businesses. Special delivery carriers deliver only special delivery mail. They try to get it out as soon as it arrives.

- **Protective services.** When you *protect* somebody, you make sure that he or she is not harmed. Many people in our nation work in the protective services job family. This family includes everyone involved in preserving our national freedom and protecting individual rights.

  Your local police officers and firefighters are part of this job family. You are probably not as familiar with the special agents in the Federal Bureau of Investigation (FBI). They try to capture bank robbers and kidnappers.

  The military is a broad category of occupations. There are many different kinds of jobs in the U.S. Army, Navy, Air Force, and Marines.

- **Public health.** Sometimes diseases, such as measles, start to spread through a community. Public health workers try to prevent this. If they can't prevent it, they try to control it. Workers who try to prevent and control diseases with public resources are in the public health job family.

  The county health officer is responsible for health services in a county. He or she manages all of the public

◀ Public utility workers make sure we are supplied with the services we take for granted, such as electricity.

health service locations. Many of these places give free shots to prevent serious diseases. Field health officers go out into the county. They try to track down people who might be carrying serious diseases. They are "disease detectives."

- **Public transportation.** The public highways, bridges, and waterways have to be built and maintained. Public transportation workers do this. You will learn more about these jobs in the next chapter.
- **Public utilities.** *Utility* means useful. A public **utility** is a business that provides water, electricity, gas, or sewage treatment. These businesses are closely regulated by the government. The workers who are involved in producing and distributing the utilities are in the public utilities job family.

  In a water plant there is a pumping station supervisor. He or she makes sure that all of the valves and pumps work. That way you get water when you turn on the faucet.

  There is also a water treatment plant operator. He or she makes sure that the right chemicals go into the water before you drink it. This prevents you from getting sick from drinking the water.

utility
useful; a public utility is a business that provides water, electricity, gas, or sewage treatment, and is regulated by the government.

In sewage treatment plants there are wastewater treatment plant operators. They make sure that all of the waste material is taken out of the water. Not until then can the water be put back into rivers and lakes.

- **Social service, rehabilitation, and correction.** Some people are unable to take care of themselves. These people need help. All the workers who provide this help are in the social service, rehabilitation, and correction job family. The different areas of help are welfare, human development, mental health, and rehabilitation.

  Welfare usually refers to money given to people who can't support themselves. The workers who help these people are called social service workers. Many state and local governments also have family service counseling. The counselors help families in need. Some people have mental problems. They are helped by mental health workers.

  Some people commit crimes. They need to be rehabilitated. To *rehabilitate* means to put back in good working condition. Rehabilitating people who commit crimes means helping them overcome their problems so they can become good citizens. Probation and parole officers are types of social workers (people who provide services directed at helping the social conditions in a community). They assist people who have committed crimes. They help them readjust to society.

- **Urban development.** Many cities are overcrowded. Many cities are polluted. People who study and try to solve the problems of cities work in the urban development job family. The term *urban* means in the city.

  Urban planners come up with plans to make sure the growth in the city doesn't ruin the city. Urban planners often use the services of urban architects.

welfare
aid in the form of money or necessities given to those in need (those unable to support themselves).

CAREER OUTLOOK

Government is growing in the United States. It is not growing as fast as the economy as a whole, however.

FASTEST-GROWING JOBS

Many of the jobs in the public services sector are projected to grow rapidly. Some of them include the following:

- Elementary or preschool teacher.
- School counselor.
- Social worker.
- Adult education worker.

- Corrections officer.
- Paralegal.

SLOWEST-GROWING JOBS

Some public services jobs will grow slowly:

- School librarian.
- Firefighter.
- Government chief executive.

▲ Do you enjoy children? Preschool teacher is one of the fastest-growing jobs in public services.

AT THE HEART OF THE PUBLIC SERVICES CLUSTER

What makes the Public Services Cluster different from the other fourteen clusters you'll be exploring? What would it really be like to work in this cluster? Let's try to get at the heart of public services.

The essence of this cluster is helping people in your community. It's all about working for the common good. Public services involve helping people in many ways. Many people are in danger. Their lives have been threatened by an epidemic, a major fire, or a criminal with a gun. Public services involve rescuing these people, even if it means putting your own life in danger. Public services can involve putting someone else's life above yours in importance.

Most public services do not involve life-threatening situations. But they all involve helping people, and helping them in very basic, important ways. People need clean water and food. They need a healthful environment. They need roads and highways to travel safely from place to place. They need heat in the winter.

All these needs are met by the workers in public services. Public services involve providing people with educations; fair treatment from employers; and clean, safe parks for recreation. They involve working to improve living conditions for all people.

Figure 19.1 lists just a few examples of occupations from this career cluster. Think about the job title, the work activities, and the work settings. Figure 19.1 just gives examples to help you get at the heart of this cluster. You don't need to read for details. Scan the entries to get a feel for the cluster as a whole.

Would you like a career in this cluster? Ask yourself the following questions:

- Do you like the sound of the occupations listed under "Who"? Would you feel good about an identity like one of these?
- Would you enjoy doing activities like those described under "What"?
- Picture yourself working in the settings described under "Where." Would you be comfortable in these settings?

Figure 19.1 Sample Occupations in the Public Services Cluster

WHO You Would Be	WHAT You Would Do	WHERE You Would Do It
Firefighter	Be prepared for emergencies; connect hose lines, operate pumps, position ladders, rescue victims, give first aid	Fire stations and sites of fires
College teacher	Teach and advise college students, give lectures, do research, write articles and books, counsel students	College campuses
Military personnel	Undertake a wide variety of jobs: mechanics, engineers, clerical workers, members of the infantry and artillery, pilots, food service workers, and health service workers are just a few	Military bases all over the world
Mail carrier	Deliver and collect mail; travel a planned route; arrange and sort mail; may walk, drive, or both	Outdoors and indoors; in neighborhoods and at post offices
Labor relations specialist	Maintain relationships with local employers, promote the use of public employment programs	Government and employers' offices
Social worker	Help individuals, families, and groups cope with problems; counsel the homeless, unemployed, and seriously ill; investigate cases	Government offices and in homes and institutions housing people being assisted

SKILLS, TRAINING, AND EXPERIENCE

Listed below are some skills common to many of the careers in the Public Services Cluster.

- Work with laws and regulations, sometimes written in legal language.
- Deal with many different kinds of people.
- Use logical thinking and special training to advise others.
- Care about other people's needs and problems.
- Gain the trust and confidence of people.
- Collect, organize, and analyze data.
- Use language and math skills to analyze and interpret documents.

- Plan and direct programs and the activities of others.

Many jobs in public services require only some skills. Others require advanced training. If you want to be a teacher, for example, you would have to go to college. The following are three categories of jobs.

JOBS REQUIRING LESS-THAN-AVERAGE TRAINING AND EXPERIENCE

- Member of the armed services.
- Building custodian.
- Electrical meter reader.
- Firefighter.
- Corrections officer.
- Garbage worker.
- Postal service worker.
- State police officer.
- Highway maintenance worker.
- Police officer.

JOBS REQUIRING AVERAGE TRAINING AND EXPERIENCE

- Crime laboratory technician.
- Detective.
- Teacher's aide.
- Legal secretary.
- Paralegal aide.

JOBS REQUIRING MORE-THAN-AVERAGE TRAINING AND EXPERIENCE

- City manager.
- FBI special agent.
- Internal Revenue Service worker.
- Parole officer.
- Probation officer.
- College teacher.
- Criminologist.
- Public librarian.
- Urban and regional planner.
- School counselor.
- School librarian.
- Social worker.
- Teacher.
- Vocational counselor.

See page 304 for a list of some of the jobs in the Public Services Cluster, along with their *DOT* numbers.

Career Decision-Making Activities

1. As soon as you can, try a summer job in public services. Contact your local or state government, or the federal government. Day-care centers, senior citizen centers, day camps, parks, libraries, and law firms are some of the places you could work.
2. Take courses in government, psychology, and sociology. If you can, also take a first-aid course and join the school safety patrol.
3. Do volunteer work to help people in any way you can. For example, you might agree to help out an aging relative after school and during the summer. You could volunteer for work at a service club or with a church or community group.

Occupations in Public Services

Here is a list of occupations mentioned in this chapter. Next to the name of each occupation is its *DOT* number. You can use the *DOT* number to locate further information about the occupation in your school or public library. For the broad occupational terms mentioned in this chapter, only one or two examples of that occupation are listed below. You can easily find more examples of the occupation in the *DOT.*

Adult Education Worker (097.227-014)
Armed Services Career (see 378 series)
Building Custodian (381.137-010)
Business Agent (187.167-018)
Carrier (230.367-010)
City Manager (188.117-114)
Civil Engineer (005.061-014)
Clerical Worker (209.587-026)
College Teacher (090.227-010)
Corrections Officer (372.667-018)
County Health Officer (070.101-046)
Crime Laboratory Technician (029.281-010)
Criminologist (054.067-014)
Detective, Plain Clothes (375.267-010)
Detective, Special Agent (375.167-042)
Electrical Meter Reader (209.576-010)
Elementary or Preschool Teacher (092.027-014)
Family Service Counselor (195.107-018)
FBI Special Agent (375.167-042)
Field Health Officer (168.167-018)
Firefighter (373.364-010)
Garbage Worker (909.687-010)
Government Counselor (045.107-010)
Highway Maintenance Worker (899.684-014)
Internal Revenue Service Worker (160.167-038)
Labor Relations Specialist (188.117-066)
Lawyer (110.107-010)
Legal Secretary (201.362-010)
Mail Carrier (230.367-010)
Mail Handler (209.687-014)
Mayor (188.117-114)
Mental Health Worker (045.107-022)
Military Personnel (see 378 series)
Paralegal Aide (119.267-026)
Parole Officer (195.167-030)
Police Officer (375.263-014)
Postal Service Worker (see Postal Worker)
Postal Worker (243.367-014)
Principal, High School (099.177-018)
Probation Officer (195.167-034)
Public Health Worker (187.117-050)
Public Librarian (100.127-167)
Public Transportation Workers (188.167-078)
Pumping Station Supervisor (954.130-010)
Safety Engineer (012.061-0140)
School Counselor (045.107-010)
School Librarian (100.127-167)
Social Service Worker (195.107-010)
Social Worker (195.107-026)
Special Agent, (FBI) (375.167-042)
Special Delivery Carrier (230.367-010)
State Police Officer (375.263-014)
Teacher, Kindergarten and Elementary (092.027-014)
Teacher, Secondary (091.227-010)
Teacher's Aide (249.367-074)
Urban Architect (see Urban Planner)
Urban Planner (199.167-014)
Vice-Principal (091.107-010)
Vocational Educational Teacher (097.227-014)
Wastewater Treatment Plant Operator (see Water Treatment Plant Operator)
Water Treatment Plant Operator (954.382-014)

Review and Enrichment

Summarizing the Chapter

Summarizing information is a critical thinking skill that will help you succeed in the world of work. Write a summary of what you learned in Chapter 19. Focus on the main points of the chapter. Then in a class discussion, compare your summary with the summaries done by your classmates. Can you improve your summary?

Improving Your Career Vocabulary

1. Learning to use new vocabulary terms will improve your communication skills, which are important in almost all areas of work. Write definitions for the terms listed below. Then for each term, write an original sentence about yourself in which you use the term correctly.
   - taxes
   - public
   - Public Services Cluster
   - administration
   - white-collar job
   - blue-collar job
   - Civil Service test
   - administration
   - regulatory
   - labor
   - labor union
   - utility
   - welfare
2. List the job families discussed in this chapter. Write a one-sentence description of each.

Finding the Facts

Finding exact information is a frequently used skill in many careers. Find the answers to the exercise below, and write the answers on a separate sheet of paper.

1. How do governments get the money to provide services for the public?
2. With what funds are postal workers paid?
3. How many job families are in the Public Services Cluster?
4. Is a city manager elected?
5. Name three public utilities.

Thinking for Yourself

To complete the exercise below you will need to use critical thinking and communication skills, which are skills valued by all employers. Write out your answers or be prepared to discuss them in class, depending on your teacher's instructions.

1. Some people think utilities and other services would operate more efficiently if they were run by private businesses. Others think these services would then be denied to people who couldn't afford them. What do you think?
2. Our prison system is so overcrowded it is difficult for any rehabilitation to take place. If there is no money to build more prisons, what do you think would improve the situation?
3. How would you describe someone you think would enjoy a public services career?
4. What values do you think would be common among people interested in public services?
5. Some people criticize the work of public officials. They say you have to "know someone" to get anything done. Do you think this is a fair criticism? Explain.

Practicing Your Basic Skills

Your career success depends greatly on your basic math and communication skills. Work hard at improving in the areas where you have trouble with the following exercises.

Math

1. LeRoy was trying to figure his income taxes. He earned $27,221 last year. He knew that about 7 percent was deducted for Social Security tax. About how much did he have to pay in Social Security tax?
2. Clarice owned two pieces of property. Property tax was 5 percent of the estimated value. She paid $2,500 on one lot and $1,700 on the other. What was the value of both lots?
3. Julio's state taxes its people 1.5 percent on the first $1,000 they earn and 3 percent on everything over that. Julio earned $15,600 last year. How much did he pay his state in taxes?

Review and Enrichment, continued

Reading and Writing

1. Read your local newspaper for one week, and clip out articles having to do with public services workers. How many articles did you find for each job family?
2. Write a one-page story about someone in a public services job.
3. Ask at your library to see books dealing with civil service examinations. Scan the books. What kinds of questions are asked? What skills seem to be required?
4. Pick at least one occupation mentioned in this chapter that you think would be interesting. Research the occupation thoroughly, and write a report. Use the career research checklist in Chapter 5 as a guide for your report. Conclude your report with an explanation of your interest in that occupation based on your findings.

Speaking and Listening

1. Pretend you are running for an elected office. Give a one-minute speech to the class members about what you will do for your community if elected and why they should vote for you.
2. Listen to your classmates' speeches. How much did the personality of the speaker affect the way you felt about the message?

Activities Working with Others

In almost all careers you must be able to get along well with other people to be successful. Work with your classmates to do the following activities. As you work together, pay attention to how well you get along. If necessary, work hard at improving your ability to do your part and to cooperate.

1. Do a survey of ten people in your neighborhood to learn whether or not they are satisfied with their public utilities. Report your findings to the class. Develop a class statement about your community's general attitude about its utilities.
2. As a class, volunteer to clean up the school grounds for one week. Develop work assignments for every class member so that everyone does an equal amount of the work.
3. Add the careers mentioned in this chapter to your database.

Decision Making and Problem Solving

You will be a big help to your employer if you can make decisions and solve problems. List all the possible ways of resolving the situations described below. Then pick the best alternative (possible choice), and tell why you chose it. If you need help, you might want to refer to Chapter 3.

1. You are in a voting booth choosing local candidates. The person whose goals you admire most wants to raise taxes, but you don't have a lot of money to spare. The other candidate wants to keep taxes at the same level but has not been doing much for the community. How will you vote?
2. You are running for public office. An important woman in town comes to you and says she will give a lot of money to your campaign if you will not stand in the way of a shopping center she wants to build. As far as you know there's no reason she should not build the shopping center, and your campaign needs the money. What will you do?

CHAPTER 20

TRANSPORTATION TECHNOLOGY CAREERS

◆ Chapter Objectives ◆

After completing this chapter you will be able to do the following:

- ◆ Define the terms listed under "New Career Terms."
- ◆ List and describe the six job families in the Transportation Technology Cluster.
- ◆ Identify several careers included in this cluster.
- ◆ Name several slow-growing and fast-growing jobs in this cluster.
- ◆ Explain what it would be like to work at a career in this cluster.
- ◆ Evaluate your own interest in this cluster.
- ◆ Identify skills common to many careers in this cluster.

◆ New Career Terms ◆

In this chapter you will learn the meanings of the following career terms:

- ✔ Transport
- ✔ Transportation Technology Cluster
- ✔ Stress
- ✔ Freight
- ✔ Destinations

When this country began more than two hundred years ago, the choices for getting from one place to another were very limited. People could walk. They could take a raft or a boat. They could ride a horse. Or they could ride in a horse-drawn carriage.

Today you still have the same choices (if you look hard enough), but there are quite a few others. You can ride in an automobile or a bus. You can ride a motorcycle. You can take a plane. You can take a train. You can take a powerboat. Some people even ride in spaceships.

People and goods are moved every instant of every day somewhere in the world. To **transport** *means to take from one place to another. The* **Transportation Technology Cluster** *is a group of jobs involved in the movement of people and goods from one place to another.*

Without our transportation network, economic life as we know it in the United States would disappear. Every business in every industry depends on our transportation system. You can become part of it.

transport
to convey (take) from one place to another.

Transportation Technology Cluster
a group of jobs involved in the movement of people and goods from one place to another.

WHAT WOULD IT BE LIKE?

Many jobs in transportation technology require that you be away from home. Think about becoming a flight attendant or an airline pilot. You would have to be away from home about half of the time. If you worked on a cargo boat, you'd be away from home even more of the time.

You could get a job in the airline, bus, or railroad areas and work in the main office. Then you would be in an office situation. You would be dealing with other people all the time. You wouldn't need to be away from home.

▶ People who move goods or passengers from place to place work in the field of transportation.

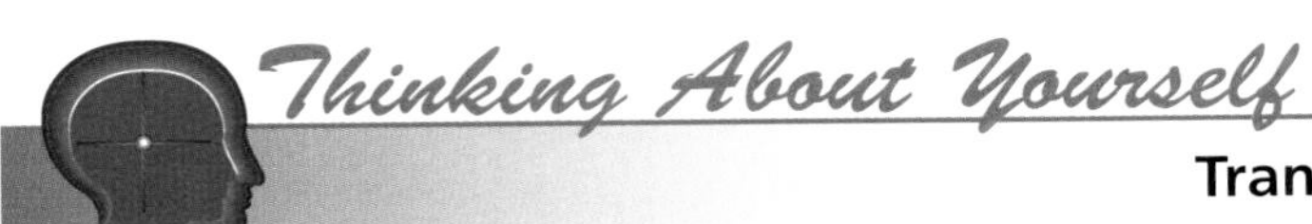

Transportation Technology

Take your time reading and thinking about the questions below. You might even want to make notes on a sheet of paper and write out your answers.

- Do you like to read magazine and newspaper articles about cars, boats, trains, or airplanes?
- Have you ever built model cars or airplanes? Did you enjoy this?
- Have you ever had an electric train set? Did you spend much time with it?
- Are you easily able to follow detailed instructions accurately?
- Do you enjoy working with your hands?

If you like being on the move and you answered yes to many of the questions above, there's a good chance you would enjoy a career in transportation technology.

If you became a mechanic for trains, automobiles, or planes you would probably work in one place. You would be using your hands. You would have to be willing to get dirty, though.

If you didn't mind **stress,** you might think about becoming an air traffic controller. Stress is physical, emotional, or mental strain. The people who work as air traffic controllers are under constant stress. They face tense situations all the time. Millions of lives a day depend on their work.

stress
physical or mental strain.

Would you enjoy working in the Transportation Technology Cluster? Do some daydreaming as you "listen" to the following conversation. Several people who enjoy working in this cluster are talking about their jobs. As you listen to what they say, imagine yourself doing their jobs.

Truck Driver: I work for a freight company. I haul all kinds of freight all over the country. You name a place, chances are I've been there. I love my job. I get to travel. I've always loved driving. Most of the time my job is pretty peaceful. I'm out there alone—just driving and thinking, listening to the radio. It's great. And then sometimes things get a little nerve-racking. Some of those winter nights with the ice, snow, and wind, I wondered if I was ever going to make it home. But I always do. And then I've got some stories to tell.

Taxi Driver: You want to hear stories? I can tell you some stories. You wouldn't believe some of the people who get in my cab. All kinds, believe me. It's fun, though. I really enjoy talking to them. That's the best part of the job. I also like wheeling around the city—in and out of traffic. I know this city like the back of my hand. Anywhere you want to go, I can find it. I get a kick out of figuring out the fastest way to get from one point to another. And by the time I get there, I've usually got another story to tell.

Locomotive Engineer: It's funny that both of you should talk about having stories to tell. Railroad people are great storytellers. They're always sitting around the yards swapping stories. Guess storytelling and traveling must go hand in hand. Actually I'm not much of a storyteller myself. I just love trains. Always have. I grew up right next to a railroad track. Used to walk up and down the track, wave at the trains as they went by. Always wanted to work on the railroad. And I got my wish! There's a lot of responsibility in being an engineer. Lots of lives depend on you. You can't let down for a moment. But I like that responsibility. Makes me feel like I'm doing something important.

Air Traffic Controller: You want to talk about responsibility—lives depending on you—you should try my job. You've got all those airplanes flying around up there—some of them with hundreds of passengers. And you've got a bunch more on the ground waiting to take off. And you've got people talking in both ears and all kinds of activity going on all around you. And somehow you've got to keep all those planes on schedule without crashing into one another. It scares me just talking about it. But really, I like the job. I need the excitement. I couldn't stand an office job where I just sat quietly at a desk all day. It's a high-stress job—no doubt about it. But I like the challenge. And we manage to get the job done, which gives all of us a sense of accomplishment.

What do you think? Do any of these careers sound appealing? Can you see yourself doing one of these jobs—or a similar job? Would you like to learn more about transportation technology careers?

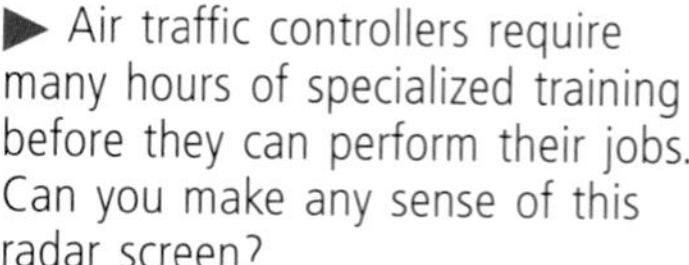

▶ Air traffic controllers require many hours of specialized training before they can perform their jobs. Can you make any sense of this radar screen?

Career Decision-Making Activities

1. Truck drivers, airplane pilots, ship captains, locomotive engineers, and astronauts all have something in common. They are responsible for moving passengers or freight safely from one location to another in a vehicle. Assume that you would like this kind of work. All that's left to be decided is in which type of vehicle you would work. Which would you choose to operate? Give at least three reasons for your choice. You can choose from the following:
   - truck
   - airplane
   - ship
   - train
   - spaceship
2. A career in transportation can mean spending many nights away from home. How would you feel about this type of lifestyle? Pretend that you are working in the career you chose for Activity 1 above. Imagine the places you might be and the working conditions. Then on a piece of paper make two lists—one list of the advantages and one list of the disadvantages of such a lifestyle. Think of as many advantages and disadvantages as possible. Compare your list with your classmates' lists in a class discussion.
3. Responsibility for the safety of passengers and freight is an important part of many transportation careers. How do you handle responsibility? On a separate piece of paper, list as many responsibility situations that you have experienced as you can. Next to each one tell how you performed and whether or not you worried about the responsibility. Then write a paragraph summarizing your attitude about responsibility. Do you like or dislike responsibility? If you don't feel you've had enough experience with responsibility to determine your attitude, imagine situations of responsibility and how you'd react. Discuss your summaries in class.

JOB FAMILIES IN THE TRANSPORTATION TECHNOLOGY CLUSTER

Each job family in the Transportation Technology Cluster is associated with either a type of transportation or a method of transportation. There are six job families in this cluster, as you can see in the diagram on page 312. Reading about the job families will help you decide which careers in this cluster you might enjoy most.

- **Water transport.** All the people who work at moving people and goods over the oceans and inland waterways are included in the water transport job family.

  The person with final responsibility for passengers, crew, and cargo is the ship captain, who is sometimes called the master or shipmaster. The captain navigates the vessel through the water. He or she makes all the decisions involved in getting the ship safely, and on time, to the next port.

  Among the other workers in this job family are the engineers. They make sure that the boats and ships have enough power and that all the machinery is working properly. Also included are baggage handlers and ticket agents,

Job Families in the Transportation Technology Cluster

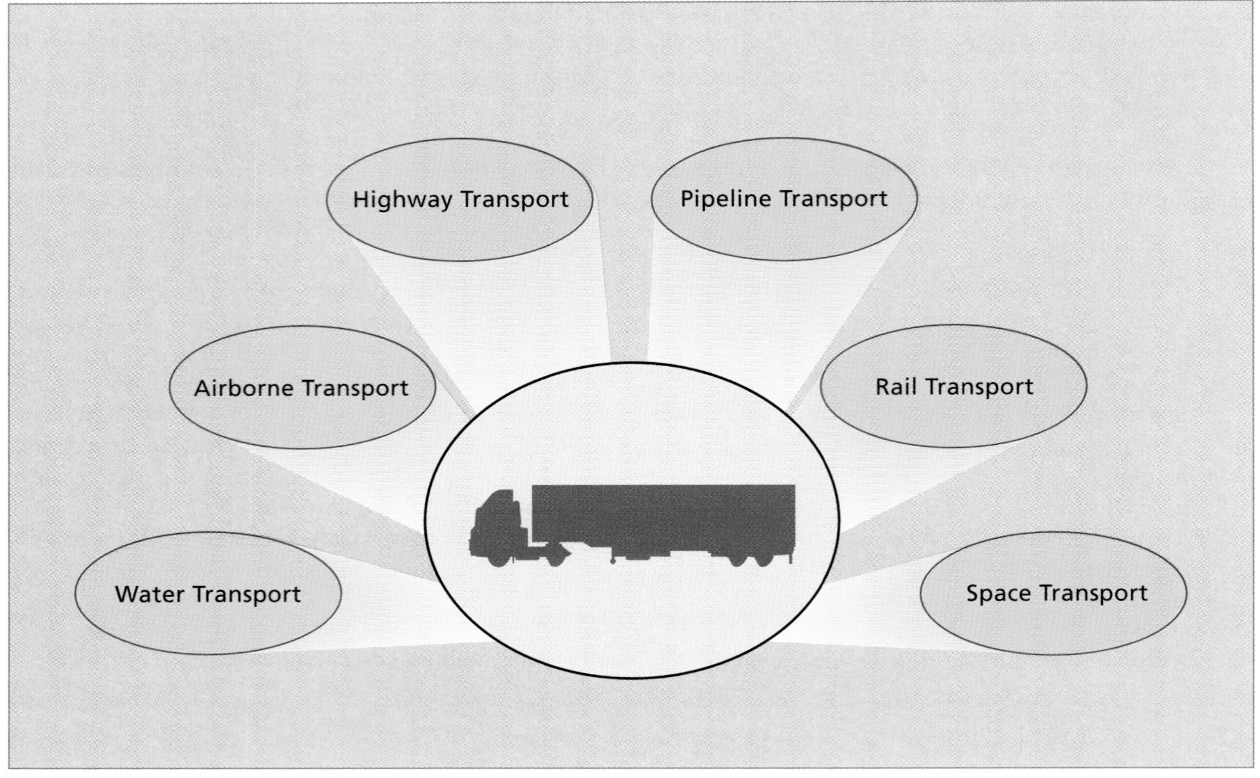

freight
goods, or cargo, to be shipped.

destination
a place that a person is traveling to, or where a thing is sent.

such as those working in other transportation technology job families.

◆ **Airborne transport.** The occupations in the airborne transport job family are involved in flying people and **freight** to their **destinations** (places to which people and things are traveling). Freight is goods, or cargo, to be shipped.

Airplanes are flown by pilots. The pilots are helped by navigators. Navigators determine the correct course for airplanes.

The navigator and the pilot are also helped by the flight engineer. This member of the flight crew checks for the proper amount of jet fuel. He or she also checks that the engines are working properly.

There are many other workers in this job family. Air traffic control specialists work in the towers at airports. They make sure that planes do not collide. Each airline has ticket agents and flight attendants. There are also reservation agents, who reserve in advance seats on different flights for customers.

- **Highway transport.** Buses, trucks, and taxis use streets and highways. They transport people and things. Occupations involved in moving people and things by bus, truck, or taxi are in the highway transport job family.

  There are different kinds of drivers. For automobiles there are also mechanics and service station attendants. For buses, taxis, and automobiles there are instructors who show students how to drive. They make sure students understand the proper way to drive.
- **Pipeline transport.** Oil and natural gas are often moved through pipelines. Sometimes coal is mixed with water, and the mixture is then moved through pipelines. All the occupations involved in moving solids and liquids by pipe are in the pipeline transport job family.

  A coal pipeline operator is in charge of the mixing of coal with water. A line walker controls the pipeline on foot, on horseback, or by small truck. He or she tries to detect leaks.

  A pipeline supervisor tells work crews where to build new pipelines. A maintenance mechanic repairs and maintains all the equipment used in pipeline operations.

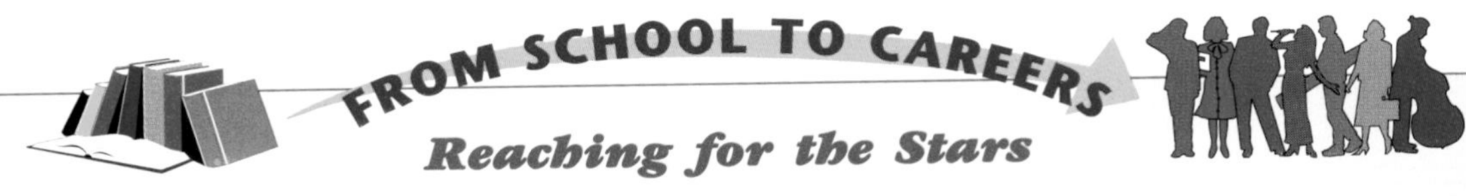

Reaching for the Stars

Forrest Dericho loved to look at stars. When he was in grammar school he learned about the constellations. These are the patterns that stars in the sky make. He even made a little display of constellations in a shoe box.

In junior high Forrest always asked his science teachers about constellations. They told him which books to read. Forrest read the books they recommended. At the school library he found even more books on his own.

When Forrest was finished with all the books on stars in the school library, he asked his mom to take him to the local community college library. There he found more books than he could read in years. He also started doing his own research on the Internet.

Forrest discovered that navigation was done using stars and constellations. He knew that navigation involved plotting a course for a ship or a plane to make sure it ended up where it was supposed to.

Forrest went to his guidance counselor and asked how he could use navigation in a career. She suggested he think about becoming a navigator on a ship or airplane.

Forrest loved airplanes. From that moment on, he chose courses that would be useful in becoming an airplane navigator.

What Do YOU Think?

How was Forrest going to make school count? Was it guaranteed that he would become what he wanted to be just by taking the right courses? What else could Forrest do to make sure he reached his career goal?

Careers for Tomorrow

BICYCLE MECHANIC

You wouldn't think that fixing bicycles would be a career for tomorrow. But this is a high-growth area. Why? Because more people than ever use bikes for recreation, health improvement, and transportation.

Bicycles are not what they used to be, either. Mountain bikes in particular are complicated. They have automatic gearshifters and complex suspension systems. They require more maintenance than do simpler bikes.

Bicycle mechanics don't have to have any formal training. But they need to be good at mechanics (working with machinery and parts). Bicycle stores often teach mechanics on the job.

For more information, write the National Bicycle Dealers Association, 2240 University Dr. #130, Newport Beach, CA 92660.

- **Rail transport.** The rail transport job family includes all the occupations involved in transporting people and freight by railroad. Many people take trains each year. Most of the work of trains, though, is moving freight.

  On a train there is an engineer and a firer. The engineer operates the train and watches the instruments and meters that measure speed, fuel, temperature, and so on. The firer acts as assistant engineer. A loading inspector makes sure that the things put in freight cars don't fall out or move around while the train trip is under way.

  A locomotive inspector makes sure that the locomotives—the engines at the fronts of trains—are working properly. If they need repairs, he or she makes sure these get done. Trains also have baggage and mail agents. They load and unload baggage and mail.
- **Space transport.** The newest form of transportation is in outer space. Workers in the space transport job family are involved in moving people and things to explore space.

  Astronauts are the people who pilot space vehicles. Aeronautical engineers design, develop, and test space vehicles. (Aeronautics is the science of making flying aircraft.)

CAREER OUTLOOK

Transportation technology is a growing field in the United States. Some of the jobs are actually disappearing, though.

◀ It takes more than just a pilot to keep planes at peak performance levels.

FASTEST-GROWING JOBS

The following transportation jobs are growing quickly:

- Auto body repairer.
- Airplane pilot.
- Flight engineer.
- Traffic engineer.

SLOWEST-GROWING JOBS

These are among the slowest-growing jobs in the cluster:

- Gas station attendant.
- Railroad maintenance worker.
- Railroad breaker.
- Railroad signaler.

Even though more people are driving cars, more gas stations are offering self-service. People use self-service, pump their own gas, and save money. That's why gas station attendant jobs are decreasing.

As more people have purchased their own cars and airline tickets have become less expensive, railroad transportation in the United States has declined. That is why railroad workers see their jobs disappearing little by little.

AT THE HEART OF THE TRANSPORTATION TECHNOLOGY CLUSTER

What makes the Transportation Technology Cluster different from the other fourteen clusters you'll be exploring? What would it really be like to work in this cluster? Let's try to get at the heart of transportation technology.

The essence of this cluster is moving from place to place in vehicles. People in this cluster are on the go. They've always got somewhere to go—another city, another state, another country. They may not be back for hours, days, or months. They'll stop over at points in between—sometimes for just a few minutes, and other times overnight. But no matter how long the stopover is, they're always on the move, living out of suitcases and duffel bags.

Working in this cluster usually means not only traveling, but traveling on schedule. There's a starting time and an arrival time. There may be lots of in-between times. Being on schedule is crucial. It's everything. Passengers are especially concerned about schedules. They plan around the transportation schedule. They expect the schedule to be met.

Vehicles are at the heart of this cluster also. Trains, planes, cars, boats—all kinds of vehicles, all with engines and parts that need constant attention. Vehicles can break down. This costs money and, more important, threatens the schedules. Therefore, the vehicles must be pampered. Everything must be in tip-top shape at all times. The people who take care of the vehicles are just as important as the drivers and pilots.

Figure 20.1 lists just a few examples of occupations from this cluster. Think about the job title, the work activities, and the work settings. Figure 20.1 just gives examples to help you get at the heart of this cluster. You don't need to read for details. Scan the entries to get a feel for the cluster as a whole.

Would you like a career in this cluster? Ask yourself the following questions:

- Do you like the sound of the occupations listed under "Who"? Would you feel good about an identity like one of these?
- Would you enjoy doing activities like those described under "What"?
- Picture yourself working in the settings described under "Where." Would you be comfortable in these settings?

SKILLS, TRAINING, AND EXPERIENCE

Listed below are some skills common to careers in this cluster:

- Understand and use techniques for controlling vehicles.
- Use judgment and make decisions that affect the lives of passengers.
- React quickly in emergencies.
- Use hand tools and machines skillfully.
- Accept responsibility for the accuracy of your work.

Figure 20.1 Sample Occupations in the Transportation Technology Cluster

WHO You Would Be	WHAT You Would Do	WHERE You Would Do It
Bus driver	Drive people from place to place; pick up and let off passengers; collect fares, answer passengers' questions; stick to schedules	Buses traveling from region to region of a state, across the country, from one part of a city to another, or to and from schools
Truck driver	Drive trucks carrying goods from one location to another, inspect trucks to see that they're in working order, pick up freight, be alert to road conditions and traffic	Trucks traveling across the country on long-distance runs, or on local runs from city to city or within the same city
Aircraft pilot	Fly airplanes to transport passengers, cargo, and mail; plan flights; communicate with dispatchers and weather forecasters; check planes before takeoff; execute takeoffs and landings safely	Airplanes on and off the ground; in airports
Automobile mechanic	Diagnose problems, test-drive vehicles; make adjustments or repairs, replace parts	Automobile repair shops
Locomotive engineer	Drive locomotives; interpret train orders, signals, rules, and regulations	Locomotives and train yards
Ship captain and pilot	Command vessels such as tugboats and ferryboats; steer vessels into and out of harbors, straits, and sounds	Ships and harbors

- Move eyes, hands, and feet together to control the movement of vehicles.

There are many entry-level jobs in the Transportation Technology Cluster of careers that require no previous training. Although some of these jobs don't pay very well, you could apply to work even before you graduate from high school. Other jobs in this field require more advanced training.

JOBS REQUIRING LESS-THAN-AVERAGE TRAINING AND EXPERIENCE

- Baggage and freight handler.
- Reservation agent.

▲ Some transportation jobs require working more with people than with things.

- Ticket agent.
- Car rental agent.
- Dockworker.
- Gas station attendant.
- Truck driver.
- Parking lot attendant.
- Railroad maintenance worker.
- Taxi driver.

JOBS REQUIRING AVERAGE TRAINING AND EXPERIENCE

- Aircraft mechanic.
- Flight attendant.
- Auto body repairer.
- Auto mechanic.
- Merchant marine engineer.
- Motorcycle mechanic.
- Railroad conductor or engineer.
- Truck terminal manager.

JOBS REQUIRING MORE-THAN-AVERAGE TRAINING AND EXPERIENCE

- Air traffic controller.
- Airline pilot.
- Airport manager.
- Flight engineer.
- Transportation engineer.
- Merchant marine captain or radio officer.
- Traffic manager.

See page 319 for a list of some of the jobs in the Transportation Technology Cluster, along with their *DOT* numbers.

Career Decision-Making Activities

1. As soon as you can, try one of the many summer jobs in transportation technology. At bus and railroad stations there are jobs for clerks and maintenance workers. Service stations and parking lots often have jobs. If you enjoy boats, you can get a job at a local marina or a boating supply company. There are fewer jobs available in the summer in air transportation, but some do exist. You need to contact your local airport and all the airlines in your area.
2. Develop your skills at repairing and maintaining vehicles. You can begin, if you haven't already, with your own bike. You can also help take care of your family car.
3. Are there driving courses or obstacle courses in your area? If so, learn to ride a bicycle over an

obstacle course. Take a driver's education class to find out how much you enjoy learning about how to operate vehicles of transportation.

4. If you are interested in railroad transportation, put together a model train layout. Demonstrate it to the class, if possible.
5. Interview a flight attendant about the kind of work he or she does. Find out what is expected on his or her job.
6. See if you can ride with a truck driver on part of his or her route. Ask questions about the driver's hours and lifestyle.
7. Arrange a visit to the local airport's traffic control tower. Ask the workers how they handle the pressure.
8. Arrange a tour through a large merchant marine ship. Talk to some of the people who work aboard the ship.

Occupations in Transportation Technology

Here is a list of occupations mentioned in this chapter. Next to the name of each occupation is its *DOT* number. You can use the *DOT* number to locate further information about the occupation in your school or public library. For the broad occupational terms mentioned in this chapter, only one or two examples of that occupation are listed below. You can easily find more examples of the occupation in the *DOT.*

Aeronautical Engineer (002.061-014)
Air Traffic Control Specialist (193.162-018)
Air Traffic Controller (193.162-018)
Aircraft Mechanic (621.281-014)
Aircraft Pilot (196.263-014)
Airline Pilot (196.263-014)
Airport Manager (184.117-026)
Assistant Engineer (007.161-018)
Astronaut (no number available)
Auto Body Repairer (807.381-010)
Auto Mechanic (620.261-010)
Baggage and Freight Handler (910.687-014)
Baggage and Mail Agent (910.137-010)
Bicycle Mechanic (639.681-010)
Bus Driver (913.463-010)
Car Rental Agent (295.477-010)
Clerk (241.367-014)
Clerk, Train (219.462-014)
Coal Pipeline Operator (914.362-010)
Dispatcher (249.167-014)
Dockworker (891.684-010)
Engineer, Locomotive (910.363-014)
Firer, Locomotive (910.363-010)
Flight Attendant (352.367-010)
Flight Engineer (621.261-018)
Gas Station Attendant (915.467-010)
Instructor (919.223-010)
Line Walker (869.564-010)
Loading Inspector (910.667-018)
Locomotive Engineer (910.363-014)
Locomotive Inspector (622.281-010)
Maintenance Mechanic (620.281-046)
Maintenance Worker (see Maintenance Mechanic)
Mechanic, Automobile (620.261-010)
Merchant Marine Captain or Radio Officer (197.167-010)
Merchant Marine Engineer (014.061-014)
Motorcycle Mechanic (620.281-054)
Navigator (196.167-014)
Parking Lot Attendant (915.473-010)
Pilot (196.263-014)
Pipeline Supervisor (914.132-022)
Railroad Breaker (910.367-010)
Railroad Conductor or Engineer (198.167-018)
Railroad Maintenance Worker (221.362-026)
Railroad Signaler (869.667-014)
Reservation Agent (238.367-018)
Service Station Attendant (915.467-010)
Ship Captain (197.167-010)
Taxi Driver (913.463-018)
Ticket Agent (238.367-026)
Traffic Engineer (005.061-038)
Traffic Manager (252.257-010)
Transportation Engineer (005.061-038)
Truck Driver (905.663-014)
Truck Terminal Manager (909.137-018)

Review and Enrichment

Summarizing the Chapter

Summarizing information is a critical thinking skill that will help you succeed in the world of work. Write a summary of what you learned in Chapter 20. Focus on the main points of the chapter. Then in a class discussion, compare your summary with the summaries done by your classmates. Can you improve your summary?

Improving Your Career Vocabulary

1. Learning to use new vocabulary terms will improve your communication skills, which are important in almost all areas of work. Write definitions for the terms listed below. Then for each term, write an original sentence about yourself in which you use the term correctly.
   - transport
   - Transportation Technology Cluster
   - stress
   - freight
   - destination
2. List the job families discussed in this chapter. Write a one-sentence description of each.

Finding the Facts

Finding exact information is a frequently used skill in many careers. Find the answers to the exercise below, and write the answers on a separate sheet of paper.

1. Name three job families in the Transportation Technology Cluster.
2. What kind of work does a line walker do?
3. What kind of work does a loading inspector do?
4. Name the slowest-growing jobs in transportation technology.
5. Name three interests that a person working in this cluster might have.

Thinking for Yourself

To complete the exercise below you will need to use critical thinking and communication skills, which are skills valued by all employers. Write out your answers or be prepared to discuss them in class, depending on your teacher's instructions.

1. Which of the following jobs would be more likely to appeal to a "people" person: auto body repairer or ticket agent? Why?
2. In your own words, describe someone who would not enjoy working in transportation technology.
3. If you were a long-distance truck driver, do you think you would get lonely? How would you plan to stay in touch with family and friends?
4. If you were an air traffic controller, what would you do to counteract stress?
5. Train travel has decreased in this country. Why do you think this is so?

Practicing Your Basic Skills

Your career success depends greatly on your basic math and communication skills. Work hard at improving in the areas where you have trouble with the following exercises.

Math

1. Jake is a train conductor. Every day he rides 20 miles to Jonesboro, 17.5 miles to Carver City, and 76.3 miles to Clinton. He then travels the same route back home. How many miles does he travel every day?
2. Cinda is a gas station attendant. Gas sells for 1.09¢ per gallon. A customer bought 16.6 gallons. How much did Cinda charge him?
3. Bus A left Carver Street at 1:10 P.M. and arrived at a point 3 miles away at 1:46. Bus B arrived at the same time but traveled half the distance. How many times faster was Bus A going?

Reading and Writing

1. Obtain a copy of a bus, plane, or train schedule, and learn to read it.
2. Write a one-page account of an interesting experience you had while riding on a plane, train, or bus.
3. Research the energy crisis of the 1970s. Write a one-page report on how it affected transportation.

Review and Enrichment, continued

4. Pick at least one occupation mentioned in this chapter that you think would be interesting. Research the occupation thoroughly, and write a report. Use the career research checklist in Chapter 5 as a guide for your report. Conclude your report with an explanation of your interest in that occupation based on your findings.

Speaking and Listening

1. Interview a truck driver or other individual who spends long hours traveling. How does the person feel about the job? Do the same routes get boring? What does the person do to prevent boredom?
2. Ride some form of public transportation. Listen to the driver. How does he or she talk to the public?

Activities Working with Others

In almost all careers you must be able to get along well with other people to be successful. Work with your classmates to do the following activities. As you work together, pay attention to how well you get along. If necessary, work hard at improving your ability to do your part and to cooperate.

1. With a classmate, obtain a commuter plane, train, or bus schedule. Make a map of your local area, and indicate on it the places nearby to which the plane, bus, or train will take you. (If you use a plane schedule, your map will show a larger area.)
2. With a classmate, make a poster or display illustrating one of the following:
   a. design of a space shuttle
   b. how radar works
   c. the effect of computers on transportation
   d. design of a cruise ship or ocean liner
   e. costs of auto body repair
   f. a parking lot of the future
3. Add the careers mentioned in this chapter to your database.

Decision Making and Problem Solving

You will be a big help to your employer if you can make decisions and solve problems. List all the possible ways of resolving the situations described below. Then pick the best alternative (possible choice), and tell why you chose it. If you need help, you might want to refer to Chapter 3.

1. You enjoy your job as a long-distance trucker. You like seeing different parts of the country. Being alone a lot doesn't bother you. However, your family complains they never see you, and they want you to stay home more. You want to make them happy but don't want to give up your job. What will you do?
2. You are a pilot for a small airline. You've gone as far as you can with this company and are looking for another job. You've been happy with your employer and would like to use her as a reference. To do that, however, you'll have to tell her you're looking for another job, and you'd rather not. Her reference would really help, but you don't want to lose her support on your current job. What will you do?

PART THREE

ON YOUR WAY TO SUCCESS

CHAPTER 21 EMPLOYMENT SKILLS

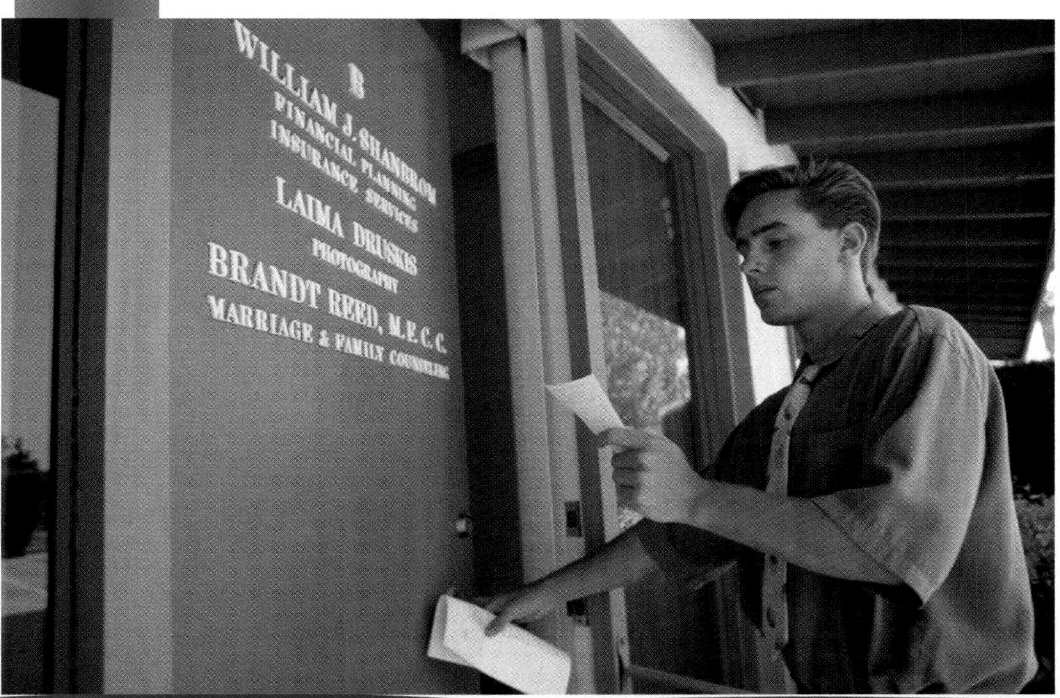

◆ Chapter Objectives ◆

After completing this chapter you will be able to do the following:

- ◆ Define the terms listed under "New Career Terms."
- ◆ List the first three steps in finding the right job.
- ◆ Name and describe four sources of job leads.
- ◆ Identify abbreviations commonly used in newspaper help-wanted ads.
- ◆ List and describe six types of information needed in preparing to apply for a job.
- ◆ Give six tips for having a successful interview.
- ◆ Explain six behaviors employers can expect from their employees.
- ◆ Describe six things you can expect from your employer.

◆ New Career Terms ◆

In this chapter you will learn the meanings of the following career terms:

- ✔ Employer
- ✔ Job lead
- ✔ Classified section
- ✔ Help-wanted ad
- ✔ Employment agency
- ✔ Fee
- ✔ Applicant
- ✔ Reference
- ✔ Résumé
- ✔ Application form
- ✔ Screen out
- ✔ Interview
- ✔ Procedures
- ✔ Punctuality
- ✔ Co-worker
- ✔ Wages
- ✔ Overtime
- ✔ Discriminate
- ✔ Compromise
- ✔ Check stub
- ✔ Deduction
- ✔ Income tax
- ✔ Gross pay
- ✔ Net pay
- ✔ Endorse

Lindsay thought her ideal job would be working in a sporting goods store. She loved sports and knew a lot about sporting goods equipment.

The day before school ended for the summer, a friend of her parents told her that his friends owned the biggest sporting goods store in town. The store owners were looking for summer help. The friend told her she could tell the owners that he had sent her. Lindsay felt very lucky.

Lindsay stopped at the store the next day after soccer practice. She was still in her soccer uniform. She asked to talk to the owner. The owner invited her back to his office to sit down.

"Hi," Lindsay said. She forgot to find out his name. "I'm here about a job."

"What sort of job?" the man asked her.

"I don't know for sure," Lindsay answered. She hadn't thought about it.

"Do you know anything about what we sell here?" the man asked doubtfully, as Lindsay looked down at her dirty sneakers.

"I'm not sure. Sporting stuff, I guess," she said, quietly gulping. She felt embarrassed that she hadn't bothered to find out.

"What sort of skills do you have?" the man looked impatiently at his watch.

"I dunno, really," Lindsay shrugged.

"I'm afraid we don't have any openings right now," the man said as he stood up and led Lindsay out the door. She left without speaking, thinking she was just unlucky.

Why do you think Lindsay didn't get the job? Did it have anything to do with bad luck? What could she have done to make a better impression? What did she do wrong during the interview?

FINDING THE RIGHT JOB

Lindsay was depending on luck alone to get a job. However, getting a job is not accidental. To find a job that is right for you takes planning and work.

Finding *a* job—any job that comes up, no matter how boring or how low the pay—can usually be done quickly and easily. Finding *the* job—the job you really want—cannot be done quickly or easily. You have to be willing to do the work of finding work. As some experts like to say, "Looking for work is the hardest work you'll ever do."

The first three steps in finding the right job are:

1. **Know yourself and what you want.** Know your skills, interests, aptitudes, abilities, and personality, as well as the kind of lifestyle you want. Know your strengths and your weaknesses. Does this advice sound familiar? It should—you spent several chapters at the beginning of this book getting to know yourself. You've completed Step 1.
2. **Know about the world of work and what kinds of jobs are possible.** Know what kind of job you are looking for. Too many people take the first job that comes along and end up with one they don't like.

This advice, too, should sound familiar. In Chapters 6 through 20 you explored a wide range of careers. By now you should have one or two definite career areas in mind. You've completed Step 2, so now it's time to think about the third step in finding the right job.

3. **Know how and where to find the people to hire you for the job you want. Employers** are the people or businesses for whom others work. Employers are the ones who own or manage the businesses. They make the decisions about hiring and firing. Chances are one in a million that they will seek you out, so you have to search them out. In this chapter you will learn several ways to identify employers who can hire you for the job you want.

employer
the person who has hired another to do a job.

Even finding a part-time job takes planning and work. More than likely you won't just "get lucky" and find a job you really like. It's important to learn how to organize your job search and how to gather job leads.

A **job lead** is information about a possible job opening. If Aunt Maria tells you she heard they were looking for a carry-out person at the grocery store, that's a job lead. If you see a sign in the window of a store that says "Hiring," that's a job lead. You will want to find as many job leads as possible. The more leads you have, the better your chances of finding the job you want.

job lead
any information about possible job openings.

Keep track of your leads on 3-by-5-inch cards or on your home computer, if you have one. Write down the name, address, and phone number of the employer. Also write appointment dates, times, and any other information you have about that lead.

There are many ways of getting job leads. The following sections discuss some of the main ones.

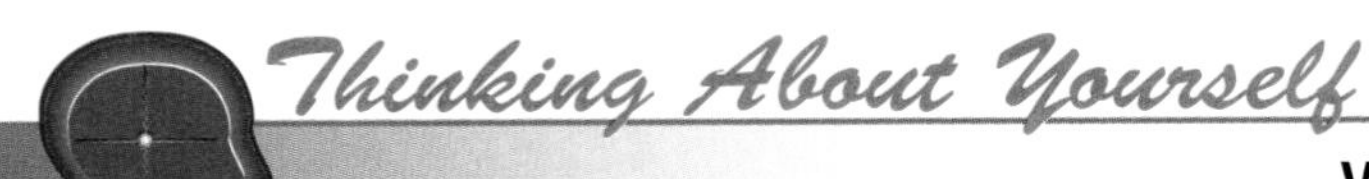

Who Do You Know?

Many young people say they don't know anyone who could give them job leads. You may feel this way, but you probably know a lot more people than you think you do. Make a list of family members, friends, and acquaintances who might help you with job leads. Include the following:

- ▲ Family members.
- ▲ Personal friends.
- ▲ Friends of your parents.
- ▲ Friends of your sisters and brothers.
- ▲ Teachers, counselors, coaches, and principals.
- ▲ Classmates.
- ▲ People you have worked for before.
- ▲ Members of your church.
- ▲ Members or leaders of clubs to which you belong.
- ▲ Parents of your friends.
- ▲ Neighbors.

FAMILY AND FRIENDS

You've probably heard someone say, "He got the job because he knew somebody," or "She got hired because she knew the right people."

Some people feel it is unfair to use "inside help" to get a job. They feel people should get jobs on their own. This is true only if the people hired are wrong for the job. Otherwise, using inside help is one of the best ways to find a job. About 20 to 30 percent of all job applicants find job leads this way.

Of course, knowing people isn't enough. Just because Lindsay's parents' friend knew the owner of the sporting goods store didn't mean she got the job. You must learn how to reach out to these people, and you must be qualified for the job. You must know your skills and be able to communicate them to the employer. Having an "inside track" isn't enough. You must still be the right person with the right qualifications.

Ask family members, friends, and acquaintances for job leads. They often know about job openings at their places of work before the openings are advertised. Tell them what kind of job you want. Give them some time to look into it, and then check back. Were there any openings?

JOB-COUNSELING CENTER

The school you go to, a school nearby, or even a local community college may have a job-counseling center. This probably is a good place to start in your search for job leads. The people working there are used to helping young people. Also, the services are usually free. Ask your school's guidance counselor if there is such a job center nearby.

► Watch for job fairs in or near where you live. They are often held at community colleges or municipal centers.

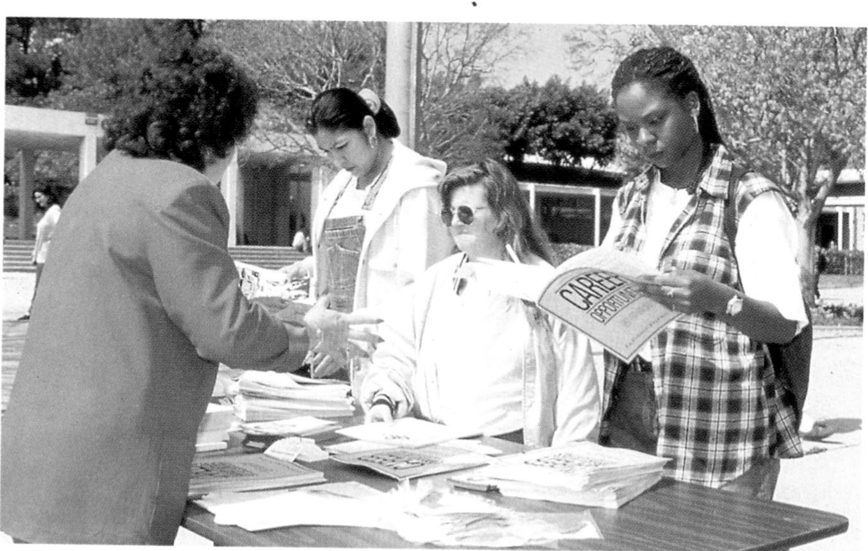

NEWSPAPER ADVERTISEMENTS

The **classified section** of the newspaper is the section with many different kinds of advertisements, such as ads for houses for rent and furniture for sale. This section includes the **help-wanted ads** (see Figure 21.1). These are the ads that employers put in the newspaper describing their job openings.

> ***classified section***
> the section of the newspaper that contains short advertisements in categories, such as "help-wanted" ads.

Figure 21.1 Sample Help-Wanted Ads

ACCOUNTING
Req's a 4 yr degree in accnt bus, xlnt PC skills (MS Office). Send resumes and cvr ltr to Silver Apple, Inc., 234 N. Sepulveda, Los Angeles, CA 90100.

★ ACTRESSES/ACTORS ★
NEEDED
NEW FACES NEEDED
FOR COMMERCIALS
- All looks and all types
- Can you create characters?
- Do you have a great voice.
- Great pay and benefits

Phone Monday 3/10, 818-987-1234

ADMINISTRATOR for 163 SNF/IMD beds. View Heights Convalescent Hospital, fax 213-123-4567

ADVERTISING SPRING IS HERE! LA Based Adv. firm just landed 3 new fortune 500 acts. Seeking 9 ind'ls this wk. No exp. req'd. Cust Serv/Area Rep to campaign. Greg 818-123-4567

AIR CONDITIONING MECHANIC: installs expansion & discharge valves in circuit. Connects motors, compressors, temp. cntrls, humidity cntrls, & crculatng-vntilatn fans to cntrl panels & connects cntrl panels to pwr source. Installs air & water filters in cmpletd instlatns. Injects small amount of refigerant into cmprsor to test systms, & adds freon gas to build up prscrbd opratng pressure. Observes prssure & vacuum gauges & adjusts cntrls to ensure efficient opratns. Tests joints & conectns for gas leaks, using gauges or soap-and-water solution. Wraps pipes in insulation batting & secures them in place w/cemnet or wire bands, Replaces defctve breaker cntrls, thrmstats, switches, fuses, & elctrcl wiring to repair installed units, using electricians's handtools. 4 yrs exp. in job ofrd. 40hrs & $ 463.20/pwk. Job Site/Intrv: LA. Send ad/res/ltr of qualif to job#60829028CCR, POB 269065, Sacramento, CA 95826-9065

ARCHITECT PERKOWITZ + RUTH architects, inc. a quality design orientated firm seeks apps w/strong ACAD skills. Construc. Admin, Entlmnt Spclst, Job Capt., & Sr. Draftrs.
FAX 567-789-2323

★ AUTO SALES ★
2 Top Sales Pros Needed, M/F
For Busy Westside Retailer.
WE OFFER:
- Great Inventory
- Positive Working Environmnt
- A Ton Of Traffic
- An Attainable 7K Monthly

Fax resume 310/123-4567

BANKING
★ OPERATIONS OFFICER ★
Independent bank in Beverly Hills seeks an Operations officer with strong orgainizational & mangeraial skills as well as heavy operations background. Must have commercial banking experience. ITI systems knowledge preferred. Fax resume attn: Tony 213/456-4567
PACIFIC SAVINGS BANK

CARPENTERS/STEEL STUD FRAMER Apprentice to Journeymen needed for commercial projects in LA, Long Beach, SF/SG Valley, and Inland Empire. Exc. benefits, 401k. Bonuses. Call 310/123-4567 M-F 7AM-5PM

CELLULAR PHONE TECH
Fast-paced, cellular syst. co. based in Beverly Hills. Min 2 yrs exp in cellular phone repair field. Coordinate the RMAs/return merchandise to mfrs. FAX resume to: 310/456-1234

CHEMIST- Newly established Medical chemical corporation, S.M. manufacturer of diagnostic agts, immediate opening for entry level manufacturing chemist. Heavy lifting required. 310/-654-2200

CIVIL (STRUCTURAL) ENGINEER: Plan, dsgn & direct civil eng. f/all devlpmnt projcts. Analysis reports, drawings, blueprints, test & aerial photogrphs on soil cmpostion, terrain hydrologcl charactristcs & other topogrphcl & geological data to plan/dsgn profct. Calculate costs/detrmn feasibility of projct applying knwldg/techniques of eng. & advnce mathematics. Prep, direct preprtns & modifctn of projts. Inspct constrctn safety stndrds. Utilize various cmptr sfwr. Bachelor's Degree-Engineering (Structural). 2 yrs exp reqd. $29.53. OT@1.5/hr 40/wk. Send ad/ltr of qualif. to American Interational Construction 11111 S. Wilshire Dr., L.A., CA 90231

COMPUTER
SOFTWARE PROJECT LEAD
Manage sftwr engrs in res/devel. of stst. level s/w prods for WindNT. Track rec. managing complex s/w proj. on sched. & meet deadlines. Prgrmmg skills in C/C++ & assembly lang. incl. design, devel, spec. writing & in-depth MS WinNT O/S. FAX: Dir of Personnel 818/012-3210.

COMPUTER. U.S. Bankruptcy court has positions avail. in L.A. dept. Web Page Design, Progrmg. (Foxpro, VB, HTML) & Systems Integration encouraged. Exclnt. benf. & opptys. Email: hr@usbankruptcycrt.com

COMPUTER C/C++/Realtime S/W $40-85K.General Employment 714/147-1471

CONSTRUCTION
LANDSCAPE ARCHITECTS
P & D Construction, Inc.
Fax Resumes 714/101-0123

CONSTRUCTION
BUILDING PERMIT TECH.
Familiarity with construction industry plans, terminology and documentation. Strong clerical, communication and people skills a must. Attention to detail. Experience in public sector desirable. Knowledge of computers necessary. Oppotunities in the High Desert. Salary dependent on qualifications. Send resumes to Recruitment Coordinator, Charles Brown Associates, Inc. 123 E. Oaks Dr., Torrance, CA 90501

COOK: Specialties, plans, menu & cooks Mexican/American style dishes. Serve food to waiters on order, seasons & cooks food according to prescribed plan, $11.50 per hour +1.5 PD OT, 4yrs exp. Verifiable ref's req'd. Job Site/interview: Lee Vining, CA. Send AD & letter of qualif. to Job#61231036HCR, P.O. Box 269065, Sacramento, CA 95826-9059

COUNSELOR
VOCATIONAL COUNSELOR &
BILINGUAL COUNSELOR
Full-time positions available with benefits. Requires a BA in a related field & experience working with persons with disabilities. Positions provide case management services to adults with disabilities in workshop setting. Bilingual English/Spanish preferred. Send resume & salary history to:
CCC
Attn: Human Resources
777 Benjamin Rd.
Los Angeles, CA 90046
FAX 213/456/4567
EOE. No phone calls please

DENTAL LABORATORY TECHNICIAN: Fabricates & repairs dental appliances, according to dentist's prescription, using hand tools, molding equipment, & bench fabricates full/partial dentures. $11.93 per hour + 1.5 FD OT, 4 yrs. Exp. verifiable ref's req's. Job Site/ interview: Monrovia, CA. Send AD & letter of qualif. to P.O. Box 269065, Sacramento CA 95826-9065

DESIGNER/STYLIST
Industry leader in home furnishings is seeking a qualified designer/stylist to coordinate our Bath Products Division. Products include shower curtains, ceramic accessories, and rugs. Some travel required. Interested applicants Submit resumes to: Bath & Showers, 2222 Western St., LA, CA 90346

DESIGNER. Mechanical designer w/Suto Cad exp. Knowledge of PCB industy or test industry a +. Benefits. Apply at 12345 S. Palacades, LA, CA 90246

DRAFTING. CAD DESIGNER
Min 4 yrs exp. in structural drafting using AutoCAD reqd. Must be very computer lit. & be able to troubleshoot & maintain ofc computer syst. Resume: Padron Associates, LLP, 1000 Oceanside, Long Beach, CA 90010

ENGR Project Engr 2-3 yrs current project mgmt exp. Engrg degree is a+. Indiv. will be exp. to complete various projects within the organization on time & on budget. Res to Krazer Aluminum, Attn: HR Department, 2000 Long Rd., West Hollywood, CA 91020

FINANCE DIRECTOR
76 year non-profit seeks candidate with degree in Bus. Admin. or related field. HR, acctg, & facilities mgmt exp. Competitive sal. + benes. Fax resume att: Arlisa 213/123-1234

HOSPITAL
HOUSEKEEPING
SUPERVISOR
Seeking an individual with 2-3 years operational exp. in Hospital Housekeeping managment. Must have the ability to speak English and Spanish fluently. Working computer knowledge, inter-personal skills. Planning, directing and organization skills. Self-motivated and creative individual.
Adobe Care Service
1000 W. 3rd. St.
Anacapa, CA 92023

HUMAN RESOURCE MANAGER
Mfg co with plants in 2 states needs HR mgr to oversee local personnel. Responsibilities will include safety, Workers Comp, benefits administration and will require light travel. Candidate must be bilingual in English/Spanish, have a minimum of 5 years exp. LA based. Please send resume with salary hist to LA Times, MSC#0000000 Los Angeles, CA 90053

Int'l Trade Analyst - Research int'l business conditions to determine sales for assisting mgmt in making import, w/sale & marketing decisions. Bach. in Int'l Trade or equiv. $2,500/mo. Job/intvw site: City of Industry, CA. Send ad/resume to Job#0000, 777 E. Circle Lp. City of Industry CA 91718

JEWELRY Mfg. co. in Burbank needs exp'd Jewelers, Bench Workers, Casters. Model Makers & Polishers Call (818) 002-0000

LEGAL
Northridge area firm seeking motivated self-starter to work in foreclosure/ bankruptcy area. Must have knowledge and at least 2yrs exp in foreclosure/ bankruptcy law or Single Family Mortgage Servicing. Requires xlnt communication, computer skills with extensive knowledge of Microsoft Word 6.0, Excel. Salary DOE. Fax resume: 818/888-9999

MECHANIC, TRUCK: Repr/maintn electrc, diesel & gasoline indstrl trucks per manuals w/ hndtools, pwr tools/knwldg of electrcl, trnsmissn, brake & othr auto systms. Read job order, detrmn malfnctn & plan wrk procdrs. Ovrhl gas/diesel engines w/ hndtools, welding eqpmnt, stndrd charts & hoists. Install, align, chnge/ rechrge various prts. Fabricate specl lifting/towing attchmnts, hydraulic systms, shields or othr devices per blueprints/schematic. 2 yrs exp reqd $18.36/hr OT @ 1.5/hr40 wk. Job site/intvw City of Industry, Ca. Snd Ad/Ltr qualifctn to Job#000, PO Box 2698 Sacramento, CA 95826-9065

NURSING RN-Medical clinic in West LA seeks RN to provide quality care, treatment, education and emotional support to IVF patients. 2 or 4 year degree in nursing and current California nursing license required. Previous experience in IVF helpful. Effective communication skills a must. Excellent benefit package. Interested parties should fax resume to 310/101-1010

PROGRAMMERS
Contract or perm. JAVA, C, C++, SQL 6.5, PowerBuilder, Data Gate, retail-wholesale distribution, COBOL, DB2. Beatrice Software, Pasadena. Call 626/999-8888, Fax 626/888-9999

SALES
Flexible Film Packaging Co. looking for a Western Regional Salesperson based in L.A area. Candidates must have packaging component direct sales experience, calling on the food, health, beauty, pharmaceutical & vitamin type of accounts. Attractive pay plan with salary, car expense + commiss. Qualified candidates, fax resume to: (818) 333-4444

RESEARCH ASSOCIATE - Manufacture medical and veterinary immuno-diagnostic kits. Participate in Research and Development leading to the development of improved testing kits. Require Bachelor's in Biology, courses in immunology, biochemistry & biology or exp must include Radio Immuno Assays, Iodination (separating & purifying Antigens & Antibodies) & Chromatography (Column, Apinity). $2,050 per month. 40hrs/wk. Job Site/Interv: Los Angeles, CA. Send ad & resume to PO Box 00, Sacramento,CA 95826

ONLINE JOB SEARCHING

The fastest-growing source of job information is online, that is, on the Internet. Career counselors say that the new technology greatly improves the whole job-seeking process. As long as your school, your parents, a friend, or even a friend of the family has access to the Internet, you can search for job openings online. These services include ones called America's Job Bank, CareerMosaic, Online Career Center, and Yahoo! Classifieds.

Employers in high-technology companies have been the most frequent users of the Internet to post job offerings. Gradually, though, most kinds of employers are finding that online posting of job openings make sense. It is up to you to discover this useful source of job leads in your quest for the right job and eventually the best career.

help-wanted ad
a newspaper notice (paid for by an employer) describing a job opening.

employment agency
an organization that tries to match qualified people with jobs, sometimes for a fee.

Each newspaper lists its help-wanted ads a little differently. You will need to learn the meanings of the abbreviated words used in the papers you'll be reading (see Figure 21.2).

When you are looking for a job, you should scan the help-wanted ads every day. Don't, however, rely only on this method for finding job leads. The best jobs are often filled before an ad ever appears in the paper. Use the help-wanted ads, but use them as one of many ways of finding leads.

EMPLOYMENT AGENCIES

An **employment agency** is an organization that helps people find jobs. Those who are looking for jobs give their names and personal information to the agency. The agency acts as a kind of go-between, matching qualified job hunters with available jobs.

There are two kinds of employment agencies—*public* and *private.* Public agencies are operated by the federal or state government. Their services are free to you. Private agencies are operated by private individuals who must make a profit. This means they must charge a **fee**—a certain amount of money or a percentage of your salary charged for helping you find a job. Sometimes a private agency will charge your new employer instead of you. Don't sign a contract with a private agency until you are sure what the fee is and who is to pay it.

When you are looking for your first few jobs, a public employment agency is probably your best bet. Find out where your state's employment office is located in your area. Visit the office, and talk to a counselor. This person will explain what that office can do for you.

ON YOUR OWN

Applying directly to an employer is one of the best ways for a young person to find a job. You can either telephone or visit possible employers without job leads. Remember—many jobs are never advertised. The employers find someone without advertising. If you call or knock on the door at the right time, you could be that someone.

Go through the Yellow Pages, and make a list of the companies that interest you. Talk to your local chamber of commerce about the kind of job you want. Then telephone or visit the companies to ask about job vacancies.

Before you contact a company, be sure to know as much as possible about it. Also be sure you know what you want to say ahead of time. Be prepared before you call or visit.

In most cases your first contact will be over the phone. Practice what you will say before you call. For your first few calls it's a good idea to write down exactly what you want to say.

Also remember that your finding a job this way will involve many calls and visits before you succeed. There is lots of competition for

Figure 21.2 Help-Wanted Abbreviations

Listed below are some of the most commonly used abbreviations in help-wanted ads. The meaning of each abbreviation is also provided. You will need to know the abbreviations and their meanings when you look in the newspaper for job openings.

Abbreviation	Meaning	Abbreviation	Meaning
Amer	American	Mo	Month
Ans	Answer; reply	Natl	National
Appt	Appointment	Nec	Necessary
Asst	Assistant	Opptys	Opportunities
Attr	Attractive	Opr	Operator
Bldg	Building	Perm	Permanent
Bus	Business	Per mo	Per month; each month
Clk	Clerk	Per wk	Per week; each week
Co	Company	Perm	Permanent
Comm	Commission	Pls	Please
Dept	Department	Proc	Processing
Dr	Drive	Prod	Production
Drv Lic	Driver's license	P/T	Part-time
Elect	Electrical	Pt time	Part-time jobs
EOE	Equal opportunity employment	Ref req	References required
Eve	Evening; night	Refs	References
Excel	Excellent	Rel	Reliable
Exper; Ex	Experience	Req; Req'd	Required or requested
Fax	Facsimile machine number	Sal	Salary; a set amount paid
Flex	Flexible	Sal open	Salary open; is flexible
F/T	Full-time	Sat	Saturday
Gd sal	Good salary	Sm	Small
Gen	General	Spec	Specialist
Hr	Hour	Sr	Senior
Hrly	Hourly	Temp	Temporary
Hskpr	Housekeeper	Trans	Transportation
Immed	Immediate; immediately	Trk	Truck
Ind	Industry	Typ	Typing
Info	Information	Vac	Vacation
Lic	License	Wk	Week or work
Lt	Light	Wkdys	Weekdays
Maint	Maintenance	Wkly	Weekly; each week
Mang	Manager	Xllent	Excellent
Mech	Mechanic; mechanical	Yr	Year
M-F	Monday through Friday	Yrly	Yearly; year
Mgr	Manager	$$	Dollars; money

Attitude makes a difference

Clothes Can Make a Difference

By the time Jason turned sixteen he had been working on cars for seven years. He felt he knew more than many mechanics already. He had a '79 Chevy that he had rebuilt. He was anxiously waiting for the day he could get his driver's license. He spent several hours a day working on his car—washing it, waxing it, and keeping it spotless. He was very proud of its beautiful appearance.

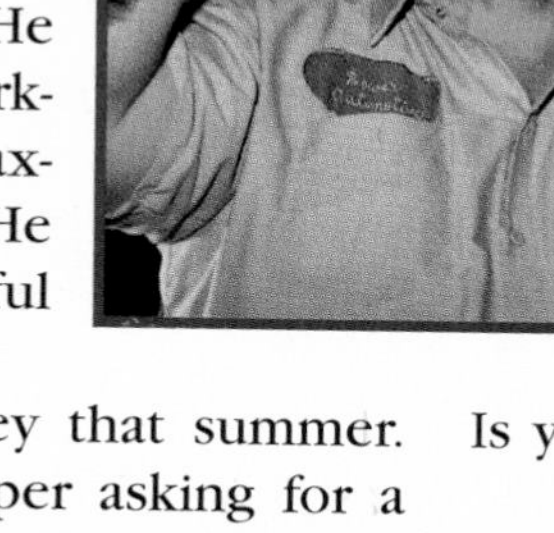

Jason wanted to earn money that summer. He read an ad in the newspaper asking for a "neat, clean, responsible young person to assist in the parts department of local auto parts store." Jason thought he could easily get the job.

After changing the oil in his Chevy, Jason went directly to visit the store. He wore his dirty coveralls. He thought the people at the auto parts store wouldn't mind, since they would understand that being a mechanic is dirty work. The owner took one look at Jason's appearance and told him the job was taken.

Jason told his friend, "If they don't like the way I look, I don't want to work there anyway."

His friend replied, "Maybe if you spent half the time preparing yourself as you do your car, you might have a better chance. Is your car worth more than you are?"

What Do YOU Think?

Why didn't Jason get the job? What was wrong with his attitude? Was his friend right?

fee
a certain amount of money or a percentage of salary charged by an agency for their help in finding you find a job.

jobs, especially the best jobs. It can be frustrating and discouraging, so it's important to keep a positive attitude! You may hear no, no, no, no, no, before you hear yes. But it takes only one yes, and it will come if you keep trying.

Career Decision-Making Activities

1. Find the classified section of a local newspaper. Bring the help-wanted ads to class. Go through the ads, looking for jobs that interest you. Pick the three ads that are of the most interest. Rewrite the ads, substituting complete words for all the abbreviations. Change papers in class, and see if you can rewrite your classmates' ads using abbreviations. Compare the abbreviated ads you've written with the actual ads. If you encounter any abbreviations you don't know, contribute them to a class list of help-wanted abbreviations. Pick a class member to compile the list. Make copies for everyone in the class. Keep and study the list.
2. Remember—most job openings are filled before they are ever advertised. Identify at least three—or more if you can—local companies that might have a job that you would enjoy. Use the Yellow

Pages of your phone book, and talk to your local chamber of commerce (the number will be in the phone book). Look at each heading in the Yellow Pages. Ask yourself if there might be a job you want in that area of work. After you have identified the three best possibilities, phone the businesses to ask about openings. First, though, write out what you'll say on a sheet of paper. Show it to your teacher or guidance counselor before you begin your calls.

APPLYING FOR THE JOB

Once you find the job you want, you will need to convince the employer that you are the best person for the job. You will probably not be the only person who wants that job. The employer will be able to choose from several **applicants** (people who apply for a job). You will have to convince the employer that *you* are the ideal person for the job.

applicant
a person applying for a job.

Remember that when you apply for a job, you become a salesperson—with you as the product. The process of applying for the job is a very important part of getting the job. Don't take it lightly.

KNOW THE EMPLOYER

Have you ever met someone for the first time and really wanted that person to like you? You are so nervous you can't think of anything to say. Or you say something that you know sounds stupid because you're trying so hard. Then that person walks away with the wrong first impression of you, which is very hard to change.

Suppose you had taken the time to learn something about that person before you were introduced. You could probably have thought of something interesting to say. That person would have been favorably impressed.

The same is true of possible employers. Find out about them and what their businesses do before you apply. You will impress the employer with your thoughtfulness and preparation. Your research will also give you a better idea of whether you could be happy working there and of how you might fit into the business. So remember—find out everything you can about the employers before you apply.

▼ Newspapers are still the largest source for job leads.

KNOW YOURSELF

It is also important to know yourself before you apply. Take out six sheets of blank paper. On the top of each page write one of the following headings. Then write the information about yourself on the appropriate sheets. Add to each page as you have more experiences. You should have collected much of this information already, in the first chapters of this book.

- **Personal information.** Include your name, address, Social Security number, date of birth, age, height, weight, and phone number.
- **Education.** Include schools you have gone to, classes you have taken, and honors you have achieved.
- **Work experience.** List any jobs you have had, including baby-sitting, mowing lawns, and volunteer work. Tell who you worked for, how much you were paid, what your duties were, how long you had the job, and why you quit. Write all this down for every job you've had. Put the jobs in order from the most recent to the one furthest in the past. Employers will want them in this order.
- **Activities and interests.** Include hobbies, clubs, sports activities, and what your interests are.
- **Special skills.** List all the skills you can think of and how you learned them.
- **References. References** are people who know you and the kind of work you are likely to do. These might be teachers or anyone for whom you have worked. They could also be leaders of any clubs or teams you belong to, or responsible people you know in the community. Ask the people you want to use if they would mind being listed as references. The employer may contact them, and you wouldn't want them to be surprised.

reference
a person who will give a favorable report of a job applicant to the prospective employer.

Employers will want to know about these main areas. It is important that you think carefully about each area before you fill out an application or go to an interview.

YOUR RÉSUMÉ

You may want to condense your personal information into one or two pages to make a **résumé.** A résumé is a description of the person seeking employment. It is written so that it can be used for any job application. Figure 21.3 shows a sample résumé.

résumé
a short written description of an applicant's personal data, education, background, and experience related to a job.

Many employers ask for résumés before they interview anyone. Sometimes only the applicants who send in the best résumés get a chance for an interview.

If you prepare a résumé, make it neat and free of errors. Your résumé may form the employer's first impression of you. Make that impression a good one by making your résumé perfect.

FILLING OUT THE APPLICATION FORM

application form
a questionnaire used by employers to obtain basic information from applicants and to determine their suitability for a job.

When you apply for a job, the employer will almost certainly give you an **application form** to fill out. Such forms are filled out for individual jobs. The forms ask the applicant to supply information that applies to the job in question. A sample application form is shown in Figure 21.4.

Figure 21.3 Sample Résumé

CAROL KINNEMAN

ADDRESS
400 W. Calhoun Street
Macomb, IL 61455
(309) 837-7524

CAREER OBJECTIVE

To further my educational experience in fields dealing with print media; to use my writing abilities in advertising, public relations, or news reporting through a summer internship program.

EDUCATION

Macomb High School, Macomb, Illinois
Will graduate June 2002
Grade Point Average: 3.1 on 4.0 scale

EXTRACURRICULAR ACTIVITIES

Soccer Team
School Newspaper

WORK EXPERIENCE

EDITORIAL PAGE EDITOR, WESTERN COURIER, Macomb, IL
Responsible for every aspect of preparing editorial pages for publication. Skills include proofreading, editing, writing headlines, formal layout and production work, and putting out weekly editorial column. Formerly part-time news reporter for the same publication. (8/98 to 1/99)

JC PENNEY COMPANY, Peoria, IL
Worked as a clerk in sportswear, juniors, cosmetics, fine jewelry, and children's departments. Gained basic knowledge in merchandising techniques, price changes, and sales techniques. (8/97 to 8/98)

HOBBIES

Writing poetry, attending plays, playing soccer.

REFERENCES

References available upon request.

Figure 21.4 Sample Application Form

Application For Employment

All qualified applicants will receive consideration for employment and promotion without regard to race, creed, religion, color, age, sex, national origin, handicap, marital status or sexual orientation. This application is effective for 90 days. If you wish to be considered for employment thereafter, you must complete a new application.

Date ______________________

Name ______________________ (Last, First, Middle Initial) Telephone (____) ______________ (Area Code)

Address ______________________ (Number & Street, Apt.#, City, State, Zip)

Length of time at that address ______________ Previous Address ______________

Position you are applying for ______________ Rate of pay expected $ ______________ per month

Were you previously employed by us? ______ If yes, when? ______________

Business Machines Operated ______________

State any other experiences, skills, or qualifications which you feel would especially fit you for work with the company

____

Applying for: Full-time ____ Part-time ____ Days ____ Evenings ____ Midnights ____ Alternating ____ Any ____

Are you at least 18 years of age? ____________ Will you take a physical examination? ____________

List any friends or relatives working for us ______________________ (Name, Relationship)

______________________ (Name, Relationship)

Referred to our company by ______________________

School	Name and Location	Course of Major	Graduated
Elementary			☐ Yes ☐ No
High School			☐ Yes ☐ No
College			☐ Yes ☐ No
Business or Trade			☐ Yes ☐ No
Other (Specify)			☐ Yes ☐ No

Do you plan any additional education? ____________ If yes, describe ______________

List in order all employers. Begin with your most recent employment:

	Name and Location of Company	From Mo Yr	To Mo Yr	Salary	Supervisor	Reason for Leaving
1)						
2)						
3)						

Describe the work you did with:

Company #1. ______________________

Company #2. ______________________

Company #3. ______________________

May we contact the employers listed above? ____ If no, indicate by number which one(s) you do not wish us to contact ______

CERTIFICATION OF APPLICANT

I hereby certify that the facts set forth in the above employment application are true and complete to the best of my knowledge. I understand that if I am employed, falsified statements on this application shall be considered sufficient cause for dismissal, and that no contractual rights or obligations are created by said employment application.

Signature of Applicant ______________________

Employers use application forms to find out basic information about job applicants. They also use them to **screen out** applicants. To screen out applicants means to eliminate the ones not wanted. For example, employers often look for misspelled words on the application forms. They might eliminate, or screen out, the applicants who made spelling errors. They would rather hire someone who knows how to spell. This fact is one reason it is so important to fill out application forms neatly, carefully, and correctly.

> ***screen out***
> to eliminate applicants that are not suited for a job.

Employers will form an impression of you based on how you fill out the application form. Here are some guidelines that will help you:

- **Read the entire application first.** This includes reading the instructions. By reading the whole application, you can judge how much space you have to write your information.
- **Be neat.** The person reading the application will think of it as an example of the kind of work you will do. If you read it first, you can plan ahead so you won't have to erase and cross out. This way you will avoid being messy. It's best to use a pen. You should bring your own pen with you. Write as clearly as you can. If you make too many mistakes, ask for another form.
- **Answer every question that applies to you.** If a question doesn't apply to you, then write *NA,* which means *not applicable.* Writing *NA* tells the employer that you didn't forget to answer one of the questions.
- **Spell all words correctly.** Misspelled words tell the employer that you are careless and sloppy or that you haven't learned your basic writing skills. Either way, the employer will prefer to hire someone else. Bring a small dictionary with you if you are uncertain about your spelling abilities.
- **Know what kind of work you want.** Do not write "Anything" when asked what kind of work you want. Be specific about the kind of work you would prefer.
- **Double-check the completed form.** Go back over everything to make sure it's correct and neat. Be sure to sign the form on the line asking for your signature.

The smartest thing you can do is to come prepared. Take the six sheets of personal information that you filled out with you. You won't be able to think of references and remember all the addresses and dates on the spot. You can never be too prepared when you look for a new job.

▼ Go to your job interview well prepared and appropriately dressed for the position for which you are applying.

INTERVIEWING FOR THE JOB

An **interview** is a formal, get-acquainted meeting between the employer and the job applicant. Very few people are hired without first being interviewed. Usually the employer is considering several people for the job. The interview is his or her way of finding out who is the best person for the job. The interview is your chance to make a good impression.

The time you spend interviewing is the most important time you will spend in your job search. Here are some tips for successful interviewing:

- **Be on time.** Being late for an interview is a sure way to lose the job to someone else. Make sure you arrive five or ten minutes early.
- **Be prepared.** Know about the company. Have the information the employer will want. Be prepared to answer questions about yourself, your education, your work experience, and your career goals or ideas about your future. Know your best skills. Be ready to tell the employer how your skills are perfect for the job.
- **Think positively about yourself.** Remember the times you went into new situations in the past and did well. Don't be bashful about your good qualities. Don't stutter or mumble. Don't look down or away from the interviewer. Be confident. Speak up. Look the person in the eye. Smile.
- **Pay close attention to your appearance.** Your grooming and dress are extremely important in an interview. Personal appearance makes an instant first impression. *Make a good one.*
- **Speak clearly.** Make sure you use standard English and correct grammar, not slang. Use complete sentences. Look at your interviewer. Listen carefully to what he or she says. Be sure to thank the interviewer for his or her time before you leave.
- **Follow up.** Send a note or call the employer a few days after your interview. Thank the employer for his or her time. Say that you are still very interested in the job.

Career Decision-Making Activities

1. Make a small booklet that will fit in your pocket to contain all the personal information you need when you apply for a job. Either rewrite or condense the information from the six sheets you prepared earlier. You can buy a small notebook, or you can fold notebook pages to make a small booklet. You can then glue or staple the pages together. Make front and back covers out of heavy construction paper. Give your booklet a title, and paint or write the title on the cover. Some possible titles are "My Job Application Booklet," "Jim's Life Story," "Everything You Want to Know about Cecily," and "Me." Take your booklet with you when you go to fill out job application forms.
2. Practice your interviewing skills. Take turns with your classmates as you pretend you are first the employer and then the person being inter-

viewed. The person playing the job applicant should describe the type of job opening and company. Before you begin, think of ten questions you will ask when you are the employer. Think of five questions you will ask when you are the applicant. Have your classmates evaluate your performance as an applicant. How can you improve?

3. Bring at least one (or more, if possible) blank job application form to class. Ask your parents, friends, and relatives if they can get forms from the companies where they work. Tell them to explain to their employers that you will be using the forms in a career class at school to learn how to fill out application forms better. Compare and discuss the forms in class. If possible, use an overhead projector, and point out the unique features of each form. Make a list on the board of the questions that appear on every form. Write out answers to these questions. Compare your answers with your classmates' answers.

ON-THE-JOB PROCEDURES AND BEHAVIOR

Let's say you did a great job in the interview—and you will. You got the job you wanted. You can't wait to get started. But now you're thinking about that first day on the job. What will be expected of you? How will you know what to do?

Don't worry. Your employer won't expect you to know everything the first day. Either the employer or someone on the job will "break you in," show you around, and help you get started. The following information will also help you know what's expected of you and what you can expect from your employer.

procedure
a rule or method of accomplishing a task.

WHAT THE EMPLOYER EXPECTS

Your employer will give you a paycheck regularly. In exchange, your employer will expect certain things from you, too. There will be certain **procedures** you will be expected to follow. A procedure is a rule or method that the employer has decided is the best way to get a job done.

The employer has probably spent many years thinking about and testing different procedures. Even if the procedures don't make sense to you at first, you will be expected to follow them. Much of your success on the job will depend on how well you meet your employer's expectations and follow the procedures.

Besides your following written and spoken procedures, your employer will expect certain other kinds of behavior from you. Have you ever been on a sports team where everyone wanted to be the star player? No one wanted to pass the ball or set up for anyone else, because everyone wanted all the glory. And what was the result? If there was no teamwork, you were almost sure to lose.

▼ Without teamwork, you're almost sure to lose—on the court or on the job.

An employer thinks of his or her workers as a team. All the team members have to behave in ways that help the team "win." The employer is a kind of coach who looks at the big picture and calls the shots.

Some of the behaviors an employer will expect are the following:

punctuality
being on time for work.

co-worker
a fellow worker.

- **Punctuality and a full day's work. Punctuality** means being on time. Most companies operate on the idea that time is money. If you are late, take long breaks, or leave early, you are costing the company money.
- **Dependability.** Just as you must be able to depend on your team members in sports, your employer has to be able to depend on you. Being dependable means that your boss and **co-workers** (the people you work with) can depend on you to do your work. You don't let them down.
- **Honesty.** Every business needs honest employees to survive. Be honest and gain the trust of your employer. Your chances of raises, promotions, and keeping your job depend on it. Honest employees don't steal from the company. They don't make up excuses for being late or not showing up for work.
- **Willingness to learn.** Make a special effort to learn everything you can about your job and business. This will make your job more interesting. You also will be promoted much faster. Some employees almost refuse to learn new tasks. If you were the employer, which kind of employee would you want: the kind who wants to learn new tasks, or the one who doesn't want to learn anything new?
- **Willingness to follow directions.** Even if you don't understand the reason yet, follow your supervisor's directions exactly. The job will get done more easily and faster. Employers are busy. They don't have time to tell you something two or three times. Do it the first time.
- **Enthusiasm.** Focus on the positive. Try to get excited about your work. Your enthusiasm will grow and will be contagious (spread to others). Do what needs to be done without having to be told every time.

WHAT YOU CAN EXPECT

wage
payment for work, usually figured by the hour.

overtime
time worked in addition to the amount normally scheduled.

In return for the work you do, you can expect certain things from your employer. In your mind the most important thing will probably be your pay. For your first few jobs you will probably be paid **wages.** Wages usually refers to an amount of money earned per hour. For example, your wages might be $6.50 per hour. If you work over forty hours a week, you will receive **overtime.** Overtime is money earned for work you do beyond the normal workweek. Overtime is usually one and one-half times the regular pay. If your wages are $6.00 an hour, overtime for you would be $9.00 per hour.

Employers have different pay periods. This means you might be paid every week, every two weeks, or once a month.

At the end of each pay period you will receive a check. You can expect your employer to pay you on a regular basis. You will learn more about your paycheck later in this chapter.

In addition to your regular pay, you can expect the following from your employer:

- **Training.** You may not believe it, but as a young worker exploring careers, the training you get on a job may be more valuable than your pay. Your employer will teach you how to do the work the way it's supposed to be done. Pay attention and learn. You'll find out whether you like this kind of work. The experience you get will help you get other, higher-paying jobs in the future.
- **Evaluations.** Your employer will let you know how you are doing. Some employers have formal evaluations (a meeting between you and your supervisor to discuss how you are doing on the job) every three months, every six months, or once a year. Listen to what your employer says about your work. Do your best to improve.
- **Fair treatment.** Employers cannot **discriminate** (show favoritism) according to race, sex, ethnic background, religion, or age. Promotions, bonuses, and other benefits are to be based on ability or shared equally. Race, sex, ethnic background, religion, or age should not be factors. The laws of the United States guarantee equal treatment for all people.
- **Fringe benefits.** You *may* receive paid holidays, paid vacation days, paid sick days, and other benefits. The amount you receive often depends on how long you work for the company. Part-time and temporary workers may not receive any benefits. Your employer will tell you what benefits you can expect.

discriminate
treating someone unfairly because of his or her race, religion, or sex

SAFETY

Both you and your employer can expect safe working conditions. You can expect your employer to provide safe equipment in a safe environment. Your employer can expect you to follow safety rules and practice safety at all times.

Most of us think that accidents happen only to other people, but they can happen to anyone. Over one million people are injured at work each year. This is why all workers must learn to protect the health and safety of themselves and those with whom they work.

Accidents cost employers billions of dollars every year in direct property losses and increased insurance expenses. Injured employees suffer a greater cost of pain and uncertain futures.

If you miss time because of an accident, your status at work can be affected. You can even lose your job. A serious accident could cost you not only a job, but your entire career. It could force you to change your personal goals and prevent you from achieving what you want in life.

Some accidents are caused by an unsafe environment. It is up to your employer to keep the work conditions safe. The U.S. government has passed laws to guide employers in keeping their work sites safe for all workers. These laws have helped reduce the number of work accidents.

Most accidents are caused by human error. There are several types of human error that you can be aware of and try to prevent from happening to you:

- **Lack of skill with equipment.** Make sure you are properly trained before you operate machinery. Don't use tools with which you are unfamiliar.
- **Lack of knowledge.** You must learn about the machines, tools, substances, and working environment. Think safety when you are using machinery or tools. Be careful with the materials with which you will be working.
- **Not knowing your physical limitations.** Fooling yourself about your abilities can cause injury and accidents. Some jobs require people to be stronger or quicker than others. Know what your limitations are. Don't try to go beyond them.
- **Fatigue.** When you suffer from fatigue, you are tired or exhausted. Fatigue can result from too little sleep, illness, poor diet, or overexertion. Whatever the cause, fatigue increases the likelihood of unsafe behavior, which leads to accidents. When you are tired, your movements and thinking are slowed down. It is your responsibility to be alert and physically fit to do the best job you can.
- **A bad attitude about safety.** People who don't care about safety are likely to have more accidents. Being tired, angry, or depressed can cause your attitude to change. Therefore, it is important to pay special attention to safety during these times. Alcohol and drugs can also lead to a poor attitude toward safety and to accidents. Remember that accidents cost money, jobs, careers, and lives. It is important to have a good attitude when it comes to safety.

GETTING ALONG WITH PEOPLE

Unless you own your own business, you won't be able to choose the people with whom you work. You will need to work with all kinds of people—even ones who think, talk, and act differently from you.

More people lose their jobs because of their poor attitudes than because of any other factor. These bad attitudes often become noticeable when workers can't get along with the boss or the other workers. Don't think that you are more important than others. You're not. On the job you will be part of a team. You must all work together equally.

Think positively about learning to get along with co-workers, employers, and customers. The good relationships you have will far outweigh the bad. The better you get along with co-workers, the more you will enjoy your job. Getting along with everyone will also increase your chances for promotions and raises.

▲ No matter how rude a customer may be, you must always treat him or her with consideration.

Here are a few tips for getting along with others on the job:

- **Accept differences.** Remember that no two people are exactly alike. Nobody is perfect, including you. But everyone has some good qualities. Try to bring out the good qualities in other people. Accept the fact that some people might not see everything the same way that you do. Be open-minded about understanding the other person's side.
- **Treat others considerately.** Treat other people the way you would like to be treated. You will find that most people will respond by treating you well in return. You may meet some people, especially if you are working with customers, who are rude or inconsiderate. If this happens, don't take it personally. If you are rude in return, it will only make matters worse. You might even be able to make a rude customer feel better or change his or her bad mood by the way you act. Then the customer will not be able to find fault with you. More important, you will feel good about how well you handled the situation.
- **Remember that you're the beginner.** Keep your eyes and ears open to learn all you can. You will probably find that your more experienced co-workers will be happy to answer your questions. If they point out a mistake, thank them. Realize that they are doing you a favor, not making fun of you or embarrassing you. Thanks to them, you probably won't make the mistake again.
- **Learn to compromise.** You've probably learned that you cannot have your own way with your friends all the time. This will be true with co-workers as well. To **compromise,** when two people disagree, means to give up something in order to come to an agreement. Both sides have to give just a little. Compromises are often necessary in the world of work.

compromise
a situation in which two sides of a differing opinion give up something to reach an agreement.

- **Remember that formality at work is usually the best way to begin.** Of course being friendly is important. But until you learn more about your place of work and those you work for, it is better to be too formal than too chummy. As you get to know everyone, you will learn more about what is expected and comfortable for all.
- **Keep your sense of humor.** If you don't already have a good sense of humor, try to develop one. Learn to laugh at yourself and look for the positive side of work situations. Your sense of humor will be very helpful during stressful times at work. It will make those around you more comfortable.

MANAGING YOUR TIME AND MONEY

In the world of work, time and money go together. This is the way many employers think. As you move further along in your career journey, you will begin to think more about the connection between time and money.

Very few people would say they have all the time and all the money they want. When you start working, you will have to learn to make *trade-offs* where time and money are concerned. That means you'll have to choose. You will have to learn the best ways to manage the new limits placed on your time. You may have to give certain things up if you want a chance to make money.

Learning to manage your time and money is part of learning to know yourself and what is most important to you. It is also part of learning good decision making. You will have to make many decisions about the best ways to spend your time and money. Don't think of it as having to sacrifice. Use the decision-making process you learned in Chapter 3 to help you make your time and money decisions.

Remember that the better you learn to manage your time and money, the more time and money you will have to spend on the things you like best.

GETTING A PAYCHECK

A paycheck usually comes in two parts. One part is the check itself. The other is the **check stub,** the part of a paycheck that shows you what you were paid and what was deducted from your earnings. A **deduction** is any money taken out for taxes, Social Security, or insurance. An important deduction is for **income tax,** which is the money deducted and paid to the government.

The check stub will show your **gross pay,** which is the total amount of your earnings. It will also show your **net pay,** which is the amount that you take home, or get to spend now, after deductions. Figure 21.5 shows a sample paycheck, including the check stub.

check stub
the part of a paycheck that lists deductions from wages.

deduction
an amount of money taken from an employee's gross pay for taxes, insurance, social security, or other benefits.

income tax
the part of earnings that people must legally give to the government to pay for government services.

gross pay
the total amount of an employee's earnings before deductions are taken out.

net pay
the amount of a paycheck after deductions are taken out.

Figure 21.5 Sample Paycheck

Restaurants, Inc. Fort Worth, Texas	Morisot, Ramona R. Pay Rate: $5.75/hr					Taxes Deductions	Year to Date
Description	Current Hours	Current Earnings	Year to Date Hours	Year to Date Earnings			
Regular	37	212.75	925	5,318.75	Federal Tax	$16.81	$433.82
Overtime	0	0.00	20	172.60	Social Security	12.76	329.48
					Medicare	0.00	0.00
					Dental	3.00	72.00
					Company Stock	0.00	0.00

	Earnings	Taxes	Deductions	Net Pay	Pay Period
Current	212.75	29.57	3.00	180.18	11-28-99
Year to Date	5,491.35	763.30	72.00	4,656.05	12-12-99

No. 311264

Restaurants, Inc.
Fort Worth, Texas 76179

Date **Dec. 3** 19**99**

Pay to the Order of **Ramona R. Morisot**

Amount **One hundred eighty and 18/100** Dollars

Dollars	Cents
180.18	

Texas Federal S&L

Ramona Morisot
2418 Hadley Street
Fort Worth, Texas 76179

Ann Winchell

Before you can cash your paycheck, you will be asked to **endorse** it. This means signing it on the back. Your signature identifies you at the bank and lets your employer know you cashed the check.

endorse
to sign the back of a paycheck made payable to you, which permits the bank to cash it.

MONEY-MANAGING TIPS

As a money earner, you have new privileges. But you also have new responsibilities. In order to get your money's worth when you shop, you need to be a skilled shopper. The following are some tips:

- **Take your time about buying decisions.** Don't be in too big a hurry. You'll end up with something you can't afford or won't like later. Wait until you have enough money to buy what you want.
- **Compare prices and services.** Learn how to shop around and find the best prices for the best quality.

- **Avoid impulse buying.** Impulse buying is buying, without much thought, an item you didn't plan to purchase. You may get home and decide it was a big mistake.
- **Look carefully at what you buy.** You can't be an expert on everything, but if you look closely you will learn to be an expert on the things you like.
- **Study labels.** Learn to read labels that describe what you are buying. That way you can make better decisions on which products to choose.

TIME-MANAGING TIPS

Managing time wisely can help you on the job and in your leisure time. Your employer will be impressed if you use every minute of company time to its fullest potential. You will impress yourself if you manage to find time for all the television shows, concerts, get-togethers with friends, and other things you'd like to do.

Here are a few quick tips on how to get the most out of each twenty-four-hour day:

- **Do the hardest work first.** Most people feel stronger, smarter, and more cheerful when they start work than when they finish. Do the most challenging job you have when you are at your peak. If it takes you a while to get warmed up, do a few easier tasks first—then tackle the hardest job.
- **Plan your day ahead of time.** Look at what you have to do and the amount of time you have to do it. Be realistic. Pick out the most important tasks. Plan to do as much as possible, but don't expect miracles.
- **Avoid interruptions.** Life—and work—is full of interruptions. Someone or something that you hadn't planned on often demands your attention. Try to put aside a time when you can deal with all the "little things."
- **Set goals.** You learned about goals early in this book. You will learn more later. Set short-, medium-, and long-term goals for big jobs. Stick to your schedule as much as possible.
- **Concentrate on finishing tasks.** Do one task at a time. While you're doing that task, devote your full attention to it. Keep the end in sight, and keep pushing toward that end. Try to finish as many tasks as you can. Don't start and stop, leaving lots of unfinished tasks.

Career Decision-Making Activities

1. Imagine what it will be like going to work on the first day of your first "real" job. You will probably be a little nervous—most people are. You will meet lots of new people. You will probably be doing work you've never done before. Write a short story or a one-act play focusing on your first day as you think it might go.
2. How good are you at getting along with people? Ask ten people who know you well to rate you on each of the following qualities. Have them rate you from 1 to 10, with 10 being very good and 1 being very bad. Rate yourself before you ask others to rate you.
   - Acceptance of the differences of others.
   - Considerate treatment of others.
   - Willingness to compromise.
   - Sense of humor.
   - Positive attitude.

   Average the ratings for each quality. How did your own ratings compare with the averages? Were you surprised by any of the ratings? Should you be working to improve in any of these areas?

◀ Today's workplace requires setting team goals and cooperative effort to reach them. You will have to plan as a team even though you may be assigned only a portion of the work required to attain the goal.

Review and Enrichment

Summarizing the Chapter

Summarizing information is a critical thinking skill that will help you succeed in the world of work. Write a summary of what you learned in Chapter 21. Focus on the main points of the chapter. Then in a class discussion, compare your summary with the summaries done by your classmates. Can you improve your summary?

Improving Your Career Vocabulary

Learning to use new vocabulary terms will improve your communication skills, which are important in almost all areas of work. Write definitions for the terms listed below. Then for each term, write an original sentence about yourself in which you use the term correctly.

- employer
- job lead
- classified section
- help-wanted ad
- employment agency
- fee
- applicant
- reference
- résumé
- application form
- screen out
- interview
- procedures
- punctuality
- co-worker
- wages
- overtime
- discriminate
- compromise
- check stub
- deduction
- income tax
- gross pay
- net pay
- endorse

Finding the Facts

Finding exact information is a frequently used skill in many careers. Find the answers to the exercise below, and write the answers on a separate sheet of paper.

1. Name the first three steps in finding the right job.
2. How many job leads should you find?
3. How do 30 to 40 percent of job applicants find job leads?
4. Name three items of personal information you should know before you apply for a job.
5. Name three behaviors an employer will expect of an employee.

Thinking for Yourself

To complete the exercise below you will need to use critical thinking and communication skills, which are skills valued by all employers. Write out your answers or be prepared to discuss them in class, depending on your teacher's instructions.

1. What do you think the advantages and disadvantages of using an employment agency might be?
2. How do you think your attitude affects a job interview?
3. Have you ever compromised in order to get a job done? How did it work out?
4. Have you ever worked with a beginner who thought he or she had all the answers? How did you relate to that person?
5. Have you ever been in a bad situation that was helped by a sense of humor? Explain.

Practicing Your Basic Skills

Your career success depends greatly on your basic math and communication skills. Work hard at improving in the areas where you have trouble with the following exercises.

Math

1. Nelson has a job interview at 11 A.M. The company is 30 minutes away from his home. He has to stop on the way to get gas, which will take 10 minutes. The highway he must travel is under repair, and he wants to allow an extra 10 minutes for delays. Since he doesn't know where the company parking lot or personnel office are, he thinks an additional 10 minutes will be needed to find his way around. What time should he leave home?
2. Ann went to an employment agency. The agency helped her find a job that paid $12,750 a year.

Review and Enrichment

The agency charged her employer an amount equal to one month of Ann's salary. How much did the company have to pay?
3. When Lupe got her first monthly paycheck, $74.50 had been taken out for taxes. She knows her taxes amount to 20 percent. How much had she earned that month before taxes?

Reading and Writing

1. Look through the help-wanted section of your local paper. Find three jobs in your area of interest. For each job, list the qualifications (abilities, skills, or requirements) and what you might need to know about the job before applying.
2. Look through the Yellow Pages of your phone book for employment agencies. Read the ads. Do any mention fees? If so, who pays?
3. Write a thank-you note to someone with whom you have just had a job interview. Say you enjoyed meeting the person and that you are very interested in the job. What else should you include in your message?

Speaking and Listening

1. As a class, practice job interviews. Your teacher will tell you for what kind of job you are applying. Take a minute to think of questions and responses. Then one class member should play the employer and another, the applicant.
2. Listen to your classmates' interviews. Take notes of things that will be helpful to remember for your own real interviews.

Activities Working with Others

In almost all careers you must be able to get along well with other people to be successful. Work with your classmates to do the following activities. As you work together, pay attention to how well you get along. If necessary, work hard at improving your ability to do your part and to cooperate.

1. Talk to parents, friends, and others regarding jobs they might know about. Make file cards giving important information. Keep the cards on hand for future reference. Share the job leads that don't match your interests with your classmates.
2. Look through your wardrobe, and choose two possible outfits for interviews. Ask a friend or family member if the outfits seem suitable. Wear them to class, and ask for constructive criticism.

Decision Making and Problem Solving

You will be a big help to your employer if you can make decisions and solve problems. List all the possible ways of resolving the situations described below. Then pick the best alternative (possible choice), and tell why you chose it. If you need help, you might want to refer to Chapter 3.

1. You live in a small town with no employment agencies and few jobs. You will have to get a job elsewhere. The nearest large city is 40 miles away, and you'd like to look there. You have access to a car only once a week. You can drive it to the city, but you'll have to make the trip worthwhile. Using your local library, weekly newspaper, and information from friends and family, how will you prepare in advance for your city visit?
2. You are having a job interview with a man in the human relations department of a company and with the woman who would be your boss. The woman is friendly, and you think you could get along with her. The man, however, challenges everything you say and is insulting. When he gets up to show you out of his office, he bumps his cup of coffee, and it spills all over your clothes. He starts to yell at you and says it is your fault. What will you do?

CHAPTER 22

FREE ENTERPRISE AND THE CHANGING WORKPLACE

◆ Chapter Objectives ◆

After completing this chapter you will be able to do the following:

- Define the terms listed under "New Career Terms."
- Give examples of how consumer demands change.
- Give examples of how the workplace changes.
- Give examples of how the population changes.
- Give examples of how economic conditions change.
- Give examples of how technology changes.
- State three ways you can learn to cope with change.

◆ New Career Terms ◆

In this chapter you will learn the meanings of the following career terms:

- ✔ Economic system
- ✔ Free enterprise system
- ✔ Enterprise
- ✔ Goods
- ✔ Democracy
- ✔ Capitalism
- ✔ Socialism
- ✔ Producer
- ✔ Profit
- ✔ Loss
- ✔ Competition
- ✔ Law of supply
- ✔ Law of demand
- ✔ Technology
- ✔ Automation
- ✔ Cope

Ray Valdez grew up in a small town outside of Pittsburgh, Pennsylvania. His father worked in the steel mills. Ray's grandfather had also worked in the steel mills. Ray was always convinced that he, too, would work in the steel industry.

All during junior high and most of high school, Ray was a good student—when he wanted to be. Unfortunately, that wasn't very often. Ray decided to drop out of school before he got his high school diploma. He went to work at the same steel factory that his father had worked in for twenty-four years. Ray was happy, at least for a few months.

Then one day Ray's boss held a meeting for all the factory workers. Ray's boss told them that in thirty days the steel mill would be closing down. It was an old mill, with old equipment. It couldn't compete with the new steel companies that had installed better, more cost-efficient equipment. A month later Ray found himself without a high school diploma, and without a job.

Do you know anyone like Ray? You probably do, because Ray's story is a familiar one in our changing workplace.

Ray had taken for granted that there would always be a job for him in the steel industry, so he did not try to get a broad range of skills while in school. As a result, Ray ended up with very few career choices. Ray needed to know about the possible changes in the American workplace.

If you are going to pursue a career—any career—in the United States, you must be prepared for *change* and be willing to adapt, too. The U.S. economy is constantly changing. You need to be aware of the current changes and learn how to anticipate future variations. In this chapter you will begin to learn about our changing workplace.

Before you or Ray can understand the changes going on in our workplace, you have to know a little something about the American economic system. You will learn a lot more about economics in future school courses. For now you need to know just a few basics. This basic understanding will help you avoid an experience like Ray's.

WHAT IS AN ECONOMIC SYSTEM?

In every nation there has to be some way for people to earn a living and find a place to live. People must buy food and clothes, get medical attention when they are sick, and provide for their old age when they can no longer work. The way in which individuals make choices about how to earn income and how to spend it depends on the **economic system** (the way a society uses to determine how it will use and distribute available resources). People either have limited choices or different kinds of choices, depending on the economic system.

Let's see how you are part of our economic system.

economic system
the method of producing, distributing, and exchanging goods and services in a society.

Career Decision-Making Activities

Let's look at a few of the changes that have taken place in the United States over the past 150 years. This may help us understand why Ray lost his job at the steel company.

Year	Major Material Used	Major Products	Jobs People Held
1840	Wood	Lumber	Lumberjack
			Sawmill operator
		Buildings	Carpenter
		Carriages	Carriage shop worker
		Barrels and boxes	Cooper
		Ships	Boat builder
		Wheels	Wheelwright
1935	Steel		Steel mill worker
			Iron ore miner
		Buildings	Structural iron worker
		Automobiles	Factory worker
		Trucks	Factory worker
		Ships	Shipwright—welder
		Wheels	Machine operator
		Heating and air conditioning units	Sheet metal worker
1990	Synthetics (polymers)		Polymer scientist
			Chemical plant operator
		Building siding, roofing, insulation	Factory worker
		Automobile parts	Factory worker
		Appliances	Factory worker
		Furniture	Factory worker
		Boats and recreational vehicles	Factory worker
		Clothing	Factory worker

Now, working as a class, take time to list the following on the blackboard:

1. Jobs related to the "steel era" that are now employing *fewer* workers. There are numerous jobs not listed in the table above.
2. Jobs related to the "polymer era" that are now employing *more* workers.

Finally, pretend that you are Ray. Compose a letter to a successful uncle describing your problem and asking for advice. After completing your letter, exchange letters with another student. Pretend you are the successful uncle, and give Ray advice.

YOUR TYPICAL DAY

In a typical day you might wake up with an alarm clock that somebody gave you last holiday season.

You take a shower or a bath using water for which your parents pay. Every month they write a check to the water department in your city.

You put on clothes that you probably picked out. Buying those clothes involved going around to different stores and making choices about what looked best on you and which clothes had the best prices.

The money that you or your parents paid to the salesclerks was probably earned by doing work for someone else. If you paid for your clothes yourself, you might have earned the money at a part-time job that you *voluntarily* chose to do. If your parents paid for the clothes, they probably earned the money in some job that they chose to do.

When you go to school, chances are you are going to a public school paid for from taxes that your parents paid. If you go to a private school, your parents pay for it directly to the owners of the school.

In the evening when you watch television, you see advertisements for products such as soap, clothes, computers, and a thousand other things. Those ads are paid for by the companies that want you or your parents to buy their products.

◀ In America's free enterprise system, you are free to make your own economic decisions.

YOUR DAY AS PART OF OUR FREE ENTERPRISE SYSTEM

free enterprise system
an economic system in which people make their own economic decisions.

enterprise
a project undertaken.

goods
tangible/useful products that are made and sold.

In the United States the typical day just described involves a lot of choices. That is because in the **free enterprise system** of the United States, most individuals get to choose where they want to work, what they want to work at, and how they want to spend their money. The word **enterprise** in *free enterprise system* simply means the effort or the attempt to accomplish something. In the U.S. free enterprise system, people are normally free to attempt whatever activity they choose to make money. They have a right to make their own economic decisions.

Businesses get to choose which **goods**—things that people might find useful—to try to sell to you. Some businesses try to sell you services, which include any help by others that you must pay for, such as dry-cleaning your clothes, polishing your car, or giving you medical care.

In your typical day, though, some of the things that you choose to do involve a government. You might buy water from your local city government. You might be going to a school provided by your government.

In some countries, the government plays a very large part in the daily lives of the people. Mainland China and Cuba are examples. The government owns and controls large parts of those countries' economies. In the United States, the government owns a relatively small amount of things and controls about one-third of all economic activity.

democracy
a system of government where the power is vested in the people.

The United States has a democratic system of government. **Democracy** is a form of government in which power is held by each citizen and the citizens we elect to represent us. Part of being a good citizen is exercising the right to vote, and taking an interest in democratic government.

As a working citizen you will be helping the nation's economy grow. The more workers continue to learn new skills and do well on the job, the better off our whole economy will be. This means more jobs will be created, and there will be more money to spend. As a talented and enthusiastic worker, you will be helping the economy grow faster.

You will also become a voter, helping to decide what policies the government will follow. You will have many opportunities to voice your opinion about the government's role in our economy. You can prepare yourself for the voter role you will play in the economy by doing the following:

- Being aware of items in the news that tell about how the economy is doing.
- Listening to the different opinions around you about the economic system.

- Reading newspapers and news magazines.
- Taking classes in school that teach you about our government and the economy.

TWO BASIC ECONOMIC SYSTEMS

The free enterprise economic system used in the United States is often called **capitalism.** This is a system based on private ownership of the goods and services people want. People make their own economic decisions. Capitalism is not the only type of economic system, however.

In some parts of the world the economic system is one of **socialism.** With socialism, the government owns some of the things used to make the goods that people want. That means that in countries with socialism, the government owns factories and machines.

Since the early 1990s, one thing has become obvious. Economic systems that were not based on free enterprise did not do as well as those that were. Consequently, most of the world is moving toward free enterprise and away from socialism.

capitalism
an economic system that allows people to make their own individual economic decisions and encourages competition.

socialism
a system where economic decisions are made by the government.

Career Decision-Making Activities

1. On a separate sheet of paper, make a list of twenty-five businesses in your area. Next to each business, tell whether the business sells *primarily* goods or services. Compare your list with your classmates' lists. Do you understand the difference between goods and services?
2. From your list of twenty-five businesses, pick the ten in which you think you'd most enjoy working. Does your list contain mostly services or goods businesses? Does this tell you anything about your interests?

CONSUMERS AND PRODUCERS

In our economy you will probably be both a consumer and a producer. In Chapter 10, you learned that a consumer is someone who buys goods and services to use them. Everybody at one time or another is a consumer. You are acting as a consumer every time you buy something in the local grocery store or drugstore, for example.

Producers are those who make the goods and services that consumers buy. All people who work are producers. If you are working, you are producing. You don't *have* to be a producer, however. You might inherit millions of dollars while you are still in school. If that happened, you wouldn't have to produce anything to earn money on which to live. That won't happen to most of us. Chances are you will not inherit a fortune or win the lottery. This is why most of us end up being both consumers and producers.

producer
one who makes and sells goods and services.

CONSUMERS MAKE THE DECISIONS

In our free enterprise system, the consumer calls the shots. Producers can spend millions of dollars advertising their products on television, on the radio, on the Internet, or in newspapers. They can make wonderful products and put them in stores all across the country. But if they haven't produced products that the consumer wants at a reasonable price, they're in trouble. Not enough of the advertised products will be sold to pay for all the advertising and for the cost of producing the products. Soon the producers will have to stop producing those products. It is the consumer, not the producer, who indirectly decides what should be produced. The consumers are in charge.

PROFITS KEEP THINGS FLOWING

Producers who come up with products that consumers want, such as a better, cheaper computer game or a music system that sounds better than all the others, end up making more profits. **Profits** are the difference between what a producer sells goods or services for and what the producer has to pay to produce them. Profits are *business earnings.* They are the money left over after the business pays all its expenses.

profit
the amount of money a business takes in that is more than the amount it spends.

Say you are in business yourself. You sell T-shirts with designs on them, which you pay your little brother to apply. You receive $15 for each T-shirt you sell.

Are you making a profit? You won't know until you add up all your costs. Let's say that the T-shirt itself costs $5. The paints cost

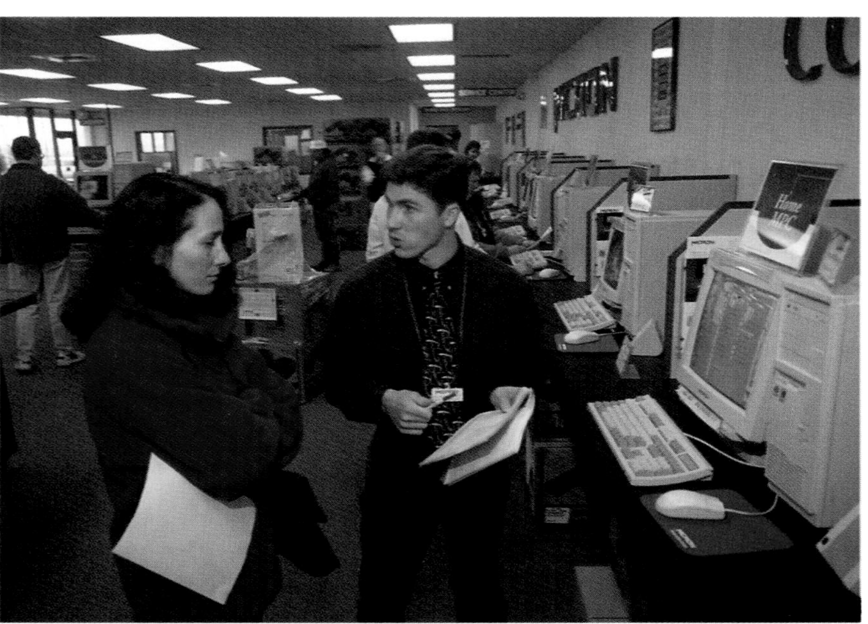

▶ Consumers control production by how they spend their money.

$2. Your little brother charges you $4 for his work. Your total costs, then, are $5 + $2 + $4, or $11. So your profits are $15 − $11, or $4 per shirt.

Businesses in the U.S. free enterprise system find out the hard way when they make something that not enough people want. Their profits fall. When their profits disappear, **losses** (more money spent than earned) occur. When companies have too many losses, they have to go out of business. That is what happened to the steel company that Ray Valdez was working for at the beginning of this chapter.

loss
the amount of money a company loses when it spends more money than it earns.

COMPETITION

You are a consumer. So are about 280 million other people in the United States. There are millions of producers and businesses trying to get you to buy their goods and services. They are in **competition** (a business trying to win customers by offering lower prices or better quality) with one another for your consumer dollars.

competition
rivalry, activities in which companies try to outsell each other.

Competition in our economic system is no different from competition on the baseball field, the football field, or the tennis court. The winner in the economic system takes home bigger profits. Because of competition, prices change all the time in the American marketplace.

SUPPLY AND DEMAND

There is another way to explain why prices change in our free enterprise system. Prices change because of *supply* and *demand.* Producers create the supply of goods and services. You and all the other consumers in the American economy generate the demand for goods and services. There are principles that determine supply and demand.

The **law of supply** states that the higher the price consumers are willing to pay, the more producers want to supply. Why? Because producers can make higher profits. The law of supply also means that the lower the price consumers are willing to pay, the less producers want to supply. Why? Because at lower prices the producers won't make many profits.

The **law of demand** states that the higher the price consumers are asked to pay, the less consumers want to buy. Why? Because consumers have limited incomes, and don't want to spend all their money on very expensive items. The law of demand also says that the lower the price, the more consumers want to buy.

law of supply
an economic rule that at higher prices a larger quantity of a product will generally be supplied than at lower prices.

law of demand
an economic rule stating that as the price of a good or service falls, a larger quantity will be bought; as the price of a good or service rises, a smaller quantity will be bought.

SUPPLY AND DEMAND IS EVERYWHERE

All around you, you can see the laws of supply and demand working. For example, when strawberries are in season, their price falls.

That is because of the law of demand. Think of it this way. When strawberries are in season, strawberry growers have many to sell. Supermarkets end up with lots of strawberries to sell to you and to the people around you. They've got to make you want to buy more. How do they do this? One way is by lowering the price.

You can think of the law of demand another way. Just ask yourself the following question: How many more compact discs would you buy if the price were cut in half? Even if you don't think you would buy any more, you probably have friends who would.

The fact is that when prices fall, we buy more of these cheaper things. When prices go up, we buy less of these more expensive things.

Career Decision-Making Activities

1. On a separate sheet of paper, make a list of six goods your family has purchased in the past month. Remember, when you purchase goods or services, you are a consumer. Next to each item on your list, write the names of two jobs necessary to produce that item. Share your list with your class. See how many goods and jobs were listed without repeating either the goods or jobs.
2. Assume that tomorrow every product and service for sale in the United States will cost one-half its current price. Make a list of ten products and services you would be able to afford that you can't afford now, or ten that you would be able to afford more often. Compare your list with your classmates' lists in a class discussion.
3. Assume that next week every product and service for sale in the United States will cost twice as much as it costs now. Make a list of ten products and services you frequently purchase now that you would no longer be able to purchase or would purchase less frequently.

CONSTANT CHANGE

Some days you spend all your free time playing computer games on the Internet. Other days you play volleyball on the beach. Some days you like to listen to techno music. Other days you listen to rap music. Some days you want to wear blue pants, and other days you want to wear black pants. As a consumer, your tastes change all the time.

Many years ago bell-bottom pants were popular. Then tastes changed, and bell-bottoms went out of style. For a few years in the 1990s, they came back in style. Clothing manufacturers had to react fast or lose business to their competitors.

Changes in consumer demands determine what producers produce. This, in turn, affects the American workplace. Producers try to keep up with American tastes by changing products and by inventing new ones.

Vinyl twelve-inch records seemed perfectly fine years ago. Then cassettes came along. Most people found cassettes easier to use. You could play them in your car and in small portable players.

Next, some producers came up with the compact disc, or CD. The sound was better than that of a record or cassette. The result? The sales of vinyl records fell dramatically. So, too, did the sales of cassettes. But the sales of compact discs went up. At the end of the 1990s, several improvements on the compact disc were introduced into the marketplace. If the public eventually prefers the improved discs, sales of old-style compact discs will eventually decline.

▲ Some businesses sell both goods and services.

CHANGES IN THE WORKPLACE

What about the people who worked in the plants that made vinyl records? What about the people who owned such plants? What has happened to them? Some of them have gone out of business. Some have had to look for other jobs. Others have taken cuts in pay and profits.

In a free enterprise system, businesses have to respond to changing supply and demand. In the music industry, major companies had to increase their output of compact discs, because so many consumers wanted them. Most of those companies eliminated virtually all of the work available for making vinyl records.

In the world of work you have to be prepared for changes. That's the nature of competition in our free enterprise system. The workers who are best able to anticipate and prepare for change are the most successful.

As a young person making career plans, you need to be aware of how important change is in our economy. Many of the jobs that will be available when you finish school haven't even been created yet. You may create new jobs yourself. Those jobs you create might disappear five, ten, or fifteen years later.

The average man entering the workplace today will work about forty years. This hasn't changed much since the turn of the century. The major change has been for women in the workplace. The number of women and the amount of time they spend working outside the home has increased greatly.

During the 1960s more and more women chose to pursue careers outside the home and to have families at the same time. Many of these women decided to begin new careers because the cost of living had risen, and more income was needed to maintain their chosen lifestyle. Other women chose to pursue both a career and a family because they wanted to achieve the satisfaction and fulfillment offered by the experience.

At first, even highly trained and educated women were placed in the more traditional, low-paying jobs. Most of the best-paying jobs, though, especially in management, were held by men. Today, there is

Attitude makes a difference

Accepting Economic Change

Frank and John had known each other all their lives. They had grown up together in a small midwestern town, and had gone to the same elementary school and high school. They had the same friends. They both worked in the town's only factory.

During the twelve years that Frank and John worked at the factory, they made very good wages. They supported their families comfortably and enjoyed their small-town lifestyles.

The company they worked for had survived, but barely. Workers with less seniority (rank based on the amount of time with the company) than Frank and John were frequently laid off for long periods. The company never got the big break it needed and constantly seemed on the verge of collapse. Frank and John often talked about what they would do if they ever lost their jobs.

Then one day it happened—everyone received the announcement that the factory was closing. It would not reopen. The company was out of business.

For the next fifteen months Frank collected his unemployment checks and looked half-heartedly for a new job. He didn't look anywhere outside his hometown, however. He was comfortable there and didn't like the uncertainty that came with meeting new people and driving in strange places. He was depressed and angry. He felt he had been cheated. Things just weren't going the way they were supposed to. He spent a lot of time telling anyone who'd listen how the breaks had gone against him.

For the rest of his life Frank worked at part-time and low-paying jobs around his small community. He always seemed grouchy, with a chip on his shoulder. He never got over the factory's closing.

John's life, however, went in an entirely different direction after the plant closed. John had seen the bad news coming and had done something about it. He had taken computer application courses at a nearby community college and done part-time work for a local architect. He had developed some new, up-to-date skills.

John had also made a big decision. He liked the small-town life just as much as Frank, but he knew that he would never be able to give his family the lifestyle they were used to if he stayed in his hometown. John had many working years ahead of him. He knew he had to broaden his job search to nearby towns, and even bordering states, if he was to have a satisfying, happy life.

John did find a new and better job. He had to move two hundred miles from his hometown. He and his family were very homesick for the first year or so. But in time they came to think of their new community as home. They made new friends, and John enjoyed his new job.

What Do YOU Think?

Do you feel sorry for Frank? Why or why not? Do you think everyone is capable of doing what John did? Explain.

still some prejudice against placing women in higher-paying jobs, but the opportunities are getting better.

It is estimated that by 2010, about 47 percent of the employed people in the United States will be women. Women will spend as much time in the workplace as men. They will also be filling positions more and more that have traditionally been held by men. Young women today have many more choices.

OUR CHANGING POPULATION

In the United States the population continues to grow. It is expected to grow for another thirty, forty, or maybe fifty years and then level off at about 340 million people. Some areas of the country are growing faster than others. For example, in Florida and California, the population is growing much faster than it is in Wyoming and North Dakota.

The makeup of our population is also changing. People live longer today than ever before, which means we have a much larger senior citizen population. When the baby boom generation reaches retirement age in another fifteen years, an even larger percentage of the population will be elderly. Immigration of people from foreign countries has also changed the makeup of our population.

Let's say you are making a decision about where to settle down when you start your career. Information about population trends is provided by the federal government. You might want to ask your librarian to help you find this information in the library. You can also do research on the Internet.

The simple fact is that jobs are easier to find in areas of our country where the population is growing than in areas where it isn't. That doesn't mean you'll be forced to leave your hometown just because it's not growing. If your town isn't growing, however, you're going to have to be more *flexible* about your career.

You may still want to stay in your hometown and even open your own business. If that's your goal, you will learn more about it in Chapter 23, which deals with starting your own business.

CHANGING ECONOMIC CONDITIONS

Sometimes cities in the United States have lots of unemployed workers—people who want to get a job, but can't find one. The workers at Ray Valdez's steel mill, for example, became unemployed when it was shut down.

During the short history of the United States, the country's economy has changed a great deal. When the United States was founded, almost all the people worked on farms. Then, during the 1800s and early 1900s, the United States changed from an *agricultural economy* to a *manufacturing economy*. More and more workers left the farms for jobs in the factories. In more recent years, the United

States has become a *service economy.* This means that many more people work at producing services than goods. Some experts even go further and describe our economy as an *information economy,* because information services employ increasingly greater numbers of workers.

You can find out from the U.S. government which industries are growing and which industries are getting smaller. Again, your local reference librarian can help you. All this information is also available on the Internet. You can look up the outlook for different career possibilities. Figure 22.1 shows what the U.S. government is predicting for a number of occupations.

If you are interested in mining or manufacturing, you can see from Figure 22.1 that the government is not predicting much growth in jobs through the year 2005. In fact, the government is predicting a decline in jobs for both industries. But if you are interested in retail trade or government work, the outlook is rosy. As you can see from the figure, the government is predicting big increases in jobs for these industries.

Figure 22.1 Percent Change in Number of People Working in Major Industries

INDUSTRY	PERCENT CHANGE IN EMPLOYMENT 1986–1996	PERCENT PROJECTED CHANGE IN EMPLOYMENT 1996–2006
Goods-Producing		
Mining	−27%	−23%
Construction	+12%	+9%
Manufacturing	−4%	−3%
Service-Producing		
Transportation and Public Utilities	+19%	+14%
Wholesale and Retail Trade	+13%	+11%
Finance, Insurance, and Real Estate	+10%	+12%
Government	+13%	+1%
Agriculture, Forestry and Fishing		
All jobs	+22%	+3%

Source: Adapted from *Occupational Outlook Handbook,* 1998–1999 Edition, Bureau of Labor Statistics. Projections for 2006 are the *Moderate* projections.

Attitude makes a difference

Coping with Technology

Olga Davis had a part-time job after school that she really liked. She worked downtown as a part-time word processor in a law firm. Most of the time she spent at a computer typing communications between her boss and the other lawyers in town. She always had to make sure that the letters looked perfect. Sometimes she then had to deliver them. Often, she sent them to the other law offices using the fax machine.

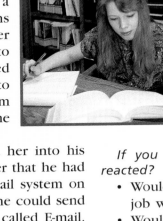

Then one day her boss called her into his office. He was smiling. He told her that he had just installed a new electronic mail system on his computer. He explained that he could send and receive electronic messages, called E-mail, to and from anywhere in the world at virtually no cost. The messages went out on the Internet. On his computer screen he even had an electronic "address book" where he had already put in many E-mail addresses of the various attorneys in town. Olga recognized their names because she had been typing letters to them all year.

After a few weeks, Olga's boss gave her fewer and fewer letters to type. She had less and less to do.

Olga's boss called her in one day and explained the situation. He said she was a great worker, but now he didn't need her as much as before. There just didn't seem to be enough work for her. He asked her if she would cut back her hours of work.

Olga said she would. She thought about her problem that night and discussed it with her parents.

The next day she went to see her boss. Olga told him she wanted to learn how to do online legal research for him. She said that she wanted to learn how to look up law cases that would help in his work. She offered this as an alternative to cutting back her hours of work. Olga's boss agreed to let her try.

What Do YOU Think?

If you were Olga, how would you have reacted?

- Would you have been angry and quit the job when the boss cut your hours?
- Would you have worked fewer hours, as the boss requested, and tried to make a good impression?
- Would you have avoided telling anyone what happened and probably been angry and unhappy at home and with your friends?
- Would you have continued the job but started looking for a better job?
- Would you have handled the situation pretty much the same as Olga did?

All of these choices reflect different attitudes that people might have in Olga's situation. How do these choices reflect "good" or "bad" attitudes? Could some of the choices reflect both kinds of attitudes?

DOING LEGAL RESEARCH ONLINE

The convenience of online legal research has revolutionized the way paralegals do their work. A paralegal now has free, or relatively inexpensive, access to virtually millions and millions of important legal research documents. Online legal research is becoming easier as quicker and more efficient methods of accessing online legal documents are developed.

technology
use of science to develop new products and new methods.

Just remember that "knowledge is power." The more information you can get about different occupations and different careers, the less chance you will make a mistake.

HOW TECHNOLOGY CHANGES WORK

Remember the example we talked about with records, cassettes, and compact discs? In that example the technology changed. **Technology** is the use of ideas and processes, as well as tools and materials, to make things. Technology is everywhere. Indeed, you could say that we live in a *technological society.*

When someone created the technology for making compact discs cheaply, they became reality. When Henry Ford developed the technology for using an assembly line to make his automobiles, the price of cars dropped. More and more people bought them. When the technology was right, airplanes became a fast, relatively cheap form of getting from one place to another.

And of course, any discussion about technology has to include computers. Computers are everywhere in our economy. Before the computer, books took longer to print and cost more.

Before the computer, hundreds of thousands of workers had to spend hours a day sorting checks for the banks around the country. Today checks are sorted by computers.

Before the computer, the cost of operating telephone systems was much higher than it is today. As a result, the real cost of making telephone calls, particularly over long distances and abroad, has fallen dramatically over the last decade.

TECHNOLOGY EQUALS CHANGE

In our technological society, just about every improvement in technology leads to a change. Those changes affect the workforce just as much as they do the goods that we buy as consumers.

Every time somebody comes up with a new idea or a new way to do things and applies it, there is going to be a change. In the music industry the development of compact disc technology led to changes in the workplace. People who used to make vinyl records weren't in demand. People who understood the more complicated compact disc technology were.

TECHNOLOGY AND AUTOMATION

automation
use of machines to replace human labor.

Technology sometimes is talked about in terms of **automation.** Automation is replacing human workers with machines made by other human workers.

For example, printers used to physically take lead type and place it in a tray. This was called setting type.

Today the letters that form the words on the printed pages you read are not set by hand with lead type. They are formed through computers attached to keyboards like those you see on regular typewriters. Printed pages are even being replaced by pages on a computer screen, received through the Internet or from a CD-ROM. In the future, fewer actual book pages will be printed.

▲ Technology changes daily. Be sure to keep abreast of changes as they occur in your occupation.

COPING WITH CHANGE

The word **cope** means to be able to deal with or handle a problem that disturbs you. Changing technology disturbs a lot of people. They do not know how to cope with it. Changing neighborhoods and changing customs also cause problems for many people.

You can learn to cope with a world that changes. The first thing that you must do is understand that *you* are often the reason the world is changing. Inventors and businesspeople usually try to come up with new things and new processes that make goods more to your liking. That is how they make the best profits.

New products are offered to you with the hopes that you will buy them. If you don't like them, you won't buy them. The makers of those new products then will lose money.

When new technology makes a job simpler and requires fewer workers, there is a reason. The businesspeople who use the new technology want to lower their costs. Why? Because they are in competition with other businesspeople. If they lower their costs, they can lower their prices. That way they can get more consumers to buy their products.

cope
to face and deal with problems or responsibilities.

The second thing you can do to cope with change is to realize the importance of education and training. No matter how our economy changes, employers will always need workers who can read, write, speak, listen, and do math calculations. Employers know that workers with these skills can quickly learn the newest skills in demand. They also know that these workers are usually willing and eager to be retrained.

A third thing you can do to cope with change is to learn to accept different beliefs, customs, and languages. The world is shrinking. People from different cultures must work together more than ever. The Chinese economy changes to become more like the U.S. economy. The U.S. economy becomes more like the Japanese economy. And more and more workers from different countries work side by side. You increase your chances for success if you are open-minded about the different methods and beliefs that you encounter. To cope with change you must be willing—even eager—to accept changes and differences.

Career Decision-Making Activities

1. Talk to some senior citizens in your community—perhaps a grandparent and some friends of your grandparents. Ask them what have been the biggest changes in our society since they were your age. On a separate sheet of paper, list at least five changes. Think of at least one way each change could have affected the workplace in our country.
2. Find the oldest copy of a magazine or newspaper that you can. Skim the publication, looking for signs of how our society, and especially the workplace, has changed over the years. Look at advertisements, prices, fashion, articles about fads and trends, and current events stories. If possible, bring the publication to class, and point out to the class the examples you've discovered. Good places to look for older publications are college libraries, bookstores that sell used books, antique sales, and attics and storage areas of relatives' and friends' older homes.
3. Examine your attitudes about authority. You know, don't you, that almost everyone has a boss? Your teacher, for example, receives instructions from the school principal. The principal gets his or her instructions from the superintendent, who gets instructions from the school board, and so on. Even the president of the United States must obey rules established by the courts, Congress, and the people.

   Another way of describing a boss is someone who has authority over you. People usually have one of three attitudes toward people who have authority over them:

   - **Attitude 1.** "I do not like the person in authority. The things she says and the things she expects me to do are wrong. I know I will not like doing what she says."
   - **Attitude 2.** "I usually get along pretty well with the person in authority. I listen carefully to what he says, and then I make my decisions."
   - **Attitude 3**. "The person in authority is wonderful. Everything she says is right. I always do exactly what she tells me."

   On a separate sheet of paper, list 12 people who have some degree of authority over you. Then, next to each authority figure, write the number 1, 2, or 3 to describe the attitude you have toward each authority figure, with 1, 2, and 3 representing the attitudes just described. This activity is designed to help you understand your attitudes better. You need not share your responses with others unless you choose to do so.
4. Most successful people display Attitude 2 more frequently than Attitudes 1 and 3. The following list contains a few characteristics of people who have Attitude 2.

   - Cooperative.
   - Tolerant.
   - Optimistic.
   - Polite.
   - Honest.
   - Diplomatic.
   - Fair.
   - Loyal.
   - Tactful.
   - Confident.
   - Punctual.
   - Reliable.

   Working as a class, list other characteristics you can think of that describe a person with Attitude 2. Also list some characteristics you can think of that might describe a person with Attitudes 1 and 3.

Review and Enrichment

Summarizing the Chapter

Summarizing information is a critical thinking skill that will help you succeed in the world of work. Write a summary of what you learned in Chapter 22. Focus on the main points of the chapter. Then in a class discussion, compare your summary with the summaries done by your classmates. Can you improve your summary?

Improving Your Career Vocabulary

Learning to use new vocabulary terms will improve your communication skills, which are important in almost all areas of work. Write definitions for the terms listed below. Then for each term, write an original sentence about yourself in which you use the term correctly.

- economic system
- free enterprise system
- enterprise
- goods
- democracy
- capitalism
- socialism
- producer
- profit
- loss
- competition
- law of supply
- law of demand
- technology
- automation
- cope

Finding the Facts

Finding exact information is a frequently used skill in many careers. Find the answers to the exercise below, and write the answers on a separate sheet of paper.

1. Name two basic economic systems.
2. Who calls the shots in the free enterprise system?
3. What is another term for *business earnings?*
4. State the law of supply and the law of demand.
5. What change took place in the U.S. economy during the 1800s and early 1900s?

Thinking for Yourself

To complete the exercise below you will need to use critical thinking and communication skills, which are skills valued by all employers. Write out your answers or be prepared to discuss them in class, depending on your teacher's instructions.

1. In your own words, describe capitalism and socialism. Tell how they differ.
2. Fifteen years ago microcomputers were too expensive for most people. Today many families can afford them. How do you think the laws of supply and demand affected the price of computers?
3. You have been reading about the importance of having a positive attitude. How do you think having a positive attitude would help a worker who had just lost a job?
4. Scientists believe that one day we will run out of oil and gasoline to power the cars we drive. How do you think such a change will affect our economy and the way we live today?
5. What more do you think you could do to better prepare yourself for technological change in your career? How could your school help you?

Practicing Your Basic Skills

Your career success depends greatly on your basic math and communication skills. Work hard at improving in the areas where you have trouble with the following exercises.

Math

1. Below is a list of items and their prices in 1955 and 1998. Calculate the percentage of increase for each one.

Item	1955	1998
Bread	35¢	$1.49
Gasoline (per gallon)	52¢	$1.28
Sofa	$562	$1,500
Man's shirt	$6.50	$25.99

2. The present U.S. population is about 280 million people. If our population grew by 20 percent each year, in how many years would it reach 480 million?
3. In 1920, Jack's grandfather earned $5 per *week* as a grocery clerk. How much did his grandfather earn in a year? Today Jack earns $5 per *hour* as a grocery clerk and works 27 hours a week. How much does Jack earn in a year?

REVIEW AND ENRICHMENT, CONTINUED

Reading and Writing

1. In recent years, many immigrants from other countries have come to the United States. As workers they have been very successful. Find and read several articles on this subject. Try to learn why the immigrants have been successful at jobs U.S. workers did not want to take. Report your findings to the class.
2. Learn to use your library reference department. Ask your librarian for help if needed. Find the answers to the following:
   a. Who was the twelfth vice-president of the United States?
   b. What is the economic system used in Cuba?
   c. What was the population of Wyoming in 1988?

Speaking and Listening

1. Pretend you are the owner of a small business. Give a one-minute speech to your class on the advantages of the free enterprise system.
2 Ask your parents and grandparents about products they used to buy that are no longer available. Listen for names that are unfamiliar to you. Make a list of the names, and identify what they were.

ACTIVITIES WORKING WITH OTHERS

In almost all careers you must be able to get along well with other people to be successful. Work with your classmates to do the following activities. As you work together, pay attention to how well you get along. If necessary, work hard at improving your ability to do your part and to cooperate.

1. Ask your parents and grandparents how technology has changed since they were children. As a class, make a list of the changes.
2. As a class, make a time line on the bulletin board showing technological changes since prehistoric times. The invention of writing might be one, and the automobile another.

DECISION MAKING AND PROBLEM SOLVING

You will be a big help to your employer if you can make decisions and solve problems. List all the possible ways of resolving the situation described below. Then pick the best alternative (possible choice), and tell why you chose it. If you need help, you might want to refer to Chapter 3.

You are the owner of a grocery store. At a meeting of local businesspeople, another store owner suggests that you should get together and agree on certain prices for certain items. That way, he says, all the store owners will make the same amount of money on the items. Another store owner argues that doing so will destroy competition. The group is to take a vote. What will you vote for?

◀ Today's AM/FM radios can be worn as headphones. Radios in your grandparents' days were pieces of furniture!

CHAPTER 23

STARTING YOUR OWN BUSINESS

◆ Chapter Objectives ◆

After completing this chapter you will be able to do the following:

◆ Define the terms listed under "New Career Terms."

◆ Identify and explain several advantages to being an entrepreneur.

◆ Identify and explain several disadvantages to being an entrepreneur.

◆ List personal traits that lead to success as an entrepreneur.

◆ Evaluate your own interest in becoming an entrepreneur.

◆ New Career Terms ◆

In this chapter you will learn the meanings of the following career terms:

✔ Entrepreneur
✔ Risk
✔ Persistence
✔ Sole proprietorship
✔ Partnership
✔ Corporation
✔ Stockholder
✔ Stock

A high school student named Steve Wozniak had a good friend named Steven Jobs. Both young men were crazy about electronics and were known as "electronic wizards" by their friends. They decided to team up to work on projects together.

They worked very hard on many projects to find out everything they could about electronics. Their most successful early project was a device to make free long-distance phone calls. From there they went on to a more legal, and much more profitable, project together.

In Steven Jobs's bedroom they designed what became the first Apple I computer. In the family garage, they built the first model. Steven Jobs was able to fill an order for twenty-five of the computers with a local electronics retailer.

Jobs and Wozniak needed money to expand, so they sold the most valuable things they owned—Jobs's Volkswagen bus and Wozniak's calculator. They borrowed more from friends in the electronics industry. They were off and running as business partners.

Within three years their new Apple II earned $140 million. The multibillion-dollar personal computer industry started with the dreams and hard work of two young men working together to start their own business.

Perhaps you've heard stories that are similar to the true story of how the Apple microcomputer got started. Perhaps you've read about Thomas Edison, Andrew Carnegie, or Henry Ford. They all started their own businesses, each of which led to multibillion-dollar industries. They made fortunes for themselves and changed the daily lives of all Americans. They had big dreams and were willing to stay true to them even when the going got rough.

These famous people are just a few of our country's great **entrepreneurs.** Entrepreneurs are people who start their own businesses or introduce new products or techniques. With their new ideas and their willingness to take **risks** (chances), entrepreneurs create businesses that give millions of Americans places to work.

entrepreneur
a person who organizes, manages, and assumes the risks of a business.

risk
a chance of possible loss.

ADVANTAGES OF ENTREPRENEURSHIP

One of the biggest advantages to entrepreneurship (being an entrepreneur) is being your own boss. Almost everyone dreams of running a business his or her way, of being in charge, and of making all the important decisions. Being your own boss also means setting your own hours and *giving* orders instead of taking them.

Another advantage is being able to create something new and different—something in which you believe. For example, maybe one of your favorite activities is helping your family and friends pick out clothes. You have a knack for putting outfits and colors together. Your friends tell you they never could have thought of the ideas you come up with. If so, you may be dreaming of having your own clothes-designing business someday.

Or maybe you enjoy bicycle racing and have lots of ideas about how bikes could be designed better. You think you could improve

▼ Did you ever imagine a computer built in a wooden box?

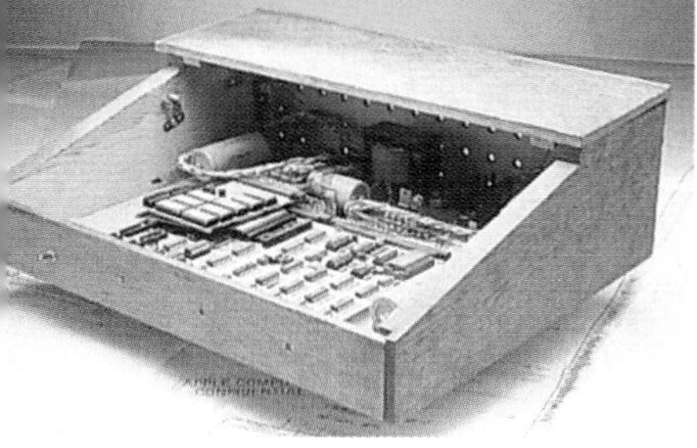

Attitude makes a difference

Baking Up a Storm

Maria got her first summer job in the bakery of a large grocery store. She didn't know the first thing about baking. All that summer she helped the baker prepare cakes, cookies, and pies. By the middle of the summer, Maria made them as well as he did.

Maria experimented with the crust and came up with a recipe that made it flakier. The customers began commenting that it was the best crust they had ever tasted. Maria made pies at home using different combinations of fillings until she came up with two that her family thought were delicious.

When Maria asked the baker if he would let her try to make some of her special-recipe pies at the grocery store, he told her it was too risky. He told her that people don't like new things, and they might stop coming to their bakery.

Maria didn't argue. She continued to experiment at home. By the following summer Maria had two new recipes for pies, two special cake recipes, and a recipe for cookies that all her friends and family loved.

The baker from the grocery store offered Maria a job that summer. He offered her a raise. Maria thought about it.

She decided to take a risk. She really believed that her recipes were good. She knew she was willing to work hard.

She thanked the baker, but told him she had decided to start her own business. He told her she was foolish. However, Maria believed in herself and wasn't afraid to take chances.

Maria used the money she had saved the summer before. She worked to organize a bake sale in her yard. She prepared her new recipes and sent out almost fifty invitations to different restaurants and gourmet food stores in town. Maria offered them free samples and drinks. Her friends and family came, along with other people in the neighborhood and five people to whom she had sent invitations.

By the end of the day, Maria had sold all her baked goods. Two people from local restaurants were favorably impressed by her goods. They were also impressed by the reactions of everyone else. They asked her if she would like to prepare some desserts for their restaurants for weekend specials. One of the gourmet stores asked her if she would be willing to make a dozen pies and twelve dozen cookies a week for them.

Maria worked hard that summer and got three more restaurants and one other store as customers. She even hired her brother to help her on a part-time basis. Her name became quite well known as one of the best dessert makers in town.

What Do YOU Think?

What kind of risks did Maria take? In this case, Maria's risks paid off. What if they hadn't? What could Maria have lost? Would you have taken the same risks that Maria did?

▲ Are you an entrepreneur?

the gears and tires so bicycles could go even faster and still be safe. Maybe you're thinking you would like to have your own custom bicycle shop. You'd design, develop, and build your own products.

As an entrepreneur you would turn your dream into a reality. If it's your own business, you can be creative. You can use your own ideas. You get a lot of satisfaction from working in an area you enjoy and coming up with new ideas.

Another advantage of having your own business is the chance to earn more money than you could working for someone else. Owners of *successful* businesses do very well financially. The work can be long and hard, but the rewards can be great.

There are added advantages for those who become entrepreneurs while still in high school. As a young entrepreneur you get an early chance to learn how things are done in the business world. This gives you a jump on almost everyone else. You also have an opportunity to meet businesspeople who can help you later in life.

DISADVANTAGES OF ENTREPRENEURSHIP

There are also disadvantages to entrepreneurship. Probably the biggest disadvantage is the possibility of failure and the financial responsibility you must accept. It's tough to start a new business and keep it going. Eight out of ten new businesses fail within five years of opening. Most entrepreneurs borrow money to get the business started. If the business fails, they can end up owing huge sums of money.

Even when a business survives and does well, the owner must constantly watch over finances. As you know, businesses must make profits. Each new month and each new year the entrepreneur must be sure there's enough money coming in to pay all the bills. This financial risk is a disadvantage of entrepreneurship.

Another disadvantage is having to work hard for long hours. Especially in a new business, entrepreneurs usually do much or all of the work themselves. This can often mean working fourteen- or fifteen-hour days and working Saturdays and Sundays with no long vacations. Entrepreneurs are willing to do this because they believe in their dreams, but it can be a disadvantage. There are many times when they'd rather go to a ball game or out to a movie than work.

Career Decision-Making Activities

1. Interview a local business owner. Ask this person to name the advantages and disadvantages of owning your own business. Also ask this person what the biggest problems and surprises were in starting the business. Report back to class with your findings.

2. An important part of most businesses is dealing with customers. For example, even if you're the best auto mechanic within a hundred miles, many people will go to other mechanics if they don't like the way you treat them. In a week's time, visit at least twenty businesses in your community. Notice the behavior of workers dealing with you or other customers.

   On a piece of paper, list the workers you see who seem to be good at dealing with customers and those who don't seem very good. Describe what you saw or heard that made you think these people were either good or bad at working with customers. Tell in what kind of business each person was working.

   Next, discuss your findings in class. Tell the class your opinion about the importance of dealing with customers in different businesses. Is it more important in some businesses than in others?

   Finally, write a paragraph telling how you would help customers. If the success of a business you started depended on your being able to deal effectively with customers, do you think the business would succeed? Include the answer in your paragraph.

3. Some people like to lead. Others prefer to follow. It's okay to be either type of person. Which type are you? On a separate sheet of paper, write down a brief, one- or two-sentence description of the last ten times you can remember being with friends when decisions were made. You might have been deciding where to go, what game to play, or how to do something together. For each of the ten events, write *leader, follower,* or *in between* to indicate the best description of your involvement in the decision-making activity. Then for each event, tell whether you were happy with your role or whether you should have taken a different role. Finally, write a paragraph telling why you think you are most comfortable being a leader or a follower.

WHAT IT TAKES TO BE SUCCESSFUL

Some people think entrepreneurs are born with what it takes to be successful. They think that you either have it, or you don't. Other people think that almost anyone can learn to be a successful entrepreneur. These people think that you can develop the needed skills if you have the ideas and the desire.

Whether entrepreneurs are born or made, most of them seem to have certain qualities. Here are some of the common traits researchers have identified in successful entrepreneurs:

- They have a lot of self-confidence.
- They like to take risks. They like challenges. They prefer risks and challenges to being safe and secure.
- They're not afraid to make decisions. They decide, and then they act on their decisions.
- They have a strong desire to achieve what they want. They don't quit, and they're not easily talked out of trying something.
- They have a lot of energy. They like to work, and work hard. They are not lazy.
- Many like to be recognized. They like being in the spotlight.
- They look for and see opportunities. They're always searching for a better way or a better product.

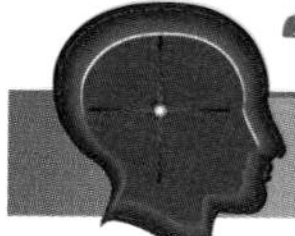

Thinking About Yourself

Do I Have What It Takes?

Starting a business isn't for everyone. It takes some special qualities. Here are a few. How many do you have?

- ▲ I know how to make decisions.
- ▲ I know how to set goals and develop a plan to achieve them.
- ▲ I am willing to put my work above everything and work long hours.
- ▲ I don't give up.
- ▲ I am not afraid to take risks.
- ▲ I am a hard worker.
- ▲ I am a good problem solver.
- ▲ I am patient.
- ▲ I believe in myself and my ideas.
- ▲ I know how to motivate people.
- ▲ I have a good imagination.
- ▲ I am a good leader.
- ▲ I come up with good ideas.
- ▲ I've got "guts."

persistence
the quality of sticking with something in spite of difficulties—not giving up.

If you become an entrepreneur, you will be the one who either takes credit for being successful or takes the responsibility for failure. No one can predict what will happen to your business. You can, however, do some things to increase your chances of success.

Many successful businesspeople agree that good planning leads to success. They say that when people start businesses they must know where they are going. Planning is extremely important. Many people get a good idea, can't wait to get started, and just jump into their new businesses. You can probably guess how long these businesses last: not long.

If you have an idea, work it out on paper first. Include your goals, the possible customers you would have, and a detailed description of how the business will operate. Estimate how much your business will cost to run and how much it will earn. Also make sure you understand your competition. How will your product compare with the competition's?

▼ Most small businesses operate as sole proprietorships under the control of one person.

Other successful businesspeople agree that you shouldn't start a business unless it involves something that you like. You must also know something about your product or service. It's natural that if you enjoy your work, you will be more motivated, work harder, and be happier. Most successful businesspeople agree that the more you know about the business you plan to go into, the better. This includes learning about laws, regulations, and tax codes that would apply to your business.

Managing money is an important part of every business. Are you good at math? Do you keep track of how you spend your money? If you're not a good money manager, you'll need to get someone to help you. Maybe a parent or other adult could help you get started.

Another key to success is **persistence.** This is the quality of sticking with something—not giving up. Those who succeed know that some things will go wrong, but they learn how to handle the unexpected. They stick with it. They learn how to keep a positive attitude and how to solve problems. They have drive. They don't give up.

Success usually takes time. Successful people have learned to be patient. They enjoy short-term success, overcome setbacks, and keep working toward the long-term success.

If you decide you would like to start your own business, here are some questions to ask yourself:

- Do I know enough about the business?
- Will I have time for the business?
- How much will it cost to start this business?
- Will I have to borrow money?
- How much competition will I have?
- Will sales be great enough to make a profit?
- Should I do it alone or have partners?
- Does this business have a chance to grow?
- Would I be able to find good employees for this business?
- What will my interest be in this business in the future?

WORKING AT HOME

One of the major benefits of the online revolution is that it has allowed many people to work at home. Today over five million Americans work out of their homes. They may communicate with their bosses through e-mail, cellular phones, and video conferencing. They can access important files anywhere in the world through the Internet. They can send files through the Internet. They can communicate with their customers and clients through the Internet. Computers, along with the online revolution, have allowed many Americans to do an office job, but not have to go to an office.

TYPES OF BUSINESS OWNERSHIP

Have you ever gone in with a friend and bought something such as a new computer game? Perhaps neither one of you had enough money for it, so you decided to share it. If so, you know that the good side of this arrangement is that you have a new computer game to play that you otherwise wouldn't have.

The bad side is that you only own half of it, so you only get to use it half the time. You don't have as much control as you would if you were the only owner.

Maybe you've had three or four friends chip in to buy something such as a package of games on CD-ROM, which you then traded with one another. You have even less control with this arrangement, but you have many more games to play on your home or school computer.

You can own things all by yourself. Or you can own them with someone else. The same is true with a business.

The most basic type of business ownership is a **sole proprietorship.** This is a business owned by one person. It is the oldest form of business ownership and the most common, especially in small businesses.

sole proprietorship a business owned by one person..

Having a sole proprietorship is like owning a new computer game of your own. You get to play it when you want to. You receive all the benefits. The owner of a business gets to keep all the profits that the business makes.

The other side of the coin is that you have all the responsibility. If you erase part of your computer game program by accident, you

partnership
a business that two or more people own and operate.

corporation
a business owned by many people but treated by the law as though it were one person.

stockholder
a person who owns stock in a company.

stock
a share of the ownership in a company.

alone have to pay to get it fixed. It's the same if you are the sole proprietor of a business. You get all the profits, but you also have all the work and financial responsibility.

A **partnership** is a business that two or more people own and operate together. They pool their money, skills, knowledge, and time to operate the business. They also share the profits and the risks.

A **corporation** is a business owned by a number of people who buy shares in the business. These people are called **stockholders. Stock** is the share of ownership that stockholders buy in the company. The stockholders get a certain part of the profits. Sometimes they get to vote about what happens in the business. There are many legal requirements involved in forming a corporation.

YOUNG ENTREPRENEURS

You may want to become an entrepreneur like Maria while you're still in school. It's not too early to start. In fact, *now* may be the perfect time. If you see a need that no one else is meeting, you may want to try meeting it yourself. People your age have started suc-

Maria Makes More Decisions

Maria, whom you were introduced to in the previous "Attitude Makes a Difference" box, planned to start college the following fall after a successful summer with her baking business. She had to make some decisions about her business and about her future. She had a steady group of restaurants and gourmet stores in town that depended on her. She still wanted to learn more about business.

Maria had already decided to make school count while she was in high school. She had taken bookkeeping, math, computer, and business courses, which she felt had helped her a lot that summer with her baking business. She wanted to learn more, though, because she wanted her business to grow.

She decided to give up some work in the short run so she could take courses that would help her in the long run. She kept her biggest customers and baked for them on weekends. She earned enough money to pay for much of her college education. She enrolled in the business management program at the local college.

Maria received her college degree four years later. She still had a small baking business in the community. She had learned so much more about marketing, advertising, and running a successful business that she came up with a long-term plan.

One year later Maria already had a statewide specialty dessert business that sold desserts to several chain restaurants and stores. She had a sole proprietorship with three employees. One was Liza, a college friend who had majored in marketing. Liza knew more about marketing than Maria did. Liza wanted to invest her own savings in Maria's company. Maria decided that this was the best way to expand the business. Liza and Maria formed a partnership together.

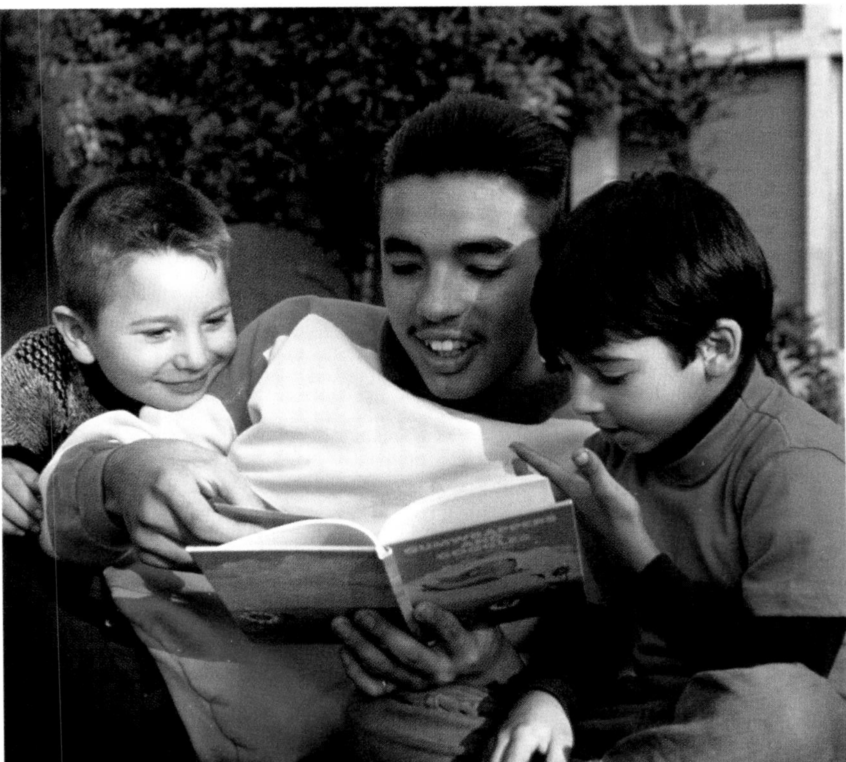

Many teens start successful small businesses while still in high school. Childcare after school would be a possible service you could offer.

cessful small businesses in lawn maintenance, baby-sitting services, cleaning services, painting, delivery services, shopping services, and many more.

In recent years, an increasing number of young people have been running their own computer-related businesses. Some of those businesses offer technical support to neighbors and local businesses. The federal government estimates that over 100,000 Americans under the age of nineteen hold part-time computer-related jobs. Many of them have started their own businesses. Lots of these businesses involve the Internet.

Suppose you want to start a new business. Where do you get information? One source is the Small Business Administration (SBA). This is a government organization that helps new small businesses get off the ground. There are SBA offices in every state. You can also write to the Small Business Administration, 1441 L Street N.W., Washington, DC 20416.

Banks also have information about becoming an entrepreneur. The library has books about how businesses work and about starting your own business. These books can also be helpful. There are also numerous sources of information readily available on the Internet.

One of the best ways to learn is by talking to other people who have started successful businesses. There are probably a number of people in your community who started businesses and have many stories to share. Most people in business for themselves are happy to share what they have learned and give tips to young people who are interested.

As a final suggestion, try reading a book you can find in many libraries called *The Teenage Entrepreneur's Guide: 50 Money Making Business Ideas,* by Sarah Riehm (Chicago: Surrey Books). In her book, Riehm provides fifty ideas for starting a business. Among these ideas are those listed here:

- Auto detailing service.
- Recycling service.
- Neighborhood directory.
- Painting business.
- Painting house numbers.
- House numbers.
- Birthday party service.
- House-sitting business.
- Word processing service.
- Home bakery.
- Delivery service.
- Handicrafts.
- Personalized greeting cards.
- T-shirts.

Riehm gives lots of suggestions for getting each business idea off the ground. She also tells what to expect regarding materials, experience, money, time, and much more. All of her ideas and suggestions were written with teenagers like you in mind. Maybe one of the fifty ideas is one that you've already been dreaming about yourself.

Career Decision-Making Activities

1. Read two newspaper or magazine articles about people who have started successful businesses recently. Magazines such as *Entrepreneur, Business Week,* and *Success* contain many such articles. Other magazines, such as *Time, Newsweek,* and *Kiplinger's Personal Finance Magazine,* also frequently have such articles, as do the business or lifestyle sections of your local newspaper. Identify the reasons you think these people were successful. Discuss your findings in class. What reasons for success were mentioned most frequently?
2. Write down on a sheet of paper your five strongest interests and five strongest skills. You should know these from reading Chapters 2 and 3 in this book. On the same sheet, list the two career clusters in which you are most interested. Now, as you look at what you've written, come up with as many ideas as you can for businesses you could start that would match your

skills, interests, and career choices. Don't rule out any ideas. Write down everything that comes to mind. Share your list with the class. Ask the members of your class which ideas they think have the greatest chance for success.

3. The success or failure of a new business often depends on how good a job the business does in advertising its products. Choose one of your business ideas from Activity 2 above. Develop one print advertisement and a marketing plan for that business. Your ad should fit on an 8½-by-11-inch sheet of paper so you can photocopy it and circulate it in your school and community. Look at newspaper and magazine ads to get ideas. Notice that most ads use photographs or drawings with a minimum number of words. Your marketing plan should list all the ideas you can think of for promoting your business. Give an estimated cost for each idea in your plan. After you've created your ad and plan, share them with the class. Ask your classmates for suggestions. If you had your own business, do you think you would create your own ads or hire someone to do this?

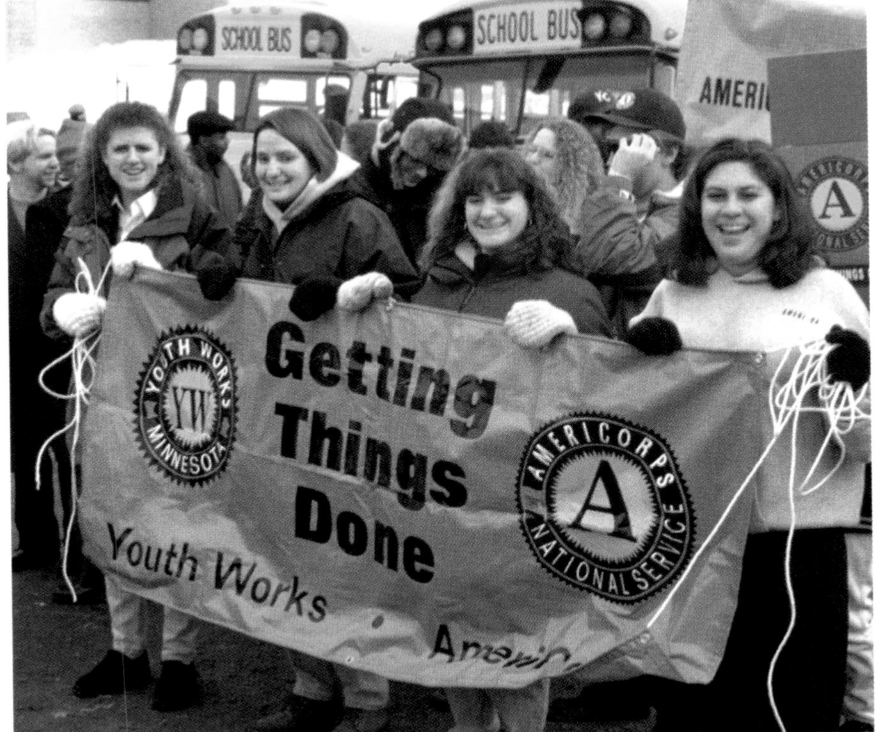

◀ Think about club or volunteer activities you've enjoyed and in which you've had success. How could these successes apply to starting your own business?

Review and Enrichment

Summarizing the Chapter

Summarizing information is a critical thinking skill that will help you succeed in the world of work. Write a summary of what you learned in Chapter 23. Focus on the main points of the chapter. Then in a class discussion, compare your summary with the summaries done by your classmates. Can you improve your summary?

Improving Your Career Vocabulary

Learning to use new vocabulary terms will improve your communication skills, which are important in almost all areas of work. Write definitions for the terms listed below. Then for each term, write an original sentence about yourself in which you use the term correctly.

- entrepreneur
- risk
- persistence
- sole proprietorship
- partnership
- corporation
- stockholder
- stock

Finding the Facts

Finding exact information is a frequently used skill in many careers. Find the answers to the exercise below, and write the answers on a separate sheet of paper.

1. Name the advantages and disadvantages of being an entrepreneur.
2. How many businesses fail within the first five years?
3. What special qualities are needed by an entrepreneur?
4. Name the types of business ownership.
5. How is a partnership different from a corporation?

Thinking for Yourself

To complete the exercise below you will need to use critical thinking and communication skills, which are skills valued by all employers. Write out your answers or be prepared to discuss them in class, depending on your teacher's instructions.

1. What do you think would be the most important personal quality of an entrepreneur?
2. What values do you think would be common among entrepreneurs?
3. Compare times you have worked on your own with times you have had a boss. Which did you enjoy most? Why?
4. Are you patient? Think of times you had to wait to get a result you wanted. Did the result seem worth it?
5. Partners must get along. What do you think is the most important quality to look for in a business partner? Explain.

Practicing Your Basic Skills

Your career success depends greatly on your basic math and communication skills. Work hard at improving in the areas where you have trouble with the following exercises.

Math

1. Bob had his own bicycle repair shop. He earned \$8,750 the first year, \$12,780 the second, and \$10,091 the third. His taxes were 24 percent of his total earnings. How much did he earn before and after taxes altogether in the three years?
2. To start her business, Debbie had to borrow \$35,000. Her local banks charge the following fees for making loans. How much would Debbie's fee be at each bank?
   a. 2¼ percent of the full amount
   b. 3 percent of the first \$30,000 only
   c. 2 percent of the first \$25,000 and 1½ percent of the remaining amount
3. Mike and Ernest opened a doughnut shop. The ingredients they used cost \$129.75. At 20¢ each, how many doughnuts must they sell to cover the cost of ingredients?

Reading and Writing

1. Read a biography of a well-known entrepreneur. Write a paragraph describing the personal quality you admired the most.

Review and Enrichment, continued

2. Obtain booklets from the Small Business Administration or a bank about being an entrepreneur. Read through the booklets. Make a list of tips to remember.
3. Think of a business you would like to start. Write a newspaper ad telling your town about your business.

Speaking and Listening

1. Talk to an entrepreneur in your town. Ask the person what advice he or she would give someone starting out.
2. Listen to the entrepreneur. How would you describe the person's attitude?

Activities Working with Others

In almost all careers you must be able to get along well with other people to be successful. Work with your classmates to do the following activities. As you work together, pay attention to how well you get along. If necessary, work hard at improving your ability to do your part and to cooperate.

1. As a class, organize a small one-time business, such as a bake sale for the PTA or a soda stand at a football game. Keep track of expenses, profits, and "employee" hours.
2. Work out an arrangement so that class members can buy "stock" in the class business. Make stock certificates (showing the name of the business and number of shares the certificate represents) and sell shares. Distribute profits depending on how many shares a stockholder owns.

Decision Making and Problem Solving

You will be a big help to your employer if you can make decisions and solve problems. List all the possible ways of resolving the situations described below. Then pick the best alternative (possible choice), and tell why you chose it. If you need help, you might want to refer to Chapter 3.

1. Your uncle owns a shoe repair shop. You like him, but he's not a hard worker. The shop is dirty and needs its own repairs. Your uncle offers you either a job or a partnership in the place. You'd like to take one or the other. The job doesn't pay too well at first, but the partnership would mean a lot of work for you. What will you do?
2. You are an independent person, and you have opened a small shop of your own. The shop is two years old but just getting by. You're tired of having no extra money. You're also tired of the long hours. A new factory has opened in town and offered you a job as a supervisor. You'd make good money at the factory. What will you do?

CHAPTER 24

EDUCATION AND TRAINING

◆ Chapter Objectives ◆

After completing this chapter you will be able to do the following:

◆ Define the terms listed under "New Career Terms."
◆ List several career advantages that often result from increased education and training.
◆ Identify several types of programs available in high schools.
◆ List several educational alternatives available after high school graduation.
◆ Explain the type of education available in four-year and two-year colleges, adult education, on-the-job training, and military training.
◆ Name careers that can be pursued as a result of the various educational alternatives.

◆ New Career Terms ◆

In this chapter you will learn the meanings of the following career terms:

✔ G.E.D. certificate
✔ Program
✔ Elective
✔ Credit
✔ Prerequisite
✔ Bachelor's degree
✔ Graduate school
✔ Associate degree
✔ Adult education
✔ Vocation
✔ Grant
✔ Trade
✔ Apprentice
✔ Tuition
✔ Scholarship

Knowing what you want out of life is a big step. Having a dream is important. Your dream isn't worth much, though, if you don't make it come true. Just thinking about it and waiting won't make it happen. Wishing won't even help. You have to take positive action.

One of the best ways to make your career dreams come true is by getting the education and training you need. By now you probably realize that almost all jobs, in any career, require some training and education. The more education and training you have, the more career opportunities you will have. When you have more choices, you will be more likely to find the career that fits your values, interests, and abilities.

Education and training can never guarantee your success. They can, however, greatly improve your chances for success. Did you know that careers requiring the most education and training will be the fastest growing (and highest paying)? That is what the government predicts. Occupations that require a college degree (or more) will average a 23 percent growth rate, which is double the growth rate projected for jobs that require less education and training.

The better education and training you have,

- The more choices you will have in your life.
- The more likely you will be to find the job that is right for you.
- The more likely you will be to spend your time doing what you like to do.

These are some of the reasons why it is so important for you to find the education and training that will lead you to your career dreams. Different careers require different kinds and levels of education and training. You will need to know the ***minimum requirements*** in the career area you have chosen. That means the *least* amount of skills and training you must have.

Thinking About Yourself

What Do You Want Out of a Career?

All of the following benefits of a career usually require more than the average amount of education and training. On a separate sheet of paper, write down which of the following benefits you want. Then decide how important education and training are to you.

- Higher salary in the long run.
- More job security.
- More chances for higher-level jobs.
- More job benefits, such as expense accounts, paid vacation time, health insurance, bonuses, and pension plans (money for when you no longer work).
- More chances for promotion and advancement.
- More chances to be given greater authority on the job.
- More chances to put your own ideas into effect.
- More chances to be in a decision-making role.
- The chance to choose from among many more jobs.

What if you don't know how much education and training you need for your chosen career? You can find out by looking in the *Occupational Outlook Handbook,* which you can find in the library and on the Internet. Your guidance counselor can also advise you. And you can talk to people working in that career field about their education and training.

Graduation from high school has become the minimum requirement for almost all jobs. Without a high school diploma your choices will be severely limited. The only jobs available will be those that no one else wants. You don't want to be limited to these choices, do you?

G.E.D. certificate (General Educational Development certificate) a document stating that a person has passed a five-part test in the areas of writing, social studies, science, reading, and math.

If you must leave high school for some reason, plan on getting a **G.E.D. certificate.** This certificate is similar to a high school diploma. To get this certificate you must pass the General Educational Development (G.E.D.) test. The test discovers whether you have learned the things that are needed for a high school diploma. The test is divided into five parts:

- Writing skills.
- Social studies.
- Science.
- Reading skills.
- Mathematics.

A high school diploma will contribute more to your career success than will a G.E.D. certificate. The G.E.D. certificate will limit your college choices. Also, it will not be looked on as favorably as a diploma by many employers.

Career Decision-Making Activities

1. Break into twelve groups with your classmates. Each group should be responsible for one of the following school subject areas: English, math, social studies, science, art, music, industrial technology, business, family and consumer sciences, agriculture, health, and physical education. Within your group, choose one person to be a recorder. The recorder should number a blank sheet of paper from 1 to 30.

   Then, as a group, take ten minutes to come up with as many careers as possible related to your assigned school subject. The recorder should write down the careers. After a group discussion, have the recorder write next to each career the required level of education, choosing from the following six choices: (a) high school diploma, (b) apprenticeship training, (c) trade school, (d) two-year college degree, (e) four-year college degree, or (f) graduate college degree. Count the number of careers you have for each of these six levels of education.

   Each group's recorder should then put the information on the board. Discuss your group's findings in a class discussion. Ask questions about the other groups' findings.
2. Interview an adult in your family about the relationship that education and training have to career success. On a separate sheet of paper, copy the following questions for your interview:
   a. What is the title of your present job?

b. Which levels of education did you obtain? High school graduation? On-the-job training? Apprenticeship program? Military training? Community college? Trade school? College (if so, years completed)? Other (please name)?

c. Overall, are you satisfied with this career?

Using the board, have the entire class tabulate the findings of the interviews. Here is an example:

Title of Job	Level of Education of Worker Polled	Is This Career Satisfying?
Automobile mechanic	Military training and trade school	Yes
Computer engineer	College, 6 years	Yes
Bookkeeper	Community college	No
Hospital aide	High School	Yes

Have a class discussion about the findings of your interviews.

EDUCATION—NOW THROUGH HIGH SCHOOL GRADUATION

Now is the time to start planning your education. *Now* is the time to start learning what you need to know to achieve your career goals. You are probably already making some of your own decisions about courses. These educational decisions become more and more important as you get older. But they are important today—right now!

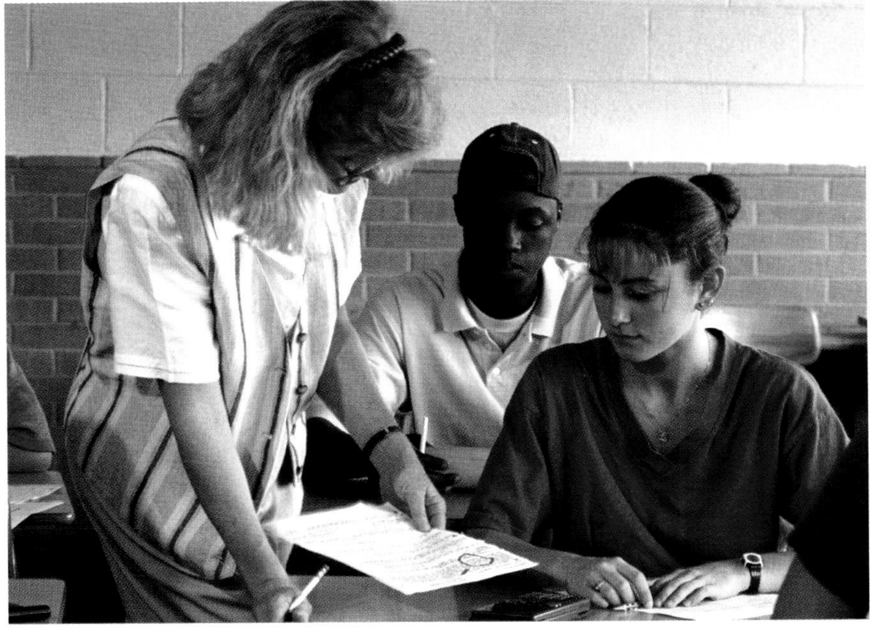

◀ Today is the right day to pay attention to your grades.

Attitude makes a difference

Raul Doesn't Give Up Easily

While Raul was in high school he worked in his father's grocery store. His two older brothers and his sister also worked there. The money they earned went toward living expenses for the family. They all worked hard, but they never seemed able to save any extra money to put away for a college education. The two older brothers decided to continue working at the store when they graduated from high school.

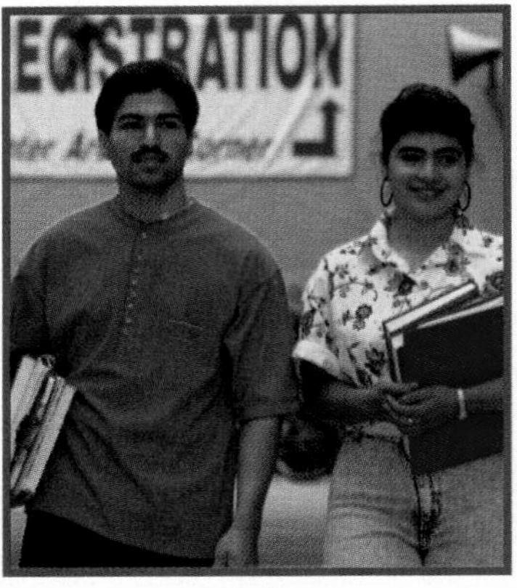

Raul had always been interested in science. He thought he would like to be a science teacher someday. Through his research, he found out that he needed a bachelor's degree. That meant he would need four years of college. He found out that the state college offered a good program. When Raul talked to his older brothers about his dreams, they told him that he would never be able to afford college. They told him to forget it and stay at the family store.

Raul talked to several of his teachers. He talked to his guidance counselor about his career dreams, too. His counselor told him which classes would help him. She told him about several scholarships he could apply for if he kept up his grades. (A scholarship is money given to students to help pay for their education.) Raul was determined to find a way to get to go to college.

During his senior year Raul applied for a scholarship that would pay for his college tuition (the money a college charges for its teaching). Because his grades were good, Raul got the scholarship. He also applied for a student loan to help pay for his other fees. He got a part-time job in a grocery store near the university to help pay for his living expenses.

Raul is now a college junior. He lives on a tight budget. He is busy, but he likes working hard. He will get his degree at the end of next year. He hopes to find a teaching job in his hometown. Raul kept a positive attitude and found a way to reach his dream.

What Do YOU Think?

If Raul had not gone to college, what could he have done instead? Could he have been just as happy? Why do you think it was important for Raul to go to college?

You've been reading about the importance of making school count in the features entitled "From School to Careers." First and most important is learning your basic skills. You must have these skills no matter what career you choose. You've also read many tips about which courses to take if you are interested in certain kinds of careers. By now you should be in the habit of automatically linking your future career and your education. When you think about your schoolwork, you should think about how it will affect your career. When you dream about a career, you should automatically think about the courses you could take to help you make your dream come true.

If you haven't already done so, you may soon be deciding on your high school **program.** A program is a group of courses that go together. Different high schools offer different programs. Some of the more common programs are called *vocational, college prep, advanced, honors,* and *advanced placement.* Your guidance counselor or teachers will explain the differences among the programs. Then you will have to decide in which one you want to be.

How will you decide? Your guidance counselor, teachers, and parents will help you. They will make suggestions. They all have your best interests in mind. They also have experience with these kinds of decisions. Listen closely to your parents, teachers, and guidance counselors.

You should also base your decisions on what you have learned about yourself in this book. You should now have some career goals—goals that match your values, interests, and abilities. You want to choose the high school program that takes you closer to those goals. Your own career research and your guidance counselor can help you match your goals with the best high school program.

For example, suppose you decided you want to be an accountant. You know from your research that you need *at least* four years of college. This means that you had better get into the college prep or similar program at your high school.

Whichever high school program you choose, you will have some required courses and some **electives.** The required courses are courses you *must* take to graduate in your program. Electives are courses that you can choose from based on your personal interests. For example, suppose that at your school you need twenty **credits** to graduate. Credits are the *units* of measurement schools use to determine whether or not students are progressing toward graduation. You usually obtain a certain number of credits for each course that you pass.

Let's say that thirteen of the units you need are taken up by required courses, such as basic English, math, and science courses. This will allow you to take seven credits of electives. From many different courses you can choose the seven that you think will help you the most. This is where you can take advantage of your career planning. Rather than pick your electives at random, you can choose the elective courses that will help you reach your career goals.

In choosing your high school courses, there's another important term you need to know—**prerequisite.** *Pre* means "before." *Requisite* looks a lot like *require,* a word you already know. Put these together, and you almost have the meaning of *prerequisite*—a course that is *required before* another. Prerequisites are courses you need to take first, in order to understand a more challenging course. For

Online Research

Research today—whether it be medical, legal, technical, political, or anything—is much different than it was a few years ago. Today, you can do research online quickly and at almost no cost. To do research, all you have to do is use one of the existing search programs (browsers) that looks through the billions of documents available on the Internet. At the speed of light, the world is at the fingertips of the researcher.

program
a group of school courses that relate to each other.

elective
a course that is not required but can be chosen by a student according to his or her interest.

credit
a unit of measurement used by schools to determine a student's progress.

prerequisite
a class that is required before another higher level course can be taken.

example, you can't take Algebra II until you've taken Algebra I. Algebra I is a prerequisite for Algebra II.

Knowing about prerequisites will help you in your educational planning. If there's a course you know you want to take, find out if there are any prerequisites to it. This way you won't miss out on the course you want because you failed to plan ahead.

Career Decision-Making Activities

It is important that you select the high school courses you will need to prepare you for the occupation you are considering. The purpose of this activity is to help you see the high school subjects that are most closely related to your career choice and how those subjects are used by workers.

On the board, make a list of the basic high school courses offered by the school you attend or will be attending when you need to choose your program. Examples would be English, science, mathematics, social studies, auto mechanics, and office education. Be sure to include vocational courses as well as college preparatory courses. You might ask the guidance counselor to send information or visit your class.

On a separate sheet of paper, make an information table for one or more occupations you are considering. An example of such a table is shown here:

My Tentative Career Choice—*Automobile Mechanic*

HIGH SCHOOL COURSE	HOW THIS COURSE HELPS ME REACH MY TENTATIVE CAREER GOAL	SOURCE OF MY INFORMATION
Mathematics	Figuring cost of parts and customer bills	Discussed it with my uncle, who is an auto mechanic
English	Reading repair manuals	*Occupational Outlook Handbook*
Automotive technology	Learning how to use tools	Guidance counselor
Computer sciences	Learning how to use new systems to test car engines	Guidance counselor

When you are finished, post your information sheet on the bulletin board for your classmates to see. They may be considering a similar career. You should study their sheets to see what you can learn as well.

EDUCATION AND TRAINING AFTER HIGH SCHOOL

When you graduate from high school, you will have many choices. You will need to make a decision about what is right for you. You will need to make decisions that will lead you along your career adventure. Knowing what your options are will save you time and money. Look carefully at your choices. Do some research to make sure you choose the educational or training program that will prepare you best.

As you know from your career research, high school doesn't provide enough education for many careers. Most professional jobs, for example, require two-year or four-year degrees after high school. You can obtain these degrees at a wide variety of colleges and universities throughout the country.

▲ Is college the right place for you after you graduate from high school?

COLLEGES AND UNIVERSITIES

A profession is a career that requires some specialized training and a period of academic (school) preparation. To enter a profession, you usually need a college degree. Some examples of professions are teacher, engineer, accountant, economist, and biologist.

Most professions require a **bachelor's degree.** A bachelor's degree is an academic title usually awarded after you have completed four years of college with an emphasis in one or two areas of study. Other professions require further study in **graduate school** to become qualified. Graduate school is the school people go to after they earn their bachelor's degrees. It's called *graduate* school because you have to *graduate* from college before you can enter. Some examples of professions requiring graduate study are physician and lawyer.

bachelor's degree
a certificate of completion awarded to people after they successfully complete a required set of college courses in both general and specific areas, usually lasting four years.

graduate school
a program of study beyond a bachelor's degree.

Every college will require you to take a certain number of general education courses. These are courses all students must take because they are thought to be needed for a complete, well-rounded education. You will also take a certain number of courses in your major area of study. This is the area in which you have chosen to specialize and get a degree. Beyond these courses, you will have the chance to choose other courses in which you are interested. For example, you may *major* (specialize) in math but take an art course as an elective just because you enjoy it.

There are over two thousand colleges and universities in the country. Selecting the right college is like selecting the right career for yourself. Some colleges are especially strong in some programs and not as strong in others. You should try to choose one that is strong in the area in which you are interested.

Compare schools based on size, location, cost, quality, and entrance and graduation requirements. When you are making your college decision, follow through with the complete decision-making process you learned in Chapter 3. Your chances of being successful and learning what you want to learn are greater if you pick the right college.

▲ Community colleges offer a wide range of 2-year associate degree programs. Explore the offerings at these colleges.

There are many sources of information about colleges. The best place to start is your guidance counselor and teachers.

COMMUNITY COLLEGES

Community colleges are also called *junior colleges* or *city colleges.* They offer two-year programs of college-level work and **associate degrees.** An associate degree is similar to a bachelor's degree, but it usually takes two years instead of four. Some examples of these two-year programs are nursing, computer programming, and medical assistant programs. Associate degrees are offered in more than sixty occupational areas.

You can transfer credit for your community college work to four-year colleges and universities. This means you can begin your studies at a community college. Then you can transfer (switch) to a four-year college to complete your degree.

Many community colleges offer courses at night. This makes it possible for you to work during the day to earn money for your education.

associate degree
a certificate of completion awarded to a person after completing a program of study in a particular area, usually lasting two years.

adult education
programs designed for adults who want to retrain for new careers or improve skills for advancement in their current career area (also called *continuing education*).

ADULT EDUCATION

Another way to get the education and training you need is through **adult education,** or continuing education. Adult education consists of programs designed for adults who want to retrain for new careers or improve their skills for advancement in their current career areas. This route will take you longer, but you can work to earn money as you continue to learn. Adult education courses are offered by colleges, local school systems, and other agencies. Many offer night courses, weekend courses, and correspondence courses (which are done through the mail or the Internet).

Adult education is a good way of advancing your career after you get a job. You can continue to pursue your career, make money, and learn more at the same time.

LEARNING A SKILL OR TRADE

Some people choose not to continue their education at a college or university. Instead, they choose to attend trade or vocational schools. These schools are often called technical schools, because they usually prepare people for jobs that involve the newest technologies. They usually don't include general courses in any areas other than the one you choose. All the courses are directly related to the career you will pursue as soon as you graduate from the school.

Some people choose vocational and trade schools because they don't think they need to learn anything besides the skills they need to do a certain job. You should realize, though, that by taking other

Outside the Classroom

Last summer Stephanie decided to find a part-time job because she wanted to start saving money for college. She saw a newspaper ad about a part-time job at the newspaper office for a messenger and office person. Because working for a newspaper had always been her dream, Stephanie eagerly applied for the job at the *Tribune* office.

The man who interviewed Stephanie told her that the newspaper had many applicants. Some of the applicants had some experience working around a newspaper office and delivering papers.

Stephanie didn't get the job. She did find a part-time job in a fast-food restaurant, and she started saving money. She found out later that the person hired at the *Tribune* had been delivering papers for the company for several years.

The following school year Stephanie wrote an article about one of the school football games and took it to her school newspaper office. The teacher who was in charge of the newspaper liked her article and asked if Stephanie would like to start working on the school newspaper. Stephanie agreed. Throughout the year she wrote articles about sporting events and other afterschool activities, as well as special features on student projects.

This summer Stephanie saw another advertisement in the *Tribune* for a part-time office person. She applied again, this time taking with her several copies of the articles she had written during the year. The same man who had interviewed her before told her they had even more applicants this year. He told her that many of the applicants had worked for the *Tribune* delivering papers, but he promised to read her articles. The next day he called Stephanie and offered her the job.

Stephanie realized that part of making school count means getting involved outside of regular classwork. She plans to continue working on the school newspaper during the school year. She's also going to apply for another job with the *Tribune* next summer. She knows her chances will be better than ever.

What Do YOU Think?

Did Stephanie have the right attitude about job seeking? What else might Stephanie do to improve her chances of getting a job at the *Tribune* next summer?

courses, some people find areas that they hadn't thought of going into before. As they find out more about themselves, they find careers in which they are more interested. Taking courses outside their fields also helps people understand the "big picture" and get ahead in their jobs more quickly.

VOCATIONAL AND TRADE SCHOOLS

Vocation is another word for occupation. Vocation is the kind of work that a person does. You can probably guess what a *vocational school* is. It's a school where people learn a vocation. Vocational schools offer work-related programs for students to learn skills that lead directly to jobs. These schools teach the basic skills that a person needs to qualify for a job. They usually offer programs during the day and evening. The programs take different amounts of time.

vocation
the kind of work a person does, occupation.

Most take less than two years. Some students work while they are enrolled in the programs.

You can take a variety of programs in vocational schools. Some of the larger schools offer training in more than forty occupations. Listed here are just a few examples of the occupations you can prepare for at vocational schools:

- Air conditioning and refrigeration repairer.
- Baker.
- Barber.
- Computer repairer.
- Dental laboratory technician.
- Engraver.
- Gemologist.
- Hotel/motel manager.
- Interior designer.
- Medical assistant.
- Office machine repairer.
- Photographer.
- Secretary.
- Travel specialist.
- Truck driver.
- Welder.
- Word processor.
- X-ray technician.

The costs of vocational schools are often low. Because the government pays for many area and regional vocational schools, students pay very little. There are several vocational school guides that will give you more information. Many of the private vocational schools are expensive, but they often offer **grants.** A grant is a certain amount of money that can be used to pay for school. This money need not be paid back. Grants are different from *loans,* which do need to be repaid.

grant
a certain amount of money to be used for school tuition and expenses, which does not need to be paid back.

trade
an occupation that requires manual (physical) or mechanical skills.

A **trade** is an occupation that requires manual (physical) or mechanical skills. The trades include such areas as plumbing, carpentry, sheet metal work, and machining. You might wonder how a trade compares with a vocation. A trade is just a certain type of vocation. A vocation can be any kind of work. Only work that requires special mechanical or manual skills is called a trade.

Trade schools operate in much the same way as vocational schools. Almost all are privately owned, so the costs may be high unless you receive a grant.

ON-THE-JOB TRAINING

Some companies offer on-the-job training that can last from a few days to several years. The pay usually starts fairly low and gradually increases as you are trained.

Some industries offer in-plant training programs. Others send their workers to outside training courses. Some examples are on-the-job training to become a factory machine operator, a store manager, a salesperson, or a nursery worker.

To find out about on-the-job training programs, you can apply to your area's job service office of the state employment service. You can also apply directly to some companies.

APPRENTICESHIPS

An **apprentice** is a person learning how to do a certain job by working alongside a skilled worker. The most popular apprenticeship programs are offered in the trades.

apprentice a person learning a job (usually a trade) by working alongside a skilled worker.

Most apprenticeship training takes place on the job, with added classroom learning. The length of time varies from several years up to six years. One advantage of apprenticeships is the cost. You can earn money while you learn. You are paid less than skilled workers, but your pay increases as your skills increase.

Many apprenticeships are registered through the federal and state governments. You can get information from your guidance counselor or your state employment office. You can also write to the Department of Labor in Washington, D.C.

MILITARY SERVICE TRAINING

Many people choose to further their education through the military services. This training can be used later in civilian occupations.

◀ These West Point cadets will spend a specified period of time in the Army following their 4-year education. The service academies are supported by tax dollars, with highly competitive admissions standards.

There are about 1,500 different jobs for which the military offers training. The military services offer training in such areas as electronics, airplane mechanics, and computer technology. For some people this is a good way to learn a skill while they earn money.

Talk to your guidance counselor about military training. You can also get information from U.S. Army, Navy, Air Force, and Marine recruiting offices.

FINANCING YOUR EDUCATION

tuition
a fee charged for taking college courses.

Tuition is the fee that colleges charge you to take their classes. Besides paying tuition, college students must buy books, pay activity fees, and pay for room and board (food) if they live away from home. The cost will vary a great deal, depending on where you want to go.

If you have decided that you want to go to college, you're probably wondering how you are going to pay for it. There are many ways of paying for your education. You don't have to depend just on your parents to help you.

Making a careful career plan also means considering the need for money to pay for it. If you plan well, you may even be able to earn money while you learn.

▼ Working part-time in high school can help pay initial college costs.

The cost of different colleges varies a great deal. Community colleges are less expensive to attend than private colleges, four-year colleges, or universities. If you attended a local junior college you might pay very little tuition. Your expenses would be for books and a small student activity fee. Going to a local school would also mean you could live at home, so you wouldn't have to pay room-and-board fees.

State colleges and universities are colleges supported by public tax money. The tuition at these schools is less than at private colleges. You must be a resident of the state, or you will be charged out-of-state tuition. This is much higher than tuition for in-state students.

START NOW AND KEEP WORKING

If you know you want to go to college, you may want to start saving money now. Get part-time jobs after school, temporary jobs during holidays, and summer jobs. Start a savings account that you don't use for anything other than future college expenses.

There are also usually plenty of part-time jobs available for college students while they go to college. Many employers in college communities like to hire students. These employers will make up work schedules that don't interfere with your class and study schedules.

You may even be able to find a part-time job that will help you learn more about your career. A part-time job can give you work experiences that will help you in college and will help you in getting a job once you graduate. Employers look favorably on students who worked while they were going to school.

WORK-STUDY PROGRAMS

There are also work-study programs available through college financial aid offices. In Chapter 5 you learned about work-study programs available in high schools. Work-study programs are jobs that the college arranges for students to fit into their school schedules. Look for one that will help you learn more about the area you are studying.

FINANCIAL AID

You may be able to get some financial help in paying for your college expenses. You can apply for a variety of **scholarships.** A scholarship is an amount of money used to pay for someone's education. The person receiving the money does not have to repay it—it is a gift. Depending on the amount of the scholarship, it may pay for some or all of the college costs.

scholarship
an amount of money (which does not have to be repaid) used to pay for part or all of a person's education.

It is important to earn good grades throughout high school if you are planning to apply for scholarships. Many are based on grades and test scores. The students with the best grades and highest scores get the scholarships. It is also important to find out about them early so you won't miss any application deadlines.

Student loans are another way to pay for education. Loans differ from scholarships and grants in that loans must be repaid. *Guaranteed student loans* are loans made by private banks that the federal government guarantees. You must show a financial need to get these loans. You also must pay them back on schedule. *National direct student loans* are other direct loans to students for which you may apply.

Are you interested in military training? If so, you should learn more about the *Reserve Officers Training Corps (ROTC).* This program will pay all your college tuition. In exchange, you agree to spend a certain number of years in the military service after you graduate from college. You begin your service as an officer. You also have to put in a certain number of hours for ROTC training while you are in college.

Check with your guidance counselor, or look in the library or on the Internet to learn more about different kinds of scholarships, grants, and loans. Remember that there are deadlines for every one of them. Plan ahead, and apply on time.

Career Decision-Making Activities

1. Now is the time to begin thinking about and planning your future education and training. Select a class committee that will contact and invite representatives to your classroom from each of the following groups:
   - High school vocational programs.
   - Nearby four-year colleges.
   - Apprenticeship programs in your area.
   - Military services.
   - Nearby community colleges.
   - Nearby technical and business schools.

   As a class, prepare a list of questions to ask these representatives. Assign a student to introduce each guest and write a follow-up thank-you letter.
2. If you decide to go to college, how much will it cost? On a sheet of paper, make a budget for one year of college expenses. You may wish to discuss with your parents some of the personal expenses you are including. Try to be as accurate as possible. Your guidance counselor and school library are sources of college catalogs and college reference books containing expense information.

   Determine expenses for each of the following categories:
   - College tuition and fees.
   - Books and supplies.
   - Room and board.
   - Entertainment.
   - Medical and dental expenses.
   - Clothing.
   - Transportation.

   You may want to substitute technical school tuition and fees, or community college tuition and fees, in place of college tuition and fees, depending on your future education or training plans.

   Volunteer to list your budget on the board. After several classmates have posted their budgets, discuss the budgets in class. Which of your items, if any, are too high? Which ones are too low? What additional expenses should be included in a college budget?

▶ People who are interested in the military services might also investigate police work.

Review and Enrichment

Summarizing the Chapter

Summarizing information is a critical thinking skill that will help you succeed in the world of work. Write a summary of what you learned in Chapter 24. Focus on the main points of the chapter. Then in a class discussion, compare your summary with the summaries done by your classmates. Can you improve your summary?

Improving Your Career Vocabulary

Learning to use new vocabulary terms will improve your communication skills, which are important in almost all areas of work. Write definitions for the terms listed below. Then for each term, write an original sentence about yourself in which you use the term correctly.

- G.E.D. certificate
- program
- elective
- credit
- prerequisite
- bachelor's degree
- graduate school
- associate degree
- adult education
- vocation
- grant
- trade
- apprentice
- tuition
- scholarship

Finding the Facts

Finding exact information is a frequently used skill in many careers. Find the answers to the exercise below, and write the answers on a separate sheet of paper.

1. In what reference book can you find the education and training required for a certain job?
2. What five parts does the G.E.D. test contain?
3. How many years of college does a bachelor's degree require?
4. Which offers a more general education, a trade school or a community college?
5. How does on-the-job training differ from an apprenticeship?

Thinking for Yourself

To complete the exercise below you will need to use critical thinking and communication skills, which are skills valued by all employers. Write out your answers or be prepared to discuss them in class, depending on your teacher's instructions.

1. Have you ever saved money for something? How did achieving your goal make you feel? Explain.
2. Does learning something new make you excited? Tell about something you learned recently that you enjoyed.
3. What do you want from school? How can school help you in your career goals?
4. Do you know an adult who went back to school? Did that person seem to regard school differently than you did? If so, how?
5. If you had the means to go to the school of your choice after high school, which school would it be? Explain your choice.

Practicing Your Basic Skills

Your career success depends greatly on your basic math and communication skills. Work hard at improving in the areas where you have trouble with the following exercises.

Math

1. Dick earned one college credit for every hour of class per week. (In other words, if he had science five hours every week, he would earn five credits.) He took three hours of math and four hours of English. For physical education he earned half what he did for math. For speech he earned one-fourth of what he did for English. How many credits did he earn altogether?
2. Julio spent $17,557 for his first year at a private college. Half of that was for room and board, a quarter was for tuition, and a sixth was for fees. How much was left for general expenses?
3. Yin earns $4.78 an hour at a part-time job. Her books for trade school will cost her $37.99 and $18.56. How many hours will she have to work to pay for them?

Reading and Writing

1. Write a paragraph describing your ultimate career goal. Tell why you chose it.
2. Write your plan for education and training. Include names of any schools and courses in which you're interested.

REVIEW AND ENRICHMENT, CONTINUED

3. Obtain from your library pamphlets for schools such as colleges and trade schools. Read through them. Do any seem right for you?

Speaking and Listening

1. Talk to your family about your educational needs and career goals. Explain what you're working on in class. What does your family think?
2. Talk to your guidance counselor about getting more education. Listen to what he or she has to say.

Activities Working with Others

In almost all careers you must be able to get along well with other people to be successful. Work with your classmates to do the following activities. As you work together, pay attention to how well you get along. If necessary, work hard at improving your ability to do your part and to cooperate.

1. Look over your grades in school so far. Choose one class in which you will do better from now on. Go to that teacher and discuss ways you can improve. Make a plan for doing so.
2. With a classmate, make a chart of the educational opportunities in your town and the nearby area. Compare costs, travel distances, and courses offered for each alternative.

Decision Making and Problem Solving

You will be a big help to your employer if you can make decisions and solve problems. List all the possible ways of resolving the situations described below. Then pick the best alternative (possible choice), and tell why you chose it. If you need help, you might want to refer to Chapter 3.

1. You have a natural talent for accounting. Your parents and teachers encourage you to go on with it. The only problem is that the education and training you need costs more money than you have. Your parents can't help. Your boyfriend or girlfriend wants you to take any job you can get so you can get married. What will you do?
2. You want to be an electrician. You have taken a job as an apprentice that pays $7 an hour. You know that good electricians earn $25 an hour. Your best friend, who works in a factory, earns $10.75 an hour. After a year you are still making $7 and your friend is making $12. He's always buying things you'd like to buy. Your friend says you should quit your apprenticeship and go where the money is. What will you do?

CHAPTER 25

PLANNING YOUR FUTURE

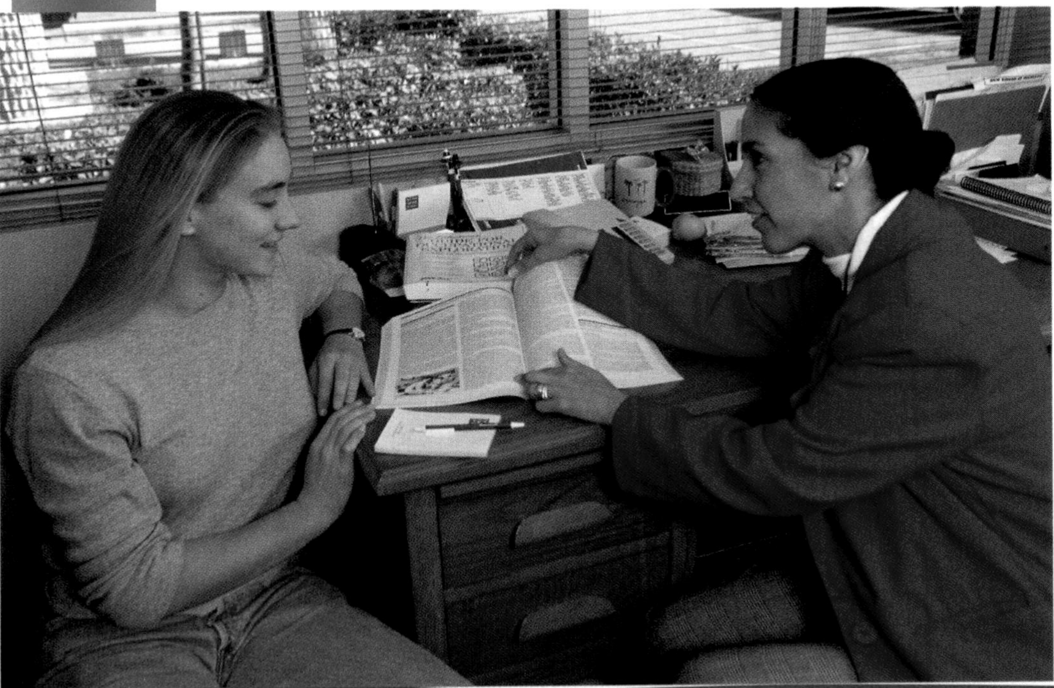

◆ Chapter Objectives ◆

After completing this chapter you will be able to do the following:

- ◆ Define the terms listed under "New Career Terms."
- ◆ List and explain at least six reasons why planning is important.
- ◆ Explain why short-term goals are important.
- ◆ Develop a personal career plan.

◆ New Career Terms ◆

In this chapter you will learn the meanings of the following career terms:

- ✔ Procrastinator
- ✔ Short-term goal
- ✔ Long-term goal
- ✔ Browser
- ✔ Flexibility
- ✔ Contingency plan

How often have you heard people say they should have done things differently? How often have you heard people say they'd like to go back in time and do things over? How often have you heard the words, "If I'd only known then what I know now"?

People who say these things probably knew more "then" than they think. If they had made a plan before they set out, though, they might not have so many regrets. They would probably be much happier. The outcomes would probably have been much more to their liking.

People will always make mistakes. No one can predict the future. But we can cut down on those mistakes and regrets. We can do this by making wise plans and following through with them.

If Roberto had planned more carefully, he wouldn't be feeling so lost. His lack of planning could affect his entire future and how happy his life will be. There is no substitute for planning if you want to reach your goals. *Having a plan doesn't guarantee success, but it greatly improves your chances.*

Roberto learned the importance of planning and will now have to make a plan of action to make up for his mistakes. He will have to work harder, but he can still make a plan to reach his dreams.

BENEFITS OF HAVING A PLAN

Have you ever opened your eyes in the morning and dreaded the day ahead because you just had too much to do? You didn't see any possible way to get everything done? You didn't even know where to begin?

You didn't finish your homework or study for the test first period. Your best friend's birthday is today, but you didn't buy a present. Worse yet, you didn't save any money for the present. You'll have to borrow money and pay it back with the money you were going to use for new shoes. You just remembered that you said you'd go to a game with your brother—at exactly the same time as a job interview you scheduled. You wish you had planned better.

A plan can save you time, effort, and money. It can make your life easier. It also helps you remember what needs to be done and when it needs to be done.

Planning will help in several ways. Here are six benefits of having a plan:

1. A plan helps you get organized so you don't miss out on things you want to do. It helps you fit everything important into your schedule. You'll be surprised how much more time it seems you have when you plan your time well.
2. A plan makes you sort through things *in order of importance.* You can *make a list* with the most important things first. This way, the important things will get done.
3. A plan helps you avoid being a procrastinator. A **procrastinator** is a person who always puts things off. The world is filled with procrastinators. They usually don't get much done. They also are the ones who complain about never having enough time.

procrastinator
a person who puts off doing things or making decisions.

Planning Will Help

Roberto decided as early as junior high that his ideal career goal would be to become a petroleum engineer, because that's what his uncle did. When he entered high school he spoke to his guidance counselor about what kind of preparations he could begin making that would lead him on the track of becoming a petroleum engineer. The counselor told Roberto that he would need math, physics, and chemistry to enter most engineering schools. The counselor explained that Roberto would need a four-year bachelor's degree and that the closest engineering school was in another state. This meant that Roberto would have to work to save money for out-of-state tuition. He also could get grades that would allow him to get a scholarship. If he did not get good grades, he would have to plan on taking out a student loan.

For the next two years Roberto was involved with the drama club and football. He found that those extra activities kept him too busy to work at all. He also decided to put off the classes he needed until he was a senior. He didn't plan. He just took whatever classes fit in with his football and drama schedule.

When Roberto went into his senior year he found out that he needed a certain math class before he could take chemistry or physics. It was too late to take them all.

Two weeks before Roberto graduated, he decided to apply to the engineering school. The guidance counselor told him that the application deadline had passed three months ago. Anyway, his grades were probably not good enough to get him in. They definitely weren't good enough to apply for a scholarship. The counselor told Roberto he hadn't taken the courses the college would look for before they accepted him.

Roberto left her office wondering how he could have let everything slip for so long. He knew his grades were poor because he hadn't spent enough time on schoolwork.

He wondered what he was going to do now. He had always thought things would just automatically fall into place. He realized how wrong he had been not to plan ahead so he could reach his goals.

What Do YOU Think?

What did Roberto do wrong? What can he do now? How would planning have helped Roberto?

The more you put off getting things done, the more they pile up and turn into big burdens. A plan helps you get things done when they need to be done.

4. A plan gives you a sense of accomplishment and satisfaction. When you complete each item on your plan, you can cross it out or check it off. You can feel like you're getting somewhere. You will feel like you are moving forward toward your goal.
5. A plan can save you energy. If you don't have a plan, you will waste energy and time doing things that aren't necessary. A plan helps you focus on what needs to be done and prevents you from wasting your energy and time.
6. A plan can save you from embarrassment and from forgetting important events. Without a plan, people sometimes schedule two things at the same time or forget important events in their lives.

▶ A plan prevents you from being a procrastinator.

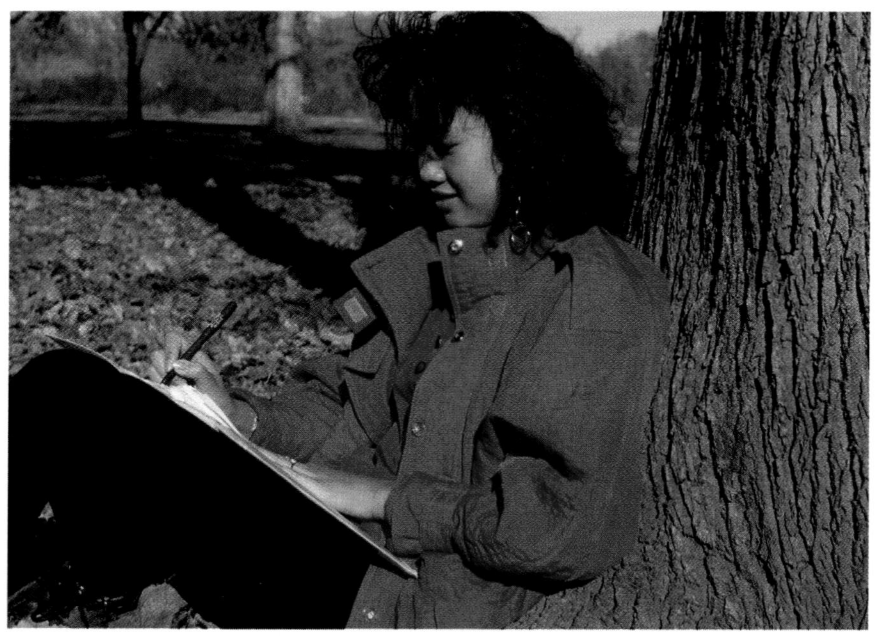

SHORT-TERM AND LONG-TERM GOALS

You know by now that goals are pictures in your mind of what you want your life to be like. Goals are all the things you want to accomplish. Without these "bigger pictures," it is easy just to drift along like a spaceship without a guidance system. You will never reach your destination—where you want to go.

Setting goals helps you move from where you are now to where you want to be. Goals are targets you aim for in your life. They give your life a sense of direction. They put meaning in what you do. They focus your energy. As you reach your goals, you will find that you gain confidence in yourself.

A **short-term goal** is something you want to achieve in a fairly short period of time. Short-term goals are stepping-stones along the way to long-term goals. They can give you daily "booster shots" as you accomplish them. You then get to think about how they help you get closer to your long-term goals. Setting short-term goals is a good way to start.

A **long-term goal** is an ultimate (final) goal that usually takes a long time to reach. Achieving each long-term goal usually takes many steps. Long-term goals take careful thought and planning. They usually involve many short-term goals along the way. Your long-term goals should be tied up with your values and dreams.

short-term goal
an objective to be achieved in a relatively short space of time that can be used as a step towards achieving a long-term goal.

long-term goal
an ultimate future target or objective, which is usually reached by first accomplishing many short-term goals.

THE IMPORTANCE OF SETTING SHORT-TERM GOALS

Setting short-term goals will help you know if your long-term goals are right for you. Let's say you have a long-term goal to become a veterinarian. You've heard that veterinarians make relatively high incomes, and the work sounds interesting.

You then set some short-term goals. One might be to take a science course where you learn about animal anatomy (structure) by dissecting (cutting into) a frog. Another might be to get a part-time job in a zoo helping clean and feed the animals. You might find out that you don't like cleaning and feeding animals. You might find out that you don't like cutting into animals and memorizing all their different body parts.

What should you do then? You might decide that you want to change your long-term goal of becoming a veterinarian. In your attempt to reach your short-term goals, you avoided a long-term mistake.

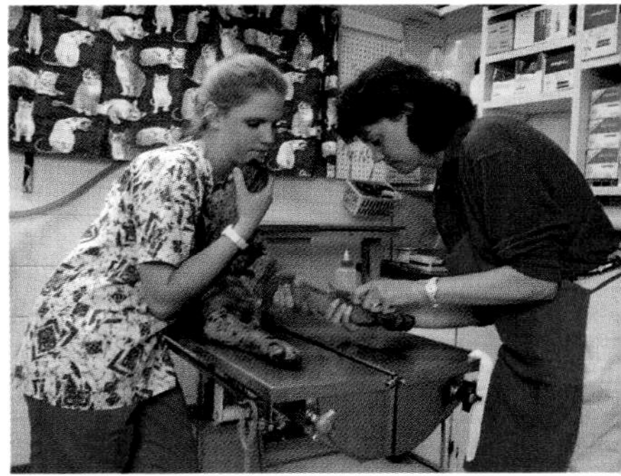

▲ What part-time jobs will help you develop the knowledge and skills needed to reach your career goal?

Attitude makes a difference

Josh Finds a Way

Josh grew up on a farm. He knew he wanted to live and work in a farm lifestyle. But he realized that most farmers in his area were not doing well. He knew he would have difficulty being successful as a farmer. Josh decided that the best career for him would be to have his own crop-dusting business. He set a long-term goal of learning to fly an airplane and buying his own plane. He wanted to start his own business in his area of the state.

Josh's guidance counselor helped him come up with a plan and some short-term goals. He took agriculture courses in school and joined Future Farmers of America. He continued working on his family's farm. He learned as much as he could about the crops in that area.

When Josh graduated, he didn't have enough money to buy an airplane or take a training program to become a pilot. It didn't look as if there were any way for him to reach his goal. Josh kept a positive attitude, though. He was determined to find a way.

Josh did some research. He found out that if he joined the air force he could become a pilot while he saved enough money for a down payment on his own airplane.

After Josh finished his time and training in the Air Force, he planned to work full-time at a fertilizer plant to save the rest of the money he needed to buy his airplane. He also planned to take night courses in business. This education would help him when he opened his crop-dusting business.

What Do YOU Think?

Write a list of all the steps in Josh's plan. What else could he have done to reach his long-term goal? Was he being realistic at first?

GOALS HELP YOU MEASURE

There's another important benefit to setting short-term goals. They help you know if you are on the right track, one that leads to your long-term goal. They help you measure your progress.

Let's say your long-term goal is to own your own service station. You may set your first short-term goal as getting a part-time job pumping gas. Your next short-term goal might be to get a full-time, on-the-job training position as a mechanic. Your next goal might be to become a service department supervisor and then work your way toward becoming a station manager.

As you reach each short-term goal, you will know you are making progress toward your ultimate goal. You can keep track of your progress.

Career Decision-Making Activities

1. Make a time diary for a week. Use a separate sheet of paper for each day. Put the name of a day at the top of each sheet. Be sure to include Saturday and Sunday. Divide each sheet into three parts:

- Morning (from getting out of bed until lunch).
- Afternoon (from lunch until dinner).
- Evening (from dinner until bedtime).

For each day write answers to the following questions in your time diary.

a. How much time did you spend doing things you were made to do by others? How much time was spent doing things you selected?

b. How do you feel about the way you spent your time during each part of the day? Did you make good use of your time? Could you have used your time more effectively?

c. What did you enjoy most today?

d. What did you enjoy least today?

e. What did you do or learn today that will help you the most with your career in the future?

f. What did you do or learn today that will be least helpful to you in the future?

For the first two questions (*a* and *b*), write answers for each of the three parts of the day (morning, afternoon, and evening). For each of the remaining questions (*c* through *f*), write *one* answer. Write your answers for *a* through *f* on the part of the day when the event you're talking about took place. At the end of the week you should have a seven-page diary. Be prepared to discuss in class what you have learned about time.

2. On a sheet of paper, write down one goal you would like to achieve before you graduate from high school. Under the goal write the short-term goals that will take you closer to your final goal. In a class discussion read your final goal. Have your classmates suggest short-term goals for your final goal. Did your classmates think of any short-term goals you didn't already have?

DEVELOPING A CAREER PLAN

Have you ever decided you wanted something very badly and then carefully planned out every step you needed to take to get it? Don't be embarrassed if your answer is no. Many people spend their whole lives without planning. They "play it by ear," "see what comes up," or "take things as they come." Then they wonder why they never get what they want.

Nothing worthwhile comes easily. Time, effort, and planning are required. Usually the biggest obstacle is making a decision. Many people can't decide what they want, so they just drift or plod along, waiting for something to happen. They can't plan how to reach their goals, because they can't decide what their goals are.

You have already learned how to take the first and most difficult step in planning: you learned about making decisions in Chapter 3. Now it's time to do some research to find out what steps you must take to reach your goals. Then you must write down a detailed plan of action for yourself.

WRITING YOUR PLAN

Even if you're tired of making lists, you've probably found out by now that they do help. They help you stay on track. They help you check your progress over the weeks and months.

Writing down your short-term goals forces you to come up with more specific plans. It lets you know if you are making progress toward your ultimate goals. Make a flexible career plan by following these steps:

1. At the top of a sheet of paper write down your career goal. Write next to it any specific wants that you have, such as where you want to live or certain responsibilities you want.
2. Take out three other sheets of paper. Write "High School" at the top of one, "Education and Training" at the top of the second, and "Work Experience" at the top of the third.
3. On each sheet list all the courses, activities, or jobs that are the short-term steps that will help you reach your career goal. Be as specific as possible. Ask teachers, guidance counselors, or people in the field you are interested in to help you.
4. Go over each list, and assign dates to each short-term step.
5. Go over your list and dates. Decide what you will have to do to take each step. Decide which steps are most important and what order they should follow.
6. On another sheet of paper write your plan of action. List every step in the order that you need to do it. List all your steps according to the dates when you must get things done.
7. Check your plan from time to time. Revise it if you need to do so. Don't change it for the wrong reasons, though, such as procrastination.

Remember that your decisions and plans are not set in cement. You can always change them. The advantage of having a plan is that you are moving ahead and that you are moving with direction. Even as you change your goals and plans, you will still be getting closer to a career that is right for you.

DEVELOPING BETTER WAYS TO SEARCH ONLINE

When you go to the library, you know that there are ways to search in the library's card catalog. The World Wide Web is bigger than any library in the world. Therefore, a way to search it quickly had to be found.

Today there are many ways to search for what you want online. There are programs with such strange names as Yahoo!, Lycos, Infoseek, and Excite. The formal name for programs that help you search online is **browsers,** for they allow you to browse, or casually look around, online. A new job today is that of a browser developer—someone who helps improve the existing online search programs.

browser
the formal name for a program that helps you browse or casually look around online.

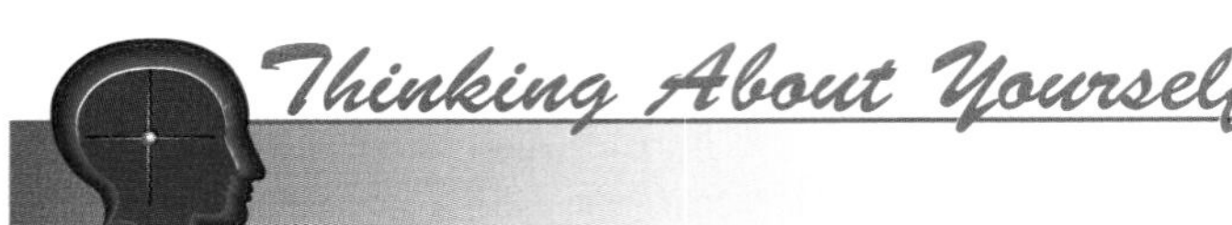

Thinking About Yourself

My Goals

Ask yourself the following questions:

- **Are my goals realistic?** Dream big, but know your limitations. If you are five feet tall, you will probably never play basketball for the Los Angeles Lakers. If you have looked closely at your aptitudes and abilities, you should be able to set realistic goals.
- **Are my goals specific?** Having specific goals makes it easier to know what to do to reach them. Saying "I want to be successful" isn't specific enough. Saying "I want to be a successful interactive video game designer" is specific.
- **Are my goals my own?** Make sure you know what you want for yourself, not what other people want you to do.
- **Do I set deadlines for my goals?** Know the difference between long- and short-term goals, but don't leave them open-ended. Set some "due dates" for yourself, and try to stick to them.
- **Are my goals in agreement with my values?** Your values are very important to consider when setting goals. Think carefully about what your values are before you set long-term goals.

If your long-term goal is to become a commercial artist, set short-term goals as well that might include entering your best work in a local art competition.

FLEXIBILITY AND CONTINGENCY PLANS

When making plans, remember to be flexible. Sometimes the unexpected will ruin your plan. **Flexibility** is the ability to adapt to changes. For example, suppose that you are planning a camping trip. At the last minute, you discover that the canoe you were going to borrow is not available. You could adjust the plan and rent a canoe instead. Of course, to do so you must have set aside some extra money that you can use to rent a canoe.

In fact, your original plan should have included setting aside some extra money to rent a canoe—just in case you couldn't borrow one. This kind of plan, which provides an alternative or backup, is called a **contingency plan.** (Something that is contingent is possible but may not happen.) It is always a good idea to have a contingency plan in case your original scheme doesn't work.

flexibility
the ability to adapt to changes in the established plan.

contingency plan
a kind of plan which provides an alternative or backup in case the established method is altered.

Career Decision-Making Activities

Now is your chance to be a guidance counselor. Pick one of the seven students below to advise. Review the career goals of your student. Then develop a plan that will lead that student to his or her career goal. In a class discussion share the career plan you have developed for that student. Ask the class to respond to your plan.

1. Rosa is a freshman in high school. Her career goal is to become an electrician as soon as possible. She is good in math and helped her uncle, who is an electrician, this past summer. She must support herself as soon as she graduates from high school.
2. Christopher is a sophomore in high school. His career goal is to become a commercial artist upon graduation from college. He is somewhat talented in drawing but does poorly in his English and social studies courses. He will have some financial help from his family when he goes to college.
3. Jennifer is a ninth grader. Her career goal is to own and manage a successful resort hotel by the time she is thirty. She will have to support herself shortly after high school. She is excellent in all subjects but is shy around adults.
4. Joji is a junior in high school. His career goal is to become a psychologist after graduation from college. He will have to support himself through college, but he can keep his expenses down by living at home. He is very good in all subjects except math.
5. Erica is a senior in high school. Her career goal is to make the world a better place by helping others. She is undecided about a career. Her favorite subjects are music, art, and science. She gets along well with everyone.
6. Carlos is a freshman in high school. His career goal is to become a commercial fisher and own his own boat by age twenty-five.
7. Samantha is a seventh grader. Her career goal is to become a biomedical researcher by the time she is twenty-four.

Review and Enrichment

Summarizing the Chapter

Summarizing information is a critical thinking skill that will help you succeed in the world of work. Write a summary of what you learned in Chapter 25. Focus on the main points of the chapter. Then in a class discussion, compare your summary with the summaries done by your classmates. Can you improve your summary?

Improving Your Career Vocabulary

Learning to use new vocabulary terms will improve your communication skills, which are important in almost all areas of work. Write definitions for the terms listed below. Then for each term, write an original sentence about yourself in which you use the term correctly.

- procrastinator
- short-term goal
- long-term goal
- browser
- flexibility
- contingency plan

Finding the Facts

Finding exact information is a frequently used skill in many careers. Find the answers to the exercise below, and write the answers on a separate sheet of paper.

1. What three things can a plan save you?
2. Name the advantages of having a plan.
3. How can a plan save energy?
4. What is the difference between a short-term goal and a long-term goal?
5. Name the five questions you should ask yourself when setting a goal.

Thinking for Yourself

To complete the exercise below you will need to use critical thinking and communication skills, which are skills valued by all employers. Write out your answers or be prepared to discuss them in class, depending on your teacher's instructions.

1. Have you ever procrastinated? How did it affect what you wanted to do?
2. Describe the last time you felt a sense of accomplishment.
3. Have you ever set a goal that was unrealistic? What happened?
4. Tell about a time when you made a plan and used it to reach a goal.
5. Have you ever missed an opportunity because you didn't have a good plan? Explain.

Practicing Your Basic Skills

Your career success depends greatly on your basic math and communication skills. Work hard at improving in the areas where you have trouble with the following exercises.

Math

1. John's plan is to choose a job when he's seventeen and work until he's sixty-five. If you could see his future, you'd know he will change jobs an average of once every five years. He will consider changing jobs and then not do so three times as often as he actually does. How many times will he need to make a job-related decision after his initial career decision?
2. Sary planned to graduate from high school in June of 2001. She would go to four years of college and three years of medical school. Then after two years of residency at a hospital, she'd get her medical degree. In what year would she become a doctor?
3. There were eighteen students in Mike's college English class. After two weeks, one-third dropped out. At midterm another one-sixth knew they had failed. How many passed the course?

Reading and Writing

1. Write a paragraph describing something in your life that would have gone better if you had developed a plan.
2. Write a one-page story about a person who drifts through life having no plan.

Speaking and Listening

1. Talk to your family and friends about plans they have made and goals they have set. How did the plans work out?

Review and Enrichment, continued

2. Listen to what your family and friends say as you do Activity 1. Did they think things through when making the plan? Were their goals realistic?

Activities Working with Others

In almost all careers you must be able to get along well with other people to be successful. Work with others to do the following activities. As you work together, pay attention to how well you get along. If necessary, work hard at improving your ability to do your part and to cooperate.

1. With a classmate, make a plan to do something after school one day soon. Write out your plan in detail.
2. The next time your family plans to do something together, make a list of the steps taken in working out the goal. Are the steps complete? What, if anything, would have made the goal easier to reach?

Decision Making and Problem Solving

You will be a big help to your employer if you can make decisions and solve problems. List all the possible ways of resolving the situations described below. Then pick the best alternative (possible choice), and tell why you chose it. If you need help, you might want to refer to Chapter 3.

1. You work on Saturday at a part-time job that doesn't pay a lot. One day your guidance counselor says she can get you a nonpaying job doing just the kind of work you want to try. The only problem is that it, too, is done on Saturday. What will you do?
2. You have just graduated from high school with good grades. You carried through with your career plan and now have a job waiting for you after a short vacation. The sun is shining, and you feel great. Your best friend calls and asks if you have plans. You say you planned to go home and watch a little TV. He invites you to a party. What will you do?

EMPLOYMENT TABLES

FASTEST GROWING OCCUPATIONS

Covered in the 1998-99 Occupational Outlook Handbook, 1996-2006
(Numbers in thousands of jobs)

OCCUPATION	Employment Change, 1996—2006 Number	Percent	MOST SIGNIFICANT SOURCE OF TRAINING
Database administrators, computer support specialists, and all other computer scientists	249	118	Bachelor's degree
Computer engineers	235	109	Bachelor's degree
Systems analysts	520	103	Bachelor's degree
Personal and home care aides	171	85	Short-term on-the-job training
Physical and corrective therapy assistants and aides	66	79	Moderate-term on-the-job training
Home health aides	378	76	Short-term on-the-job training
Medical assistants	166	74	Moderate-term on-the-job training
Desktop publishing specialists	22	74	Long-term on-the-job training
Physical therapists	81	71	Bachelor's degree
Occupational therapy assistants and aides	11	69	Moderate-term on-the-job training
Paralegals	76	68	Associate's degree
Occupational therapists	38	66	Bachelor's degree
Teachers, special education	241	59	Bachelor's degree
Human services workers	98	55	Moderate-term on-the-job training
Data processing equipment repairers	42	52	Postsecondary vocational training
Medical records technicians	44	51	Associate's degree
Speech-language pathologists and audiologists	44	51	Master's degree
Dental hygienists	64	48	Associate's degree
Amusement and recreation attendants	138	48	Short-term on-the-job training
Physician assistants	30	47	Bachelor's degree

EMPLOYMENT TABLES

OCCUPATIONS WITH LARGEST PROJECTED JOB GROWTH

Covered in the 1998-99 Occupational Outlook Handbook, 1996-2006
(Numbers in thousands of jobs)

OCCUPATION	Employment Change, 1996—2006 Number	Percent	MOST SIGNIFICANT SOURCE OF TRAINING
Cashiers	530	17	Short-term on-the-job training
Systems analysts	520	103	Bachelor's degree
General managers and top executives	467	15	Work experience plus bachelor's and/or higher degree
Registered nurses	411	21	Associate's degree
Salespersons, retail	408	10	Moderate-term on-the-job training
Truck drivers, light and heavy	404	15	Short-term on-the-job training
Home health aides	378	76	Short-term on-the-job training
Teacher aides and educational assistants	370	38	Short-term on-the-job training
Nursing aides, orderlies, and attendants	333	25	Short-term on-the-job training
Receptionists and information clerks	318	30	Short-term on-the-job training
Teachers, secondary school	312	22	Bachelor's degree
Childcare workers	299	36	Short-term on-the-job training
Clerical supervisors and managers	262	19	Work experience in related occupation
Database administrators, computer support specialists, and all other computer scientists	249	118	Bachelor's degree
Marketing and sales worker supervisors	246	11	Work experience in related occupation
Maintenance repairers, general utility	246	18	Long-term on-the-job training
Food counter, fountain and related workers	243	14	Short-term on-the-job training
Teachers, special education	241	59	Bachelor's degree
Computer engineers	235	109	Bachelor's degree
Food preparation workers	234	19	Short-term on-the-job training

GLOSSARY

(Number in parentheses indicates chapter number in which term first appears)

accommodate to give others something they need or want. (14)

accommodations places to stay while on a trip, such as a hotel or resort. (14)

administration management or supervisory personnel. (19)

adult education programs designed for adults who want to retrain for new careers or improve skills for advancement in their current career area (also called *continuing education*). (24)

advertise to inform people about a product by means such as radio, television, the Internet, newspapers, and magazines. (17)

advocate to speak or write in favor of a cause or causes. (10)

aerobics a type of physical conditioning. (14)

agribusiness the entire process or business of producing, processing, and distributing agricultural products. (6)

Agribusiness and Natural Resources Cluster a group of occupations involved in producing, regulating, conserving, and guaranteeing the quality of the raw materials used for food, shelter, energy, and comfort. (6)

agriculture the science of cultivating the soil and producing crops (farming) and raising livestock. (6)

applicant a person applying for a job. (21)

application form a questionnaire used by employers to obtain basic information from applicants and to determine their suitability for a job. (21)

apprentice a person learning a job (usually a trade) by working alongside a skilled worker. (24)

aptitude ability or potential for learning new skills. (2)

aquaculture cultivating or growing marine life under controlled conditions, usually to be sold for consumption. (16)

associate degree a certificate of completion awarded to a person after completing a program of study in a particular area, usually lasting two years. (24)

attitude a person's outlook on life, usually positive or negative. (1)

automation use of machines to replace human labor. (22)

bachelor's degree a certificate of completion awarded to people after they successfully complete a required set of college courses in both general and specific areas, usually lasting four years. (24)

bacteria special types of microorganisms that have only one cell. (11)

blue-collar job a job having to do with industrial or factory work. (19)

body image the way you look, and a mental picture of how you *think* you look. (4)

browser the formal name for a program that helps you browse or casually look around online. (25)

budget a plan for spending and saving money over a specific period of time. (10)

Business and Office Technology Cluster a group of occupations involved in managing and organizing businesses and offices. (7)

CAD/CAM Computer-Aided Design/Computer-Aided Manufacturing—translating an engineering design into a manufactured product with the use of computers. (15)

capitalism an economic system that allows people to make their own individual economic decisions and encourages competition. (22)

career work done over a period of years in one area of interest. (1)

Career Cluster a group of similar occupations. (6)

chain of command the way that authority is distributed in an organization. (4)

check stub the part of a paycheck that lists deductions from wages. (21)

civil service test a preemployment test developed by the federal government for specific government jobs. (19)

classified section the section of the newspaper that contains short advertisements in categories, such as "help-wanted" ads. (21)

co-worker a fellow worker. (21)

commission a percentage of what an agent sells, which is received by the agent as income. (7)

communications ways in which people share ideas and information (for example, conversation and the media). (8)

Communications and Media Cluster a group of occupations involved in designing, preparing, and sending information and messages. (8)

competition rivalry, activities in which companies try to outsell each other. (22)

compromise a situation in which two sides of a differing opinion give up something to reach an agreement. (21)

computer-aided design (CAD) using a computer and special software to create designs. (9)

conflict of values when you have one or more values that you can't satisfy at the same time. (2)

Construction Technology Cluster a group of occupations involved in planning, designing, building, and repairing structures of all kinds. (9)

consumer one who buys and uses goods and services. (10)

contingency plan a kind of plan which provides an alternative or backup in case the established method is altered. (25)

cope to face and deal with problems or responsibilities. (22)

corporation a business owned by many people but treated by the law as though it were one person. (23)

cosmetology improving the appearance of skin, hair, and nails. (18)

credit a unit of measurement used by schools to determine a student's progress. (24)

curator a person who is in charge of the whole museum and its research. (12)

data information (facts, numbers, measurements, etc.) used as a basis for reasoning, discussion or calculation important to business. (7)

decision choosing between two or more possibilities. (3)

decision-making process steps that can be taken to help you make the best decision. (3)

deduction an amount of money taken from an employee's gross pay for taxes, insurance, social security, or other benefits. (21)

democracy a system of government where the power is vested in the people. (22)

destination a place that a person is traveling to, or where a thing is sent. (20)

dietitian a person who plans and directs food service programs, including preparation and delivery in hospitals and cafeterias. (10)

discriminate treating someone unfairly because of his or her race, religion, or sex. (21)

distraction anything that draws attention away from what you really want to be doing. (4)

distribute the act of getting a product to consumers (distribution decisions include where to sell, how to sell, how to ship, etc.). (17)

domestic of or relating to the household or family. (18)

DOT *Dictionary of Occupational Titles*—a guide containing descriptions of jobs organized by numbered code into related groups. (5)

drive motivation, the ambition and energy to do something productive. (12)

economic system the method of producing, distributing, and exchanging goods and services in a society. (22)

elective a course that is not required but can be chosen by a student according to his or her interest. (24)

employer the person who has hired another to do a job. (21)

employment agency an organization that tries to match qualified people with jobs, sometimes for a fee. (21)

endorse to sign the back of a paycheck made

payable to you, which permits the bank to cash it. (21)

engineering the use of science and math to solve problems in manufacturing and other industries. (15)

enterprise a project undertaken. (22)

entrepreneur a person who organizes, manages, and assumes the risks of a business. (23)

entry-level job a job for a beginner to start with to train for higher-level jobs. (5)

environment everything around us including air, water, minerals, plants, animals, and insects. (11)

Environmental Sciences Cluster a group of occupations involved in the conservation and protection of our environment and also the safe and healthful use of products made from our natural resources. (11)

environmental scientist a person involved in helping to protect our air, water, animals, plants, and other natural resources from pollution or its effects. (11)

ergonomics the study of office environments and how to improve them. (7)

ethics the rules or principles by which a person lives. (4)

evaluate to look at closely and judge. (3)

experience duties or jobs you have done that will help your performance in future jobs. (5)

extraction the act of removing or "taking out." (16)

Family and Consumer Sciences Cluster a group of occupations involved in developing, producing, and managing goods and services that improve the quality of home life. (10)

family interaction the experiences that take place involving family members. (10)

fee a certain amount of money or a percentage of salary charged by an agency for their help in finding you a job. (21)

fine arts activities concerned with the creation of beautiful performances or objects such as symphonies, ballets, paintings, and sculptures. (12)

Fine Arts and Humanities Cluster careers that are grouped together because they all involve developing, promoting, and preserving the social and moral values of a culture and the value of art and beauty. (12)

flexibility the ability to adapt to changes in the established plan. (25)

free enterprise system an economic system in which people make their own economic decisions. (22)

freight goods, or cargo, to be shipped. (20)

G.E.D. certificate (General Educational Development certificate) a document stating that a person has passed a five-part test in the areas of writing, social studies, science, reading, and math. (24)

goal an objective or target to be reached by directing your thoughts and energy. (1)

GOE *Guide for Occupational Exploration*—book giving information on career areas. (5)

goods tangible/useful products that are made and sold. (22)

graduate school a program of study beyond a bachelor's degree. (24)

grant a certain amount of money to be used for school tuition and expenses, which does not need to be paid back. (24)

gross pay the total amount of an employee's earnings before deductions are taken out. (21)

Health and Medical Cluster the group of all occupations involved in providing the services necessary to meet people's physical and mental health needs. (13)

help-wanted ad a newspaper notice (paid for by an employer) describing a job opening. (21)

hospitality the friendly reception and treatment of guests. (14)

Hospitality and Recreation Cluster occupations involved in providing pleasure for people involved in leisure-time activities. (14)

human resources employees or workers. (15)

humanities the study of subjects having to do with people. (12)

income tax the part of earnings that people must legally give to the government to pay for government services. (21)

individual responsibility being accountable, or

responsible, for ourselves and our actions. (4)

initiative doing something that needs to be done without having to be asked. (18)

integrity the quality of being honest, both to yourself and others. (4)

interest something a person enjoys doing or thinking about. (2)

interest inventory a questionnaire that helps people determine what their interests are. (2)

interrelate to communicate with and get along with other people. (10)

interview a formal meeting between an employer and job applicant to help both parties make a decision about whom to hire. (21)

job being employed by a person or company to perform certain tasks and being paid for the work. (1)

job duty a task you are expected to perform on the job. (5)

job family groups of jobs with similar characteristics. (6)

job lead any information about possible job openings. (21)

labor the resource of employed workers. (19)

labor union a group of workers who have organized to increase their wages or improve their working conditions. (19)

laser a device that produces a very concentrated beam of intense light that can pierce through solid objects, such as metal. (15)

law of demand an economic rule stating that as the price of a good or service falls, a larger quantity will be bought; as the price of a good or service rises, a smaller quantity will be bought. (22)

law of supply an economic rule that at higher prices a larger quantity of a product will generally be supplied than at lower prices. (22)

life values things that are important in your life such as family values and social values. (2)

linguistics the structure of speech. (12)

lodging a place to spend the night or stay for a short time. (18)

long-term goal an ultimate future target or objective, which is usually reached by first accomplishing many short-term goals. (25)

loss the amount of money a company loses when it spends more money than it earns. (22)

low self-esteem a poor self-concept or self-image. (4)

manufacturing the process of making from raw materials products that people can use. (15)

Manufacturing Technology Cluster a group of occupations involved in the design and assembly of goods. (15)

marine of or relating to the sea. (16)

marine science the study of the sea and the plants and animals that live in it. (16)

Marine Science Cluster jobs that discover, develop, and improve marine life and the products we can use from the ocean. (16)

market research a study to determine what influences someone's buying decisions. (17)

Marketing and Distribution Cluster a group of occupations involved in getting products from the producer to the consumer and in influencing the customer to buy a product. (17)

mass media means of communication by which information is distributed to the general public (newspapers, magazines, radio, television, the Internet). (4)

media means of communication such as newspapers, television, radio, magazines, and the Internet that influence people widely. (8)

merchandise the vast array of products bought and sold by businesses. (17)

microorganism extremely small living things that are only visible under a microscope. (11)

module units that fit or work together (for example, prefabricated houses are made from separate factory-made modules put together on the home site). (9)

natural resource a useful material provided by nature; natural resources include soil, gold, trees, water, and minerals. (6)

needs things you must have to survive. (3)

net pay the amount of a paycheck after deductions are taken out. (21)

nutritionist a person who studies the effects of food on the human body. (10)

occupation the type of job a person is employed in. (1)

offshore drilling the activity of obtaining oil and natural gas off the shore of a continent or island. (16)

OOH *Occupational Outlook Handbook*—a guide for researching careers. (5)

organism an individual living thing, such as a person, animal, or plant. (11)

overtime time worked in addition to the amount normally scheduled. (21)

part-time job a job less than 40 hours per week, such as an after-school or weekend job. (5)

partnership a business that two or more people own and operate. (23)

perfectionist a person who is uncomfortable with mistakes or flaws. (4)

persistence the quality of sticking with something in spite of difficulties—not giving up. (23)

Personal Services Cluster occupations that involve providing people with the services they want to make their lives more pleasurable. (18)

petroleum an oily, flammable liquid obtained from wells drilled in the ground, which is refined into gasoline, fuel oils, and other products. (6)

pharmacy a store for dispensing medical drugs, a drugstore. (13)

plan the method or course you decide to take after going through the decision-making process. (3)

plant factory (most manufactured goods are made in factories). (15)

pollution the introduction of harmful elements (such as man-made waste) into the environment. (11)

prerequisite a class that is required before another higher level course can be taken. (24)

procedure a rule or method of accomplishing a task. (21)

processing a series of actions or operations as a means to conclusion (for example, processing data would involve entering, storing, sorting, retrieving, and editing the data). (7)

procrastinator a person who puts off doing things or making decisions. (25)

producer one who makes and sells goods and services. (22)

profession a career that requires specialized training and academic preparation. (13)

professional a person who works in a profession (a career that requires special knowledge and usually many years of schooling). (13)

profit the amount of money a business takes in that is more than the amount it spends. (22)

program a group of school courses that relate to each other. (24)

promote to advertise and encourage people to purchase a product. (17)

public the people of our nation as a whole. (19)

Public Services Cluster a group of occupations involved in providing services to the public (most are paid for with tax dollars). (19)

punctuality being on time for work. (21)

quarry a big pit from which limestone and other kinds of stone are removed. (6)

radiation particles of energy (given off by certain natural elements in nature; also produced by X-ray machines; and present in nuclear power plant waste). (11)

recreation a means of refreshing yourself by relaxation and enjoyment. (14)

reference a person who will give a favorable report of a job applicant to the prospective employer. (21)

regulatory controlling how things occur; to direct according to rule. (19)

research finding out more by reading and talking to people. (5)

resource any skill or advantage you have. (3)

résumé a short written description of an applicant's

personal data, education, background, and experience related to a job. (21)

retail the sale of goods to the final consumer. (17)

risk a chance of possible loss. (23)

satellite dish a bowl-shaped receiver that gathers signals from satellites in space. (8)

scholarship an amount of money (which does not have to be repaid) used to pay for part or all of a person's education. (24)

screen out to eliminate applicants that are not suited for a job. (21)

seasonal work or activity done only during part of the year. (16)

self-concept the way in which a person views his or her or own self-worth and personal abilities. (1)

self-esteem to have a high regard for, or feel good about, yourself. (4)

self-management a key personal skill—organizing your time so as not to waste yours or that of others. (4)

semiskilled worker a person with partial or some skills required to perform a task. (15)

services tasks other people or machines do that cannot be physically weighed or measured. (18)

short-term goal an objective to be achieved in a relatively short space of time that can be used as a step towards achieving a long-term goal. (25)

sibling a brother or sister. (4)

sincerity honest or genuine feeling. (4)

skill ability to perform a certain activity well. (2)

skilled worker a person with the skills, training, and experience to perform a task. (15)

socialism a system where economic decisions are made by the government. (22)

sole proprietorship a business owned by one person. (23)

stock a share of the ownership in a company. (23)

stockholder a person who owns stock in a company. (23)

stress physical or mental strain. (20)

subcontractor people who agree to supervise part of a construction job for an agreed-upon amount of money. (9)

taxes money that citizens pay to the government to provide for public services. (19)

technology use of science to develop new products and new methods. (22)

telecommunications sending and receiving messages over the telephone system. (8)

telemarketing using the telephone to sell goods (one of the fastest-growing sales areas). (17)

temporary job a job obtained for the summer or any other time period that is limited. (5)

tentative the best decision you can decide on at a certain time, which can be changed later as you learn more. (3)

textile a woven or knit cloth. (15)

theology the study of different religions. (12)

trade an occupation that requires manual (physical) or mechanical skills. (24)

transport to convey (take) from one place to another. (20)

Transportation Technology Cluster a group of jobs involved in the movement of people and goods from one place to another. (20)

tuition a fee charged for taking college courses. (24)

unskilled laborer a person not required to have special skills or training to perform a task. (15)

unstructured varied; an unstructured job would involve doing many different things throughout the day. (18)

utility useful; a public utility is a business that provides water, electricity, gas, or sewage treatment, and is regulated by the government. (19)

values personal views or ideas that a person feels are important. (2)

vocation the kind of work a person does, occupation. (24)

volunteering doing a job, which you are not paid for, to gain the experience. (5)

wage payment for work, usually figured by the hour. (21)

wants things you would like to have, but don't have to have—luxuries. (3)

welfare aid in the form of money or necessities given to those in need (those unable to support themselves). (19)

white-collar job a job having to do with clerical, professional, or business work. (19)

wholesale goods obtained directly from manufacturers. (17)

work productive activity resulting in something useful. (1)

work ethic a set of values based on hard work. (1)

work-study program jobs that give students a chance to explore careers while earning school credit. (5)

work values represent what is important in work such as the money you earn, job security, and your work environment. (2)

GLOSARIO

(los números entre paréntesis corresponden a los capítulos)

accommodate/adecuarse brindar a los otros algo que necesitan o desean. (14)

accommodations/alojamiento cuartos donde permanecer durante un viaje, como puede ser un hotel u hostería. (14)

administration/administración personal de gerencia o supervisión. (19)

adult education/educación para adultos programas para adultos que desean entrenarse en carreras nuevas o superarse, para mejorar su presente posición laboral (llamado también *continuing education/educación incorporada)*

advertise/publicar informar a la gente sobre un producto, por medio de la radio, la televisión, el Internet, los periódicos y revistas. (17)

advocate/defender hablar o escribir en favor de una causa o causas. (10)

aerobics/ejercicios aeróbicos tipo de entrenamiento físico. (14)

agribusiness/administración agropecuaria el proceso completo o el negocio de producir, procesar y distribuir productos agrícolas. (6)

Agribusiness and Natural Resources Cluster/ Ramo de la Administración Agropecuaria y de Recursos Naturales grupo de ocupaciones dedicadas a producir, regular, conservar y garantizar la calidad de las materias primas usadas en la alimentación, vivienda, energía y confort del hogar. (6)

agriculture/agricultura(producción agropecuaria) ciencia del cultivo del suelo y la producción de cosechas (agricultura) y criado de ganado (ganadería). (6)

applicant/aspirante persona que solicita un empleo, candidato. (21)

application form/solicitud de empleo cuestionario usado por los empleadores, para obtener información básica de los candidatos y para determinar su aptitud para el empleo. (21)

apprentice/aprendiz persona que está aprendiendo el oficio, mientras trabaja junto a un obrero especializado. (24)

aptitude/aptitud dote o capacidad para incorporar nuevas habilidades. (2)

aquaculture/piscicultura cultivo y criado de vida marina, bajo condiciones controladas, por lo general para consumo del público. (16)

associate degree/título intermedio certificado otorgado a una persona luego de haber completado un programa de estudios sobre un área específica; por lo general, es un curso de dos años. (24)

attitude/actitud visión de una persona ante la vida, puede ser positiva o negativa. (1)

automation/automatización uso de máquinas para reemplazar la labor humana. (22)

bachelor's degree/bachiller certificado de estudios otorgado a una persona luego de haber aprobado una serie de cursos universitarios, tanto en areas generales como específicas; por lo general, estos cursos duran cuatro años. (24)

bacteria/bacteria tipo especial de microorganismos de una sola célula. (11)

blue-collar job/trabajo de operario trabajo de fábrica o industria. (19)

body image/aspecto físico forma en que uno luce; visión mental que uno tiene sobre su propia imagen. (4)

browser/navegar nombre formal que se da al programa que ayuda a curiosear o panear dentro del Internet

budget/presupuesto plan para gastar y ahorrar dinero, dentro de un período específico. (10)

Business and Office Technology Cluster/Ramo de la Administración y Tecnología de Empresas grupo de profesiones dedicadas a la dirección y organización de negocios y oficinas. (7)

CAD/CAM Diseño por Computación/Fabricación por computación transformar un diseño de ingeniería en un producto manufacturado, mediante el uso de computadoras. (15)

capitalism/capitalismo sistema económico que permite a la gente tomar sus propias decisiones financieras y que estimula la competencia. (22)

career/carrera trabajo que se realiza dentro de un cierto número de años, dentro de un área de interés. (1)

Career Cluster/Ramo Profesional grupo de ocupaciones similares. (6)

chain of command/cadena de mando forma en que se distribuye la dirección dentro de una organización. (4)

check stub/talón de cheque parte de un cheque de sueldo, en el que se indican todos los descuentos salariales. (21)

civil service test/prueba para administración pública exámen tomado por el gobierno federal, para emplear a un individuo en un trabajo público específico. (19)

classified section/clasificados sección de un periódico que contiene pequeños avisos según categorías, tales como "empleos ofrecidos." (21)

co-worker/colega compañero de trabajo. (21)

commission/comisión ingreso de dinero que un agente recibe por el porcentaje de ventas que este agente realiza. (7)

communications/comunicación modos en que la gente comparte ideas e información; por ejemplo, conversaciones o medios de difusión. (8)

Communications and Media Cluster/Ramo de la Comunicación y Difusión grupo de profesiones dedicadas al diseño, preparación y envío de información o mensajes. (8)

competition/competición rivalidad; actividades mediante las cuales las compañías tratan de superar las ventas entre sí. (22)

compromise/compromiso situación por la que las partes con distinta opinión, tratan de llegar a cierto acuerdo, dando alguna concesión. (21)

computer-aided-design (CAD)/diseño por computación (CAD) uso de la computadora y un programa especial, para crear diseños. (9)

conflict of values/conflicto de valores cuando existe uno o más valores que no se pueden satisfacer al mismo tiempo. (2)

Construction Technology Cluster/Ramo de la Tecnología de la Construcción grupo de profesiones dedicadas al planeamiento, diseño, construcción y reparación de estructuras de todo tipo. (9)

consumer/consumidor persona que compra y utiliza artículos y servicios. (10)

contingency plan/plan de emergencia tipo de plan que provee una alternativa o apoyo, en caso de que fuera alterado el método original. (25)

cope/enfrentar encarar y tratar problemas o responsabilidades. (22)

corporation/corporación empresa que pertenece a muchas personas, pero que está considerada por la ley como si perteneciera a una persona sola. (23)

cosmetology/cosmetología mejorar el aspecto de la piel, el cabello y las uñas. (18)

credit/crédito unidad de medida usada por las escuelas, para determinar el progreso del estudiante. (24)

curator/celador persona encargada de un museo y su investigación. (12)

data/datos información tal como hechos, números, medidas, etc., usada como base de razonamiento, discusión y cálculo, necesarios para una empresa. (7)

decision/decisión elección entre dos o más posibilidades. (3)

decision-making process/proceso de toma de decisiones pasos de razonamiento que ayudan a una persona a tomar la mejor decisión. (3)

deduction/deducciones monto substraído de la paga de un empleado por impuestos, obra social, jubilación, u otros beneficios. (21)

democracy/democracia sistema de gobierno en el que el poder pertenece al pueblo. (22)

destination/destino lugar hacia donde una persona viaja, o algo es enviado. (20)

dietitian/dietólogo(a) persona que planifica y dirige los programas de alimentación, incluyendo la preparación y despacho de comida a hospitales y comedores. (10)

discriminate/discriminar tratar a alguien con injusticia, debido a su raza, religión o sexo. (21)

distraction/distracción algo que lleva la atención afuera de lo que uno desearía hacer. (4)

distribute/distribución acto de llevar un producto hasta el consumidor. Las decisiones sobre la distribución involucran la venta, el modo de venta, el transporte, etc. (17)

domestic/doméstico perteneciente o relativo al hogar o la familia. (18)

DOT Dictionary of Occupational Titles/DOT Diccionario de Profesiones guía que contiene la descripción de distintos trabajos, ordenados por grupo según un código. (5)

drive/impulso motivación, ambición y energía para hacer algo productivo. (12)

economic system/sistema económico método de producir, distribuir e intercambiar artículos y servicios, dentro de una sociedad. (22)

elective/materia electiva curso que no es obligatorio pero que puede ser elegido según los intereses del estudiante. (24)

employer/empleador persona que toma a otra persona para hacer un trabajo. (21)

employment agency/agencia de empleos organización que intenta colocar a gente capacitada en posiciones de trabajo, en general, a cambio de una comisión. (21)

endorse/endosar firmar el reverso de un cheque pagadero a uno mismo, para que el banco pueda cobrarlo. (21)

engineering/ingeniería uso de las ciencias y las matemáticas para resolver problemas en fábricas u otras industrias. (15)

enterprise/empresa encargarse de un proyecto. (22)

entrepreneur/empresario persona que organiza, dirige y encara los riesgos de un negocio. (23)

entry-level job/nivel básico trabajo para que un principiante inicie su capacitación hacia empleos de mayor jerarquía. (5)

environment/medio ambiente todo lo que está a nuestro alrededor: aire, agua, minerales, plantas, animales e insectos. (11)

Environmental Sciences Cluster/Ramo de la Ecología grupo de profesiones dedicadas a la conservación y protección de nuestro medio ambiente y también al empleo en forma saludable y sin riesgos, de los productos de las fuentes naturales. (11)

environmental scientist/ecólogo científico dedicado a proteger el aire, el agua, los animales, las plantas y otras fuentes naturales, de la contaminación u otros efectos. (11)

ergonomics/ergonomía estudio del ambiente dentro de una oficina y la forma de mejorarlo. (7)

ethics/ética reglas o principios bajo los cuales vive una persona. (4)

evaluate/evaluar mirar con detenimiento y juzgar. (3)

experience/experiencia trabajos u obligaciones que uno ha realizado, y que lo capacitan para trabajos futuros. (5)

extraction/extracción acto de eliminar o "quitar" algo. (16)

Family and Consumer Sciences Cluster/Ramo de Ciencias de la Familia y el Consumidor grupo de profesiones dedicadas al desarrollo, la producción y la administración de artículos y servicios, destinados a mejorar la vida hogareña. (10)

family interaction/interacción familiar experiencias que tienen lugar entre los miembros de una familia. (10)

fee/arancel suma de dinero o porcentaje de un sueldo, que carga una agencia, para ayudar a uno a encontrar un empleo. (21)

fine arts/bellas artes actividades dedicadas a representaciones hermosas o a objetos exquisitos, tales como sinfonías, ballets, pinturas y esculturas. (12)

Fine Arts and Humanities Cluster/Ramo de Bellas Artes y Humanidades Carreras que están todas agrupadas porque involucran el desarrollo, la promoción y la conservación de los valores sociales y morales de una cultura y el valor del arte y la belleza. (12)

flexibility/flexibilidad capacidad para adaptarse a cambios, dentro de un plan establecido. (25)

free enterprise system/sistema de libre empresa sistema económico en el que la gente toma sus propias decisiones financieras. (22)

freight/flete despacho de artículos o carga. (20)

G.E.D. certificate/certificado G.E.D. (Desarrollo de Educación General) documento que indica que la persona ha aprobado un exámen de cinco partes, en las áreas de redacción, estudios sociales, ciencias, lectura y matemáticas. (24)

goal/objetivo meta o logro al que se aspira, concentrando los pensamientos y la energía. (1)

GOE Guide for Occupational Exploration/GOE Guía para Explorar las Profesiones libro que da información sobre las distintas carreras. (5)

goods/artículos productos tangibles y útiles, que se producen o se venden. (22)

graduate school/carrera de post-grado programa de estudios más allá de un título de bachiller. (24)

grant/donación cierta suma de dinero para poder cursar estudios, la cual no necesita ser devuelta. (24)

gross pay/salario bruto monto total de los ingresos de un empleado, antes de descontar las deducciones. (21)

Health and Medical Cluster/Ramo de Salud y Medicina grupo de profesiones dedicadas a proveer los servicios necesarios para mantener la salud mental y física de la gente. (13)

help-wanted ad/aviso de trabajos ofrecidos anuncio en un periódico, pagado por el empleador, que describe la oportunidad de empleo disponible. (21)

hospitality/hospitalidad recepción amistosa y modo amable de tratar a los invitados. (14)

Hospitality and Recreation Cluster/Ramo de Hospitalidad y Recreación profesiones que proveen diversiónes a las personas dedicadas a actividades de entretenimiento. (14)

human resources/recursos humanos empleados o trabajadores; mano de obra. (15)

humanities/humanidades estudio de los temas que se refieren a las personas. (12)

income tax/impuesto a los ingresos parte de los ingresos de una persona, que se deben entregar legalmente al gobierno, en pago por los servicios que el gobierno brinda. (21)

individual responsibility/responsabilidad individual estar obligados, o ser responsables de nosotros mismos, o de nuestras acciones. (4)

initiative/iniciativa hacer algo que se debe hacer, sin que alguien lo solicite. (18)

integrity/integridad cualidad, honestidad hacia nosotros mismos y hacia los demás. (4)

interest/interés algo en que el individuo disfruta en hacer o pensar. (2)

interest inventory/guía de vocaciones cuestionario que ayuda a determinar en qué se interesan las personas. (2)

interrelate/interrelacionarse comunicarse o llevarse bien con otras personas. (10)

interview/entrevista encuentro formal entre un empleador y un aspirante a un trabajo, con el objeto de ayudar a ambas partes a tomar una decisión sobre el candidato a emplear. (21)

job/trabajo estar empleado por una persona o compañía, para realizar ciertas tareas y recibir pago por las mismas. (1)

job duty/obligación tarea que se espera que uno cumpla durante su trabajo. (5)

job family/familia de empleos grupo de trabajos que tienen características similares. (6)

job lead/referencia sobre oportunidades cualquier información sobre posibles trabajos. (21)

labor/laboral fuente de trabajadores que están empleados. (19)

labor union/sindicato grupo de trabajadores que han organizado un aumento de salarios y una mejora en sus condiciones de trabajo. (19)

laser/laser dispositivo que produce un rayo muy concentrado de intensa luz, que puede perforar a través de objetos sólidos, tales como el metal. (15)

law of demand/ley oferta y demanda regla económica que establece que si el precio de los artículos o los servicios baja, se producen mayores compras; y si ese precio sube, se vende menos. (22)

law of supply/ley del suministro regla económica que establece que a mayores precios, se venden, por lo general, mayores cantidades de un producto, que a menores precios. (22)

life values/valores vitales aquello que es importante en nuestra vida, como ser, la familia y la sociedad. (2)

linguistics/lingüística estructura de la palabra. (12)

lodging/alojamiento lugar donde pasar la noche o permanecer por poco tiempo. (18)

long-term goal/objetivo a largo plazo alcance futuro, o meta final adonde se debe llegar, logrando primero muchos objetivos a corto plazo. (25)

loss/pérdida monto de dinero que una compañía pierde, cuando gasta más de lo que ingresa. (22)

low self-esteem/poca confianza imagen pobre o concepto bajo, de uno mismo. (4)

manufacturing/fabricación proceso que utiliza materias primas, para lograr productos que la gente usa. (15)

Manufacturing Technology Cluster/Ramo de la Technología Industrial grupo de profesiones dedicadas al diseño y armado de productos. (15)

marine/marino perteneciente o relativo al mar. (16)

marine science/ciencias marinas estudio del mar y de las plantas y animales que viven en él. (16)

Marine Science Cluster/Ramode las Ciencias Marinas trabajos que descubren, desarrollan y mejoran la vida marina y los productos que se pueden extraer del océano. (16)

market research/estudio de mercado estudio para determinar lo que influye en las decisiones de compra de las personas. (17)

Marketing and Distribution Cluster/Ramo del Mercado y la Distribución grupo de profesiones dedicadas a llevar productos desde el fabricante al consumidor y también para promover la compra de cierto producto. (17)

mass media/medios masivos medios de comunicación mediante los cuales la información es distribuida al público en general: periódicos, revistas, radio, televisión, Internet. (4)

media/medios medios de comunicación, tales como periódicos, televisión, radio, revistas y el Internet, que tienen gran influencia en la gente. (8)

merchandise/mercadería amplia gama de productos comprados y vendidos en los negocios. (17)

microorganism/microorganismos seres vivos, extremadamente pequeños, que sólo son visibles bajo el microscopio. (11)

module/módulo unidades que se encajan o que trabajan juntas; por ejemplo, casas prefabricadas que son construídas en base a módulos armados en la obra. (9)

natural resource/recurso natural material útil provisto por la naturaleza. Son recursos naturales el suelo, el oro, los árboles, el agua y los minerales. (6)

needs/necesidades cosas que la gente debe tener para sobrevivir. (3)

net pay/sueldo neto monto final por pago de sueldo, luego de haber hecho los descuentos. (21)

nutritionist/nutricionista persona que estudia los efectos de la alimentación en el cuerpo humano. (10)

occupation/ocupación tipo de trabajo que realiza un empleado. (1)

offshore drilling/perforación de altamar extracción de petróleo y gas natural que se realiza fuera de los límites del continente o isla. (16)

OOH Occupational Outlook Handbook/OOH Manual de Orientación Ocupacional guía para buscar una carrera. (5)

organism/organismo ser viviente único; por ejemplo, una persona, animal o planta. (11)

overtime/hora extra tiempo de trabajo agregado al horario normal de trabajo. (21)

part-time job/período parcial trabajo de menos de 40 horas por semana, como después de clase o en fines de semana. (5)

partnership/sociedad cuando dos o más personas operan y poseen un negocio. (23)

perfectionist/perfeccionista persona que no admite errores o defectos. (4)

persistence/persistencia mantenerse en algo con firmeza a pesar de las dificultades; sin rendirse. (23)

Personal Services Cluster/Ramo de Servicios Personales profesiones que se dedican a proveer a las personas, los servicios que desean para llevar una vida más placentera. (18)

petroleum/petróleo líquido oeloso, inflamable, que se obtiene perforando pozos subterráneos, y que luego es refinado hasta lograr gasolina, gasoil (aceite combustible) y otros productos. (6)

pharmacy/farmacia negocio que provee drogas medicinales; droguería. (13)

plan/plan método o camino que uno decide tomar, luego de haber cumplido un proceso de toma de decisiones. (3)

plant/planta fábrica. La mayoría de los artículos manufacturados, son elaborados en fábricas. (15)

pollution/contaminación introducción, dentro del medio ambiente, de elementos dañinos, tales como desperdicios creados por el hombre. (11)

prerequisite/requisito previo clase que se debe tomar antes de tomar otro curso de nivel mayor. (24)

procedure/procedimiento regla o método para realizar algo. (21)

procrastinator/moroso persona que posterga el hacer cosas o tomar decisiones. (25)

producer/productor persona que elabora o vende artículos o servicios. (22)

profession/profesión carrera que requiere entrenamiento especializado y preparación académica. (13)

professional/profesional persona que trabaja en una profesión. Carrera que requiere un conocimiento especial y por lo general, muchos años de educación. (13)

profit/ganancia monto de dinero que produce un negocio, y que es mayor que los gastos. (22)

program/programa grupo de cursos educativos que se relacionan entre sí. (24)

promote/promocionar anunciar y propiciar la venta de un producto. (17)

public/público la gente de nuestra nación, en su totalidad. (19)

Public Services Cluster/Ramo de Servicios Públicos grupo de ocupaciones dedicadas a proveer servicios al público. La mayoría de estos servicios son pagados mediante la recaudación de impuestos. (19)

punctuality/puntualidad llegar a tiempo al trabajo. (21)

quarry/cantera pozo grande del que se extrae mármol y otros tipos de piedras. (6)

radiation/radiación partículas de energía, emanadas de ciertos elementos naturales; producidas también por los rayos X y presentes en los residuos de las usinas de energía nuclear. (11)

recreation/esparcimiento medio de revitalizarse mediante descanso y diversión. (14)

reference/referencia persona que da, a un futuro empleador, un informe favorable sobre un posible candidato a un puesto. (21)

regulatory/reglamentario que controla cómo suceden las cosas; que dirige de acuerdo con las reglas. (19)

research/investigación hallar más información mediante la lectura o hablando con la gente. (5)

resource/recurso cualquier habilidad o ventaja que uno tiene. (3)

résumé/curriculum breve descripción escrita de los datos de un aspirante a un puesto. Incluye datos personales, educación, antecedentes y experiencia relacionada con el trabajo. (21)

retail/venta minorista venta de artículos al consumidor final. (17)

risk/riesgo posibilidad de perder. (23)

satellite dish/satélite parabólico receptor con forma de disco que toma señales desde satélites espaciales. (8)

scholarship/beca suma de dinero, que no necesita ser devuelta, usada para pagar parte o todos los gastos de educación de una persona. (24)

screen out/filtrado eliminar candidatos que no tienen capacidad para un trabajo. (21)

seasonal/de temporada actividad o trabajo que se realizan durante alguna parte del año. (16)

self-concept/concepto propio forma en que una persona se ve a sí misma, o considera su propio valor y habilidades personales. (1)

self-esteem/autoestima tener un gran concepto o sentirse bien con uno mismo. (4)

self-management/auto-disciplina tributo personal clave: organizar el tiempo sin desperdiciar el de uno ni el de los demás. (4)

semiskilled worker/trabajador semi capacitado persona con capacidad parcial o ligera, para poder realizar cierta labor. (15)

services/servicios tareas que realizan algunas personas o máquinas, y que se pueden medir o pesar físicamente. (15)

short-term goal/objetivo a corto plazo meta a la que se debe llegar en un plazo relativamente corto, la cual puede ser utilizada como paso para lograr un objetivo a largo plazo. (25)

sibling/hermanos hermano o hermana. (4)

sincerity/sinceridad sentimiento honesto y genuino. (4)

skill/capacidad habilidad para realizar bien alguna actividad. (2)

skilled worker/trabajador capacitado persona que tiene habilidad, entrenamiento y experiencia para realizar una tarea. (15)

socialism/socialismo sistema en el que las decisiones económicas son tomadas por el gobierno. (22)

sole proprietorship/propietario único negocio perteneciente a una sola persona. (23)

stock/acciones compartir la posesión de una compañía. (23)

stockholder/accionista persona que posee acciones de una compañía. (23)

stress/tensión esfuerzo físico o mental. (20)

subcontractor/contratista persona que accede a supervisar parte de una construcción, por un precio acordado de antemano. (9)

taxes/impuestos dinero que los ciudadanos pagan al gobierno para la provisón de servicios públicos. (19)

technology/tecnología uso de las ciencias para desarrollar nuevos productos y métodos. (22)

telecommunications/telecomunicaciones enviar y recibir mensajes a través del sistema telefónico. (8)

telemarketing/comercio por vía telefónica emplear el teléfono para la venta de productos; una de las áreas de más rápida venta. (17)

temporary job/trabajo temporario trabajo obtenido durante el verano o durante cualquier otro período limitado. (5)

tentative/tentativa la mejor decisión que uno puede tomar en cierto momento, la cual se puede cambiar con posterioridad, a medida que uno aprende más. (3)

textile/textil tela entramada o tejida. (15)

theology/teología estudio de distintas religiones. (12)

trade/oficio ocupación que requiere habilidades manuales (físicas) o mecánicas. (24)

transport/transportar transladar (llevar) de un lugar a otro. (20)

Transportation Technology Cluster/Ramo de la Tecnología del Transporte grupo de tareas dedicadas al translado de gente y productos, de un lugar a otro. (20)

tuition/arancel derecho que se cobra para tomar cursos universitarios. (24)

unskilled laborer/operario inexperto persona que no necesita tener capacidad especial o entrenamiento, para realizar una tarea. (15)

unstructured/no estructurado variado. Durante un trabajo no estructurado se realizan distintas tareas a lo largo de todo el día. (18)

utility/servicio utilidad; un servicio público es una empresa que provee agua, electricidad, gas natural o tratamiento cloacal y está administrada por el gobierno. (19)

values/valores ideas o conceptos personales que uno considera que son importantes. (2)

vocation/vocación tipo de trabajo que una persona realiza; ocupación. (24)

volunteering/trabajo voluntario realizar una labor con el objeto de obtener experiencia, pero sin recibir paga. (5)

wage/salario pago por un trabajo, estimado, por lo general, en base a horas. (21)

wants/deseos cosas que uno quiere tener pero que no necesita. Lujos. (3)

welfare/beneficencia ayuda en forma monetaria que se brinda a los necesitados o a aquellos que no se pueden mantener a sí mismos. (19)

white-collar job/trabajo de cuello duro trabajo que tiene que ver con las tareas de oficinistas, profesionales o empresarios. (19)

wholesale/venta por mayor productos que se obtienen directamente del fabricante. (17)

work/trabajo actividad productiva que resulta en algo útil. (1)

work ethic/ética laboral conjunto de valores basados en el trabajo duro. (1)

work study program/programa de trabajo y estudio trabajos que dan a los estudiantes la posibilidad de conocer las profesiones, al mismo tiempo que obtienen créditos por sus estudios. (5)

work values/valores laborales representar lo que es importante en un trabajo, como puede ser, el sueldo que se gana, la seguridad del mismo y el ambiente en que se trabaja. (2)

INDEX

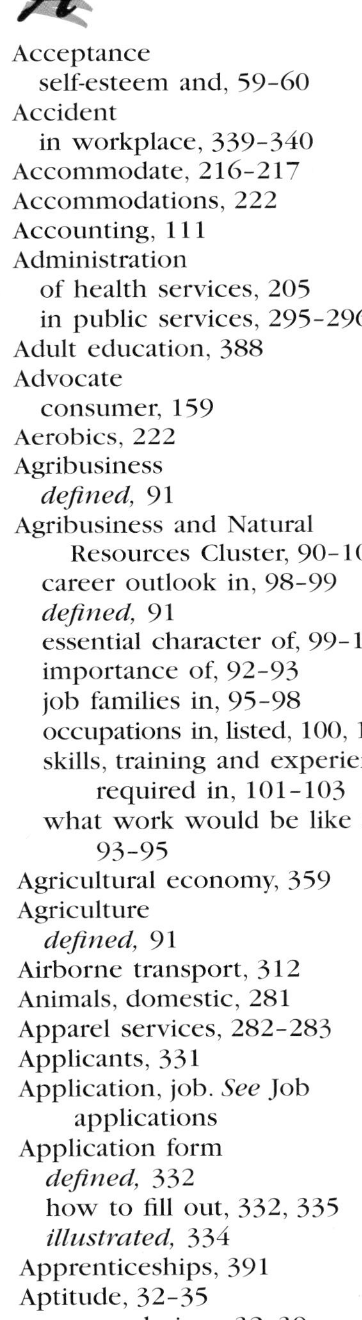

E

E

I

J

PHOTO CREDITS

Unit Openers
1 Digital Stock;
3 Image ©1998 PhotoDisc, Inc.;
71 Image ©1998 PhotoDisc, Inc.;
322 Digital Stock

Chapter 1
4 ©Robert Brenner/PhotoEdit;
5 Image ©1998 PhotoDisc, Inc.;
7 ©Michael Newman/PhotoEdit;
8 Image ©1998 PhotoDisc, Inc.;
12 ©Mark Kate Denny/PhotoEdit;
13 Image ©1998 PhotoDisc, Inc.;
15 ©Mary Kate Denny/PhotoEdit

Chapter 2
21 ©Michael Newman/PhotoEdit;
24 ©Richard Hutchings/PhotoEdit;
26 ©Michael Newman/PhotoEdit;
28 bottom ©Cleo Photography/PhotoEdit;
28 top ©Tony Freeman/PhotoEdit;
33 ©Mark E. Gibson

Chapter 3
42 ©Mark Richards/PhotoEdit;
45 Image ©1998 PhotoDisc, Inc.;
48 ©David Young-Wolff/PhotoEdit;
50 ©David R. Frazier Photolibrary;
52 ©David Young-Wolff/PhotoEdit

Chapter 4
56 Image ©1998 PhotoDisc, Inc.;
57 ©Tony Freeman/PhotoEdit;
59 ©Myrleen Ferguson/PhotoEdit;
62 ©David Young-Wolff/PhotoEdit;
63 ©Myrleen Fersguson Cate/PhotoEdit;
66 Image ©1998 PhotoDisc, Inc.;
68 ©David Barber/PhotoEdit

Chapter 5
72 Image ©1998 PhotoDisc, Inc.;
74 Digital Stock;
78 ©Tony Freeman/PhotoEdit;
83 ©Myrleen Ferguson Cate/PhotoEdit;
84 ©Mark Richards/PhotoEdit

Chapter 6
90 Image ©1998 PhotoDisc, Inc.;
91 ©David R. Frazier Photolibrary;
92 ©David R. Frazier Photolibrary;
94 Image ©1998 PhotoDisc, Inc.;
97 Digital Stock
99 Image ©1998 PhotoDisc, Inc.;
101 left Image ©1998 PhotoDisc, Inc.;
101 right Image ©1998 PhotoDisc, Inc.;
102 Image ©1998 PhotoDisc, Inc.

Chapter 7
107 ©David R. Frazier Photolibrary;
109 ©Jose Carillo/PhotoEdit;
111 ©MIchael Newman/PhotoEdit;
115 ©Billy E. Barnes/PhotoEdit

Chapter 8
122 ©Batt Johnson/Unicorn;
124 Image ©1998 PhotoDisc, Inc.;
128 Image ©1998 PhotoDisc, Inc.;
129 Image ©1998 PhotoDisc, Inc.;
130 ©Spencer Grant/PhotoEdit;
133 Skjold Photographs

Chapter 9
138 Image ©1998 PhotoDisc, Inc.;
139 ©Mark E. Gibson;
141 Image ©1998 PhotoDisc, Inc.;
144 ©Elena Rooraid/PhotoEdit;
146 Image ©1998 PhotoDisc, Inc.;
149 Image ©1998 PhotoDisc, Inc.

Chapter 10
154 Image ©1998 PhotoDisc, Inc.;
155 ©Laura Dwight/PhotoEdit;
157 ©Bill Aron/PhotoEdit;
161 ©Stephen McBrady/PhotoEdit;
164 ©Tom McCarthy/PhotoEdit;
165 ©Tony Freeman/PhotoEdit

Chapter 11
169 ©Mark Burnett/David R. Frazier Photolibrary;
171 Digital Stock;
175 Image ©1998 PhotoDisc, Inc.;
177 ©Davis Barber/PhotoEdit

Chapter 12
183 ©Kathy Sloane;
185 bottom ©MIchael Newman/PhotoEdit;
185 top ©Bonnie Kamin/PhotoEdit;
189 ©MIchael Newman/PhotoEdit;
190 ©MIchael Newman/PhotoEdit;
192 ©Mark E. Gibson

Chapter 13
199 ©MIchael Newman/PhotoEdit;
200 ©Jonathan Nourok/PhotoEdit;
201 ©Tony Freeman/PhotoEdit;
206 Digital Stock;
208 Digital Stock

Photo Credits, continued

Chapter 14
215 ©Mark E. Gibson;
216 ©Jeff Greenberg/PhotoEdit;
218 ©Michael Newman/PhotoEdit;
219 ©Jeff Greenberg/PhotoEdit;
221 ©W.B. Spunbarg/PhotoEdit;
225 ©MIchael Newman/PhotoEdit;
227 Image ©1998 PhotoDisc, Inc.

Chapter 15
231 Digital Stock;
232 Image ©1998 PhotoDisc, Inc.;
234 ©MIchael Newman/PhotoEdit;
237 ©Michael Newman/PhotoEdit;
239 Digital Stock

Chapter 16
247 Digital Stock;
248 ©Mark E. Gibson;
253 Image ©1998 PhotoDisc, Inc.;
254 Digital Stock;
255 ©David R. Frazier Photolibrary

Chapter 17
262 ©Myrleen Ferguson Cate/PhotoEdit;
265 Image ©1998 PhotoDisc, Inc.;
269 Image ©1998 PhotoDisc, Inc.;
270 ©David Young-Wolff/PhotoEdit;
273 Image ©1998 PhotoDisc, Inc.

Chapter 18
277 ©David R. Frazier Photolibrary;
278 Image ©1998 PhotoDisc, Inc.;
280 ©Tony Freeman/PhotoEdit;
282 ©David Young-Wolff/PhotoEdit;
283 ©Mark E. Gibson

Chapter 19
291 ©David R. Frazier Photolibrary;
292 ©Paul Conklin/PhotoEdit;
294 ©David R. Frazier Photolibrary;
296 ©Tony Freeman/PhotoEdit;
298 ©Mark E. Gibson;
299 Image ©1998 PhotoDisc, Inc.;
301 Image ©1998 PhotoDisc, Inc.

Chapter 20
307 Image ©1998 PhotoDisc, Inc.;
308 ©David R. Frazier Photolibrary;
310 Image ©1998 PhotoDisc, Inc.;
315 Digital Stock;
318 Image ©1998 PhotoDisc, Inc.

Chapter 21
323 ©Elena Rooraid/PhotoEdit;
326 ©Amy C. Etra/PhotoEdit;
330 ©Spencer Grant/PhotoEdit;
331 Image ©1998 PhotoDisc, Inc.;
335 ©David Young-Wolff/PhotoEdit;
337 Digital Stock;
341 Image ©1998 PhotoDisc, Inc.;
345 Image ©1998 PhotoDisc, Inc.

Chapter 22
348 ©David R. Frazier Photolibrary;
351 ©David Young-Wolff/PhotoEdit;
354 ©David R. Frazier Photolibrary;
357 Image ©1998 PhotoDisc, Inc.;
358 ©Paul Conklin/PhotoEdit;
361 ©Spencer Grant/PhotoEdit;
363 Image ©1998 PhotoDisc, Inc.;
366 Digital Stock

Chapter 23
367 Image ©1998 PhotoDisc, Inc.;
368 Courtesy of Apple Computer, Inc.
369 Image ©1998 PhotoDisc, Inc.;
370 ©David Young-Wolff/PhotoEdit
372 Image ©1998 PhotoDisc, Inc.;
375 ©Mary Kate Denny/PhotoEdit;
377 Skjold Photographs

Chapter 24
380 ©Mark Richards/PhotoEdit;
383 Image ©1998 PhotoDisc, Inc.;
384 ©David Young-Wolff/PhotoEdit;
387 ©Paul Conklin/PhotoEdit;
388 ©Jeff Greenberg/PhotoEdit;
391 ©David R. Frazier Photolibrary;
392 ©Myrleen Ferguson/PhotoEdit;
394 Image ©1998 PhotoDisc, Inc.

Chapter 25
397 ©Michelle Bridwell/PhotoEdit;
400 ©David R. Frazier Photolibrary;
401 bottom Image ©1998 PhotoDisc, Inc.;
401 top ©David R. Frazier Photolibrary;
404 ©Michael Newman/PhotoEdit